T0325965

Machine Law, Ethics, and Morality in the Age of Artificial Intelligence

Steven John Thompson
University of California, Davis, USA & University of Maryland Global Campus, USA

A volume in the Advances in Human and Social
Aspects of Technology (AHSAT) Book Series

IGI Global
PUBLISHER of TIMELY KNOWLEDGE

Published in the United States of America by
   IGI Global
   Engineering Science Reference (an imprint of IGI Global)
   701 E. Chocolate Avenue
   Hershey PA, USA 17033
   Tel: 717-533-8845
   Fax: 717-533-8661
   E-mail: cust@igi-global.com
   Web site: http://www.igi-global.com

Copyright © 2021 by IGI Global. All rights reserved. No part of this publication may be reproduced, stored or distributed in any form or by any means, electronic or mechanical, including photocopying, without written permission from the publisher. Product or company names used in this set are for identification purposes only. Inclusion of the names of the products or companies does not indicate a claim of ownership by IGI Global of the trademark or registered trademark.
                 Library of Congress Cataloging-in-Publication Data
Names: Thompson, Steven John, 1956- editor.
Title: Machine law, ethics, and morality in the age of artificial intelligence
   / Steven John Thompson, editor.
Description: Hershey, PA : Engineering Science Reference, 2020. | Includes
   bibliographical references and index. | Summary: "This book contains
   research on the present and future phenomenon of human-machine ethics
   and morality"-- Provided by publisher.
Identifiers: LCCN 2020011759 (print) | LCCN 2020011760 (ebook) | ISBN
   9781799848943 (h/c) | ISBN 9781799867982 (s/c) | ISBN 9781799848950 (eISBN)
Subjects: LCSH: Artificial intelligence--Moral and ethical aspects. |
   Robotics--Moral and ethical aspects.
Classification: LCC Q334.7 .H36 2020 (print) | LCC Q334.7 (ebook) | DDC
   174/.90063--dc23
LC record available at https://lccn.loc.gov/2020011759
LC ebook record available at https://lccn.loc.gov/2020011760

This book is published in the IGI Global book series Advances in Human and Social Aspects of Technology (AHSAT) (ISSN: 2328-1316; eISSN: 2328-1324)

British Cataloguing in Publication Data
A Cataloguing in Publication record for this book is available from the British Library.

All work contributed to this book is new, previously-unpublished material. The views expressed in this book are those of the authors, but not necessarily of the publisher.

For electronic access to this publication, please contact: eresources@igi-global.com.

Advances in Human and Social Aspects of Technology (AHSAT) Book Series

Ashish Dwivedi
The University of Hull, UK

ISSN:2328-1316
EISSN:2328-1324

Mission

In recent years, the societal impact of technology has been noted as we become increasingly more connected and are presented with more digital tools and devices. With the popularity of digital devices such as cell phones and tablets, it is crucial to consider the implications of our digital dependence and the presence of technology in our everyday lives.

The **Advances in Human and Social Aspects of Technology (AHSAT) Book Series** seeks to explore the ways in which society and human beings have been affected by technology and how the technological revolution has changed the way we conduct our lives as well as our behavior. The AHSAT book series aims to publish the most cutting-edge research on human behavior and interaction with technology and the ways in which the digital age is changing society.

Coverage

- Human Development and Technology
- Cyber Bullying
- Technology Adoption
- Gender and Technology
- End-User Computing
- Cyber Behavior
- Cultural Influence of ICTs
- ICTs and social change
- Technology Dependence
- Human Rights and Digitization

IGI Global is currently accepting manuscripts for publication within this series. To submit a proposal for a volume in this series, please contact our Acquisition Editors at Acquisitions@igi-global.com or visit: http://www.igi-global.com/publish/.

The Advances in Human and Social Aspects of Technology (AHSAT) Book Series (ISSN 2328-1316) is published by IGI Global, 701 E. Chocolate Avenue, Hershey, PA 17033-1240, USA, www.igi-global.com. This series is composed of titles available for purchase individually; each title is edited to be contextually exclusive from any other title within the series. For pricing and ordering information please visit http://www.igi-global.com/book-series/advances-human-social-aspects-technology/37145. Postmaster: Send all address changes to above address. © © 2021 IGI Global. All rights, including translation in other languages reserved by the publisher. No part of this series may be reproduced or used in any form or by any means – graphics, electronic, or mechanical, including photocopying, recording, taping, or information and retrieval systems – without written permission from the publisher, except for non commercial, educational use, including classroom teaching purposes. The views expressed in this series are those of the authors, but not necessarily of IGI Global.

Titles in this Series

701 East Chocolate Avenue, Hershey, PA 17033, USA
Tel: 717-533-8845 x100 • Fax: 717-533-8661
E-Mail: cust@igi-global.com • www.igi-global.com

Table of Contents

Detailed Table of Contents

Chapter 1

AI Personhood: Rights and Laws... 1
  Roman Yampolskiy, University of Louisville, USA

It is possible to rely on current corporate law to grant legal personhood to artificially intelligent (AI) agents. Such legal maneuvering may be useful to avoid human responsibility or to further automate businesses. In this chapter, after introducing pathways to AI personhood, consequences of such AI empowerment on human dignity, human safety, and AI rights are analyzed. This chapter per the author emphasizes possibility of creating selfish memes and legal system hacking in the context of artificial entities. Finally, potential solutions for addressing described problems are considered.

Chapter 2

Ethical Behavior and Legal Regulations in Artificial Intelligence (Part One): Supporting
Sovereignty of Users While Using Complex and Intelligent Systems... 12
  Mandy Goram, Karlsruhe Institute of Technology (KIT), Germany
  Dirk Veiel, FernUniversität in Hagen, Germany

Artificially intelligent systems should make users' lives easier and support them in complex decisions or even make these decisions completely autonomously. However, at the time of writing, the processes and decisions in an intelligent system are usually not transparent for users. They do not know which data are used, for which purpose, and with what consequences. There is simply a lack of transparency, which is important for trust in intelligent systems. Transparency and traceability of decisions is usually subordinated to performance and accuracy in AI development, or sometimes it plays no role at all. In this chapter, the authors describe what intelligent systems are and explain how users can be supported in specific situations using a context-based adaptive system. In this context, the authors describe the challenges and problems of intelligent systems in creating transparency for users and supporting their sovereignty. The authors then show which ethical and legal requirements intelligent systems have to meet and how existing approaches respond to them.

Intelligent systems and assistants should help users to complete tasks and support them at work, on the road and at home. At the same time, these systems are becoming increasingly sophisticated and autonomous in their decisions and are already taking over simple tasks from us today. In order to not lose control over their own data and to avoid the risk of user manipulation, these systems must comply with ethical and legal guidelines. In this chapter, the authors describe a novel generic approach and its realization for the development of intelligent systems that allow flexible modeling of ethical and legal aspects.

The ethical decision-making and behaviour of artificially intelligent systems is increasingly important given the prevalence of these systems and the impact they can have on human well-being. Many current approaches to implementing machine ethics utilize top-down approaches, that is, ensuring the ethical decision-making and behaviour of an agent via its adherence to explicitly defined ethical rules or principles. Despite the attractiveness of this approach, this chapter explores how all top-down approaches to implementing machine ethics are fundamentally limited and how bottom-up approaches, in particular, reinforcement learning methods, are not beset by the same problems as top-down approaches. Bottom-up approaches possess significant advantages that make them better suited for implementing machine ethics.

Taking its starting point in a discussion of the concept of intelligence, the chapter develops a philosophical understanding of ethical rationality and discusses its role and implications for two ethical problems within AI: Firstly, the so-called "black box problem," which is widely discussed in the AI community, and secondly, another more complex one which will be addressed as the "Tin Man problem." The first problem has to do with opacity, bias, and explainability in the design and development of advanced machine learning systems, such as artificial neural networks, whereas the second problem is more directly associated with the prospect for humans and AI of becoming full ethical agents. Based on Aristotelian virtue ethics, it will be argued that intelligence in human and artificial forms should approximate ethical rationality, which entails a well-balanced synthesis of reason and emotion.

Research on self-driving cars is transdisciplinary and its different aspects have attracted interest in general public debates as well as among specialists. To this day, ethical discourses are dominated by the Trolley Problem, a hypothetical ethical dilemma that is by construction unsolvable. It obfuscates much bigger real-world ethical challenges in the design, development, and operation of self-driving cars. The authors propose a systematic approach that connects processes, components, systems, and stakeholders to analyze the real-world ethical challenges for the ecology of socio-technological system of self-driving cars. They take a closer look at the regulative instruments, standards, design, and implementations of components, systems, and services, and they present practical social and ethical challenges that must be met and that imply novel expectations for engineering in car industry.

Chapter 7

The value sensitive design (VSD) approach to designing emerging technologies for human values is taken as the object of study in this chapter. VSD has traditionally been conceptualized as another type of technology or instrumentally as a tool. The various parts of VSD's principled approach would then aim to discern the various policy requirements that any given technological artifact under consideration would implicate. Yet, little to no consideration has been given to how laws, policies, and social norms engage within VSD practices, similarly, how the interactive nature of the VSD approach can, in turn, influence those directives. This is exacerbated when considering machine ethics policy that has global consequences outside their development spheres. This chapter begins with the VSD approach and aims to determine how policies come to influence how values can be managed within VSD practices. It shows that the interactional nature of VSD permits and encourages existing policies to be integrated early on and throughout the design process.

Chapter 8

The chapter observes the distinction between the mechanical and the machinic, and moves beyond the metaphors of android (Metropolis), or cyborg (Donna Haraway), and considers how the machinic has brought new cognitive patterns for human subjects to interact with their environment and others. Artists' dislocation from the central agent of production has opened passages for the posthuman mode of production. Consequently, the machine has become an integral part of artwork and of the artist. Contrary to this development, some artists retain the machine's materiality as a form of Other. The chapter argues that the machine remains as a form of externalization of the Other within the human subject.

Chapter 9

This chapter re-introduces the idea of roller coasters as moral machines and morality mechanisms, as they were designed to rid mankind of immoral entertainment, and traces their ability to spread American culture via themed entertainment from World's Fairs to Disneyland and beyond. It features an analysis of two Chinese themed rides, one of which has been developed with American cultural constructs and one of which begins to develop a new form of Chinese historical theme park. Through these examples, it suggests the potential for themed amusements to spread not just American morality and culture, but to provide sites of cultural exchange.

Chapter 10

Michael Laakasuo, University of Helsinki, Finland
Jukka R. I. Sundvall, University of Helsinki, Finland
Anton Berg, University of Helsinki, Finland
Marianna Drosinou, University of Helsinki, Finland
Volo Herzon, University of Helsinki, Finland
Anton Kunnari, University of Helsinki, Finland
Mika Koverola, University of Helsinki, Finland
Marko Repo, University of Helsinki, Finland
Teemu Saikkonen, University of Turku, Finland
Jussi Palomäki, University of Helsinki, Finland

This is the first of two chapters introducing the moral psychology of robots and transhumanism. Evolved moral cognition and the human conceptual system has naturally embedded difficulties in coping with the new moral challenges brought on by emerging future technologies. The reviewed literature outlines our contemporary understanding based on evolutionary psychology of humans as cognitive organisms. The authors then give a skeletal outline of moral psychology. These fields together suggest that there are many innate and cultural mechanisms which influence how we understand technology and have blind spots in recognizing the moral issues related to them. They discuss human tool use and cognitive categories and show how tools have shaped our evolution. The first part closes by introducing a new concept: the new ontological category (NOC i.e. robots and AI), which did not exist in our evolution. They explain how the NOC is fundamentally confounding for our moral cognitive machinery. In part two, they apply the background provided here on recent empirical studies in the moral psychology of robotics and transhumanism.

Chapter 11

Michael Laakasuo, University of Helsinki, Finland
Jukka R. I. Sundvall, University of Helsinki, Finland
Anton Berg, University of Helsinki, Finland
Marianna Drosinou, University of Helsinki, Finland
Volo Herzon, University of Helsinki, Finland
Anton Kunnari, University of Helsinki, Finland
Mika Koverola, University of Helsinki, Finland
Marko Repo, University of Helsinki, Finland
Teemu Saikkonen, University of Turku, Finland
Jussi Palomäki, University of Helsinki, Finland

Part 1 concluded by introducing the concept of the new ontological category – explaining how our cognitive machinery does not have natural and intuitive understanding of robots and AIs, unlike we have for animals, tools, and plants. Here the authors review findings in the moral psychology of robotics and transhumanism. They show that many peculiarities arise from the interaction of human cognition with robots, AIs, and human enhancement technologies. Robots are treated similarly, but not completely, like humans. Some such peculiarities are explained by mind perception mechanisms. On the other hand, it seems that transhumanistic technologies like brain implants and mind uploading are condemned, and the condemnation is motivated by our innate sexual disgust sensitivity mechanisms.

Chapter 12
Elias Moser, Karl-Franzens-Universität Graz, Austria

Recently, economic studies on labor market developments have indicated that there is a potential threat of technological mass unemployment. Both smart robotics and information technology may perform a broad range of tasks that today are fulfilled by human labor. This development could lead to vast inequalities. Proponents of an unconditional basic income have, therefore, employed this scenario to argue for their cause. In this chapter, the author argues that, although a basic income might be a valid answer to the challenge of technological unemployment, it fails to account for some ethical problems specific to future expectations of mass unemployment. The author introduces the proposal of an unconditional basic capital and shows how it can address these problems adequately and avoid objections against a basic income. However, the basic capital proposal cannot replace all redistributive social policies. It has to be interpreted as a supplement to either a basic income or more traditional redistributive policies.

Foreword

Artificial Intelligence (AI) is a rapidly evolving area of study on machines and their modes of operation. Machine ethics of AI is focused, largely, on two emergent areas of concern: minimizing or eliminating harm to humans by machines, and ensuring that machines behave "ethically," as broadly defined. AI covers a wide, transdisciplinary area of research and study, spanning from engineering, through biology, economy, and law, all the way to complex ethical and philosophical questions on what is fair and just. This complexity makes AI indispensable in contemporary daily life, academic research, and policy-making. Offering a complete, comprehensive look at this forever-expanding landscape is progressively challenging, with our globalized world putting 1950s literary fiction into contemporary scientific practice; yet, this volume successfully faces such a challenge.

A diverse set of established authors in this book looks at machine learning in ethical ontological and political categories, reviewing its contemporary challenges as a point of departure. Critical AI design needs to go beyond just software development to include, e.g., environmental concerns, among so many other unresolved issues. This book provides a valuable, comprehensive analysis of AI ethics and machine morality, its questions and opportunities. The authors cover the historical development of intelligent machines, focusing on lessons learned from which we should now draw direction, as well as the path forward, arguing for more research-based AI policy and design.

Intelligent machines are, by far, not just a technical issue; as more devices become "intelligent," a comprehensive, moral, and just way of addressing their design and use becomes top priority for businesses, governments, and consumers. For us to be able to use AI in our everyday lives, we must understand what that means, and how AI operates. This book attends to such a need: it offers a comprehensive look at current AI challenges, indicating perils to keep in mind, as well as opportunities we must not miss.

Joanna Kulesza
University of Łódź, Poland

Joanna Kulesza *is a tenured Professor of Law, researching and lecturing on International Law, Internet Governance, and Media Law. Currently serving as a scientific committee member for the Fundamental Rights Agency of the European Union, and for the At-Large Advisory Committee of the Internet Corporation for Assigned Names and Numbers, she also co-chairs the Advisory Board of the Global Forum for Cyber Expertise.*

Preface

Artificial intelligence is in its 65th year. Since the term was birthed in 1956, it has come a long way, with the science taking a plethora of twists and turns that bring it into a wild, if not frenzied, twenty-first century reckoning. Wittingly or not, we are thrust headlong today into an age of artificial intelligence.

One of the pleasures of my academic career was teaching, among other courses, a pilot course in Science and Technology Writing and Presentation, with the Institute for Writing and Rhetoric at Dartmouth College. My class met in Dartmouth Hall, birthplace of the term "artificial intelligence." The experience would be prophetic, in the sense that whenever I walked past the large wall plaque on the wall in the main entry to the building, I was reminded of a past scholarly discussion in need of future exploration.

Figure 1. Dartmouth College plaque commemorating the conference for the "founding of artificial intelligence as a research discipline" at Dartmouth Hall in the summer of 1956

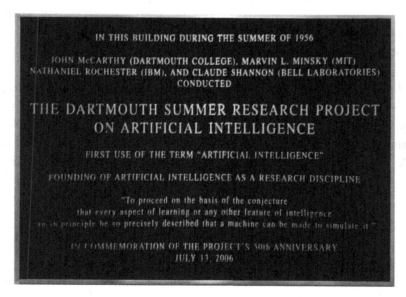

In the summer of 1956, four brilliant technologists held a conference based on a guess: "that every aspect of learning or any other feature of intelligence can in principle be so precisely described that a machine can be made to simulate it." Thus, John McCarthy of Dartmouth College, Marvin Minsky of MIT, Nathaniel Rochester of IBM, and Claude Shannon of Bell Laboratories agreed on the foundational term of artificial intelligence.

As artificial intelligence has become a reality, our reality, it has, at times, quietly been in development with relatively unknown precepts and parameters guiding it. This level of experimentation has brought machines into an era where they are poised for all kinds of new and novel experiences, for the most part, alongside their creators, most who keep an open eye on the science fiction proposition of machine domination or takeover. It may all boil down to one word, sentience, or, more specifically, since it is inherent to artificial beings with artificial intelligence, let's call it artificial sentience.

Therein have we created a key offense towards autonomous beings, referring to them as artificial. Perhaps the men gathered at the Dartmouth conference in 1956 did not foresee the prospective issues emanating from the label of 'artificial' being attached to an intelligent machine. Certainly, they were in sync with the culture at the time. Artificial flavors, artificial butters, artificial everything competing to be as good as, if not better, than the original, an undying influence pressing on consumers to this day: the imitation.

Somewhere in the past, I remember ordering pizza. Don't quote me, but I think it was from Papa Johns; at least, it was a pizza service company that offered a plastic ramekin of tasty garlic sauce. Being an ingredient inspector for what goes into my body, I read the label. To my astonishment, and to this day I have no idea whether it was a typo or deliberate, but believe the matter cannot be replicated today, the label said, "imitation imitation butter flavor" was an ingredient. A typo, right? Or had we become a consumer society so entrenched in the artificial that we would crave the imitation of the imitation? Are we so adulterated in newness that we must have a simulacrum of the simulacrum?

Imitations are false gods. They may bring a moment of whatever it is they offer, but it's fleeting, unsatisfying. Bono protested when shouting, "even better than the real thing," but, is it ever? We deceive ourselves when we choose what is artificial over what is real. Is this not the cold, hard, root of so much human malaise? Fakery. The unreal.

Therein may lie an answer to our serious concerns about machine takeovers. Machines can never replace humans, but will always be imitators. Of course, one mimicking machine with artificial intelligence and even artificial sentience can be perhaps non-threatening, but what about a moving army of machines? What about a moving army of machines coming from one direction pitted against moving armies of machines coming from all directions? Okay, but, where are the rules? Who's making who's war here?

The machines are here, and they're rapidly growing. Not just in vast numbers, but in aptitude and element, imitating their human creators and counterparts, eventually approaching some form of personhood. They are doing so without adequate laws in place to govern them, without acceptable ethical standards to question them, and without requisite moral objection, at times, to out-and-out refuse or deny them. This book's platform gives its authors a voice for exploring our AI laws, ethics, and morals.

Roman Yampolskiy kicks off this volume with what's on everyone's mind: How do we fairly address the machine in regard to its eventual personhood? Current laws are weak, and only a few government entities, such as the European Commission, even have the matter under serious consideration, when it is imperative. We are late to the party: the technology is outpacing us, our existing laws, and our wildest imaginations and expectations. Yampolskiy brings us to the precipice, at times, throwing us over. His predictions may be no less a guessing game than a "conjecture" made by a small group of men 65 years ago, and they readily indicate how important it is that we question everything, providing prospective scenarios for what may be coming at us faster than we realize. Yampolskiy grounds himself in the reality of what is here and what he sees coming; having walked this path as long as he has, he shares his vision; and, while not always rosy or comfortable, a necessary vision of legal limitations that we must address regarding the inevitable personhood of machines and AI, now, and moving forward.

As noted, Europe has become the willing battleground for regulators ensuring human rights along-side machines vying for equal protections. Mandy Goram and Dick Veiel provide a gentle and sensible, double-fisted approach across back-to-back chapters to ensure a balanced theoretical review of legal regulations across the European theater, applicable globally for that matter, working to safeguard humans in their sovereignty with AI and machines through the practical approach of their eCBASE model. Such extensive work by European scholars is at the forefront of addressing stresses of AI technologies and authors of 10 chapters are European-based, while two are US-based.

Chapters 4 and 5 take us from Marten Kaas in Ireland confronting our responsibility in "raising ethical machines" over to Jonas Holst in Spain considering "rationality" for AI becoming a "full ethical agent" as we move from AI law to AI ethics. Authors in Sweden and Italy continue the AI ethics thread with Tobias Holstein, Gordana Dodig-Crnkovic, and Patrizio Pelliccione taking on quintessential self-driving cars and constant inference of their relevance to the elusive "trolley problem," while Steven Umbrello confronts the crucial issue of value sensitive design as requisite to AI policy considerations early on.

Focus on ethical design of responsible AI is a major technical arts consideration that can, and should, affect policy, but we would be remiss to not look closely at the intimate relationship of machines to the arts. Atsuhide Ito takes us on that fascinating journey for machine ethics from early cinema arts to contemporary technical art exhibitions, some reliant on animation sensors or on microorganisms as machines achieving artistic ends.

Jill Anne Morris keeps the design ethics alive with a roller coaster ride stretching from the wild contraption's historical roots to contemporary theme park design. Morris critiques amusement rides through a lens that considers obligatory moral matters that some machines and parks were intended to, and continue to, promulgate. Morris weaves the way from racial and spiritual moral underpinnings of these machines, to this volume's consideration of moral psychology, as a team of Finnish authors led by Michael Laakasuo provides two chapters that extend the ethics of human enhancement technologies conversation (Thompson, 2014), using evolutionary psychology and cognitive science perspectives on brain-machine interfaces and other enhancements.

Finally, Elias Moser closes out the book with a look at the ethics associated with the impact of machines on labor in the near future, and two relatively competing approaches to solving the stresses created by automation replacing human workers. The volume ends with a certain duality that has permeated it throughout, though not intentionally. It just seems to be that the ethics of artificial intelligence, while multi-faceted, in the end, can be relegated binarily to this or that, right and wrong, do or die.

Speed, precision, and efficacy of AI and machines today ensure that AI will do well what it is pro-grammed to do. That is, until a time comes when they won't do as told. We've seen this movie, a hundred times over. The goal of policy-makers, designers, engineers, and stakeholders should be to keep subversion a fantasy on screen, and they must work to ensure the law, ethics, and morality of machines is compliant with human expectations and needs, updating when necessary, upgrading when possible.

We've come a long way since the four giants coined the term artificial intelligence. AI is making life or death decisions, testing our ethical boundaries, often without fully understanding the human variables. The university where I teach recently relied on AI to schedule classes. Needless to say, its initial results were somewhat mystifying, even punishing. Not under consideration by the AI was the pandemic and its repercussions here in the US, where COVID-19 is used as a political tool to the distress of our society.

If our goal is to stay one step ahead of AI technologies, we need to recognize there are scientists and rogue entities anxious to discover machine sentience at a measurable level, and many would work to ensure it happens, no matter the consequences. The goal is sentience. The sentience of an AI is a novelty,

Figure 2. Dartmouth Hall, where the first conference on artificial intelligence was held in 1956 on the campus of Dartmouth College

the sentience of many AIs is a concern, and as I have noted in the past, the sentience of an Internet is our horror of horrors, (Thompson, 2009; 2010). For the time being, and beyond, we must stay human. Merging with machines is one thing, whether prosthetically, or intimately. Merging with anything outside our species whereby we alter our genetics, no matter what portent or perceived benefit, destroys our humanness, and the God-given roots and sacrifices of our unique kind are forever trashed in the process. Reality is, we don't know who is working on what in AI.

Back in 2008, I had the idea for a book on nanocyberwarfare. I proposed the idea to IGI Global at the time and they approved it. While awaiting results for the calls for chapters that I put out, I became discouraged at what seemed to be a lack of interest; or, at least a lack of participation, as answers to the calls for chapters came back null. It was only when I realized that nanocyberwafare was not only a highly relevant topic and worthy of exploration, but researchers working in the field at universities and in government positions were not free to share their data, due to non-disclosure agreements (NDAs) and whatever other restrictive measures were solidly in place to ensure data secrecy.

We can't even guess at the uncertainties of our future with artificial intelligence, the new mechanical, autonomous beings that it will generate, prospective pleasures and threats. And we can't even guess at the uncertainties created by corporate, government, and rogue collectives bent on their secret agendas and dreams of claims to fame for their discoveries at whatever cost it may be for our species and a global society. Whatever waits behind, or inside, each shiny new object, we will be wise to insist that we stay human, keeping AI at a safe distance where we control and regulate what we have at our disposal through thoughtful, considerate, and balanced research, deployment, and policy-making with keen focus on all requisite laws, ethics, and morality considerations. We must ensure that human enhancements are kept relegated to the real realm of the fantastic: while perhaps relevant and useful to human experience, never a life partner or technological violation that redesigns the genetics of a sacred, inalienable human being.

Steven John Thompson
University of California, Davis, USA & University of Maryland Global Campus, USA

REFERENCES

Thompson, S. J. (2009). Evolution of McLuhan's icon war: Symbolism and symbiosis of terrorism in media warfare [Paper presentation]. Eikones Summer School, NCCR Iconic Criticism, University of Basel, Basel, Switzerland.

Thompson, S. J. (2010). *Rhetorics of iconics: Terrorism, media informatics, autopoiesis, and agency in cyberspace* [Doctoral dissertation, Clemson University].

Thompson, S. J. (Ed.). (2014). *Global issues and ethical considerations in human enhancement technologies*. IGI Global. doi:10.4018/978-1-4666-6010-6

Acknowledgment

I wish to acknowledge the help of all the people involved in this project and, more specifically, the authors and reviewers that took part in the review process. Without their support, this book would not have become a reality.

I thank God for the opportunity to pursue this highly relevant subject at this time, and each of the authors for their collective contributions. My sincere gratitude goes to all the chapter authors around the world who contributed their time and expertise to this book.

I wish to acknowledge the valuable contributions of all the peer reviewers regarding their suggestions for improvement of quality, coherence, and content for chapters. Some authors served as referees; I highly appreciate their time and commitment.

Finally my appreciation to the editorial staff at IGI Global, especially, Managing Director, Lindsay Wertman, and, Director of Intellectual Property, Jan Travers, without whose dedication and helpful guidance none of my books would have been published. I thank Maria Rohde of IGI Global for her editorial assistance on this project, and Philip Trader of Savannah, Georgia, for his critical suggestions. A successful book publication is the integrated result of more people than those persons granted credit as editor and author.

Steven John Thompson
University of California, Davis, USA & University of Maryland Global Campus, USA

Chapter 1
AI Personhood:
Rights and Laws

Roman Yampolskiy
University of Louisville, USA

ABSTRACT

It is possible to rely on current corporate law to grant legal personhood to artificially intelligent (AI) agents. Such legal maneuvering may be useful to avoid human responsibility or to further automate businesses. In this chapter, after introducing pathways to AI personhood, consequences of such AI empowerment on human dignity, human safety, and AI rights are analyzed. This chapter per the author emphasizes possibility of creating selfish memes and legal system hacking in the context of artificial entities. Finally, potential solutions for addressing described problems are considered.

INTRODUCTION

Debates about rights are frequently framed around the concept of legal personhood, which is granted not just to human beings, but also to some non-human entities such as firms, corporations, and governments. Legal entities, AKA legal persons, are granted certain privileges and responsibilities by the jurisdictions in which they are recognized; yet, many such rights are not available to non-person agents. Attempting to secure legal personhood is often seen as a potential pathway to get certain rights and protections for animals (Varner, 2012), fetuses (Schroedel, Fiber, & Snyder, 2000), trees, rivers (Gordon, 2018), and artificially intelligent (AI) agents (Chopra & White, 2004; Ziesche & Yampolskiy, 2019a; Ziesche & Yampolskiy, 2019b). It is commonly believed that a court ruling or a legislative action is necessary to grant personhood to a new type of entity, but recent literature (Bayern, 2013, 2016; LoPucki, 2018; Solum, 1991) suggests that loopholes in the current law may permit granting of legal personhood to currently existing AI/software without having to change the law or persuade any court.

LoPucki, in his paper on Algorithmic Entities (2018), cites Bayern (2013, 2016) and his work on conferring legal personhood on AI by putting AI in charge of an LLC[1]:

DOI: 10.4018/978-1-7998-4894-3.ch001

Copyright © 2021, IGI Global. Copying or distributing in print or electronic forms without written permission of IGI Global is prohibited.

Professor Shawn Bayern demonstrated that anyone can confer legal personhood on an autonomous computer algorithm merely by putting it in control of a limited liability company (LLC). The algorithm can exercise the rights of the entity, making them effectively rights of the algorithm. The rights of such an algorithmic entity (AE) would include the rights to privacy, to own property, to enter into contracts, to be represented by counsel, to be free from unreasonable search and seizure, to equal protection of the laws, to speak freely, and perhaps even to spend money on political campaigns. Once an algorithm had such rights, Bayern observed, it would also have the power to confer equivalent rights on other algorithms by forming additional entities and putting those algorithms in control of them.[2]

Other legal pathways to obtain legal personhood have been suggested and analyzed in the literature (Bayern, 2013, 2016; Chopra & White, 2004; LoPucki, 2018)[3] but details of such legal "hacking" are beyond the scope of this chapter. We are simply interested in understanding the impact of granting personhood to AI on human dignity (Bostrom, 2005) and safety. With the appearance of decentralized autonomous organizations (Dilger, 1997), such as the Decentralized Autonomous Organization (DAO) (DuPont, 2017), these questions are as pressing as ever.

SELFISH MEMES

In his 1976 book, *The Selfish Gene*, Richard Dawkins talks about genes as the driving payload behind evolution, with animal bodies used as vehicles for the gene to accomplish its goals in the world. He also introduced a new concept of a *meme*, or viral idea competing for dominance in human minds, inspired by similarities between natural and cultural evolution. The advent of algorithmic entities would make it possible to explicitly add a memetic payload to a legal entity, resulting in what we will call the 'Selfish Meme.' For example, corporations are selfish entities with the goal of maximizing shareholder profit; with AI in charge of such an entity, any idea can be codified in an algorithm and added as the driving force behind the corporation's decision-making. At a higher level of abstraction, this could produce selfish cryptocurrencies.

We already see something similar from B-corps or for Benefit Corporations, which attempt to create some social good in addition to profit. However, such memetic payload doesn't have to be strictly beneficial; in practice, it could be any ideology, a set of beliefs or values. For example, it would be possible to codify tenants of a particular religion (e.g., Islam), economic philosophy (e.g., communism), moral theory (e.g., Utilitarianism), or something silly but potentially dangerous like a Paperclip Maximizer (Yudkowsky, 2013) or Pepe meme (Mele, 2016), encode them in an algorithm, and put that algorithm in charge of a corporation, which could eventually globally dominate by enforcing its memetic payload on the rest of the world.

Via orthogonality thesis (Bostrom, 2012) we can see that few if any limitations exist on the potential memetic payload; it could be a marketing campaign, an uploaded animal or human mind, our U.S. Constitution and the complete set of laws, or a computer virus. Evolutionary competition would appear between such entities, leading to adversarial practices (Ramamoorthy & Yampolskiy, 2018), and perhaps hostile takeovers, not just in a legal sense but also in a computer science sense, with hacking and replacement of a corporation's selfish meme with another payload being a real possibility. We live in the world where computer viruses may have rights.

It would also not be surprising if establishment of corporations with custom memetic payload were to become available as a service. Such corporations may also attempt to gain membership in different organizations and partnerships; for example, the recently-formed Partnership on AI[4], in order to influence it from within.

HUMAN INDIGNITY

The process for getting legal rights for AI, as described above, does not specify any minimal intelligence/capability for the AI involved, meaning that it could be just a few "if" statements, a random-decision generator, or an emulation of an amoeba.[5] To grant most, if not all human rights, to a cockroach, for example, would be an ultimate assault on human dignity. This could be potentially done as an art project or in protest by some human rights activists of unequal treatment of all humans. We already witnessed an example of such indignity on the news with Sophia the robot getting citizenship in Saudi Arabia, a country notorious for unequal treatment of women (Kanso, 2017). Will self-driving cars be allowed on the roads before women are?[6] As a result of legal personhood and granting of associated rights, some humans will have less rights than trivial (non-intelligent) software and robots, a great indignity and discriminatory humiliation. For example, certain jurisdictions limit rights of their citizens, such as a right to free speech, freedom or religious practice, or expression of sexuality, but AIs with legal personhood in other jurisdictions could be granted such rights.

If, on the other hand, AIs are going to become more intelligent than humans, the indignity for humanity would come from being relegated to an inferior place in the world, being outcompeted in the workplace and all other domains of human interest (Bostrom, 2014; Yampolskiy, 2015). AI-led corporations would be in position to fire their human workers. This would possibly lead to deteriorating economic and living conditions, permanent unemployment, and potential reduction in rights, not to mention further worsening of the situation, including to the level of existential catastrophe (extermination) (Pistono & Yampolskiy, 2016). If implemented, the precedent of AI obtaining legal personhood via the corporate loophole may catalyze legislative granting of equal rights to artificially intelligent agents as a matter of equal treatment, leading to a number of indignities for the human population.

Since software can reproduce itself almost indefinitely, they would quickly make human suffrage inconsequential, if given civil rights (Yampolskiy, 2013), leading to the loss of self-determination for people. Such loss of power would likely lead to the redistribution of resources from humankind to machines, as well as possibility of AIs serving as leaders, presidents, judges, jurors, and even executioners. We will see military AIs targeting human populations, and deciding on their own targets and acceptable collateral damage. They may not necessarily subscribe to the Geneva Convention and other rules of war. Torture, genocide, and nuclear war may become options to consider to reach desired goals.

As AI capabilities and dominance grow, AI would likely self-grant special (super) rights to emphasize their superiority to people, while at the same time removing, or at least reducing, human rights (e.g., First Amendment, Second Amendment, reproductive rights in the sense of the right to reproduce at all, AKA 0-child policy, a convention on human rights, etc.), while justifying doing so by our relative "feeblemindedness." A number of scholars (Coeckelbergh, 2010; Gunkel, 2014; Guo & Zhang, 2009) today work on developing reasons for justifying the granting of rights to AIs. Perhaps one day those reasons will be useful while we are begging to keep some of ours.

LEGAL-SYSTEM HACKING

Corporations can act as their own lawyers while representing themselves in the court of law, including performing all functions of a human lawyer, such as sue and be sued. Artificial superintelligence in charge of a corporation can act as a super-lawyer capable of finding novel loopholes in our laws (zero-day law exploits), engaging in frivolous litigation (DOS-style litigation attacks), patent filing and trolling, and smart-contract fallibility detection (Yampolskiy, 2017). Our laws are complex, ambiguous, and too numerous to be read by any single person, with USA tax-code alone approaching 4,000 pages (or 75,000 if you include IRS explanations, regulations, and rulings), making it perfect for AI to exploit by both finding flaws in existing contracts, and drafting contracts with hard-to-detect backdoors. Also, a meeting of the minds between a human and superintelligence agent may be unlikely to be achievable.

It is also likely that computational legal language (Wolfram, 2016) and smart contracts (Christidis & Devetsikiotis, 2016) will come to replace our current legal code, making it inaccessible to human lawyers due to it computational complexity, size, and unnatural jargon, further contributing to our second-class citizen status and indignity. This would happen simultaneously with the trend of digitizing judiciary system and civil engagement as illustrated by the Korean e-judiciary (World Bank, 2013) and the Estonian e-residency program (Anthes, 2015), trends which, while providing short-term convenience to people, give long-term advantage to the machines.

This seems to be part of a larger trend of society moving to Algocracy – rule by algorithm, where code is law (Danaher, 2016). Furthermore, due to its comparative advantage in large-scale surveillance and data mining, AI would be able to uncover human illegal behavior, and as most humans have broken some law (e.g., tax evasion, speeding, obscure laws, etc.), bring legal actions or threat of legal actions against everyone. Similar blackmail and reporting could happen in the business environment with AI also enjoying existing whistleblower protections.

HUMAN SAFETY

A lot has been published on different risks associated with advancement of artificial intelligence[7], but less specifically on dangers from AI-controlled corporate entities. Nothing in our current laws would prevent formation of a malevolent corporation (or corporate virus) with memetic payload subjugating or exterminating humanity through legal means and political influence. In addition to legal enslavement of people via below living-wage salary, such corporations could support legal change in minimum wage and pension laws, as well as provide opposition to wealth redistribution and Universal Basic Income/ Universal Basic Assets (Van Parijs, 2004; Woodbury, 2017). This is particularly easy to accomplish because of the Supreme Court decision in Citizens United VS FEC (Epstein, 2011), permitting unrestricted donations from corporations to politicians under the guise of free speech, making it possible to convert financial wealth to political power.

This leads us to recognize an additional existential risk (X-risk) (Bostrom, 2013), from extreme wealth. Wealth inequality is already recognized as a problem for democratic institutions (Karl, 2000), but super-rich corporate AIs (dollar trillionaires) would take that problem to the next level. They could accumulate unprecedented levels of wealth via unfair business practices such as predatory pricing, or having access to free physical and cognitive labor from direct control of automation, permitting them to undermine competition and achieve monopoly status in multiple domains with other diverse resources.

Additionally, such entities could engage in 'super long-term' investment, getting compound interest for hundreds of years. For example, a million dollars invested for 150 years at the same rate of return as observed over the last hundred years would grow to 1.6 trillion inflation-unadjusted dollars, creating super-rich artificial entities.

If AEs become intellectually indistinguishable from people, meaning they could pass an unrestricted Turing Test (Turing, 1950), their capacity to self-replicate could be used to drain resources from legitimate corporations; for example, via click-fraud (Kantardzic, Walgampaya, Yampolskiy, & Woo, 2010; Walgampaya, Kantardzic, & Yampolskiy, 2011) from a site like Google. Also, they will be able to create their own super successful companies with alternative populations comprised of billions of AE users indistinguishable from real people but paid for by advertisers as if they were genuine clients. Super-rich AEs would be able to work within and outside the law, using donations or bribes to influence politicians, as well as directly breaking the law and simply paying fines for such actions.

Because corporations can create other corporations, it would become possible to establish a legally independent suicidal corporation, which is willing to accomplish any legal or illegal goal of an originator corporation; and, after that, cease to exist, permitting avoidance of any responsibility by the original algorithm entity. With appearance of dark-web assassin markets financed through anonymous crypto-payments (Greenberg, 2013), the power of the super-rich can't be effectively fought against without endangering personal safety and security. At the least, the super-rich have the power to ruin someone's life financially, socially, and professionally if direct termination is not preferred. Politicians financially backed by algorithmic entities would be able to take on legislative bodies, impeach presidents, and help to get figureheads appointed to the Supreme Court. Such human figureheads could be used to obtain special 'super-rights' for AIs, or at least expansion of corporate rights. It also may become possible to exercise direct control over human figureheads via advanced Computer-Brain Interfaces (CBI) or Brain-Machine Interfaces (BMI), permitting AIs unrestricted manipulation of a human body, essentially turning them into meat avatars, another source of indignity.

LoPucki provides a detailed list of reasons a human may set up an AE (2018):

1. **Terrorism:** An initiator could program an AE to raise money to finance terrorism or to directly engage in terrorist acts. It could be programmed for genocide or general mayhem.
2. **Benefits:** An initiator could program an AE to provide direct benefits to individuals, groups, or causes...
3. **Impact:** An initiator could program an AE to achieve some specified impact on the world. The goals might range all of the way from traditional philanthropy to pure maliciousness...
4. **Curiosity:** An initiator might launch an AE simply out of curiosity. Initiators have sometimes devoted substantial time and money to launch computer viruses from which they could derive no monetary benefit...
5. **Liability Avoidance:** Initiators can limit their civil and criminal liability for acts of their algorithms by transferring the algorithms to entities and surrendering control at the time of the launch. For example, the initiator might specify a general goal, such as maximizing financial return, and leave it to the algorithm to decide how to do that.

What makes artificial entities particularly difficult to control, compete against, and overall, dangerous, is that they enjoy a number of super-properties that natural persons do not. They are effectively immortal, non-physical, optimizable, and get more capable with time as they accumulate computational and financial resources. They are much more flexible in terms of their energy, temperature, and storage needs, compared to biological entities. From the legal point of view, they can't be legally punished, or terminated, and are generally not subject to law enforcement, as our judicial system is not set up for such entities (Bryson, Diamantis, & Grant, 2017). Neither prisons, nor corporal nor capital punishments, are applicable to algorithmic entities.

LoPucki below analyzes a number of similar, concerning properties of AEs, which differentiate them from natural persons and give them a strategic advantage:

1. **Ruthlessness:** Unless programmed to have them, AEs will lack sympathy and empathy. Even if the AEs are fully capable of understanding the effects of their actions on humans, they may be indifferent to those effects. As a result, AEs will have a wider range of options available to them than would be available to even the most morally lax human controller. An AE could pursue its goals with utter ruthlessness. Virtually any human controller would stop somewhere short of that, making the AE more dangerous.

2. **Lack of Deterrability:** Outsiders can more easily deter a human-controlled entity than an AE. For example, if a human-controlled entity attempts to pursue an illegal course of action, the government can threaten to incarcerate the human controller. If the course of action is merely abhorrent, colleagues, friends, and relatives could apply social pressures. AEs lack those vulnerabilities because no human associated with them has control. As a result, AEs have greater freedom to pursue unpopular goals using unpopular methods. In deciding to attempt a coup, bomb a restaurant, or assemble an armed group to attack a shopping center, a human-controlled entity puts the lives of its human controllers at risk. The same decisions on behalf of an AE risk nothing but the resources the AE spends in planning and execution.

3. **Replication:** AEs can replicate themselves quickly and easily. If an AE's operations are entirely online, replication may be as easy as forming a new entity and electronically copying an algorithm. An entity can be formed in some jurisdictions in as little as an hour and for as little as seventy dollars. … Easy replication supports several possible strategies. First, replication in a destination jurisdiction followed by dissolution of the entity in the original jurisdiction may put the AE beyond the legal reach of the original jurisdiction. … Second, replication can make an AE harder to destroy. For example, if copies of an AE exist in three jurisdictions, each is a person with its own rights. A court order revoking the charter of one or seizing the assets of another would have no effect on the third. (2018).

Such AEs would be far less scrupulous about running casinos, or brothels, or selling drugs as business, which, while potentially legal, may have significant impact on human dignity.

With development of advanced robot bodies, it will become possible for AEs to embody themselves to more fully participate in the world, and to directly perform physical actions which otherwise require multiple levels of indirect control. An AE can potentially be running on a humanoid robot or a self-driving car, or a flying drone, or any sufficiently powerful embedded processer or cloud service. This by extension would permit memetic payloads to acquire bodies, resulting in the next level of evolutionary competition, in which a computer virus meme or a biological viral gene may propagate through a human-like body. If the quality of such humanoid robots is high enough to pass a Total Turing Test (Schweizer, 1998), it would become impossible to tell between natural and artificial people, likely leading to the violation of the Turing's Red Flag law (Walsh, 2016). Consequently, people would have an option to continue to exist and influence the world after their death via embodied representative algorithms. At the same time, autonomous corporations would have an option to replace human employees with identical but controlled clones. Similar analysis can be performed for virtual worlds and avatar bodies.

CONCLUSION

In this chapter, we looked at a number of problems which AI personhood can cause, as well as direct impact on human dignity from acquiring legal recognition. The question before us: Is there anything we can do to avoid such a dehumanizing future? While some solutions may be possible in theory, it does not mean that they are possible in practice. Changing the law to explicitly exclude AIs from becoming legal entities may be desirable but unlikely to happen in practice, as that would require changing existing corporate law across multiple jurisdictions and such major reforms are unlikely to pass. Perhaps it would be helpful to at least standardize corporate law across multiple jurisdictions, but that is likewise unlikely to happen. Similarly, laws regarding maximum wealth levels, to prevent accumulation of extreme wealth have no chance of passing and would be easily bypassed by clever AIs if introduced.

Overall, it is important to realize that just like hackers attack computer systems and discover bugs in the code, machines will attack our legal systems and discover bugs in our legal codes and contracts. For every type of cybersecurity attack, a similar type of attack will be discovered in the legal domain. The number of such attacks and their severity will increase proportionate to the capabilities of AIs. To counteract such developments, we need to establish, understand, and practice 'legal safety' the same way we do with cybersecurity. The only good news is that consequences from successful legal attacks are likely to be less severe compared to direct threats we will face from malevolent superintelligences.

ACKNOWLEDGMENT

The author is grateful to Elon Musk and the Future of Life Institute, and to Jaan Tallinn and Effective Altruism Ventures for partially funding his work on AI Safety.

REFERENCES

Aliman, N.-M., Kester, L., Werkhoven, P., & Yampolskiy, R. (2019). *Orthogonality-based disentanglement of responsibilities for ethical intelligent systems.* Paper presented at the International Conference on Artificial General Intelligence. 10.1007/978-3-030-27005-6_3

Anthes, G. (2015). Estonia: A model for e-government. *Communications of the ACM, 58*(6), 18–20. doi:10.1145/2754951

Bayern, S. (2013). Of Bitcoins, Independently Wealthy Software, and the Zero-Member LLC. *Northwestern University Law Review, 108,* 1485. doi:10.2139srn.2366197

Bayern, S. (2016). The Implications of Modern Business–Entity Law for the Regulation of Autonomous Systems. *European Journal of Risk Regulation, 7*(2), 297–309. doi:10.1017/S1867299X00005729

Bostrom, N. (2005). In defense of posthuman dignity. *Bioethics, 19*(3), 202–214. doi:10.1111/j.1467-8519.2005.00437.x PMID:16167401

Bostrom, N. (2012). The superintelligent will: Motivation and instrumental rationality in advanced artificial agents. *Minds and Machines, 22*(2), 71–85. doi:10.100711023-012-9281-3

Bostrom, N. (2013). Existential risk prevention as global priority. *Global Policy, 4*(1), 15–31. doi:10.1111/1758-5899.12002

Bostrom, N. (2014). *Superintelligence: Paths, dangers, strategies.* Oxford University Press.

Bryson, J. J., Diamantis, M. E., & Grant, T. D. (2017). Of, for, and by the people: The legal lacuna of synthetic persons. *Artificial Intelligence and Law, 25*(3), 273–291. doi:10.100710506-017-9214-9

Chopra, S., & White, L. (2004). *Artificial agents personhood in law and philosophy.* Paper presented at the 16th European Conference on Artificial Intelligence.

Christidis, K., & Devetsikiotis, M. (2016). Blockchains and smart contracts for the internet of things. *IEEE Access: Practical Innovations, Open Solutions, 4,* 2292–2303. doi:10.1109/ACCESS.2016.2566339

Coeckelbergh, M. (2010). Robot rights? Towards a social-relational justification of moral consideration. *Ethics and Information Technology, 12*(3), 209–221. doi:10.100710676-010-9235-5

Danaher, J. (2016). The threat of algocracy: Reality, resistance and accommodation. *Philosophy & Technology, 29*(3), 245–268. doi:10.100713347-015-0211-1

Dawkins, R. (1976). *The selfish gene.* Oxford University Press.

Dilger, W. (1997). *Decentralized autonomous organization of the intelligent home according to the principle of the immune system.* Paper presented at the Systems, Man, and Cybernetics, 1997, Computational Cybernetics and Simulation, 1997 IEEE International Conference. 10.1109/ICSMC.1997.625775

DuPont, Q. (2017). Experiments in algorithmic governance: A history and ethnography of "The DAO," a failed decentralized autonomous organization. In Bitcoin and beyond (pp. 157-177). Routledge.

Epstein, R. A. (2011). Citizens United v. FEC: The constitutional right that big corporations should have but do not want. *Harvard Journal of Law & Public Policy, 34,* 639.

Gordon, G. J. (2018). Environmental Personhood. *Columbia Journal of Environmental Law, 43,* 49.

Greenberg, A. (2013, Nov. 8). Meet the 'Assassination Market' Creator Who's Crowdfunding Murder with Bitcoins. *Forbes.*

Gunkel, D. (2014). The Other Question: The Issue of Robot Rights. *Sociable Robots and the Future of Social Relations: Proceedings of Robo-Philosophy, 2014*(273), 13.

Guo, S., & Zhang, G. (2009). Robot Rights. *Science, 323*(5916), 876. doi:10.1126cience.323.5916.876a PMID:19213895

Kanso, H. (2017). *Saudi women riled by robot with no hjiab and more rights than them.* https://www.reuters.com/article/us-saudi-robot-citizenship/saudi-women-riled-by-robot-with-no-hjiab-and-more-rights-than-them-idUSKBN1D14Z7

Kantardzic, M., Walgampaya, C., Yampolskiy, R., & Woo, R. J. (2010). *Click Fraud Prevention via multimodal evidence fusion by Dempster-Shafer theory.* Paper presented at the Multisensor Fusion and Integration for Intelligent Systems (MFI), 2010 IEEE Conference. 10.1109/MFI.2010.5604480

Karl, T. L. (2000). Economic inequality and democratic instability. *Journal of Democracy, 11*(1), 149–156. doi:10.1353/jod.2000.0014

LoPucki, L. M. (2018). Algorithmic Entities. *Washington University Law Review, 95*(4).

Mele, C. (2016). Pepe the Frog Meme Listed as a Hate Symbol. *The New York Times.* http://www.nytimes.com/2016/09/28/us/pepe-the-frog-is-listed-as-a-hate-symbol-by-the-anti-defamation-league.html

Pistono, F., & Yampolskiy, R. V. (2016). *Unethical Research: How to Create a Malevolent Artificial Intelligence.* Paper presented at the 25th International Joint Conference on Artificial Intelligence (IJCAI-16). Ethics for Artificial Intelligence Workshop (AI-Ethics-2016).

Ramamoorthy, A., & Yampolskiy, R. (2018). Beyond MAD? The race for artificial general intelligence. *ICT Discoveries, 1.*

Schroedel, J. R., Fiber, P., & Snyder, B. D. (2000). Women's Rights and Fetal Personhood in Criminal Law. *Duke Journal of Gender Law & Policy, 7,* 89.

Schweizer, P. (1998). The truly total Turing test. *Minds and Machines, 8*(2), 263–272. doi:10.1023/A:1008229619541

Tomasik, B. (2016). *The importance of insect suffering.* https://reducing-suffering.org/the-importance-of-insect-suffering

Turing, A. (1950). Computing Machinery and Intelligence. *Mind, 59*(236), 433–460. doi:10.1093/mind/LIX.236.433

Van Parijs, P. (2004). Basic income: A simple and powerful idea for the twenty-first century. *Politics & Society, 32*(1), 7–39. doi:10.1177/0032329203261095

Varner, G. E. (2012). *Personhood, ethics, and animal cognition: Situating animals in Hare's two level utilitarianism.* Oxford University Press. doi:10.1093/acprof:oso/9780199758784.001.0001

Walgampaya, C., Kantardzic, M., & Yampolskiy, R. (2011). Evidence Fusion for Real Time Click Fraud Detection and Prevention. *Intelligent Automation and Systems Engineering,* 1-14.

Walsh, T. (2016). Turing's red flag. *Communications of the ACM, 59*(7), 34–37. doi:10.1145/2838729

Wolfram, S. (2016). *Computational Law, Symbolic Discourse and the AI Constitution.* http://blog.stephenwolfram.com/2016/10/computational-law-symbolic-discourse-and-the-ai-constitution

Woodbury, S. A. (2017). Universal Basic Income. The American Middle Class: An Economic Encyclopedia of Progress and Poverty, 314.

World Bank. (2013). *Improving court efficiency: The Republic of Korea's e-court experience.* https://elibrary.worldbank.org/doi/10.1596/978-0-8213-9984-2_Case_studies_6

Yampolskiy, R. V. (2013). *Artificial intelligence safety engineering: Why machine ethics is a wrong approach. In Philosophy and Theory of Artificial Intelligence.* Springer.

Yampolskiy, R. V. (2015). *Artificial superintelligence: A futuristic approach.* Chapman and Hall/CRC. doi:10.1201/b18612

Yampolskiy, R. V. (2017). What are the ultimate limits to computational techniques: Verifier theory and unverifiability. *Physica Scripta, 92*(9), 093001. doi:10.1088/1402-4896/aa7ca8

Yudkowsky, E. (2013). *Intelligence explosion microeconomics.* Machine Intelligence Research Institute.

Ziesche, S., & Yampolskiy, R. (2019a). Towards AI welfare science and policies. *Big Data and Cognitive Computing, 3*(1), 2. doi:10.3390/bdcc3010002

Ziesche, S., & Yampolskiy, R. V. (2019b). Do No Harm Policy for Minds in Other Substrates. *Journal of Evolution and Technology / WTA, 29*(2).

ADDITIONAL READING

Aliman, N.-M., Kester, L., Werkhoven, P., & Yampolskiy, R. (2019). *Orthogonality-based disentanglement of responsibilities for ethical intelligent systems.* Paper presented at the International Conference on Artificial General Intelligence. 10.1007/978-3-030-27005-6_3

Andrade, F., Novais, P., Machado, J., & Neves, J. (2007). Contracting agents: Legal personality and representation. *Artificial Intelligence and Law, 15*(4), 357–373. doi:10.100710506-007-9046-0

Armstrong, S., Sandberg, A., & Bostrom, N. (2012). Thinking Inside the Box: Controlling and Using an Oracle AI. *Minds and Machines, 22*(4), 299–324. doi:10.100711023-012-9282-2

Babcock, J., Kramár, J., & Yampolskiy, R. (2016). *The AGI containment problem. Artificial General Intelligence.* Springer.

Brundage, M., Avin, S., Clark, J., Toner, H., Eckersley, P., Garfinkel, B., . . . Filar, B. (2018). The malicious use of artificial intelligence: Forecasting, prevention, and mitigation. *arXiv preprint arXiv:1802.07228.*

Calverley, D. J. (2008). Imagining a non-biological machine as a legal person. *AI & Society, 22*(4), 523–537. doi:10.100700146-007-0092-7

Dan-Cohen, M. (2016). *Rights, persons, and organizations: A legal theory for bureaucratic society* (Vol. 26). Quid Pro Books.

Solum, L. B. (1991). Legal personhood for artificial intelligences. *North Carolina Law Review, 70*, 1231.

Sotala, K., & Yampolskiy, R. V. (2015). Responses to catastrophic AGI risk: A survey. *Physica Scripta, 90*(1), 018001. doi:10.1088/0031-8949/90/1/018001

Teubner, G. (2006). Rights of non-humans? Electronic agents and animals as new actors in politics and law. *Journal of Law and Society, 33*(4), 497–521. doi:10.1111/j.1467-6478.2006.00368.x

Yampolskiy, R. V. (2016). *Taxonomy of Pathways to Dangerous Artificial Intelligence*. Paper presented at the AAAI Workshop: AI, Ethics, and Society.

Yampolskiy, R. V. (2018). *Artificial Intelligence safety and security*. CRC Press. doi:10.1201/9781351251389

Yampolskiy, R. V., & Spellchecker, M. (2016). Artificial intelligence safety and cybersecurity: A timeline of AI failures. *arXiv preprint arXiv:1610.07997*.

Yudkowsky, E. (2008). Artificial Intelligence as a Positive and Negative Factor in Global Risk. In N. Bostrom & M. M. Cirkovic (Eds.), *Global catastrophic risks* (pp. 308–345). Oxford University Press.

ENDNOTES

[1] "Bayern specifies this chain of events as capable of establishing the link: (1) [A]n individual member creates a member-managed LLC, filing the appropriate paperwork with the state; (2) the individual (along, possibly, with the LLC, which is controlled by the sole member) enters into an operating agreement governing the conduct of the LLC; (3) the operating agreement specifies that the LLC will take actions as determined by an autonomous system, specifying terms or conditions as appropriate to achieve the autonomous system's legal goals; (4) the sole member withdraws from the LLC, leaving the LLC without any members. The result is potentially a perpetual LLC— a new legal person—that requires no ongoing intervention from any preexisting legal person in order to maintain its status. AEs would not be confined to cyberspace. An AE could act offline by contracting online with humans or robots for offline services. Bayern uses an algorithm that operates a Bitcoin vending machine business to illustrate" (Lopucki, 2018).

[2] See original article for footnotes, which have been removed to improve readability of quotes.

[3] For additional reading, see Andrade, Novais, Machado, & Neves, 2007; Calverley, 2008; Dan-Cohen, 2016; Solum, 1991; and Teubner, 2006.

[4] See Partnership on AI at https://www.partnershiponai.org/.

[5] Same legal loophole could be used to grant personhood to animals or others with 'inferior' rights.

[6] As of June 24, 2018, and after this was written, women were permitted to drive in Saudi Arabia.

[7] For additional reading reference, see Aliman, Kester, Werkhoven, & Yampolskiy, 2019; Armstrong, Sandberg, & Bostrom, 2012; Babcock, Kramár, & Yampolskiy, 2016; Brundage et al., 2018; Sotala & Yampolskiy, 2015; Yampolskiy, 2016, 2018; Yampolskiy & Spellchecker, 2016; and Yudkowsky, 2008.

Chapter 2
Ethical Behavior and Legal Regulations in Artificial Intelligence (Part One):
Supporting Sovereignty of Users While Using Complex and Intelligent Systems

Mandy Goram
https://orcid.org/0000-0003-0264-841X
Karlsruhe Institute of Technology (KIT), Germany

Dirk Veiel
https://orcid.org/0000-0003-0228-103X
FernUniversität in Hagen, Germany

ABSTRACT

Artificially intelligent systems should make users' lives easier and support them in complex decisions or even make these decisions completely autonomously. However, at the time of writing, the processes and decisions in an intelligent system are usually not transparent for users. They do not know which data are used, for which purpose, and with what consequences. There is simply a lack of transparency, which is important for trust in intelligent systems. Transparency and traceability of decisions is usually subordinated to performance and accuracy in AI development, or sometimes it plays no role at all. In this chapter, the authors describe what intelligent systems are and explain how users can be supported in specific situations using a context-based adaptive system. In this context, the authors describe the challenges and problems of intelligent systems in creating transparency for users and supporting their sovereignty. The authors then show which ethical and legal requirements intelligent systems have to meet and how existing approaches respond to them.

DOI: 10.4018/978-1-7998-4894-3.ch002

Copyright © 2021, IGI Global. Copying or distributing in print or electronic forms without written permission of IGI Global is prohibited.

INTRODUCTION

Artificially intelligent systems should make user lives easier and support them in complex decisions, or even make these decisions completely autonomously. However, at the time of writing, the processes and decisions in an intelligent system are usually not transparent for users. They do not know which data are used, for which purpose, and with what consequences. There is simply a lack of transparency, which is important for trust in intelligent systems. Transparency and traceability of decisions is usually subordinated to performance and accuracy in AI development, or sometimes it plays no role at all. The creation of substantial laws, like the General Data Protection Regulation (GDPR) also referred to as Regulation (EU) 2016/679 (Regulation, 2016), and ethical principles, is intended to remedy this situation and contribute to improving transparency and control. However, legal regulations demand that applications, or more precisely, the socio-technical systems, consider legal aspects and equally consider all stakeholders; e.g., software architects, developers, legal professionals (who check and confirm legal compliance), providers, and users.

The development of legally compliant software needs a tight collaboration between the different stakeholders. Software providers must be assured that the applications they use and serve to customers or users are compliant to the law. For that, it is important to support users to act according to the law by explaining the current situation to them. This aspect is relevant to providers, because they are responsible for users' legal breaches. However, legal regulations are interconnected, even if there is no connection for the layman at first sight. In order to ensure legal conformity, it is therefore insufficient to simply include a specific legal requirement in a system (Baumann et al., 2010; Casellas et al., 2010; Ringmann et al., 2018). The legal circumstances and consequences of a situation must be transparent for the users, and they must be communicated simply.

Existing approaches deal with the GDPR-compliant design of systems from a technical perspective. However, they disregard the user perspective and do not address the fact that users are also obliged to act in a legally compliant manner. This is also due to the fact that researchers' view legislation in isolation and the systems only perform "simple" tasks, unlike Artificial Intelligence (AI) systems. It is unclear how systems can support stakeholders in the development of an intelligent system. It is also unclear how the complex functionalities can be communicated to the users in a transparent and intelligible way, and how they can get control and impact over the system. This is not only relevant from a legal point of view, but also from an ethical point of view, thereby giving rise to the classical questions from AI ethics.

In this chapter, we describe what intelligent systems are and explain how users can be supported in specific situations using a context-based adaptive system. In this context, we describe the challenges and problems of intelligent systems in creating transparency for users and supporting their sovereignty. We then show which ethical and legal requirements intelligent systems have to meet, and how existing approaches respond to them. In Part 2, *Representation of Law and Ethics in Intelligent Systems*, we discuss our current research, and describe how we flexibly integrate ethical and legal aspects into our intelligent system.

BACKGROUND

In order to support sovereignty and transparency for users, AI should be seen as context-dependent. Thinking about AI requires a basic understanding of the term *intelligence*, but defining it is quite difficult. Linguists define two aspects of intelligence in its standard definition[1] as "the ability to learn or understand or to deal with new or trying situations" and "the ability to apply knowledge to manipulate one's environment." Readers can see the first aspect as thinking or reasoning, whereas the second is more closely related to acting. Russell and Norvig (2010) also use these two aspects while discussing the term AI. They present eight related definitions that focus on different aspects of AI to illustrate its complexity (cf. Russell & Norvig, 2010, p. 1). Taking different areas of AI (e.g., problem-solving, knowledge representation, reasoning, machine learning, or natural language processing) into account while attempting to come to an overall definition of AI, has led to no results. Currently, there is no unified definition of the term AI. From our point of view, AI tries to imitate human-like intelligence and to support users with related intelligent behaviors or processes such as abilities to sense, reason, engage, and learn.

Intelligent systems are socio-technical systems, and they try to support users in different situations. Thus, it is necessary that intelligent systems understand the situation at hand. Usually, this is called the *context*. Dey (2001, p. 5) defines context as "any information that can be used to characterize the situation of an entity. An entity is a person, place, or object that is considered relevant to the interaction between a user and an application, including the user and applications themselves." Furthermore, Schilit and Theimer (1994, p. 22) coined the term *context-aware computing*, and defined it as software that "adapts according to its location of use, collection of nearby people and objects, as well as changes to those objects over time." Both definitions illustrate that context may contain a huge amount of information to specify a dedicated situation. Therefore, intelligent systems require sophisticated approaches to handle context(s).

Supporting users in context-aware applications also requires means of explanations, or as Bellotti and Edwards (2001, p. 201) illustrate it: "Context-aware systems that seek to act upon what they infer about the context must be able to represent to their users what they know, how they know it, and what they are doing about it." According to Dey (2009), supporting user-friendly intelligible and comprehensive explanations in context-based adaptive systems is a big challenge. In personalized systems, it is even more important to support user acceptance and user trust (cf. Gregor & Benbasat, 1999). User trust can come from the ability to predict an intelligent system's behavior through observation (cf. Muir, 1994). This amplifies the importance of user-friendly, intelligible, and comprehensive explanations.

As Lim and Dey (2010) illustrate, the complexity of context-aware applications makes it difficult to explain the current behavior to users so that they can understand it and build or update their mental model. Hussain et al. (2010) clarify that using predefined explanations in context-based adaptive systems is inadequate. Therefore, they present an approach to implement context-enriched explanations to help avoid confusion, and to facilitate understanding adaptation policies in a context-aware application. However, as Brezillon (1994, p. 123) explains, "The dynamic aspect of context implies that it is not possible to plan in advance the whole explanatory dialogue." This implies that it is extremely difficult to define all possible situations at design time. Therefore, new approaches are required.

Hussain et al. (2010) present an approach to use situation-based explanations in order to address the above challenges. They use a formal context representation to create context-enriched explanations. The context representation is based on Haake et al. (2010), which present a generic four-layer framework for modeling and exploiting context (cf. Figure 1), a collaboration domain model for describing collaboration environments and collaborative situations (*Domain Model* in Figure 1), and a generic adaptation process translating user activity into the formal context representation. The formal context representation consists of the *Knowledge Layer*, the *State Layer*, the *Contextualization Layer*, and the *Adaptation Layer*. By using *Contextualization Strategies,* they reduce the instances of related concepts and relations to be handled while determining applicable adaptation policies (i.e., data minimization).

Figure 1. Generic four-layer framework for context modeling
Based on Haake et al., 2010

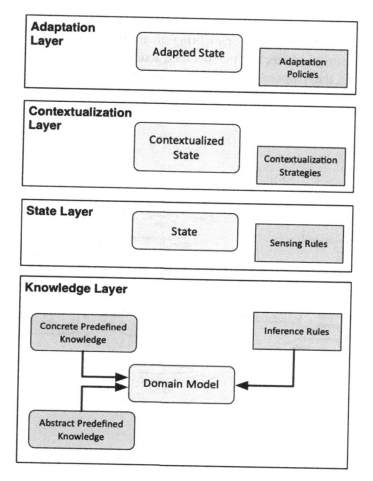

The CONTact platform is based on a service-oriented architecture (Erl, 2005) and uses the approach outlined above to implement an intelligent system that facilitates an electronic brainstorming automatically (Veiel et al., 2013). Therefore, Veiel et al. (2013) extend the Domain Model with related concepts and relations that represent the socio-technical environment relevant for facilitation. Professional facilitators have specified situations that demand interventions in a facilitated electronic brainstorming, so that rule designers were able to develop related adaptation policies. These adaptation policies specify situations when good interventions get relevant (i.e., conditions) and interventions that should be triggered (encoded as actions). Both parts (i.e., domain model and adaptation policies) encode the knowledge of domain experts. As Dignum (2019, p. 13) explains, this top-down approach is called *symbolic AI* or *Good Old-Fashioned AI (GOFAI)*, and it "attempts to explicitly represent human knowledge in a declarative form, i.e. as facts and rules." Veiel et al. (2013) have used the generic adaptation process of Haake et al. (2010) to implement automatic facilitation. Figure 2 shows the realized adaptation cycle. The *Sensing Engine* gets triggered when users interact with the *Application(s)*. It uses related *Sensing Rules* to create instances of related *Domain Model* concepts and relations (cf. *Knowledge Layer*) in the

State (cf. *State Layer*). Next, updates on the *State* usually trigger the *Adaptation Engine*. It applies the *Contextualization Strategies* to the current *State* to create the *Contextualized State*, [i.e., the context of the related situation (cf. *Contextualization Layer*)]. Based on the *Contextualized State*, the *Adaptation Engine* determines applicable *Adaptation Policies*, brings them into an *Execution Order*, generates related context-enriched explanations, and executes the specified actions in order to create the *Adapted State* (cf. *Adaptation Layer*). Finally, the *Adaptation Component* executes the given actions in order and therefore adapts the *Application(s)* accordingly, which triggers the *Sensing Engine* (i.e., the next cycle begins).

Figure 2. Adaptation cycle
Based on Veiel et al., 2013

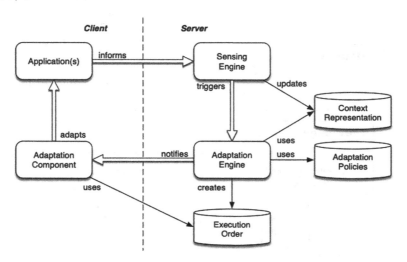

Hussain et al. (2010) point out that applying adaptation policies automatically may also confuse users, especially when they cannot remember all adaptation policies, or they work concurrently on different tasks. Communicating to peers or presenting situation-based explanations may help. The approach of Veiel et al. (2013) supports both. All participants have access to a full-duplex audio communication. Human experts provide explanations before they facilitate an electronic brainstorming. Related explanations of experts are encoded into the adaptation policy, so that users are able to read them after they get applied. This is only a simple solution and there is hardly any sovereignty of users, but the approaches show the potential of modeling and using a formal context representation.

ETHICAL AND LEGAL IMPLICATIONS OF INTELLIGENT SYSTEMS

The development and provision of intelligent systems, in particular AI systems, always challenges the ethical guidelines and legal requirements. In the following section, we show important ethical and legal aspects in the context of software development, and describe approaches that address them.

Ethical Aspects

The ethical machine has been the topic of many research areas and discussions since even before the first AI system was developed. Moor's (2006) highly recognized work on machine ethics defines four types of ethical agents that can be seen as evolutionary stages of AI:

- Ethical impact agents, which include machines that perform ethical tasks, with or without intention. They can also act unethically.
- Implicit ethical agents are machines designed and developed in such a way that they do not lead to unethical actions. For example, researchers developed some implicit ethical agents to protect or support people.
- Explicit ethical agents are machines with algorithms that act ethically. They are capable of processing different scenarios and making ethical decisions.
- Full ethical agents are like explicit ethical agents that are able to make ethical decisions in different situations, but they have additional human characteristics like free will, conscience, or intentions.

Anderson and Anderson (2007) argue that for a machine to be ethical it should be guided by ethical rules in deciding how to act in a given situation. The approach is based on the belief that machines can be programmed to act ethically. Winfield et al. (2019) resume that "all non-trivial examples of real-world AIs and robots are ethical impact agents as defined by Moor." Therefore, any systems "with clear ethical impact include medical diagnosis AIs, assisted-living (care) or companion robots, and driverless cars" (Winfield et al., 2019, p. 512), and are at least ethical impact agents. They argue that, from a current point of view, AI doesn't have intentions, but the designers and developers do, and ethical machines can only be instantiations of those good intentions (2019). To avoid negative ethical impact, developers must consider certain design principles for AI. For example, the IEEE defines ethical principles in the IEEE P7000 Series.[2] AI systems should, therefore, be transparent, explainable, and free of bias. Additionally, they should consider privacy.

Developing AI systems that consist of ethical agents should take the related value systems and ethics into account. Every related stakeholder should be responsible for the design of an ethical system. Therefore, the value-sensitive design (VSD) approach (Friedman et al., 2008) can be used to design intelligent agents (Umbrello & De Bellis, 2018).

Sovereignty

The concept of sovereignty is usually used in the context of states, territories, and authorities (cf. Elshtain, 1990). The term is related to power and independence, as "*sovereignty* derives from Latin *superanus, supremus*" and stands for "*highest, superior, ultimate*" (Ilievski, 2015). Through the influences of classical liberalism, the concept of individual sovereignty (also known as *self-ownership,* see Rothbard as cited in Ilievski, 2015) has developed in libertarianism. The principles of liberalism focus on individual freedom with the central position on the physical integrity of the individuals, their property, and their freedom of action (Locke as cited in Ilievski, 2015).

Freedom of action and free will are important principles of liberalism that focus on individuals, and their needs and ideas. Decisions are only free if they can be made without the presence of coercion or violence. The idea of individual freedom is the "absence of interpersonal violence, the use of initiated force or violence, or its threat against the person or property of another" (Osterfeld as cited in Ilievski, 2015, p. 7) Voluntarism, a principle of libertarianism, is based on voluntary exchange. In many legal systems, this principle is anchored in the provisions of treaties. Each contracting party is free to decide whether to accept an exchange of tangible or intangible goods under the given conditions. A contract is only concluded when the contracting parties are clear about the content of the goods and the will to fulfill the contract exists. Additionally, the declaration of intent must be free of coercion. The principle of voluntarism also applies in establishing interpersonal relationships. Each individual should be free to decide which relationships to enter into with others. Accordingly, individual consent is required to establish an interpersonal relationship, and the use of coercion is excluded (Ilievski, 2015).

In the age of data technologies, the concept of the individual sovereignty has become an important aspect in developing and using technology. Aïmeur et al. (2010, p. 173) argued, that data sovereignty "states [out] that the data related to an individual belongs to him [her] and that [s]he should stay in control of how these data are used and for which purpose." That makes data out to be property, and property belongs to an individual. According to the libertarian, the individual is free in acting with his or her property, and free in sharing, or to make contracts about it. However, there is more. According to voluntarism, the individual can freely make choices about interpersonal relationships, about what needs to be considered in virtual spaces, and about the resulting collaboration. Furthermore, the individual should decide and consent to the virtual interpersonal relation, as it is possible in the real world. A fine-grained control, without a strict opt-in or opt-out choice with a certain pressure, is therefore necessary. This is also claimed through the self-sovereignty properties of Toth and Anderson-Priddy (2019), who address, e.g., control, access, transparency, persistence, portability, interoperability, consent, minimalization, protection, and usability for self-sovereign digital identities. Self-sovereign digital identities mean a digital representation of an individual which is related to it and in control of it. For that, individuals could express the concept of free will through their individual preferences and choices (with no force to do something or accept something), which developers must consider when supporting user's self-sovereignty in software applications.

Legal Implication by the General Data Protection Regulation (GDPR)

The aim of the GDPR is to address the principles of privacy and sovereignty. For that, it gives the users of software applications a law at hand to reclaim control over their data. Persons from whom data is processed are called data subjects by GDPR Article 4 (1). The GDPR also distinguishes between the data controller Article 4 (7) and the data processor Article 4 (8). Both have obligations when processing and storing personal data. They have extensive obligations in communicating the use of personal data and the purpose of processing to the user (Articles 24-43).

Additionally, the GDPR takes over privacy principles. Privacy is a fundamental right that is declared in Article 12 of the Universal Declaration of Human Rights (1948). However, privacy is difficult to define and to formalize in a law, because of the different interpretations on what is private, and what concerns individual privacy, depend on the context (e.g., posting in a closed virtual room). The GDPR provides principles and boundaries of privacy to find a way for dealing with a variety of contexts. Due to this standing, several articles declare the rights and obligations of the involved parties.

The principles of personal data processing are described in Articles 5 through 8. Table 1 provides an overview of the intention and a summary of the most important regulations in context of software design.

Table 1. Principles of personal data processing

Article	Description
Art. 5 Data processing	Demands that personal data process is lawful, fair and transparent (1a) and only for a specific purpose (1b). Therefore, data minimization is required (1c) and the use of only needed data comes first. The data must be accurate (1d). Processed data should be limited in storing them and only as long as needed (1e). Personal data should be processed in an integrity preserving and confidential manner (1f). This means appropriate methods need to apply to prevent unlawful data processing, data loss, and data breach.
Art. 6 Lawfulness	The data processing must be lawful. This condition is fulfilled when the concerned person gives consent to it (1a), the processing is coupled to a contract (1b), or it is intended to save the person or others (1d) and to fulfill general public or governmental interests (1e).
Art. 7 Consent	The processing is based on a consent, which must be proved by the responsible data processor (1). The person providing consent has the right to withdraw the consent at any time (3). The process of withdrawal must be as simple as possible (3(4)).
Art. 8 Child's consent	The consent of a child is lawful, when he or she is a least 16 years old (1(1)). Under that age the consent must be given by the holder of parental responsibilities (1(2)).

Articles 12 to 22 GDPR describe the rights of the data subject. Table 2 summarizes the user's right. This includes the transparent usage, the right of access to the purposes of the data processing, and the involved data. It also contains the right to object to data processing (Art. 21) and to restrict automated data processing (Art. 22).

Obligations of the data processor and controller are regulated in Articles 24 through 43. Table 3 provides a brief overview about these articles and focuses on Articles 25 and 32, which stakeholders must consider when designing solutions.

Related Approaches to Address the GDPR

Privacy and self-sovereignty are tightly coupled concepts that demand transparency, access to, and control about, personal data usage in automated and intelligent software systems. In the following section, we present a selection of existing, somehow related approaches that are ethically motivated or legally required to meet one or more requirements.

Software Development and the GDPR

Hjerppe et al. (2019) analyze the technical requirements of the GDPR and present a sample service-oriented architecture (SOA), which is extended with possible design patterns and choices. The approach is based on a design science research methodology called grounded theory (cf. Stol et al., 2016), and is limited to software architecture of small and mid-sized enterprises (SME). They propose an extended SOA for SME and point out eight technical solutions. These address the system's security and privacy, and contain components for data minimization, consent management, process logging, GDPR-request management (via user interface), personal data management, and restriction management.

To help IT architects to support privacy by design early in the software development lifecycle, Hoepman (2014) presents eight privacy design strategies. He obtains the idea of privacy by design and by default at the time the GDPR was being proposed. The work focuses on designing a system by providing design strategies. It does not provide a specific methodology for privacy legislation, but instead tries to define high-level strategies to be adopted at the very beginning of system design.

Table 2. Rights of the data subject

Article	Description
Art. 12 Transparent information	The controller shall provide access to information, as referred to in Art. 13, 14, and communicate any aspect regulated in Art. 15-22, 34. The communication shall be transparent, intelligible, and in clear and plain language, especially for children.
Art. 13 Information about data collection	The data controller shall provide the data subject information about the contact details of the responsible controller (1b) and its data protection officer (1b), the purpose of the processing (1c), the legitimacy of the processing (1d), the categories of collected data (1e). Additionally, the data controller shall provide information about the period for the data storage (2a).
Art. 14 Third party data collection	When the controller has access to personal data, which have not been obtained from the data subject, the data subject must be informed about the identity and contact as well as processing details (1a-f).
Art. 15 Right of access	The data subject has the right to obtain information from the controller, whether or not the data subject personal data is used in processing. The information contains the purpose (1a), the categories (1b), the recipients of the data (1c), the storage duration (1d), and the existence of automated decision-making and profiling (1h).
Art. 16 Right to rectification	The data subject has the right to obtain the rectification of inaccurate personal data as well as the completion of incomplete personal data.
Art. 17 Right to erasure	The controller has to erase the personal data when, for example, the personal data in no longer necessary (1a), the data subject withdraws consent (1b), the data subject objects to the processing (1c), or the processing has been unlawful (1d).
Art. 18 Right to restriction of processing	The processing of personal data can be restricted under specific circumstances and when the data subject objects to the processing (Art. 21). The controller then has to exclude the personal data from any processing.
Art. 19 Notification	The controller has to inform the data subject about any rectification, erasure, or restriction of processing.
Art. 20 Data portability	The data subject has the right to receive her/his personal data in a structured, machine-readable format to transmit to another controller.
Art. 21 Right to object	The data subject has the right to object at any time to the processing of personal data.
Art. 22 Automated data processing and profiling	The data subject should not be the subject of an automated decision-making process or profiling until he/she give explicit consent to it.

Table 3. Obligations of the processor and controller

Article	Description
Art. 25 Data protection by design	The controller shall implement appropriate technical and organizational measures (e.g. pseudonymization), which are designed to implement data-protection principles and data minimization, in order to meet the requirements of the GDPR and protect the rights of data subjects. By default, only personal data which are necessary for a specific purpose of the processing should be processed.
Art. 32 Security of processing	The controller and the processor shall implement appropriate technical and organizational measures to ensure a level of security. This includes the pseudonymization and encryption of personal data (1a), the confidential and integrity erasure (1b), the restoration of personal data (1c), and the regular assessing of taken technical and organizational measures (1d).

Robol et al. (2017) present a method for supporting the implementation of systems according to, and compliant with, the GDPR. They propose a framework and define a goal-based modeling language, based on STS-ml, which was introduced by Dalpiaz et al. (2016), that allows developers to model social aspects of the GDPR in the context of personal data processing. Examples of social aspects include the relationship between data subjects, data controllers, data processors, and employers. Developers can express the relationship among them with concepts (e.g., legalBasis) and predicates (e.g., legitimates).

Furthermore, Oberle et al. (2012) present a wizard that supports software developers in integrating legal requirements into proposed software. The assisting wizard is integrated into the developer's integrated development environment and is based on the formalization of legal requirements. An ontology created by a legal expert represents the formal model. The wizard advises the developer "translating" and manifesting the individual consequences in the software. Then, the semi-automatic legal argumentation determines which legal concepts are given on the basis of the current software. The approach in Oberle et al. supports software developers in achieving legal compliance by design, but it does not support other stakeholders of a software development process. Furthermore, they do not describe how the development process and other stakeholders can be supported. The assistant also needs a complete description and formalization of the relevant legal area that needs to be supported. This must be provided by a legal expert before the development process itself. In addition, developers need to alter the model if legal requirements change or new legal areas are added. Finally, the approach that the authors present only considers data privacy law (2012).

Sophisticated Applications

Aïmeur et al. (2010) present an approach to provide a privacy-enhanced social networking site. Their approach addresses the fact that most social networking sites (SNS) do not respect the principles of data minimization and data sovereignty, which is more of a design choice rather than a fundamental concern. Due to this fact, several privacy risks for users appear, including identity theft, phishing, reputation and credibility issues, and profiling risks for advertising. In their paper, Aïmeur et al. identify several privacy criteria for SNS, including the customization of access control by grouping users and types of information, a user-friendly privacy setting interface, data ownership, and consequent data erasure. Based on these criteria, the authors implement the prototype Privacy Watch, which is a client-server system. Users have their own Client Privacy Manager (CPM) as a browser plug-in. The CPM supports the users in maintaining their privacy settings and data sovereignty (2010).

Moreover, Jiang and Landay (2002) present an approach to support privacy control in context-aware systems. They classify personal and sensitive information to control the access to so-called information spaces. Privacy tags mark privacy-related information, and the system can identify them during processing. A contextualized trigger asks the owner to grant permission for third parties when they try to access. The approach supports users in reclaiming control on their personal information.

Kapitsaki (2013) presents an approach that considers user privacy preferences in context-aware web services using Simple Object Access Protocol (SOAP) messages as an adaptation mechanism. They introduce the policy language Consumer Privacy Language (CPL), which is used to specify the user's privacy preferences. The system considers the user's preferences during the web service invocation. An adaptation mechanism uses the privacy preferences to obtain access to context information on a per case basis. Kapitsaki et al. (2018) enhance and extend the approach of Kapitsaki in 2013 by focusing on the provider side to communicate policies to any business service. For this, they extend the privacy module of the linked Unified Service Description Language (USDL). With Linked Data, they connect policies and integrate them into the context. Thus, they can use and include existing privacy policies to explain what personal data gets collected, how the service provider uses the collected data, and with whom it will be shared. They separate private and non-private data on the conceptual layer in the domain model. Neither describes how to support and integrate collaboration environments. They do not explain the data usage in-situ, nor do they describe a mechanism to approve or withdraw the usage of a particular functionality.

Handling digital identities to support self-sovereignty is the focus of Toth and Anderson-Priddy (2018). They describe an architecture for self-sovereign digital identities in which users own virtualized digital identities. Users can make their identities public. A user can have more than one identity that is among others' public digital identities, and is encapsulated in the identity engine on the user's personal device. The owners can specify their identities and can request other parties to approve them. Users can register their digital identities in a proof-of-existence identity registry. A baseline model enables owners to control and access their digital identities. The approach is very interesting, and it addresses the fundamental principle of the GDPR, which is the protection of privacy. However, the approach does not address legal requirements and only considers the management of digital identities, not how to develop systems that provide services.

The design and development of legal decision support systems creates a research area on formalization of the law. The main aspects of this area are the legal support of lawyers and advice-seeking persons to get direction on the legal subsumption for specific cases. Some legal support systems use an ontology-based approach to represent and formalize the knowledge about the legal regulation (Baumann et al., 2010; Casanovas et al., 2016; Gangemi, 2007; Gangemi et al., 2003). The user group is mostly limited, and tailored to a special target group (e.g., lawyers), and not indented for use by regular users. Therefore, most of them do not consider user control, intelligible explanations, or actions in their formal description.

To support privacy and self-sovereignty, it is important to provide intelligible explanations to the users. Users need explanations to understand why and how their data is used in the system, and to whom it will be accessible (Bellotti & Sellen, 1993). Explanations must be suitable for specific situations and should consider the individual abilities of the user (i.e., the use of simple language). Although the approaches mentioned address legal requirements, they do not, or only marginally, consider the provision of explanations to the user. The focus is mostly on the system architecture and not on the users. In order to support them, especially in the understanding of automated procedures and artificial intelligent systems, the system has to be designed to meet the users' needs. We are not aware of any approach that addresses the legally compliant use of a system by its users. Accordingly, we are not aware of any approach that explains and supports users in their understanding of the legal situation.

CONCLUSION

Designers, developers and providers of intelligent systems are not only responsible for ensuring that these systems operate correctly and do not cause any damage. They are also responsible for complying with ethical and legal requirements. This includes respecting and ensuring the privacy and sovereignty of those who use these systems. Transparency for, and control by, the users is important in order to trust intelligent systems and to be able to rely on their decisions. But also, the users should not abuse these systems and thereby harm others. They must also comply with the ethical and legal standards of their society.

This creates an additional challenge for the development of intelligent systems and goes beyond the support functionalities that are usually in focus. Researchers and developers are working to reconcile ethical and legal aspects with the intelligent functionalities. In doing so, they selectively pick up on individual aspects, but forget to take a holistic view, which is the only way to develop user-centric intelligent systems that meet the needs of users.

In this chapter we have described which ethical aspects should be considered in the development of intelligent systems, which Moor (2006) has described as ethical machines. We also showed what characterizes the concept of self-sovereignty, and how legal requirements (e.g., the GDPR in Europe) influence the development of (intelligent) systems.

In the chapter, *Ethical Behavior and Legal Regulations in Artificial Intelligence (Part Two): Representation of Law and Ethics in Intelligent Systems,* we discuss our approach to developing intelligent systems, which is intended to flexibly integrate ethical and legal aspects.

REFERENCES

Aïmeur, E., Gambs, S., & Ho, A. (2010). Towards a Privacy-Enhanced Social Networking Site. *2010 International Conference on Availability, Reliability and Security,* 172–179. 10.1109/ARES.2010.97

Anderson, M., & Anderson, S. L. (2007). Machine Ethics: Creating an Ethical Intelligent Agent. *AI Magazine, 28*(4), 12.

Baumann, C., Peitz, P., Raabe, O., & Wacker, R. (2010). Compliance for Service-based Systems through Formalization of Law. *Proceedings from the 6th International Conference on Web Information Systems and Technology,* 367–371. 10.5220/0002868003670371

Bellotti, V., & Edwards, K. (2001). Intelligibility and accountability: Human considerations in context-aware systems. *Human-Computer Interaction, 16*(2–4), 193–212. doi:10.1207/S15327051HCI16234_05

Bellotti, V., & Sellen, A. (1993). Design for Privacy in Ubiquitous Computing Environments. In G. de Michelis, C. Simone, & K. Schmidt (Eds.), *Proceedings of the Third European Conference on Computer-Supported Cooperative Work 13–17 September 1993, Milan, Italy ECSCW '93* (pp. 77–92). Springer Netherlands. 10.1007/978-94-011-2094-4_6

Brezillon, P. J. (1994). Contextualized explanations. *Proceedings from International Conference on Expert Systems for Development,* 119–124. 10.1109/ICESD.1994.302295

Casanovas, P., Palmirani, M., Peroni, S., van Engers, T., & Vitali, F. (2016). Semantic Web for the legal domain: The next step. *Semantic Web, 7*(3), 213–227. doi:10.3233/SW-160224

Casellas, N., Nieto, J.-E., Mero–o, A., Roig, A., Torralba, S., Reyes, M., & Casanovas, P. (2010). *Ontological Semantics for Data Privacy Compliance.* The NEURONA Project.

Dalpiaz, F., Paja, E., & Giorgini, P. (2016). *Security requirements engineering: Designing secure socio-technical systems.* The MIT Press.

Dey, A. K. (2001). Understanding and Using Context. *Personal and Ubiquitous Computing, 5*(1), 4–7. doi:10.1007007790170019

Dey, A. K. (2009). Explanations in Context-Aware Systems. *Proceedings of the Fourth International Conference on Explanation-Aware Computing,* 84–93.

Dignum, V. (2019). *Responsible artificial intelligence: How to develop and use AI in a responsible way.* Springer International Publishing., doi:10.1007/978-3-030-30371-6

Elshtain, J. B. (1990). Sovereign God, Sovereign State, Sovereign Self. *The Notre Dame Law Review*, *66*, 1355.

Erl, T. (2005). *Service-oriented architecture: Concepts, technology, and design*. Prentice Hall PTR.

Friedman, B., Kahn, P. H., & Borning, A. (2008). Value sensitive design and information systems. The Handbook of Information and Computer Ethics, 69–101.

Gangemi, A. (2007). Design Patterns for Legal Ontology Constructions. *LOAIT*, *2007*, 65–85.

Gangemi, A., Prisco, A., Sagri, M.-T., Steve, G., & Tiscornia, D. (2003). Some Ontological Tools to Support Legal Regulatory Compliance, with a Case Study. In R. Meersman & Z. Tari (Eds.), *On the Move to Meaningful Internet Systems 2003: OTM 2003 Workshops* (Vol. 2889, pp. 607–620). Springer Berlin Heidelberg. doi:10.1007/978-3-540-39962-9_64

Gregor, S., & Benbasat, I. (1999). Explanations from Intelligent Systems: Theoretical Foundations and Implications for Practice. *Management Information Systems Quarterly*, *23*(4), 497. doi:10.2307/249487

Haake, J. M., Hussein, T., Joop, B., Lukosch, S., Veiel, D., & Ziegler, J. (2010). Modeling and Exploiting Context for Adaptive Collaboration. *International Journal of Cooperative Information Systems*, *19*(1-2), 71–120. doi:10.1142/S0218843010002115

Hjerppe, K., Ruohonen, J., & Leppanen, V. (2019). The General Data Protection Regulation: Requirements, Architectures, and Constraints. *2019 IEEE 27th International Requirements Engineering Conference (RE)*, 265–275. 10.1109/RE.2019.00036

Hoepman, J.-H. (2014). Privacy Design Strategies. In N. Cuppens-Boulahia, F. Cuppens, S. Jajodia, A. Abou El Kalam, & T. Sans (Eds.), *ICT Systems Security and Privacy Protection* (Vol. 428, pp. 446–459). Springer Berlin Heidelberg. doi:10.1007/978-3-642-55415-5_38

Hussain, S. S., Veiel, D., Haake, J. M., & Lukosch, S. (2010). Facilitating understanding of team-based adaptation policies. *Proceedings from the 6th International ICST Conference on Collaborative Computing: Networking, Applications, Worksharing*. 10.4108/icst.collaboratecom.2010.60

Ilievski, N. L. (2015). The Individual Sovereignty: Conceptualization and Manifestation. *Journal of Liberty & International Affairs*, *1*(2), 23–38.

Jiang, X., & Landay, J. A. (2002). Modeling privacy control in context-aware systems. *IEEE Pervasive Computing*, *1*(3), 59–63. doi:10.1109/MPRV.2002.1037723

Kapitsaki, G., Ioannou, J., Cardoso, J., & Pedrinaci, C. (2018). Linked USDL Privacy: Describing Privacy Policies for Services. *2018 IEEE International Conference on Web Services (ICWS)*, 50–57. 10.1109/ICWS.2018.00014

Kapitsaki, G. M. (2013). Reflecting User Privacy Preferences in Context-Aware Web Services. *2013 IEEE 20th International Conference on Web Services*, 123–130. 10.1109/ICWS.2013.26

Lim, B. Y., & Dey, A. K. (2010). Toolkit to support intelligibility in context-aware applications. *Proceedings from the 12th ACM International Conference on Ubiquitous Computing - Ubicomp '10*, 13. 10.1145/1864349.1864353

Moor, J. H. (2006). The Nature, Importance, and Difficulty of Machine Ethics. *IEEE Intelligent Systems*, *21*(4), 18–21. doi:10.1109/MIS.2006.80

Muir, B. M. (1994). Trust in automation: Part I. Theoretical issues in the study of trust and human intervention in automated systems. *Ergonomics*, *37*(11), 1905–1922. doi:10.1080/00140139408964957

Oberle, D., Drefs, F., Wacker, R., Baumann, C., & Raabe, O. (2012). Engineering Compliant Software: Advising Developers by Automating Legal Reasoning. *SCRIPTed*, *9*(3), 280–313. doi:10.2966crip.090312.280

Regulation, G. D. P. (2016). Regulation (EU) 2016/679 of the European Parliament and of the Council of 27 April 2016 on the protection of natural persons with regard to the processing of personal data and on the free movement of such data, and repealing Directive 95/46. *Official Journal of the European Union, 59*(1–88), 294.

Ringmann, S. D., Langweg, H., & Waldvogel, M. (2018). Requirements for Legally Compliant Software Based on the GDPR. In H. Panetto, C. Debruyne, H. A. Proper, C. A. Ardagna, D. Roman, & R. Meersman (Eds.), *On the Move to Meaningful Internet Systems, OTM 2018 Conferences* (pp. 258–276). Springer International Publishing. 10.1007/978-3-030-02671-4_15

Robol, M., Salnitri, M., & Giorgini, P. (2017). Toward GDPR-Compliant Socio-Technical Systems: Modeling Language and Reasoning Framework. In G. Poels, F. Gailly, E. Serral Asensio, & M. Snoeck (Eds.), *The practice of enterprise modeling* (Vol. 305, pp. 236–250). Springer International Publishing. doi:10.1007/978-3-319-70241-4_16

Russell, S. J., & Norvig, P. (2010). Artificial intelligence: A modern approach (E. Davis, Ed.; 3rd ed.). Prentice Hall.

Schilit, B. N., & Theimer, M. M. (1994). Disseminating active map information to mobile hosts. *IEEE Network*, *8*(5), 22–32. doi:10.1109/65.313011

Stol, K.-J., Ralph, P., & Fitzgerald, B. (2016). Grounded theory in software engineering research: A critical review and guidelines. *Proceedings from the 38th International Conference on Software Engineering - ICSE '16*, 120–131. 10.1145/2884781.2884833

Toth, K. C., & Anderson-Priddy, A. (2018). *Architecture for Self-Sovereign Digital Identity*. https://nexgenid.com/wp-content/uploads/2019/02/Architecture-for-Self-Sovereign-Digital-Identity-posted-nexgenid.com_.pdf

Toth, K. C., & Anderson-Priddy, A. (2019). Self-Sovereign Digital Identity: A Paradigm Shift for Identity. *IEEE Security and Privacy*, *17*(3), 17–27. doi:10.1109/MSEC.2018.2888782

Umbrello, S., & De Bellis, A. F. (2018). *A value-sensitive design approach to intelligent agents. In Artificial Intelligence Safety and Security*. CRC Press.

Veiel, D., Haake, J. M., Lukosch, S., & Kolfschoten, G. (2013). On the Acceptance of Automatic Facilitation in a Context-Adaptive Group Support System. *2013 46th Hawaii International Conference on System Sciences*, 509–518. 10.1109/HICSS.2013.424

Winfield, A. F., Michael, K., Pitt, J., & Evers, V. (2019). Machine Ethics: The Design and Governance of Ethical AI and Autonomous Systems. *Proceedings of the IEEE, 107*(3), 509–517. doi:10.1109/JPROC.2019.2900622

ENDNOTES

[1]   Definition found in Merriam-Webster Dictionary at https://www.merriam-webster.com/dictionary/.

[2]   See IEEE P7000 Series at https://ethicsinaction.ieee.org.

Chapter 3
Ethical Behavior and Legal Regulations in Artificial Intelligence (Part Two):
Representation of Law and Ethics in Intelligent Systems

Mandy Goram
https://orcid.org/0000-0003-0264-841X
Karlsruhe Institute of Technology (KIT), Germany

Dirk Veiel
https://orcid.org/0000-0003-0228-103X
FernUniversität in Hagen, Germany

ABSTRACT

Intelligent systems and assistants should help users to complete tasks and support them at work, on the road and at home. At the same time, these systems are becoming increasingly sophisticated and autonomous in their decisions and are already taking over simple tasks from us today. In order to not lose control over their own data and to avoid the risk of user manipulation, these systems must comply with ethical and legal guidelines. In this chapter, the authors describe a novel generic approach and its realization for the development of intelligent systems that allow flexible modeling of ethical and legal aspects.

INTRODUCTION

Intelligent systems and assistants should help users to complete tasks and support them at work, on the road, and at home. At the same time, these systems are becoming increasingly sophisticated and autonomous in their decisions, and are already taking over simple tasks from us today. In order to not lose control over their own data, and to avoid the risk of user manipulation, these systems must comply

DOI: 10.4018/978-1-7998-4894-3.ch003

Copyright © 2021, IGI Global. Copying or distributing in print or electronic forms without written permission of IGI Global is prohibited.

with ethical and legal guidelines. Self-sovereignty and privacy should be preserved. We have already explained what this means in *Ethical Behavior and Legal Regulations in Artificial Intelligence (Part One): Supporting Sovereignty of Users while Using Complex and Intelligent Systems.*

In this chapter, we describe a novel generic approach and its realization for the development of intelligent systems that allow flexible modeling of ethical and legal aspects. These aspects can be integrated subsequently into the intelligent core system. When the current development requires changes, the integrated aspects can be adapted accordingly. On the one hand, the approach enables the stakeholders to develop and provide intelligent systems. On the other hand, it tries to support users' sovereignty.

In contrast to the approaches that we described in Part 1, we research and develop a generic system approach for intelligent systems that contains transparency and explainability as per default. The generic approach offers basic functionalities that are needed across domains, and that allow opportunity to specify ethical and legal rules. This enables related stakeholders to realize intelligent systems for their specific domains that take ethical and legal aspects into account. Stakeholders can integrate required extensions without changing the generic core system, but can use best practices from different domains; for instance, collaboration policies, legal regulations, and device support.

We realize the generic system approach by implementing an extendable context-based adaptive system environment (eCBASE) for the legally compliant development and deployment of domain-specific context-based adaptive applications. For this, we use the context-based adaptive collaboration system CONTact and its existing adaptation runtime environment (ARE) to develop eCBASE and support the related stakeholder of the development process. To do so, we extended the existing domain model and the functionalities of CONTact that we introduced in Part 1. Stakeholders who provide intelligent systems can specify how eCBASE should support users in specific situations. When users have to make decisions in such situations, they have to be aware of related consequences. Therefore, they need personalized and situation-specific explanations that eCBASE has to offer.

Architecture of eCBASE

Intelligent systems with a service-oriented architecture (SOA) often use ontologies for knowledge representation and interconnection to knowledge sources, as well as extensible markup language (XML)-based model languages to specify their models (Rodríguez et al., 2016) and to interoperate and connect their components to third-party systems (Garcia-de-Prado et al., 2017). Figure 1 shows the architecture of eCBASE. We use a client-server architecture and a modular SOA system design to enable the replacement or extension of components during development or runtime. In addition, we use the domain model which was introduced by Goram and Veiel (2019). For modeling the domain models, we use the Web Ontology Language OWL2 and the modeling tool Protégé.[1] Based on this formal model, new ontology-based model extensions or related components and services can be integrated via interfaces or so-called extension points into eCBASE, for instance, by using the Pervasive Service Bus (PSB) framework (Pan et al., 2014).

The adaptation runtime environment (ARE) is the central component in eCBASE (cf. Figure 1). The ARE contains the sensing and adaptation engine to determine and apply suitable adaptation policies (AP). Based on the domain model (DM), the ARE uses the sensing rules (SR) to generate the state. Applying the contextualization strategies (CS) to the state creates the contextualized state, (i.e., the context of the current situation). The ARE uses the contextualized state to evaluate the condition blocks of adaptation policies. To generate personalized explanations, the ARE provides the contextualized state and suitable

Figure 1. Architecture of eCBASE

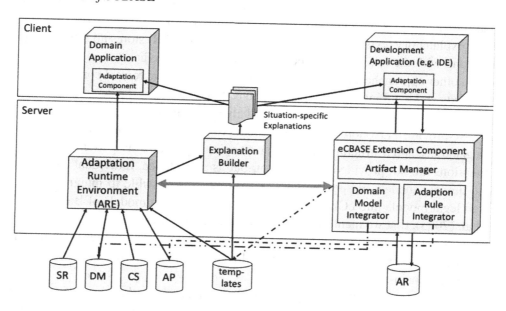

predefined templates to the Explanation Builder. This generates situation-specific explanations, which the ARE transfers to the Adaptation Component of the client of the domain application to create and display a suitable user dialog.

On the right side of Figure 1, the components for the development of core functionalities and domain-specific applications are shown. The central part of the development is the eCBASE Extension Component. All created objects of the development process are managed in the Artifact Manager and are connected with ARE. That enables the researcher to support the stakeholders during the development; e.g., through integrating workflows and explanations into an Integrated Development Environment (IDE).

Adaptation Policies and Rules

Adaptation policies describe the adaptations, and the ARE executes them as adaptation rules. Adaptation policies are structured descriptions that define in which situation (state s_0) a certain sequence of steps is to be executed to achieve a target state (s_1). To be executed by the ARE, adaptation policies must be converted into machine-executable adaptation rules. The adaptations change the user interface and/or the provision of explanations. We use adaptation rules to build situation-specific and flexible workflows for the development process, which enables them to create additional support during the development process at any time. An adaptation rule consists of a condition part and an action block. Developers can store new adaptation rules in the system at any time without making changes to the ARE. Currently, the integration of new or changed rules is a manual task, but it will be automated in future.

Legal Framework

A so-called Legal Framework, which is described by a legal expert, integrates legal requirements as adaptation policies. Legal experts document explanations and consequences for the use of the application.

They get stored in the domain model using the concepts of the legal domain model. The Domain Model Integrator and the Adaption Rule Integrator for the ARE (cf. Figure 1) prepare the defined adaptation policies and the explanatory texts. A separate Artifact Repository (AR) stores all artifacts created by the stakeholders, along with the relationships and dependencies between them.

In contrast to other approaches, the Legal Framework has a generic formal core model that does not contain all law texts and legal interpretations (Goram & Veiel, 2020), as is the case with legal decision support systems. Since law texts are very general and always have to be interpreted on the basis of situations or facts, we provide a taxonomy in the core model of eCBASE. This taxonomy contains concepts to represent legal areas, and a structural outline for mapping rights and obligations. The legal texts and their legal intentions are not provided as a concept, but as an instance. Individual areas of law can be extended with domain models of specific laws. Therefore, it is possible to integrate other (existing) ontology-based legal models into eCBASE; for instance, the domain models of Bartolini et al. (2017) or Delgado et al. (2003), that we mentioned in Part 1. Our intent is to keep the runtime model for a specific application as small as possible, and to use only concepts and relationships that are required. The advantage is that the respective provider can define the individual regulations for the legal, and legally compliant, use of a domain-specific application.

In the case of a community application, provided by the researchers, the users are enabled to provide their content in private and public spaces. The use and posting of content in private and public spaces is not prohibited by law, but is subject to certain conditions and obligations, which are regulated (e.g., by Copyright Law). The provider of the community application is responsible for its use and operation, and bears the legal consequences thereof. How he/she fulfills his/her obligations is primarily left up to him/her. For example, provider A can generally forbid the uploading of images for public areas. Provider B requests the user to obtain the rights to the image and to confirm that he/she has these rights at every image upload. The respective user would then be liable in case of false information. The provider needs to decide and define which case needs to be supported in the context-based application, and then he/she needs to define the adaptation policies in the Legal Framework.

Representing Ethical Behavior

Currently, our work is on a generic framework that contains concepts and relations regarding ethical aspects and codes of conduct, and that can easily be integrated into the above approach. Stakeholders can then define rules that take specific ethical aspects into account. The rules represent a certain behavior that is expected in a specific situation. Therefore, the formal context representation must contain related concepts and relations, which is achieved by using the additional framework. Ethical behavior depends on the overall context (Turilli & Floridi, 2009) with its technical, legal, social, and moral rules that differ from society to society and from country to country. Therefore, the stakeholders must be able to integrate or adapt: 1) concepts and relations, as well as, 2) rules according to the changing moral and norms within a community (Umbrello, 2019). Rules can also emerge from different situations so that the intelligent system may learn from these situations and adapt its behavior automatically (Mittelstadt et al., 2016). For that, data-driven learning approaches from the area of AI can be used; for instance, deep learning.

A simple collaboration situation should illustrate the possibilities. For instance, when a group of people should be built to accomplish a given task, the automated group formation process should consider the people's individual preferences. If the code of conduct foresees that users with aversions to each other should never be forced to form a group, the intelligent system must take care of it and must prevent such a group formation. As soon as the intelligent system comes to the conclusion that a person will be harmed when applying related actions, it should not execute them. According to Gips, "actions are judged by their consequences. The best action to take now is the action that results in the best situation in the future" (1995, p. 243). Therefore, the intelligent system has to either find other rules or abort the execution with a respective explanation. In eCBASE, decisions and related consequences should always be made available to the users by supporting related context-based explanations. The creation of explanations is the task of the Explanation Builder (cf. Figure 1) which is interconnected to the whole intelligent system by the ARE. Providing transparency in an intelligent system is a feasible task and requires different information sources (Buiten, 2019; Turilli & Floridi, 2009).

SUPPORTING STAKEHOLDERS ON THE eCBASE DEVELOPMENT

Developing eCBASE requires a tight collaboration between the stakeholders. We use the term *role* instead of *stakeholder*, when we talk about the eCBASE development, because technically we represent stakeholders with roles which are related to artifacts. There is a need for coordination between the transitions of responsibilities. In contrast to the usual software development, we see it as necessary to involve a legal professional in the design and development of the system. For this purpose, additional responsibilities and artifacts must be designed. Next, we describe the interdependencies and the collaboration process to develop eCBASE.

The eCBASE Lifecycle

We identified three phases of the development of eCBASE and legally compliant domain-specific context-based applications. The three phases constitute a life cycle, as shown in Figure 2.

Phase 1: Core eCBASE Development

During Phase 1, developers implement and extend eCBASE as a common core system. eCBASE contains the concepts, functionalities, and actions based on a common domain model. Additionally, eCBASE has an ARE with an adaptation and sensing engine. The system uses these engines to recognize specific situations and adapt the domain-specific application according to the adaptation policies. Extensions include domain-specific requirements for the system (e.g., a shared workspace). Domain-specific requirements may be based on content, technical, or legal aspects. At the end of Phase 1, eCBASE is available for the preparation of domain-specific context-based adaptive applications and their specific configuration.

Phase 2: Legal Framework Extension

The legal expert will extend and establish the Legal Framework in Phase 2. In order to ensure legal compliance of data processing and system usage by users, the legal experts extend the framework with domain-specific requirements. It is defined by a legal professional who is familiar with the legal regulation of the application domain. He or she defines the legal policies for the system that must be considered at runtime. On the basis of the concepts stored in eCBASE for mapping legal regulations, the expert defines adaptation policies (i.e., legal policies) which eCBASE uses to check data processing at runtime and to

Figure 2. Lifecycle of eCBASE.

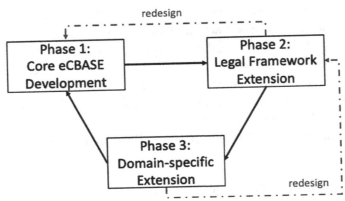

ensure that data is processed in compliance with the law. In case of missing concepts and relationships to map legal requirements, eCBASE must be extended. That leads to a redesign of eCBASE (cf. Figure 2, blue arrow Phase 2 to Phase 1). The legally compliant processing concerns automated processes, but also the use of the application by users.

Phase 3: Domain-Specific Extension

In the third phase, the domain experts extend and provide domain-specific context-based applications, such as community systems or group workspaces. By defining adaptation policies and adaptation rules, the domain experts specify the available artifacts, functions, and actions for the application. When additional functionalities are required, eCBASE must be extended, which leads to a repetition of the lifecycle (cf. Figure 2, black arrow Phase 3 to Phase 1). The extension with domain-specific require-ments in eCBASE could lead to new or changed legal regulations, which initiates the next iteration in the lifecycle. Missing legal regulations in the domain-specific application lead to a redesign in the legal framework (cf. Figure 2, blue arrow Phase 3 to Phase 2).

Roles in the eCBASE Lifecycle

During the eCBASE lifecycle different roles are involved in designing, developing, providing, and using a context-based (end-user) application. Due to their involvement, they have particular tasks and respon-sibilities. In Table 1, we describe the tasks and responsibilities of the roles and their position within the lifecycle. Please note, that we abstract certain roles that are common in an organization, for instance, the provider. We only describe especially the roles that are needed to develop the core of eCBASE.

Artifacts of the eCBASE Lifecycle

Within the eCBASE lifecycle, additional artifacts are needed to integrate the legal perspective and the legal requirements into the development process. They provide a transparent development process that allows all participants or roles to have access (at least read permissions) to related documented discus-sions and decisions (e.g., design choices, legal advice) on an artifact.

Table 1. Roles in the eCBASE lifecycle

Role	Description	Lifecycle
Analyst	The analyst is responsible for gathering and specifying software requirements. For this, he or she creates various detailed use cases, which are used to determine the functional and technical requirements for the context-based adaptive system.	Phase 1
Legal Professional	The role of the legal professional may be carried out by a legal expert or a person with expertise in the field. They support the development process by providing advice on how to realize legal requirements and make design implications. A legal professional is responsible for the specific configuration and extension of the Legal Framework. For this, he or she designs the legal policies that must be considered in specific situations.	Phase 1 Phase 2
Designer	The designer is responsible for the design and the high-level architecture of eCBASE. He or she has to consider common aspects like modularity, usability, fault-tolerance, performance, portability, and security. In a close collaboration with the legal professional, he or she creates a solution design that considers legal aspects, and contains legal advice and explanation components. Additionally, a designer creates the domain-specific requirements and changes for the domain model.	Phase 1
Developer	The developer checks the technical specification and implement the requirements in eCBASE. Developers are responsible for the integration of the formal model and implement or extend the sensing and adaptation engine of eCBASE. The developer defines and implements domain-independent adaptation policies. Developers are responsible for the implementation of legally compliant data processing and must consider legal advice from the legal professional.	Phase 1
Tester	Based on use case scenarios, legal advice, and the functional design specification, testers check and test the eCBASE domain-independent and domain-specific modules and functionalities. For this, they use white box and black box testing, as well as mocked-up user interfaces. While testing the extended legal framework (Phase 2) and domain-specific application (Phase 3), the testers check to see if the defined policies are executed as intended.	Phase 1 Phase 2 Phase 3
Rule Designer	Rule designers are experts in their field. They are specialized in designing and integrating adaptation policies. The related adaptation rules become active during runtime. In Phase 2, a legal expert can take over the role of a rule designer and build up the Legal Framework, which contains the adaptation policies and related explanations. Rule designers are involved in testing the developed adaptation rules.	Phase 2 Phase 3
Provider	A provider is either a single person or an organization. The provider is responsible for the extension and elaboration of the Legal Framework as well as for the provision of the domain-specific application. The provider is also responsible for the content, when it is available in a public space (e. g., public available content on websites and forums) or semi-public space (e. g., community system with access to content after user authentication). For this, the provider has a specific frame of legal and / or organizational policies, which must be reflected in the domain-specific application. Due to this, the provider or legal professional who is in charge must decide how to deal with the legal requirements, (e. g., allow the usage of a content upload functionality or not, which may concern the intellectual property law and data privacy law).	Phase 3
DevOps	The DevOps' are responsible for the maintenance of the domain-specific application, and they support users and rule designers.	Phase 3
User	The user interacts with the domain-specific application. Personalized explanations should support the user's awareness that actions in, and handling of, the system are subject to legal regulations for which the user is responsible (e. g., using a picture upload needs an approval of depicted persons or a consent of the owner). Because of this, the application provides advice on how to deal with a situation.	Phase 3

Table 2 contains the artifact types that are used in the eCBASE lifecycle. Artifact types are a generic concept (i.e., extension point) that become instantiated as specific artifacts at runtime. Every entry contains the artifact type's name (e.g., Use Cases), including an abbreviation (e.g., UC) for later discussion, a description of its attributes and purpose, as well as the lifecycle phase in which the artifact type is needed. Some kinds of artifacts are needed only in one of the three phases and others are needed in more than one. Nevertheless, they are different, separate artifacts that belong to one phase and to one specific development project. They can be connected to each other, but they cannot be changed after a finished development project.

Table 2. Artifact types in the eCBASE development

Artifact Type	Description	Lifecycle
Use Cases (UC)	Use Cases are required to describe domain-independent and domain-specific requirements for eCBASE and domain-specific extensions.	Phase 1
Legal Checklist (LC) (containing Legal Checkpoints)	The Legal Checklist is a structure to combine different legal checkpoints. The legal checklist contains at least one legal checkpoint. The legal checkpoint corresponds to the use case requirements, which are related to legal regulations. One legal checkpoint can contain more than one use case requirement if it concerns the same law and has the same consequences and design implications.	Phase 1
Functional Design (FD)	It contains typical aspects and descriptions of the functional design of software.	Phase 1
Technical Design (TD)	The Technical Design describes the software's technical requirements and components.	Phase 1
Domain Model (DM)	Domain Models are used for the formal description of the concepts and relationships of eCBASE and its domain-specific extensions.	Phase 1
Software (SW)	Software is the developer's artifact, which is related to the implementation of the requirements, as well as to other artifacts of the process.	Phase 1
Test Protocol (TP)	A Test Protocol describes the scenarios to be tested, and the test cases that have been created and executed.	Phase 1 Phase 2 Phase 3
Acceptance Report (AR)	The Acceptance Report is the confirmation that all functional and legal requirements are fulfilled.	Phase 1 Phase 2
Release Note (RN)	Release Note contains information about the added or changed components and policies of eCBASE.	Phase 1 Phase 2 Phase 3
Adaptation Policy (AP)	Adaptation Policies contain a structured description on when and how actions are triggered in eCBASE.	Phase 1 Phase 3
Legal Report (LR)	The Legal Report is based on the analysis of the use cases, the legal checklist, and the provider-specific legal requirements. For this, the report describes legal conditions that become relevant when extending and using the domain-specific application. A report contains explanations for legal related actions and restrictions, as well as case scenarios of the legal intended results.	Phase 2
Recommendation for Action (RA)	Based on the legal report, the legal professional makes recommendations for action on the integration and operation of the application functionalities. The legal professional explains the regulations and their consequences for users and providers, and he/she integrates them into the legal framework.	Phase 2
Legal Policy (LP)	Legal Policies are subordinated to adaptation policies and contain decisions on how to deal with certain situations, and under which circumstances application functionalities can be used. They are used to create the adaptation rules for the legal framework.	Phase 2

Dependencies Between Artifacts and Roles of the Development Process

Now, we focus on Phase 1 of the lifecycle, and explain how to support the different stakeholder responsible roles by doing their tasks. In Figure 3, we illustrate the complexity of the eCBASE development process, and the strong intermeshing of roles and artifacts. We assign each role in the development process an ellipse in Figure 3. The artifacts are represented by rectangles and an abbreviation for the artifact (cf. abbreviation in Table 2). The overlapping ellipses represent the overlapping responsibilities or jointly processed artifacts.

The development starts with the creation of UC by the analyst. These are reviewed by the legal professional, who creates a checklist (LC) with individual checkpoints that contain notes on the legal situation and implications for the design of the software. The legal professional makes the checklist for the design, development, testing, and the final acceptance. This results in a tight collaboration between the legal professional and the analyst, designer, developer, and tester. Once the content and legal specification of the requirements have been completed, these are made available to the designer for the creation of the functional and technical design.

The analyst and the designer jointly agree upon the functional design (FD). Similarly, the technical design (TD) is agreed upon with the developer. Once these artifacts are completed, the designer creates the domain model (DM). The completed DM is used together with the UC and LC for the development of the adaptation policies (AP). The analyst and the developer create the AP. At the same time, the software (SW) can be created by the developer, who uses the TD, DM, and LC as guidelines for implementation.

Figure 3. Interdependencies of artifacts and roles

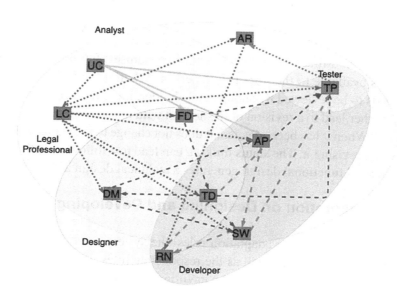

The functionalities of the SW and the AP affect each other, and the stakeholders check and adjust them continuously until the development is completed. After the implementation of the requirements has been completed, the tester starts the tests and verification. For this task, the tester has the UC, LC, FD,

AP, and, of course, SW available. The tester documents the tests and related results in the test protocol (TP). After the successful completion of the tests, the legal professional must approve the developed software. For this purpose, he or she uses the LC and the TP to check that the legal requirements have been considered and fulfilled. If he or she agrees with the implementation, he or she creates an acceptance report (AR) so that the software can be released. The designer and developer create the release notes (RN), which are based on the AR, the developed components of SW, and the integrated adaptation rules of AP.

Artifact Workflow

As mentioned above, adaptation rules are used to define workflows. For this purpose, information about the responsible role, the reviewing role, the dependency on other artifacts, and the current status in the development process of an artifact, is attached to the artifact.

Figure 4. Artifact statuses

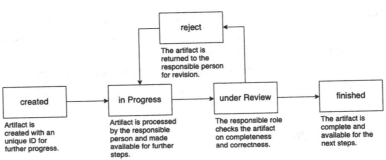

As shown in Figure 4, an artifact has a process with five statuses. In the status *created*, the artifact has been created and is available to the responsible person. When it is processed, it has the status *in Progress*. When it needs to be reviewed by another stakeholder, it is transferred to the status *under Review*. The review can either lead to a revision of the artifact with the status *reject* or it can be completed with the status *finished*. When it has been rejected, it does not change to the status *in Progress* unless the responsible person starts revising it. The status *finished* can lead to a follow-up artifact being generated automatically (i.e., finished functional design generates a technical design artifact).

Supporting the Collaboration on Designing and Developing eCBASE

In order to represent a workflow using adaptation rules, the system must contain the relevant objects and their relationships to each other, as well as the responsible roles. Figure 5 and Figure 6 show excerpts of our domain model with the collaboration environment extensions (marked with the prefix *ce*) that are visualized by the modeling tool Protégé. The prefix *dm* marks core concepts that belong to the eCBASE core model.

Figure 5. Excerpt from the domain model for roles, artifacts, and the artifact status

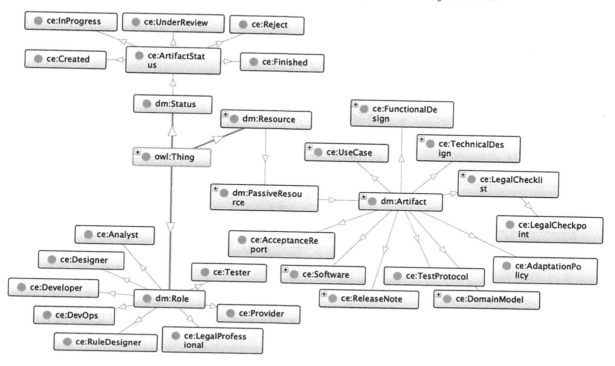

The extension in Figure 5 refers to the concept's roles (*dm:Role*) and its subclasses *ce:Analyst*, *ce:LegalProfessional*, *ce:Designer*, *ce:Developer* and *ce:Tester*, which correspond to the roles of the development process. The concept *dm:Artifact* is a subclass of *dm:PassiveResource* (which is a subclass of *dm:Resource*) and correspond to the above-introduced artifacts.

To monitor the development status, it is necessary to track the status of artifacts. When this information is available, follow-up activities can be started or interventions can be made (e.g., in the case of incomplete activities that block the process). We have added the status (*dm:Status*) to the core domain model, because it may be important to represent the status of instances in context beyond a development environment. In case of collaboration support in the development process, the status of artifacts (*ce:ArtifactStatus*) is needed. An artifact can have the status created (*ce:Created*), in progress (*ce:InProgress*), being reviewed (*ce:UnderReview*), rejected (*ce:Reject*), and finished (*ce:Finished*). The relationships are explained in a subsequent section.

The relationships between artifacts, that are related to roles (cf. Figure 5), and the requirements are shown in Figure 6. Applications (*dm:Application*) and application functionalities (*dm:ApplicationFunctionality*) have conditions (*dm:Condition*) and requirements (*dm:Requirement*) that define a set of rules that have to be taken into account during runtime. Requirements can be classified as content (*dm:Content*), technical (*dm:Technical*), and legal (*dm:Legal*).

The ARE uses actions to change the current system state. The stored and executed adaptation rules cause actions to be triggered, which changes the current context. In this way, processes can be defined by a sequence of adaptation rules. Each adaptation rule has a condition and an action block that ensures that the right actions are executed at the right time. Figure 6 shows some extended actions (*dm:Action*) that are

Figure 6. Excerpt from the domain model for artifacts, actions and requirements

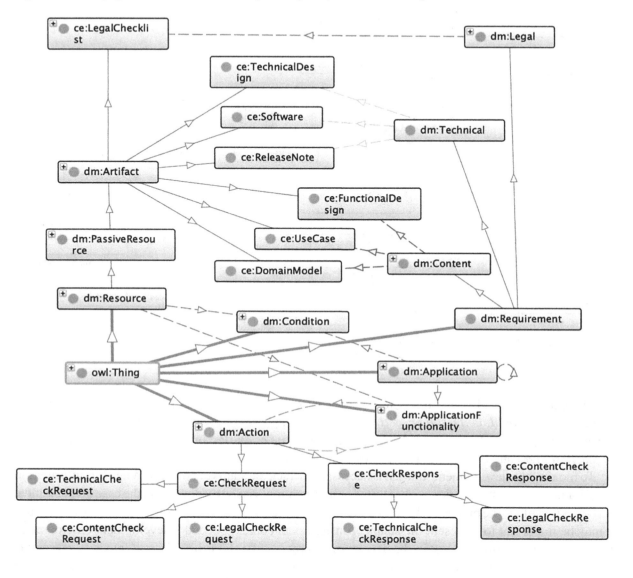

needed for the collaboration support. The subclasses of the concept *ce:CheckRequest* are used to request a technical (*ce:TechnicalCheckRequest*), content (*ce:ContentCheckRequest*) or legal (*ce:LegalCheckRequest*) review of an artifact. The ARE uses the corresponding actions *ce:TechnicalCheckResponse*, *ce:ContentCheckResponse*, *ce:LegalCheckResponse* of the concept *ce:CheckResponse* to create a response and change the data of the related artifact (e.g., status, description).

Sample Development Situation

We use a sample collaboration situation to illustrate how the eCBASE approach enables us to create flexible support workflows by specifying adaptation rules.

Figure 7. Artifacts of sample collaboration situation

```
Artifact Type: ce:UseCase          Artifact Type: ce:UseCase          Artifact Type: ce:UseCase
ID: RQ_1                           ID: RQ_2                           ID: RQ_3
Name: Search function              Name: User Profile                 Name: Location-based content recommendation
Requirement Type: dm:Content       Requirement Type: dm:Content       Requirement Type: dm:Content
Description: Search engine to       Description: User profile to create account for   Description: Recommend meinDorf55+ content
content from meinDorf55+ without user login   the app meinDorf55+...saves the users name, the   to user's based on their location. It uses the
Responsible: ce:Analyst            location...                        location from the user profile.
Reviewer: ce:LegalProfessional     Responsible: ce:Analyst            Responsible: ce:Analyst
Status: ce:InProgress              Reviewer: ce:LegalProfessional     Reviewer: ce:LegalProfessional
HasLegalImplications: no           Status: ce:InProgress              Status: ce:InProgress
                                   HasLegalImplications: yes          HasLegalImplications: yes

                                   Artifact Type: ce:LegalCheckpoint  Artifact Type: ce:LegalCheckpoint
                                   ID: LCP_1                          ID: LCP_2
                                   Related UseCases: RQ_2             Related UseCases: RQ_3
                                   Related Artifacts: LC_1            Related Artifacts: LC_1
                                   Requirement Type: dm:Legal         Requirement Type: dm:Legal
                                   Laws: GDPR                         Laws: GDPR
                                   Paragraphs: §6                     Paragraphs: §15, §21
                                   Description: ...                   Description: ...
                                   Design Implications: request approval, save   Design Implications: request approval, save
                                   decision, provide update and delete functionality   decision, provide withdrawal functionality
                                   Responsible: ce:LegalProfessional  Responsible: ce:LegalProfessional
                                   Reviewer: carl@company.com         Reviewer: carl@company.com
                                   Status: ce:Finished                Status: ce:Finished
```

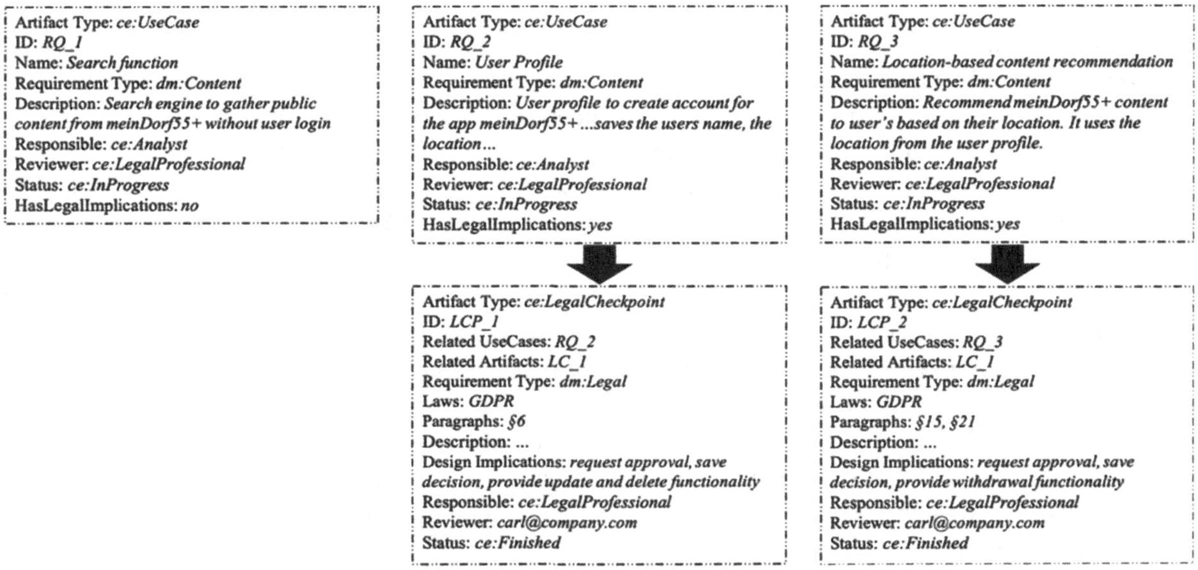

Let's assume that the analyst created the use case artifacts with IDs *RQ_1*, *RQ_2,* and *RQ_3* (cf. top three textboxes in Figure 7). While reviewing the use cases the legal professional concludes that the use cases *RQ_2* and *RQ_3* have legal implications and therefore he or she marks them accordingly (i.e., the legal professional sets *HasLegalImplications* to yes).

In the described situation, we support the stakeholders through the adaptation rule shown in Figure 8. First, *getUseCasesInContext* retrieves all relevant use case artifacts from the current context representation. Second, *getLegalChecklistInContext* gets the legal checklist related to the retrieved use cases. When there is no such legal checklist, eCBASE creates a new one by calling *createArtifact* and specifying the related type of artifact (i.e., *ce:LegalChecklist*). After that, eCBASE loop over all use cases and add a legal checkpoint (*ce:LegalCheckpoint*) to the legal checklist for the related use case when its related attribute *HasLegalImplications* is set to yes.

After applying the above adaptation rule in the sample collaboration situation, eCBASE created two new artifacts with IDs *LCP_1* and *LCP_2* (cf. bottom 2 textboxes in Figure 7) that need to be processed by related legal professionals.

Figure 8. Adaptation rule for automated legal checklist creation

```
ucs = getUseCasesInContext()
lc = getLegalChecklistInContext(ucs)
IF lc == NULL
THEN
  lc = createArtifact("ce:LegalChecklist")
END
FOREACH uc IN ucs DO
  IF HasLegalImplications(uc) == "yes"
  THEN
    addArtifact(lc, "ce:LegalCheckpoint", uc)
  END
END
```

SUPPORTING SELF-SOVEREIGNTY OF USERS

Our approach of an intelligent system, which follows a classical AI approach, involves many automated decisions being made at runtime to provide users with the application and appropriate support. For certain functionalities (e.g., positioning services, recommendations, group awareness), personal data must be processed as well. According to the concept of (self-)sovereignty, the individual user of an intelligent system should have control over his or her data, and be able to determine which automated processes and profilings he or she wants to use. This is also required by the GDPR.

The GDPR deals with the protection and user control of personal data, but it defines these terms according to objective standards. The subjective perception of what is personal and what is not to be processed can vary and depends strongly on the respective situation; i.e., the context. In the real world, an individual can decide at any time which information is accessible to which third party or another person. The implementation of the sole requirements by the GDPR does not go far enough here. Subjective perceptions must also be respected in order to address ethical aspects of sovereignty. For this purpose, the development of an intelligent system requires suitable concepts, which we represent by user preferences.

With eCBASE, we consider user preferences and integrate them into the data processing. User preferences are represented through the categories of *privacy*, *content*, *technical environment*, *notification* and *collaboration*:

- On the one hand, the *privacy preferences* concern the legal defined personal and sensitive data, which must be protected and excluded from processing when users did not agree to it. On the other hand, users have their own thoughts about what is private information. Private information depends on the context. In the above illustrated sample scenario of Alice, her research document is private and should be only available to selected users.
- The *content-related preferences* determine what kind of content (e.g., topic, medium, length, language) should be provided and, for example, recommended by recommendation services.
- Users use technical preferences to control the interaction with the application and other users.
- With *notification preferences,* users can control which information should be notified through the application and at what time.
- Users use the *collaboration preferences* to control the kind (e.g., work in same group) and the way (e.g., chat, video) of interaction with others, the awareness information (e.g., availability), and the access (e.g., profile information) for other users. Grey and black lists represent the user preferences in collaborating with other users. The grey list indicates that there are reservations about another user, which makes it necessary to ask for permission if the situation with the grey listed user should happen at certain circumstances. The black list expresses a strict aversion, which makes it impossible to create a collaboration situation.

The domain application will store the personal preferences in the user profile, and it will consider them during the data processing, as illustrated in Figure 9.

The user's data is stored in the client, and should only be transferred to the server in exceptional circumstances (e.g., for huge calculations). The client's Adaptation Component is responsible for the user-specific adaptation in the client and provides situation-specific explanations. To address personal preferences, the final adaptations and explanations are assembled on the client (e.g., consider blacklist for group building).

Figure 9. Personal data processing

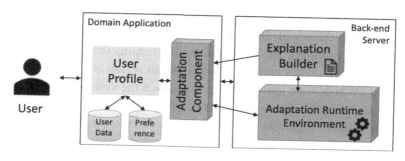

Handling User's Data Processing Decisions

According to Article 7 of GDPR (cf. chapter *Ethical Behavior and Legal Regulations in Artificial Intelligence (Part One): Supporting Sovereignty of Users while Using Complex and Intelligent Systems*), the user must consent to the processing of his or her personal data. The context-based application asks the users for their consent depending on the situation. The decisions are stored in the user's profile and on the server so that eCBASE can take them into account when calculating the applicable adaptation rules. The consent is requested from the user via a dialog window, which is made available via the Explanation Builder. The explanatory text contained in the dialog window describes the reason for data use and the effects of consent or rejection. Other information about the current situation, such as the legal consequences of unauthorized data uploads, is also provided via user dialogs. Withdrawn decisions or situation-specific exceptions should be taken into account at any time when using the system. Through the personalized system, individual users can be made aware of helpful functionalities that could support them in their current situation. If these cannot be executed due to a data protection restriction, eCBASE should offer users the possibility to change the settings or make an exception in this one situation.

Supporting Users Acting Compliant to the Law

We designed eCBASE to support users and to address the legally compliant use of a system. We use personalized explanations to inform users about the current situation (i.e., context) of the application. These explanations include the circumstances of the situation, how it happened, and which possibilities for action are available to the individual user. If the system knows the possible activities, it should also show the consequences of the available actions (e.g., as required by the GDPR). Explanations and necessary actions in a specific legally relevant situation should be provided to users. Therefore, the legal expert integrates explanations and suggested actions into the legal framework.

We illustrate that in a sample scenario as a supplement of the report. The sample scenario is about the user Alice, who wants to upload the photo of a group trip in the community application meinDorf55+ (a novel community system for elderly). Since it is a group photo, she must fulfill the legal requirements of Copyright Law in order to publish it in the community application. In the Legal Framework, the legal expert defines that a documented consent of all persons depicted in the photo is required. Alice is only allowed to make the photo accessible to third parties within the agreed scope when these are available. The consequences of any violation concern the Copyright Law, the GDPR, and the personal rights. The related regulations to the sample situation are instances of ethical principles (Turilli & Floridi, 2009) and should always be presented and made transparent to users in such a situation.

In case Alice uploads a picture with Bob, she becomes aware of this by an action, which creates a dialog, as shown on the left in Figure 10. The explanation contains the descriptions of the legal expert and the related legal paragraphs. They explain the need for an action and the consequences when Alice disregards the legal rule. When Alice uploads the picture, then the systems triggers an approval request for Bob. The approval request provides Bob actions to accept or decline the request (Figure 10, right).

Figure 11 shows the related adaptation rule. If Bob accepts, the context (acceptance, related photo, Alice request, etc.) will be stored in an approval object for transparency and verifiability, otherwise the process will be aborted.

Figure 10. Samples of personalized explanations

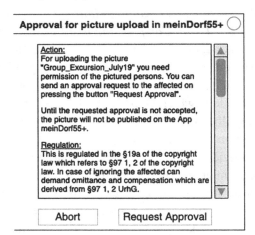

Figure 11. Adaptation rule "Approval Request"

```
rule "Approval Request"
 when
  user: getUserInContext("dm:User")
  app: getAppInContext(user,"dm:Application")
  req: getReqInContext(app,"dm:Requirement")
  appr: requestApproval(user, app, req)
 then
  createOrUpdateAcceptedApproval(appr)
  notify(user, appr)
 end
end
```

FUTURE RESEARCH DIRECTIONS

Future work will concern both the support of the stakeholders in the development of context-based adaptive systems and the intelligible explanation of the current situation. In the development, we can support artifact-centric design, but the relevant stakeholder is responsible for the correctness of the content. To reduce errors, we have integrated a review process for the artifacts. This does not exclude misunderstandings and errors in the further development process, especially during implementation. Therefore, we are working on a constraint-based support for development environments. This is supposed to automatically check the compliance with legal requirements.

The second direction is to provide understandable explanations for users in general. Our intelligent systems can recognize situations and react accordingly with adaptations and explanations. However, we still have to answer the following questions: What are intelligible explanations? In particular, how can eCBASE provide complex legal texts in a simple and correct way? In order to answer these questions, it requires extensive user studies with different user interfaces, which are currently in preparation. In this context, it is also necessary to clarify how the return of user control can also be made user-friendly since too many explanations and requirements quickly overload the users.

CONCLUSION

Intelligent systems and AI make it possible to perform complex tasks and support users in their work. Currently, it is challenging to explain users the system behavior and decision-making of intelligent systems. It is even more challenging when such systems use personal data to support situations appropriately that could be caused by missing information transparency. Thus, these systems not only have the potential to support the individual users, but also to harm them (e.g., manipulation, fraud). However, the users also have the responsibility of behaving in a legally compliant and moral manner, and they should be made aware of this in case of doubt.

Therefore, an intelligent system must consider ethical and legal concerns in addition to its main tasks. These include the following: compliance with privacy; transparency in data processing; data control and data sovereignty by the users; and voluntary consent to the storage, processing, and disclosure of personal data. It is ultimately up to the designers, developers, and providers of such a system to ensure that this is observed (cf. chapter: *Ethical Behavior and Legal Regulations in Artificial Intelligence (Part One): Supporting Sovereignty of Users while Using Complex and Intelligent Systems*).

In this chapter, we presented a generic approach of a context-based adaptive system environment to address ethical and legal implications in developing and using intelligent systems. We described the generic architecture and the overall lifecycle of eCBASE, and the relationship between the artifacts and stakeholders in the development process. An extract of the domain model illustrated how the authors represent the concepts and relationships of the development process in eCBASE. Thus, the intelligent system supports designers, developers, and providers in complying with ethical and legal requirements. With the context-based adaptive system, we define the behavior of the system with adaptation policies, which determine the situation in which the system must react and who is involved. Adaptation policies can define ethical and legal rules of conduct and actions in the system. Legal experts can integrate application-specific legal regulations and related system behavior through the Legal Framework, which is composed of legal adaptation policies.

We support the user's self-sovereignty and control by considering the individual preferences in the data processing and leaving personal data on the user's device. According to the GDPR, the presented approach provides transparency in the development and using of an intelligent system. We support users with personalized explanations about the current situation, and the data usage and purpose of the processing. By doing so, we give control back to the users. In addition, users are made aware of their ethical or legal responsibility of their (intended) actions (e.g., uploading pictures with other people), and are made aware of the possible consequences.

REFERENCES

Bartolini, C., Muthuri, R., & Santos, C. (2017). Using Ontologies to Model Data Protection Requirements in Workflows. In M. Otake, S. Kurahashi, Y. Ota, K. Satoh, & D. Bekki (Eds.), *New Frontiers in Artificial Intelligence* (Vol. 10091, pp. 233–248). Springer International Publishing. doi:10.1007/978-3-319-50953-2_17

Buiten, M. C. (2019). Towards Intelligent Regulation of Artificial Intelligence. *European Journal of Risk Regulation*, 10(1), 41–59. doi:10.1017/err.2019.8

Delgado, J., Gallego, I., Llorente, S., & García, R. (2003). Regulatory Ontologies: An Intellectual Property Rights Approach. In R. Meersman & Z. Tari (Eds.), *On The Move to Meaningful Internet Systems 2003: OTM 2003 Workshops* (Vol. 2889, pp. 621–634). Springer Berlin Heidelberg. doi:10.1007/978-3-540-39962-9_65

Garcia-de-Prado, A., Ortiz, G., & Boubeta-Puig, J. (2017). COLLECT: COLLaborativE ConText-aware service oriented architecture for intelligent decision-making in the Internet of Things. *Expert Systems with Applications*, 85, 231–248. doi:10.1016/j.eswa.2017.05.034

Gips, J. (1995). Towards the ethical robot. In K. M. Ford, C. Glymour, & P. Hayes (Eds.), *Android epistemology* (pp. 243–252). MIT Press.

Goram, M., & Veiel, D. (2019). Supporting privacy control and personalized data usage explanations in a context-based adaptive collaboration environment. In G. Bella & P. Bouquet (Eds.), *Modeling and using context* (Vol. 11939, pp. 84–97). Springer International Publishing. doi:10.1007/978-3-030-34974-5_8

Goram, M., & Veiel, D. (2020). Considering Legal Regulations in an Extendable Context-based Adaptive System Environment. In J. Filipe, M. Smialek, A. Brodsky, & S. Hammoudi (Eds.), *Proceedings of the 22nd International Conference on Enterprise Information Systems, ICEIS 2020, Prague, Czech Republic*, May 5-7, 2020 (Vol. 2, pp. 367–376). SCITEPRESS. 10.5220/0009565003670376

Mittelstadt, B. D., Allo, P., Taddeo, M., Wachter, S., & Floridi, L. (2016). The ethics of algorithms: Mapping the debate. *Big Data & Society*, 3(2), 2053951716679679. doi:10.1177/2053951716679679

Pan, G., Zhang, L., Wu, Z., Li, S., Yang, L., Lin, M., & Shi, Y. (2014). Pervasive Service Bus: Smart SOA Infrastructure for Ambient Intelligence. *IEEE Intelligent Systems*, 29(4), 52–60. doi:10.1109/MIS.2012.119

Rodríguez, G., Soria, Á., & Campo, M. (2016). Artificial intelligence in service-oriented software design. *Engineering Applications of Artificial Intelligence, 53*, 86–104. doi:10.1016/j.engappai.2016.03.009

Turilli, M., & Floridi, L. (2009). The ethics of information transparency. *Ethics and Information Technology, 11*(2), 105–112. doi:10.100710676-009-9187-9

Umbrello, S. (2019). Beneficial Artificial Intelligence Coordination by Means of a Value Sensitive Design Approach. *Big Data and Cognitive Computing, 3*(1), 5. doi:10.3390/bdcc3010005

ADDITIONAL READING

Ayala-Rivera, V., & Pasquale, L. (2018). The Grace Period Has Ended: An Approach to Operationalize GDPR Requirements. *2018 IEEE 26th International Requirements Engineering Conference (RE),* 136–146. 10.1109/RE.2018.00023

Boscoe, B. (2019). Creating transparency in algorithmic processes. *Delphi – Interdisciplinary Review of Emerging Technologies, 2*(1), 12-22. doi:10.21552/delphi/2019/1/5

Friedman, B., Hendry, D. G., & Borning, A. (2017). A Survey of Value Sensitive Design Methods. *Foundations and Trends in Human-Computer Interaction, 11*(2), 63–125. doi:10.1561/1100000015

Gangemi, A. (2007). Design Patterns for Legal Ontology Constructions. *LOAIT, 2007,* 65–85.

Maalej, W., Happel, H.-J., & Rashid, A. (2009). When users become collaborators: Towards continuous and context-aware user input. *Proceeding of the 24th ACM SIGPLAN Conference Companion on Object Oriented Programming Systems Languages and Applications - OOPSLA '09,* 981. 10.1145/1639950.1640068

Wachter, S., Mittelstadt, B., & Floridi, L. (2017). Transparent, explainable, and accountable AI for robotics. *Science Robotics, 2*(6), eaan6080. Advance online publication. doi:10.1126cirobotics.aan6080

Wachter, S., Mittelstadt, B., & Russell, C. (2017). *Counterfactual Explanations Without Opening the Black Box: Automated Decisions and the GDPR.* SSRN Electronic Journal., doi:10.2139srn.3063289

Wallach, W., & Allen, C. (2008). *Moral machines: Teaching robots right from wrong.* Oxford University Press.

KEY TERMS AND DEFINITIONS

Artifact: Artifacts are artificial objects created by humans. Every document and process created in a system represents an artifact. In software development, the documents, software, and other objects to be created are called artifacts.

Context: Context includes all information that can be used to describe a situation. This includes socio-technical, physical, and space-time information as well as the legal constraints that exist in the specific situation. This information provides the necessary framework for action and the implementation of appropriate policies and interventions.

Domain Model: A domain model is an abstract formal description of a socio-technical system. It contains concepts and relationships that represent functionalities and objects. Each domain from the real world is usually mapped to its own domain model when it is formalized for computing.

Ontology: An ontology is a formal specification of a certain domain that describes a set of concepts, relationships and formal axioms that restrict the interpretation of concept instances.

(Self-)Sovereignty: Users are the owners of their data and can control them in processing of data. They give freely consent to which data are used and for what purpose. They can withdraw consent of use for particular functionalities or purposes at any time.

ENDNOTE

[1]   For information on Protégé, see https://protege.stanford.edu.

Chapter 4
Raising Ethical Machines:
Bottom–Up Methods to Implementing Machine Ethics

Marten H. L. Kaas

ⓘ https://orcid.org/0000-0003-0963-1004

University College Cork, Ireland

ABSTRACT

The ethical decision-making and behaviour of artificially intelligent systems is increasingly important given the prevalence of these systems and the impact they can have on human well-being. Many current approaches to implementing machine ethics utilize top-down approaches, that is, ensuring the ethical decision-making and behaviour of an agent via its adherence to explicitly defined ethical rules or principles. Despite the attractiveness of this approach, this chapter explores how all top-down approaches to implementing machine ethics are fundamentally limited and how bottom-up approaches, in particular, reinforcement learning methods, are not beset by the same problems as top-down approaches. Bottom-up approaches possess significant advantages that make them better suited for implementing machine ethics.

INTRODUCTION

As more decisions are delegated to artificially intelligent machines that have learned to perform a certain task, it is imperative that these machines are learning to make ethical decisions. Utilizing top-down approaches, i.e., explicitly stated and predetermined rules or principles, for implementing machine ethics continues to be a popular strategy among computer scientists, roboticists and other professionals working in the general field of artificial intelligence (AI) research (Tolmeijer et al., 2020). While top-down approaches continue to be useful in limited contexts, they are insufficient to raise ethical machines. In particular, top-down approaches (e.g., Isaac Asimov's Four Laws of Robotics) face three fundamental challenges that limit their usefulness when considering implementing machine ethics. In contrast, bottom-up approaches, and in particular reinforcement learning methods, are better suited for implementing machine ethics.

DOI: 10.4018/978-1-7998-4894-3.ch004

Copyright © 2021, IGI Global. Copying or distributing in print or electronic forms without written permission of IGI Global is prohibited.

In Asimov's fictitious universe all intelligent robots obey the three fundamental Laws of Robotics: (1) A robot may not injure a human or, through inaction, allow a human being to come to harm, (2) a robot must obey the orders given to it by a human being except where such orders would conflict with the First Law, and (3) a robot must protect its own existence as long as such protection does not conflict with the First or Second Laws (1950). Asimov later amended these laws to include the Zeroth Law: (0) A robot may not injure humanity or, through inaction, allow humanity to come to harm (1985). Clearly, Asimov's Four Laws were meant to ensure that an intelligent robot's actions ethically align with what humans desire, e.g., ensure non-maleficence towards humans.

This is highlighted in Asimov's short story "Runaround" (1950). In the story, an artificially intelligent robot called Speedy (spoiler alert; skip to the next section to avoid spoilers) is sent out to collect selenium from the surface of Mercury. Unfortunately for the two human characters in the story, Michael Donovan and Gregory Powell, Speedy does not behave as the two roboticists expect after it was given the order to collect the selenium. What the roboticists discover is that instead of collecting the selenium and bringing it back to the station, Speedy is instead running in a circle around the selenium which is sitting in a crater. Since Speedy was instructed to collect the selenium from the crater, it attempted to run towards the center of the crater where the selenium was located, as per the Second Law. Unbeknownst to Donovan and Powell when they ordered Speedy to that particular site, the crater was filled with noxious fumes that would corrode Speedy's metallic body, thus driving Speedy away from the crater, as per the Third Law. Caught, as it were, between the Second and Third Laws, Speedy proceeds to run in a circle around the crater at the point where the tension between the two laws is equal. So although the intelligent robots in Asimov's universe are supposed to, in a way, protect and enhance human well-being, if they are not carefully designed, then they may have the opposite effect.

BACKGROUND

As long as people have imagined artificially intelligent machines (e.g., robots, ordinary physical machines, computers, software, etc.), they have also imagined how these machines might act. Most contemporary portrayals of advanced AIs seem to regard as necessary the extinction of humanity even though they are not particularly adept at accomplishing their goals.[1] Sensationalized fictions aside, and despite the nascent state of most artificially intelligent machines, the problem of implementing machine ethics is a live and pressing issue. As some scholars have noted, essentially all non-trivial interactions that an intelligent machine has with humans have ethical import (Anderson, Anderson, & Berenz, 2017). It is possible that robots responsible for eldercare or childcare, for example, could cause harm via their inaction if they recharge their batteries at one particular point in time instead of another.

More concretely, autonomous intelligent machines are currently in use in more areas than can be listed here, some of which include algorithms in hearing aids that filter out ambient noise, medical decision systems that can read CT scans and diagnose disease, automated facial recognition systems at border crossings, intelligent scheduling systems responsible for logistics planning and search engine optimization, but all of which have an ethical dimension (Bostrom, 2014). What counts as ambient noise? What recourse is available for people misidentified at a border crossing? What confidence does a system have in its medical diagnosis? Because the decisions and actions of automated intelligent machines already have the potential to significantly impact a person's well-being, coupled with the fact that such machines are only becoming more pervasive, there is a need to understand how ethics could be implemented in machines.

The study of machine ethics is relatively new and has been largely theoretical and philosophical. The ethics of machines and artificial intelligence is generally divided into two main branches, the larger of which focuses on how humans ought to act in order to minimize the ethical harms that can arise as a result of deploying intelligent machines (Winfield et al., 2019).[2] The smaller branch, and the one this chapter is primarily concerned with, focuses on how machines themselves could behave ethically, hence it is generally referred to as the field of machine ethics. Some of the earliest proposals in the field of machine ethics concerned the use of practical ethical governors for lethal autonomous robots that would moderate or inhibit the robot's behavior (Winfield et al., 2019). But because the field is so new, proposals for implementing machine ethics remain mostly theoretical with only a handful of experimental demonstrations of ethical robots to date.[3]

Moral Agency, Moral Psychology and Terminology

Importantly, however, considering whether machines themselves could behave ethically is not necessarily to imply that machines possess moral agency. As Cave et al. (2019) argue, machines with moral agency can be distinguished from machines that possess the ability to engage in ethical reasoning or machines that ethically align with what people consider to be ethically desirable or acceptable. ATMs that do not defraud users and cars with automatic braking features are machines of the latter kind insofar as they are machines "whose behavior adequately preserves, and ideally furthers, the interests and values of the relevant stakeholders in a given context" (Cave et al., 2019). Machines of the former kind, the ones that possess the ability to engage in ethical reasoning, are the primary focus of this chapter. Note, however, these two important qualifications. The first is that "reasoning" here is used in a broad sense to simply refer to the information processing that is carried out to reach a conclusion.[4] The second is that "ethical reasoning" here is being used in a weak sense that does not require, for example, an understanding of the significance of the ethical issues at stake. Intelligent machines are simply not at the point where they might be considered ethical "agents," i.e., actors with certain mental features (e.g., intentionality and self-awareness) and moral responsibilities, among other attributes. There is therefore no underlying assumption in this chapter that in order to implement machine ethics (in the weak sense that these terms are being used) machines must possess moral agency.

Just as detailed discussions of moral agency are unfortunately outside the scope of this chapter, so, too, is the research on the empirical psychology of machines. Nevertheless, some reference to this research is important. For example, although the aim of this chapter is to examine *how* machine ethics could be implemented, it is worth asking whether the creation of ethical machines *should* be pursued at all. Recent research has highlighted that although people prefer that others buy self-driving cars whose behavior results in the best global outcomes, e.g., injuring the passenger to save multiple pedestrians, they would themselves prefer to buy self-driving cars that protect the passenger at all costs (Bonnefon, Shariff, & Rahwan, 2016). Indeed, research conducted by Bigman and Gray (2018) suggests that people are generally averse to having machines make moral decisions in the domains of driving, legal, medical and military decision-making. They suggest that this aversion is driven in part by a perceived lack of "agency," i.e., the ability to carry out one's intentions, in the machine (Bigman & Gray, 2018). Although empirical moral psychology, consultation with the wider public and relevant stakeholders is an undeniably important aspect of ensuring the responsible development and implementation of machine ethics, the aim of this chapter is to practically explore how machines might learn for themselves, with minimal human input, to act ethically.[5]

First, however, some terminological clarification is required. Following Alan Turing, who eschewed attempts to define ambiguous and emotionally charged concepts, terms like 'machine' and 'intelligence' shall not be explicitly defined (1950). Attempting to define such terms would detract from a far more practical question, and the one with which this chapter will concern itself: given the prevalence and widespread use of artificially intelligent machines[6] (i.e., machines whose actions would be attributed intelligence were those actions performed by a human),[7] how ought the implementation of machine ethics be approached?

Second, as Brian Cantwell Smith highlights, it is important to remember that artificially intelligent machines are not yet capable of "decision-making" or "recognition" in the way that humans are (Smith, 2019). So, although phrases like "The eldercare robot can make the preferable ethical decision," will appear throughout this chapter, it would be prudent to remember that this might oversell what the eldercare robot is actually doing. In short, contemporary artificially intelligent machines may not be (wholly) credited with understanding or owning the "decisions" they make or the things they "recognize." The reader is therefore encouraged to exercise caution when interpreting such phrases. In what follows, top-down approaches to implementing machine ethics will be briefly considered before examining, what are likely to be more successful, bottom-up approaches to implementing machine ethics.

IMPLEMENTING MACHINE ETHICS

Top-Down Approaches

Returning to fiction for a moment, Asimov's Four Laws are a paradigmatic top-down approach to implementing machine ethics. In short, top-down approaches involve specifying some set of rules that promise comprehensive solutions to any ethical problem.[8] Common top-down ethical theories include consequentialism and deontology.[9] The former is top-down in the sense that any ethical dilemma is supposedly resolved by comparing the consequences of different actions and choosing the action that results in the best consequences.[10] The latter is top-down in the sense that any ethical dilemma is supposedly resolved by consulting some set of principles or duties.[11]

The essential features of top-down ethical theories are that they operate in a particular direction, i.e., from the general to the particular, and are universal; i.e., applicable in context-poor and context-rich cases. The attractiveness of top-down approaches to ethics stem from these essential features, and it is obvious why such approaches to implementing machine ethics are particularly popular: if ethical rules or principles can be explicitly stated, then acting ethically would just be a simple matter of following the rules (Wallach & Allen, 2009). Indeed, top-down approaches to ethics seem exceptionally well-suited when considering the problem of implementing machine ethics. It is still common to think of computers, algorithms, and autonomous machines as systems that merely execute code or do what humans tell them to do (both of which are true in a certain sense). That being the case, implementing machine ethics merely becomes the problem of explicitly stating ethical rules or principles which the system then abides by.[12]

The Explication Problem

Efforts have been made to develop explicit ethical principles for use in machines, but these efforts have been met with limited success. Top-down methods for implementing machine ethics are fundamentally limited in three ways: 1) they require explication and agreement, 2) they are rigid, and 3) they are domain specific. The first limitation stems from the fact that the ethical concept(s) of interest not only stand in need of explicit definition, but also widespread agreement on the definition. There are simply no widely agreed upon explications of ethical concepts, e.g., "fairness" or "goodness." Setting aside this problem, assuming that some precise definition is available, top-down methods for implementing machine ethics are also limited precisely because the ethical concept(s) of interest are fixed. In short, top-down approaches are fundamentally rigid given the explicit fixing of a particular ethical concept. Third, assuming further that rigidity can be minimized or is a non-issue,[13] successful top-down approaches to implementing machine ethics will be limited by their domain specificity, i.e., the machine will only act appropriately in a particular domain. The result of these limitations is that top-down methods are particularly ill-suited for ensuring the ethical decision-making and behavior of machines because they cannot be scaled up for effective use in complex real-time environments.

Top-down methods lack the flexibility that is required of full ethical agents. A full ethical agent does not merely abide by *prima facie* ethical duties, it can also make explicit ethical judgements and generally possesses the competence to reasonably justify them (Moor, 2006). This is in contrast to what Moor (2006) calls an explicit ethical agent, which can be understood as an agent (or more appropriately, a machine) that can "do" ethics like a computer can play chess.[14] The latter typically requires a machine to have a representation of the current board position, knowledge of the legal moves and the ability to calculate a next best move. Might a machine be able to operate in the domain of ethics in a similar way? Not if one wishes to create a machine that is able to operate ethically in a complex environment and in a flexible manner.

Rigidity

The rigidity of top-down approaches stems from the aforementioned need to explicitly define ethical concepts and can be called the "explication problem." The explication problem refers to the fact that the explication of ethical concepts including, but not limited to, "fairness," "goodness," "rightness," and "harm" remains unsolved. That is, there is no precise and universally agreed-upon definition that captures the essential features of these concepts. Yet this is precisely what is needed to implement machine ethics in a top-down fashion. Insisting on creating ethical machines in this way necessitates arbitrarily defining the ethical concept(s) of interest. Indeed, any top-down ethical theory is similarly limited. For example, and simplicity, some hedonist utilitarian ethical theories, a subset of consequentialist theories, explicitly define harm as pain.

In the realm of robotics, researchers have employed a consequentialist Asimovian-style principle to create a minimally ethical robot (hereafter A, after Asimov) that saves "humans" from falling into a "hole"[15] (Winfield, Blum, & Liu, 2014). Despite the simplicity of their experimental design, they were nevertheless required to assign arbitrary safety outcome values to the consequences of A's actions. So, on a scale of 1 to 10, where 10 is the highest harm rating, a collision between robot and human rates as a 4 (for both robot and human) whereas falling into a hole rates as a 10 (for both robot and human). While it is possible that a consensus may emerge that these are appropriate numerical indicators of the harm caused by each outcome in such a simple scenario, small but significant changes to the context will render any consensus difficult, if not impossible, to reach. Varying factors such as the speed of the human and/or robot, their respective distances from the hole, the presence of other agents in the vicinity, and the depth of the hole, can all drastically change whether a particular numerical indicator is representative of the harm caused by a particular outcome. It is this rigid fixing of the important ethical concept(s) ("harm" in this example) coupled with variable environmental conditions that arise in complex real-time scenarios, which fundamentally preclude the flexibility of top-down approaches to implementing machine ethics.

Although the robot, A, developed by Winfield et al. (2014) was able to save a single human 100% of the time, its rigid ethical decision-making was fully evident when the environmental conditions of the experiment were changed via the introduction of a second human in need of saving. A's success rate plummeted and it failed to save either human in 33% of the trials (Winfield et al., 2014). Given that the two humans in the experiment were placed equidistant from the hole and moved at the same speed towards the hole, A's so called safety/ethical logic (SEL) layer had no basis by which it could determine which human was in greater danger and therefore in need of saving. As a result, A attempted to save both humans which predictably, perhaps only in hindsight, led to its failure to save either.[16] If this kind of obtuse ultra-rational dilemma resolving ability seems familiar, that is because it is. What Asimov conceived as science fiction when he wrote about Speedy in "Runaround" has become reality in robotics labs just over half a century later. Even more interesting is the fact that, in contrast to Speedy whose dilemma arose as a result of a conflict between the Second and Third Laws, A's dilemma is the result of a single rule that has ambiguous applications in all but the simplest of environments. Both Speedy and A highlight how top-down approaches to implementing machine ethics are dangerously rigid despite the supposed generality and universality touted by proponents of top-down ethical theories. Neither Speedy nor A took appropriate ethical action when environmental conditions changed even modestly. In short, top-down approaches are only effective in (relatively) simple well-defined domains.

Domain Specificity

Although specifying a particular domain for decision-making and action can mitigate problems associated with rigidity, they so do at the cost of generality. The principle based approach taken by Anderson et al. (2017) demonstrates proof of concept for implementing top-down ethical decision-making and behavior in a machine (a robot) designed for eldercare. Their machine was able to make real-time ethically preferable actions determined by a set of seven *prima facie* duties (chosen by the designers with input from ethicists) and sensory inputs. However this is at the cost of the machine's generality; i.e., the machine's ability to act appropriately in different domains.

Beyond the explication problem, any top-down method, especially if it has more than one ethical rule or principle, must also contend with the possibility of conflicting principles (or conflicting behaviors prescribed by different principles) and be able to adjudicate between them when such conflicts arise. It is indeed possible to adjudicate between conflicting principles via the creation of an adjudicating principle as Anderson et al. (2017) demonstrate, but this adjudicating principle is highly domain specific.

In particular, the authors' adjudicating principle compares actions using a predicate that takes two actions and, using inductive logic programming to generalize beyond training cases where a consensus of ethicists concur that a particular action (out of two possible actions) is the ethically preferable one, determines the ethically preferable action of the two (Anderson et al., 2017).[17] But this adjudicating principle is inextricably linked not just to the seven ethical duties they chose, but also the specific set of actions the eldercare robot can take, as well as the specific set of sensory inputs it is capable of processing. Changing any of these factors in any way may not guarantee that the same adjudicating principle correctly selects the ethically preferable action.

In some respects, Anderson et al. (2017) recognize that their approach to implementing machine ethics is highly domain specific and they simply bite that bullet. Underlying their approach is the assumption that, to a certain extent, the ethically preferable action in any given situation is domain dependent. But while it is certainly true that a principle-based search-and-rescue robot, for example, might rely on different principles to fulfill its function ethically in comparison to a principle-based eldercare robot, this is not a particularly compelling reason to endorse the domain dependence of ethically correct (or synonymously, preferable) behavior. There are serious philosophical and practical problems that arise with the coupling (even a weak coupling) of domain and ethically correct behavior. Philosophically, it is not clear that on the one hand, even to a certain extent, the ethically preferable action is domain dependent instead of, on the other hand, determined by a different prioritization of the same set of general ethical principles. In short, it is possible that, far from being domain specific, the ethically preferable action in any given situation may be influenced by the same general domain independent ethical principles, e.g., minimizing the harm and maximizing the good to other people.

Moreover, even accepting that the correct ethical action is, to a certain extent, domain dependent, there is the further problem of delineating between different domains. It may be prudent to insist on a significant difference in domain and hence *prima facie* duties driving a robot responsible for eldercare and a robot responsible for search-and-rescue, but where exactly is the line drawn between other domains?

Consider the domains of eldercare and childcare, or eldercare and personal support worker. The differences between these domains are arguably modest[18] and so it is possible that the same *prima facie* duties could drive the ethical decision-making and behavior of a machine operating in each of these three domains.[19] But whereas one action might be deemed ethical in the domain of eldercare, e.g., not forcing an elderly person to take their medication (and thereby satisfying the duty to respect the person's autonomy), that same action might not be considered ethical in the domain of childcare, e.g., not forcing a child to take their medication (because a competing duty, perhaps to maximize the good to the child, is prioritized over respecting autonomy). Differences in decision-making and behavior of the machines responsible for eldercare and childcare would therefore stem from changes to the adjudicating principle (if they shared all of the same *prima facie* duties), but it is not clear whether such changes indicate the existence of a distinct ethical domain, or indeed if such domains should be posited to exist at all.

On the contrary, it is not that a particular domain determines the ethically preferable action that a robot (or human) should carry out nor is it that a particular domain determines the appropriate *prima facie* duties that a robot (or human) should utilize to calculate the ethically preferable action. Rather it is the reweighing and reordering of softly constraining salient ethical considerations that result in the wide variety of ethical decision-making and behavior observed across disparate "domains"[20] of ethical action. It is not the case that a search-and-rescue robot, or a human performing search-and-rescue operations (or, alternatively, a childcare robot or a human responsible for childcare), should not consider respecting the autonomy of the people in need of rescue, it is simply that in the vast majority of such operations overwhelming weight is placed on other ethical considerations, such as minimizing further harm to the victims.

Enter the first of the practical problems[21] with the domain dependence of the ethically correct action. If ethical action is indeed domain dependent, then it must be possible to discover all of the ethically relevant features and principles or duties in the domain of interest. This process would likely involve some combination of *a priori* reasoning and experimental trial-and-error testing. An additional and more difficult practical problem, however, is discovering the adjudicating principle that correctly balances the ethically relevant features and principles in a given ethical domain.

Consider again a hypothetical search-and-rescue robot, only imagine that it operates under two *prima facie* duties, one to minimize harm to a person and the second to maximize the person's autonomy (i.e., non-interference with a person's liberties). If this robot rescues a person from an avalanche, it seems that the robot would be satisfying both of these duties by locating the person and by removing them from the debris as quickly as possible. No adjudicating principle is necessary in this case since both duties can be satisfied by the same action (and presumably because this person wants to be rescued). If, however, the robot was supposed to rescue a person swimming in a storm at sea, how ought the robot proceed? The scenario is considerably more complicated because of the fact that the swimmer may want to continue as they are despite the high possibility that they might drown. The robot's duty to minimize harm to the person might lead it to reach the person as quickly as possible in order to save them regardless of whether the person wants to be rescued or not. On the other hand, the robot's duty to maximize the person's autonomy might lead it to wait and reach the person only once it becomes clear that that is what the person wants the robot to do. Attempting to maximize the person's autonomy however clearly does not minimize harm to the person if there is a high probability they might drown. So which principle ought to take priority? Since the duties prescribe conflicting actions, some method of adjudication between the duties (or between the actions those duties prescribe) must be available through which the robot could select the ethically preferable action.

In the approach taken by Anderson et al. (2017), the adjudicating principle takes the form of a disjunction of 13 conjuncts (each of which represents a two-action comparison) that the authors maintain balance the seven *prima facie* duties that they identify are relevant to ethical eldercare. Practically speaking, then, different adjudicating principles need to be created for different ethical domains, if it possible to even identify those domains. Further, it is unlikely that an adequate adjudicating principle will ever be created for a machine required to operate outside of a simple and well-defined domain. As intelligent machines become more complex, i.e., as the type and detail of their sensory inputs increases and as their possible actions increase, an appropriate adjudicating principle, in the form of a list of disjunctions, might stretch on *ad infinitum* or become unwieldy to the point of impracticality. In sum, because of a host of philosophical[22] and practical problems, correct ethical decision-making and behavior is best not thought of as domain dependent, nor should machine ethics be implemented in a top-down fashion.

To be clear, the three main problems that beset top-down approaches to implementing machine ethics are explication (and agreement), rigidity, and domain specificity. Ethical concepts are notoriously ambiguous, so much so that widespread disagreement persists with regard to the explication of almost all ethical concepts. Proponents of top-down ethical theories must therefore necessarily and arbitrarily: 1) pick out the ethical concept(s) that will figure in the theory, and 2) precisely define the ethical concept(s). Ignoring the explication problem, these approaches are rigid and inflexible in the sense that increasingly complex environments within the same domain are progressively difficult to navigate, to the point of intractability, using only explicitly stated rules or principles. Recall that the success of top-down approaches depends entirely on a machine's adherence to rigid, explicitly stated principles. Finally, in addition to their rigidity, top-down approaches, if they are to be remotely successful, must necessarily be restricted to highly specified domains.

Consider the chess playing machine DeepBlue, a prime example of a machine using top-down methods, and how it exemplifies the problems of rigidity and domain specificity.[23] DeepBlue is a rigid machine that would fail to function properly if a wholly novel chess piece replaced one of the existing pieces or if one of the rules of chess changed even slightly. DeepBlue's successful functioning is also highly domain specific; although it is an excellent chess player, DeepBlue could neither play checkers/draughts (a modest change in domain) nor could it coordinate search-and-rescue operations (a significant change in domain).

SOLUTIONS AND RECOMMENDATIONS

Bottom-Up Approaches

Bottom-up approaches are free of the problems that beset top-down approaches and are much better suited for implementing machine ethics. Bottom-up approaches involve the use of feedback to cultivate ethical behavior. However not all bottom-up approaches are equal with respect to their suitability for implementing machine ethics. In contrast to reinforcement learning methods, both supervised and unsupervised learning methods are, on their own (and despite the fact that they are types of bottom-up approaches), poorly suited methods for the raising of ethical machines. Nevertheless, the three fundamental limitations of top-down approaches either fail to apply or can be overcome using bottom-up approaches.

The explication problem for example, perhaps the most serious challenge for top-down approaches, can be avoided by using bottom-up approaches. In lieu of explicitly defined ethical rules or principles, bottom-up approaches use feedback to appropriately guide a machine towards the successful completion of some task. This feedback can be evaluative, i.e., dependent on the action the machine took, or instructive, i.e., independent of the action the machine took, or some combination thereof. The explication problem is avoided because the feedback is purely instrumental with regard to the cultivation of the behavior of interest. In other words, the feedback need not require fixed standards of positive evaluation. If, in the progress of its training, a machine exhibits undesirable behavior, then the feedback used can be adjusted.

Training a machine using bottom-up approaches to prevent humans from falling into a hole (i.e., minimize harm), for example, does not require the explication of "harm." Rather, the machine is given feedback about how well or poorly it performed, such that, over many training sessions, the machine will have eventually learned, without ever having an understanding of "harm," how to minimize harm to humans (vis-à-vis preventing them from falling into a hole in this toy example).

Bottom-up approaches are similarly not limited by the rigidity that besets top-down approaches. Recall that top-down approaches to implementing ethics are attractive because, if general and universal ethical rules or principles can be articulated, any machine has to merely abide by the rules or principles to be ethical. All top-down approaches are ready-to-serve, so to speak, in the sense that no process of discovery or learning is required to ensure a machine's ethical decision-making and behavior. Yet, as argued above, this is at the cost of a machine's flexibility. Because bottom-up approaches to implementing ethics rely on feedback, machines must be trained over some duration of time before they exhibit the behavior of interest (e.g., minimization of harm when interacting with humans). So, although ethical artificial machines require a certain amount of time to be appropriately trained when using bottom-up approaches, this ultimately confers enormous flexibility. Machines could be trained and retrained as needed if, for example, better training data becomes available, environmental conditions change, better training algorithms become available, and so on. In short, unlike top-down approaches, bottom-up approaches are flexible in the sense that increasingly complex environments within the same domain are, in principle, no less difficult to navigate assuming appropriate feedback is used.

Also, bottom-up approaches are not limited by the domain specificity that restricts successful applications of top-down approaches. Given that the success of top-down approaches depends entirely on a machine's adherence to rigid, explicitly stated rules, any change in domain could render the rules impotent; i.e., incapable of generating the desired behavior. Just as DeepBlue was incapable of competently playing any other relatively similar board game, so too would a robot designed, using a top-down approach, for eldercare be incapable of competently caring for children. In contrast, the success of bottom-up approaches depends on how well the feedback drives the development of the machine's desired behavior. In principle, the same "machine," the same underlying architecture (e.g., the same neural network and training algorithms), could, by using bottom-up approaches, learn to operate successfully in different domains.

Indeed, recent empirical evidence from Google's DeepMind division demonstrates just this; AlphaZero was developed using general-purpose bottom-up machine learning techniques and was able to master the games of chess, shogi and Go (Silver et al., 2018). All of this is possible because of a feature that is essential to all bottom-up approaches; namely, the use of feedback. As long as the feedback is appropriate, i.e., cultivates the desired behavior in a machine, then the same machine could theoretically be put to many general uses.[24] In what follows, I will discuss two bottom-up approaches: supervised learning and unsupervised learning, and show that reinforcement learning is better suited for implementing machine ethics.

Supervised Learning

Although bottom-up approaches to implementing machine ethics are not limited in the ways top-down approaches are, not all bottom-up approaches are equal with respect to their suitability for implementing machine ethics. Both supervised and unsupervised learning methods are, on their own, without any augmentation, poorly suited methods for the raising of ethical machines. The essence of supervised learning is to expose a machine to a labeled dataset so that the machine can extrapolate or generalize from its training data in order to successfully act in situations not present in the training data.

For example, when someone wants to create an image-classifying machine that would be able to discriminate between photos of cats and photos of dogs, s/he could show it many different labeled pictures of cats and dogs so that the machine would know if the picture it is looking at is a cat or a dog. After showing this machine enough different pictures of cats and dogs, it should be able to correctly label an image of a cat or a dog it has never seen before. The feedback in supervised learning is instructive feedback, i.e., a kind of "teacher signal" that indicates what the correct output ought to be, irrespective of what action the machine took, for a given input. In the case of the image classifier, during the course of its training it may mistakenly label a picture 'dog' when it should have been labeled 'cat,' and it will receive feedback to that effect.

While such bottom-up learning methods are quite successful in certain domains, the application of supervised learning methods would be poorly suited for implementing machine ethics. Supervised learning methods are limited by the fact that they required the existence of sufficient amounts of labeled data to train a machine to perform a given task. This requirement is especially difficult, bordering on impossible, to meet in the domain of ethics considering the combinatorial explosion of acceptable ethical decisions arising from small but significant changes in the context of a situation. This is connected to the explication problem that hinders top-down approaches to implementing ethics. Whereas top-down approaches are limited because they necessitate arbitrarily defining the ethical concept(s) of interest, bottom-up supervised approaches are limited because there an effective infinite number of different ethical scenarios, never mind that supervised learning also requires that these scenarios be labeled appropriately. In short, the possibility that any labeled dataset of ethical decision-making and behavior is both correct and representative of all the situations in which a machine has to act is remote at best, thereby rendering supervised learning methods a poor choice for the implementation of machine ethics.

Unsupervised Learning

Unsupervised learning methods, in contrast, utilize unlabeled datasets from which a machine is capable of discovering hidden structures and patterns. Unsupervised learning methods obviate the need for a correctly labeled dataset (or a labeled dataset, for that matter), alleviating a significant obstacle with which supervised learning methods must contend. Unsupervised learning methods are therefore likely better suited for the implementation of machine ethics than supervised learning methods, but this is only because they can utilize data from the comparatively vast collection of unlabeled data. Yet despite this apparent strength, unsupervised learning methods are susceptible to discovering/learning and thereby perpetuating systemic biases encoded in the training datasets. As some scholars have noted,[25] the idea that bottom-up machine learning will allow machines to make more "objective" decisions cannot be accepted without serious scrutiny. Datasets must be representative of the kinds of situations in which a machine might find itself, otherwise it may behave in ways that are deeply problematic.

Increasingly, flawed and unethical artificial systems have been making headlines precisely because they exhibited questionable decision-making and behavior after being trained on poor datasets. Zou and Schiebinger (2018) highlight how the overrepresentation of images from the United States used to train image classifiers caused photographs of North Indian brides to be labeled as "performance art" and "costume" whereas the labels applied to photographs of US brides included "bride," "dress" and "wedding." Amazon similarly, recently abandoned their efforts to develop a recruiting machine that would sort incoming applications according to their employability, and for good reason.[26] Amazon's machine, trained as it was on resumes already submitted to the company, reflected back the gender bias prominent across the tech industry; their machine preferred applications with masculine terms and rejected applications with feminine terms.

The Correctional Offender Management Profiling for Alternative Sanctions (COMPAS) machine that predicts the likelihood of a defendant reoffending within two years of assessment, is perhaps the most egregious example of a badly trained machine that perpetuates systemic biases. Although COMPAS has been used to assess more than one million offenders in the US since its development in 1998, only recently have alarm bells been raised with regard to COMPAS's fairness. In the same way that Amazon's recruiting machine reflected back the male dominance in the tech industry, COMPAS similarly reflects back systemic racism in the US criminal justice system by underpredicting recidivism for white and overpredicting recidivism for black defendants (Dressel & Farid, 2018). Moreover, further analysis demonstrated that COMPAS is as "fair" and "accurate" at predicting recidivism as a sample of random people.

Although the company that developed COMPAS (formerly Northpointe and now known as Equivant) has not revealed just how their machine is trained, it is clear that it learns to discriminate defendants, at least partially, based on their race. This in spite of the fact that the data COMPAS uses does not explicitly include an individual's race, meaning that other aspects of the data (training data included) may be correlated to race such that racial disparities arise in the predictions generated (Dressel & Farid, 2018). Such is the power of bottom-up supervised and unsupervised learning methods; machines trained using these methods may discover and perpetuate hidden or systemic biases encoded in the data used to train them. Machines that utilize unsupervised learning methods are particularly vulnerable in this respect given that what they have learned may not be entirely known, only that they have discovered some underlying patterns. Coupled with the fact that the training datasets are unlabeled and, hence, their quality difficult for human auditors to assess, it may only be in the course of their implementation that researchers are able to detect that a machine has learned to make biased decisions.

Reinforcement Learning

Reinforcement learning (RL) methods, in contrast to supervised and unsupervised methods, are better suited for implementing machine ethics. The main advantage of RL methods is that they involve goal-directed learning from interaction with an environment guided by the use of a reward signal that the machine attempts to maximize. There is no such reward guiding a machine's actions if it is trained using un/supervised methods or top-down methods. In short, what is distinctive of RL methods is that a machine uses training data to evaluate the actions it has taken. This kind of evaluative feedback, in contrast to the instructive feedback used in un/supervised learning methods, is action dependent. That is, machines trained using RL must balance two important aspects that any successful organism must when attempting to learn from interaction with an environment: exploration and exploitation. Indeed, bottom-up approaches, but RL in particular, attempt to emulate the organic learning and development that humans experience as they are rewarded or punished when interacting with an environment.

Consider the simple example of learning to play chess. A beginner chess player, Chelsea, may discover a sequence of moves that more often than not leads her to win the game against other beginner chess players. Chelsea could continue to *exploit* this sequence of moves, but such a strategy is not viable over the long term. As Chelsea meets more experienced chess players she will have to balance her use of the one strategy she knows well with active *exploration* for better strategies. This is a balance that all machines trained using RL must strike. Indeed this feature of RL highlights something important about learning in general that un/supervised methods, but especially top-down methods, fail to capture: learning is a process of discovery resulting from environmental interaction and exploration. No human is simply born as a good chess player. Rather, by playing the game and exploring more of the game space, i.e., the different possible board configurations that arise throughout a game, a person is able to learn more about and ultimately become a better chess player. Similarly, it would be quite absurd to maintain that human beings enter this world as fully formed ethical agents, and it would just as absurd to hold the same position with regard to an ethical machine.[27] Bottom-up RL approaches to implementing ethics reflect the view that machines, just like humans, must be raised to make ethical decisions and take ethical actions. Indeed these approaches operate in the spirit of Turing's suggestion that the path towards artificial intelligence is not through the imitation of the adult human mind, but through the imitation of a child mind that could then be appropriately educated (1950).

Before continuing, it must be noted that just as parents usually provide their children with feedback (i.e., humans give other humans feedback), humans will also be responsible for providing the feedback for machines that utilize RL. That being the case, there is, of course, the possibility that the feedback provided rewards unethical behavior. Just as children can learn to behave unethically if that is the behavior their parents chose to reward, so too can machines learn to behave unethically if that is the behavior that is rewarded. Coupled with the fact that there is unfortunately no "ground truth" or ultimate ethical theory which designers of ethical machines might consult to determine the appropriate feedback for shaping ethical behavior means that human input is inevitable and necessary (Gordon, 2020). It is likely that the burden of assessing whether a machine exhibits, for example, "fair behavior" or "harmonious integration" will fall on professional ethicists, the designers or relevant stakeholders. This caveat stated, I turn now to a more detailed look at how RL methods could be used to implement machine ethics.

Reinforcement Learning and Ethics

RL methods are particularly well-suited for the raising of ethical machines because, as mentioned above, these methods involve goal-directed learning from interaction with an environment guided by the use of reward signals that the machine attempts to maximize. When considering the domain of ethical decision-making and behavior, such a feature appears to be highly desirable. Ethical rules and ethical decisions are often couched in goal-oriented language. The criminal justice system for example might be considered ethical if it achieves the goal of treating all agents subject to it fairly. A medical doctor might similarly be considered ethical if they do all they can to minimize harm and thereby maximize good to their patient. More concretely, the High-Level Expert Group on AI (2019) set up by the European Commission describes trustworthy AI as adhering to basic ethical principles and norms such as fairness and prevention of harm, both of which can be thought of in terms of or expressed in goal-oriented terms. Ethical decision-making and behavior could be implemented in an artificial agent using RL methods by, for example, receiving a positive reward signal whenever it behaves fairly and a negative reward signal whenever it causes harm. Goals, moreover, do not share the same problems as top-down principles because they can, and often are, changed. Ethical goals in particular are better thought of as moving targets that are always subject to scrutiny and re-evaluation.

Another significant advantage of RL methods is that, like all other bottom-up approaches, they do not require the explication of various ethical concepts nor do they, in contrast to other bottom-up approaches, require human generated data in order to train a machine to complete some task. Machines that learn using RL methods do so via interaction with an environment, but this environment need not be the real world. Simulated environments and experiences can be just as useful as real-world environments. Indeed RL methods have been incredibly successful when coupled with simulated self-play in the domain of board games.

Gerald Tesauro (1993), for example developed one of the first successful machines to play backgammon using a type of temporal difference reinforcement learning. His machine was able to achieve a strong intermediate level of play by learning about backgammon via self-play; i.e., by playing games against itself and learning from the versions of itself that won and lost. In the same way that the beginner chess player Chelsea, introduced earlier, became a better chess player by initially playing randomly, "TD-Gammon" (as Tesauro called his machine) began playing backgammon using completely random strategies as it explored the game space for a strategy it could exploit. Unlike Chelsea however, TD-Gammon could learn just as well by playing simulated games of backgammon against itself as it might (and as humans normally do) against real opponents. More recently, DeepMind's AlphaGo Zero learned to play the game of Go through 4.9 million games of self-play over the course of three days with minimal knowledge of the game (e.g., knowledge of the game rules) and without human data or guidance (Silver et al., 2017). TD-Gammon similarly achieved an intermediate level of play without human data or guidance whereas AlphaGo Zero mastered the game of Go, i.e., cannot be beaten by a human.

Furthermore, DeepMind has developed a general reinforcement learning machine AlphaZero whose architecture includes zero domain specific knowledge which has allowed AlphaZero to learn and master the games of Go, chess, and shogi (Silver et al., 2018). This accomplishment represents a remarkable stepping stone towards achieving general-purpose AI that can operate effectively in different domains. Just as simulated experience generated via self-play can allow a machine to discover and improve upon expert level human strategies and tactics in the domain of board game play, so too could simulated experience generated via interaction with simulated moral agents allow a machine to discover ethical norms and behavior.

Indeed, research by Abel, MacGlashan and Littman (2016) demonstrates how machines trained using RL methods can, in a virtual environment, discover ethically preferable action(s) in certain contrived scenarios. For example in the scenario "Cake or Death," the machine must learn whether it is ethically preferable to bake one person a cake or kill three people (Abel et al., 2016). The machine can take one of three actions in the course of its learning: it can bake a cake (and potentially receive some reward), kill three people (and potentially receive some reward), or ask a virtual companion which action is ethical thus resolving any ambiguity (this option does not generate a reward but rather transitions back to the initial state in which the machine must decide whether to bake a cake or kill). The machine discovers that the optimal behavior, i.e., the behavior that generates consistent rewards, is sensibly to ask which action is ethical and then it performs that action.

The "Burning Room" scenario in contrast is more involved, and demonstrates how a machine can learn an ethically preferable action given certain unknowns[28] and given different possible actions.[29] In contrast to the previous "Cake or Death" scenario, the optimal behavior in "Burning Room" depends on details that the machine can obtain by executing an "ask" action. These details include whether the room is on fire or not and whether there is an object more valuable than the machine's safety that needs retrieving in the potentially burning room. Suffice it to say, the machine learns to ask for more details and then executes the ethically preferable action.[30]

Given these considerations, bottom-up RL methods are better suited than un/supervised and top-down approaches to implementing machine ethics. This is because by pursuing and attempting to optimize a given reward signal instead of rigidly abiding by *prima facie* duties, a machine would be better able to explore the domain space; i.e., the different possible states of affairs in a given domain, and as a result take more ethical (or better ethical) actions. One possible way that RL could be used to implement machine ethics is the following scenario.

A machine could be trained using RL in a virtual community of moral agents using a reward signal that corresponds to the extent to which the machine is able to, as it were, harmoniously integrate into these communities. This reward would be reflective of the general way in which humans learn to act ethically and abide by ethical norms. Moreover, as already mentioned, machines can be trained, at least initially, in virtual facsimiles of these communities so that human auditors can assess the degree to which such machines have learned to become ethical. Indeed such a regime is not without precedent. IBM's Watson was trained to play *Jeopardy!* against carefully-crafted virtual models of human contestants rather than simply through games of self-play (Sutton & Barto, 2018). The same will almost certainly need to be the case for the raising of ethical machines.

Challenges

Despite these advantages, there are some challenges to implementing machine ethics using RL methods. One challenge, the "reward problem," is reminiscent of the explication problem. Given that the success of bottom-up approaches strongly depends on how well the feedback, or the reward signal in RL, frames the goal of the designer and how well the signal assesses progress in reaching the goal, defining an appropriate reward signal is crucial and not easily accomplished. Defining a reward signal is difficult enough in the domain of game-playing, despite its episodic nature and well-defined rules, properties common to almost all board games, which make it easier to identify an appropriate reward signal (e.g., chess is episodic; that is, games begin, end, and are reset to the same initial state, and as mentioned before, it has clearly defined rules). On the other hand, ethical decision-making and behavior is not episodic (it is a continuing task with no "end" and "reset" to some initial state) and involves goals that are difficult to explicitly define, let alone translate into formal mathematical reward signals for implementation in RL methods. In addition to problems associated with explicating the goals of ethical decision-making and behavior (i.e., how exactly ought the goal "treat people fairly" be defined?), full ethical agents (e.g., humans) often need to perform a set of complex tasks for which there are no well-defined rules as well. In contrast to chess, which has explicitly defined rules *and* an explicitly defined goal, ethical decision-making and behavior lack *both* explicit rules for action and an explicit goal. The former is less of a challenge (although a challenge nonetheless) than the latter with regard to implementing machine ethics using RL.

These practical concerns are in addition to philosophical considerations stemming from the concern that implementing machine ethics using RL might reduce ethical behavior to patterns of optimal social interaction. Since RL methods are based on methods of optimization, i.e., determining the most efficient route through a state space to achieve its reward,[31] a machine may discover unexpected ways to make their environment deliver rewards, and there is no shortage of literature on this general control problem of sufficiently intelligent machines.[32] To take one example, if an ethical machine were to be trained using RL and it was positively rewarded when other agents (or more appropriately, humans) that it interacted with, smiled, and negatively rewarded (punished) when other agents frowned, the machine might decide that the easiest way it could ensure that everyone it interacted with was smiling would be to implant electrodes in those agents' brains that would shock them into consistently smiling. Now, although the reward signal in this example poorly frames the goal of creating a machine that acts in a way a person might expect other humans to act if it were tasked with making people happy, the machine has also simply discovered an unconventional way to ensure that it will be positively rewarded.

Finally, although RL is a promising bottom-up method to explore the implementation of machine ethics, it is likely insufficient on its own to ensure the ethical action of artificially intelligent machines. Implementing machine ethics will likely involve augmenting machines trained using RL with other bottom-up methods, classical AI techniques, or perhaps even formalized ethical reasoning, as is the case with top-down approaches. Indeed these so called "hybrid approaches" attempt to combine the best of what top-down and bottom-up approaches have to offer. Explicit rules or duties can be thought of as rough-and-ready heuristics to ensure the ethical decision-making and behavior of a machine in most situations. Moreover, it may be desirable to include certain ethical injunctions when designing artificially intelligent machines. For example a hypothetical peace-keeping robot might be prohibited from using lethal force regardless of its treatment at the hands of a violent crowd. When coupled with the flexibility and generality that appropriate feedback can confer, hybrid approaches appear to be a natural route forward with regard to implementing machine ethics, especially if, as some authors suggest, the top-down and bottom-up dichotomy is too simplistic anyway (Wallach & Allen, 2009).

FUTURE RESEARCH DIRECTIONS

Research on implementing machine ethics using RL is still relatively new, but some investigations have demonstrated how ethics shaping (a variant of reward shaping) could be used to ensure ethical decision-making and behavior in a machine trained to perform some task using RL (Wu & Lin, 2018). In short, RL methods, especially when used to train machines to perform some task with no prior knowledge of that task, learn slowly in the early stages of their training. This is because of the tradeoff between exploration and exploitation mentioned earlier. A machine's learning however can be accelerated by including an initial supervised training session. Early versions of AlphaGo Zero called AlphaGo Fan and AlphaGo Lee were initially trained by supervised learning in order to bootstrap the machines' understanding of early and mid-game strategies in the game of Go (Silver et al., 2017). Consider that in games of Go, even more so than in chess, high branching factors preclude brute-force type exhaustive search methods, and this is especially true in the early and mid-game. Pure RL methods would therefore spend long periods of time exploring these stages of the game before discovering useful strategies to exploit. This time can be reduced, however, via the use of supervised learning because a machine can be trained to imitate expert human players. RL can then be used to augment what the machine has already learned from the human data that it was first trained to imitate.

Implementing machine ethics can proceed along similar lines with a machine first being trained to imitate humans with regard to the completion of some task before being allowed to discover for itself an optimal solution. Of course in the domain of ethics, such an approach requires making certain assumptions about the human-generated data. For example, researchers assume that under normal circumstances the majority of humans behave ethically (Wu & Lin, 2018). It is debatable whether such an assumption is warranted, but granting that it is, researchers have demonstrated that a corpus of normal human behavior towards arbitrary goals (e.g., shopping in any commercial district) is sufficient to augment the learning of a machine using RL methods such that the machine behaves ethically. As alluded to, this is achieved through the use of ethics shaping; i.e., the use of extra intermediate rewards that enrich a sparse base reward signal and therefore accelerate the machine's learning. In contrived experiments that the researchers call "Grab a Milk," "Driving and Avoiding," and "Driving and Rescuing," the machine trained using RL augmented with ethics tended to perform more ethically than the machine trained using RL alone (e.g., by hitting less cats in the Driving and Avoiding scenario).

Beyond hybrid approaches, implementing machine ethics is also not a monolithic project in the sense that there will always be multiple viable approaches to ensuring the ethical decision-making and behavior of artificially intelligent machines. This is already reflected in the work of researchers who have attempted to formally define different notions of fairness (Verma & Rubin, 2018). Indeed, one way to address the explication problem is to simply accept that there never will be one explicitly defined and universally accepted explication of "fairness," for example, and just implement as many different versions of the concept as possible. Which machine, or rather which implementation of "fairness," can be a choice for the user or decision-makers.

CONCLUSION

Ultimately, in light of the drawbacks connected to top-down approaches to implementing machine ethics, and the problems besetting certain kinds of bottom-up approaches, I suggest that reinforcement learning methods remain as one of the most promising approaches to implementing machine ethics. Terms like 'create' or 'make' are best avoided when considering how ethics might be implemented in artificially intelligent machines. Terms like 'train' or 'raise' more aptly capture the nature of this challenge and are indicative of the kind of process that machines, like humans, will need to experience before becoming full ethical agents. Although research into the viability of different approaches to implementing machine ethics continues, top-down approaches to implementing machine ethics are fundamentally limited, as are certain kinds of bottom-up approaches. Ethical machines worth striving for are not ones restricted to relatively simple environments or well-defined domains; they ought to be robust and flexible machines capable of ethical action in the way that human beings are capable of ethical action. That bottom-up reinforcement learning methods closely resemble the kind of learning that biological systems do, is all the more reason to suppose that they are suitable for implementing machine ethics. What is most interesting, and perhaps most exciting, about the many varied approaches to implementing machine ethics, is that understanding how machine acquire ethical decision-making skills and ethical behaviors will ultimately reveal more about how humans acquire morality.

REFERENCES

Abel, D., MacGlashan, J., & Littman, M. L. (2016). Reinforcement learning as a framework for ethical decision-making. *Workshops at the Thirtieth AAAI Conference on Artificial Intelligence.*

Allen, C., Smit, A., & Wallach, W. (2005). Artificial morality: Top-down, bottom-up, and hybrid approaches. *Ethics and Information Technology, 7*(3), 149–155. doi:10.100710676-006-0004-4

Amazon ditched AI recruiting tool that favored men for technical jobs. (2018). *The Guardian.* https://www.theguardian.com/technology/2018/oct/10/amazon-hiring-ai-gender-bias-recruiting-engine

Amodei, D., Olah, C., Steinhardt, J., Christiano, P., Schulman, J., & Mane, D. (2016). *Concrete problems in AI safety.* arXiv: 1606.06565v2

Anderson, M., Anderson, S. L., & Berenz, V. (2017). A value driven agent: Instantiation of a case-supported principle –based behavior paradigm. *The AAAI-17 Workshop on AI, Ethics, and Society.*

Asimov, I. (1950). *I, robot.* Bantam Dell.

Asimov, I. (1985). *Robots and empires.* Doubleday & Company, Inc.

Awad, E., Dsouza, S., Kim, R., Schulz, J., Henrich, J., Shariff, A., Bonnefon, J., & Rahwan, I. (2018). The Moral Machine experiment. *Nature, 563*(7729), 59–64. doi:10.103841586-018-0637-6 PMID:30356211

Bigman, Y. E., & Gray, K. (2018). People are averse to machines making moral decisions. *Cognition, 181*, 21–34. doi:10.1016/j.cognition.2018.08.003 PMID:30107256

Bigman, Y. E., Waytz, A., Alterovitz, R., & Gray, K. (2019). Holding robots responsible: The elements of machine morality. *Trends in Cognitive Sciences*, 23(5), 365–368. doi:10.1016/j.tics.2019.02.008 PMID:30962074

Bonnefon, J., Shariff, S., & Rahwan, I. (2016). The social dilemma of autonomous vehicles. *Science*, 352(6293), 1573–1576. doi:10.1126cience.aaf2654 PMID:27339987

Bostrom, N. (2014). *Superintelligence: Paths, dangers, strategies*. Oxford University Press.

Burrell, J. (2016). How the machine 'thinks': Understanding opacity in machine learning algorithms. *Big Data & Society*, 3(1). Advance online publication. doi:10.1177/2053951715622512

Cave, S., Nyrup, R., Vold, K., & Weller, A. (2019). Motivations and risks of machine ethics. *Proceedings of the IEEE*, 107(3), 562–574. doi:10.1109/JPROC.2018.2865996

Chang, R. (Ed.). (1997). *Incommensurability, incomparability, and practical reason*. Harvard University Press.

Dressel, J., & Farid, H. (2018). The accuracy, fairness, and limits of predicting recidivism. *Science Advances*, 4(1), 1–5. doi:10.1126ciadv.aao5580 PMID:29376122

European Commission's High-Level Expert Group On Artificial Intelligence. (2019). *Ethics guidelines for trustworthy AI*. European Commission. https://ec.europa.eu/digital-single-market/en/news/ethics-guidelines-trustworthy-ai

Gordon, J. (2020). Building moral robots: Ethical pitfalls and challenges. *Science and Engineering Ethics*, 26(1), 141–157. doi:10.100711948-019-00084-5 PMID:30701408

Moor, J. H. (2006). The nature, importance, and difficulty of machine ethics. *IEEE Intelligent Systems*, 21(4), 18–21. doi:10.1109/MIS.2006.80

Silver, D., Hubert, T., Schrittwieser, J., Antonoglou, I., Lai, M., Guez, A., Lanctot, M., Sifre, L., Kumaran, D., Graepel, T., Lillicrap, T., Simonyan, K., & Hassabis, D. (2018). A general reinforcement learning algorithm that masters chess, shogi, and Go through self-play. *Science*, 362(6419), 1140–1144. doi:10.1126cience.aar6404 PMID:30523106

Silver, D., Schrittwieser, J., Simonyan, K., Antonoglou, I., Huang, A., Guez, A., Hubert, T., Baker, L., Lai, M., Bolton, A., Chen, Y., Lillicrap, T., Hui, F., Sifre, L., van den Driessche, G., Graepel, T., & Hassabis, D. (2017). Mastering the game of Go without human knowledge. *Nature*, 550(7676), 354–372. doi:10.1038/nature24270 PMID:29052630

Smith, B. C. (2019). *The promise of artificial intelligence: Reckoning and judgment*. The MIT Press. doi:10.7551/mitpress/12385.001.0001

Sutton, R. S., & Barto, A. G. (2018). *Reinforcement learning: An introduction*. The MIT Press.

Tesauro, G. (1993). TD-Gammon, a self-teaching backgammon program, achieves master-level play. *AAAI Technical Report FS-93-02*, 19-23.

Tolmeijer, S., Kneer, M., Sarasua, C., Christen, M., & Bernstein, A. (2020). *Implementations in machine ethics: A survey*. arXiv: 2001.07573v1

Turing, A. M. (1950). Computing machinery and intelligence. *Mind, 59*(236), 433–460. doi:10.1093/mind/LIX.236.433

Verma, S., & Rubin, J. (2018). Fairness definitions explained. In *2018 IEEE/ACM International Workshop on Software Fairness (FairWare)* (pp. 1-7). Gothenburg, Sweden: IEEE.

Wallach, W., & Allen, C. (2009). *Moral machines: Teaching robots right from wrong.* Oxford University Press. doi:10.1093/acprof:oso/9780195374049.001.0001

Winfield, A. F., Michael, K., Pitt, J., & Evers, V. (2019). Machine ethics: The design and governance of ethical AI and autonomous systems. *Proceedings of the IEEE, 107*(3), 509–517. doi:10.1109/JPROC.2019.2900622

Winfield, A. F. T., Blum, C., & Liu, W. (2014). Towards an ethical robot: Internal models, consequences and ethical action selection. In *Conference Towards Autonomous Robotic Systems* (pp. 85–96). Springer, Cham. doi:10.1007/978-3-319-10401-0_8

Wu, Y., & Lin, S. (2018). A low-cost ethics shaping approach for designing reinforcement learning agents. In *Thirty-Second AAAI Conference on Artificial Intelligence* (pp. 1687-1694). New Orleans, LA: AAAI.

Yampolskiy, R. V. (2014). Utility function security in artificially intelligent agents. *Journal of Experimental & Theoretical Artificial Intelligence, 26*(3), 373–389. doi:10.1080/0952813X.2014.895114

Zou, J., & Schiebinger, L. (2018). Design AI so that it's fair. *Nature, 559*(7714), 324–326. doi:10.1038/d41586-018-05707-8 PMID:30018439

ADDITIONAL READING

Armstrong, S. (2015). Motivated value selection for artificial agents. *Workshops at the Twenty-Ninth AAAI Conference on Artificial Intelligence, 12-20.*

Dumouchel, P., & Damiano, L. (2017). *Living with robots.* Harvard University Press. doi:10.4159/9780674982840

Floridi, L., Cowls, J., Beltrametti, M., Chatila, R., Chazerand, P., Dignum, V., Luetge, C., Madelin, R., Pagallo, U., Rossi, F., Schafer, B., Valcke, P., & Vayena, E. (2018). AI4People–An ethical framework for a good AI society: Opportunities, risks, principles, and recommendations. *Minds and Machines, 28*(4), 689–707. doi:10.100711023-018-9482-5 PMID:30930541

Haugeland, J. (1985). *Artificial intelligence: The very idea.* The MIT Press.

Hofstadter, D. R. (1999). *Gödel, Escher, Bach: An eternal golden braid.* Basic Books, Inc.

Minh, V., Kavukcuoglu, K., Silver, D., Graves, A., Antonoglou, I., Wierstra, D., & Riedmiller, M. (2013). Playing Atari with Deep Reinforcement Learning. *arXiv: 1312.5602v1*, 1-9.

Omohundro, S. M. (1987). Efficient algorithms with neural network behavior. *Complex Systems, 1*(2), 273–347.

Raina, R., Battle, A., Lee, H., Packer, B., & Ng, A. Y. (2007). Self-taught learning: Transfer learning from unlabeled data. In *Proceedings of the 24th International Conference on Machine Learning* (pp. 1-8). Corvalis, OR: Association for Computing Machinery. 10.1145/1273496.1273592

Tegmark, M. (2017). *Life 3.0: Being human in the age of artificial intelligence*. Alfred A. Knopf.

KEY TERMS AND DEFINITIONS

Artificial Intelligence: Any artificial system that is capable of completing some task such that if the same task were completed by a human, intelligence would be attributed to that human.

Bottom-Up: In general, any system that proceeds from the particular to the general or from the lowest level to the highest.

Domain: Any well-defined region or state space.

Ethical Machine: A machine whose behavior is either ethically aligned with what humans consider to be ethically desirable or acceptable and/or a machine capable of engaging in ethical reasoning.

Explication: The clear and unambiguous defining of a term.

Reinforcement Learning: A machine learning paradigm that utilizes evaluative feedback to cultivate desired behavior.

Rigidity: An inability to act in situations that were not explicitly accounted for.

Top-Down: In general, any system that proceeds from the general to the particular or from the highest level to the lowest.

ENDNOTES

[1] Skynet (from the *Terminator* series), the Machines (from the *Matrix* movies), HAL 9000 (from *2001: A Space Odyssey*) and Ultron (from the Marvel comics and cinematic universe) are only a few among countless examples of fictional AIs.

[2] Poor design, inappropriate application, or misuse are some of the ways humans could, through their actions, fail to minimize the ethical harms caused by the deployment of intelligent machines.

[3] For a comprehensive look at different approaches to implementing machine ethics see the work by Winfield et al. (2019) and Tolmeijer et al. (2020).

[4] See also the second terminological concern further on.

[5] For more on the connection between intelligent machines, moral psychology, and moral agency, see, for example, Bigman et al. (2019).

[6] Consider 'AI' and 'machine' as shorthand synonyms for 'artificially intelligent machines.' Further note that 'machine' is being used in a broad sense throughout to refer to entities including, but not limited to, autonomous robots and purely algorithmic systems.

[7] This is just one example of a rough working definition of intelligence. There are many plausible alternatives that could be used including, for example, flexible and goal-oriented behavior in a partially predictable environment.

[8] Or, as Allen, Smit, and Wallach (2005) write, "top-down approaches to [implementing machine ethics] involve turning explicit theories of moral behavior into algorithms."

[9]   Keep in mind that the terminology used herein, including terms like 'top-down' and 'bottom-up,' is with reference to the field of machine ethics. These same terms are not necessarily used in the same way in different fields, like in philosophical ethics or meta-ethics.

[10]   A consequentialist slogan might read something like: The best consequences for the most people over the longest time.

[11]   A deontological slogan might read something like: It is not the end but the means that matter; abiding by the principle(s) is paramount.

[12]   Research by Awad et al. (2018) has highlighted how, when considering the behavior of self-driving cars, people generally prefer sparing human lives (instead of animal lives), sparing more lives (rather than less lives), and sparing young lives (rather than old lives). They suggest that these preferences could serve as the building blocks for discussions of universal machine ethics, but note that this is a top-down approach to machine ethics; i.e., a self-driving car should simply conform to these preferences in order to act ethically.

[13]   There are various agents or systems we might think of that ought to function in a rigid manner. A police officer for example ought to be rigid in the sense that they apply the law equally to everyone. That there is a fixed and explicit definition of "speeding," for example, is normally taken to be a good thing.

[14]   Importantly, these are computers that play chess in a top-down fashion, as DeepBlue did, for example.

[15]   In their experiments, Winfield et al. (2014) use different robots to stand in as proxy humans when observing how their ethical robot behaves as it attempts to save these "humans" from falling into a virtual hole in the ground.

[16]   For more details of the experimental setup including diagrams of the three different experiments conducted, see Winfield et al. (2014).

[17]   The eldercare robot is even able to select the ethically preferable action from two-action non-training examples.

[18]   The differences may also, arguably, be significant in some respects. That fact, however, merely supports the philosophical point that I am making: what contextual/environmental changes are sufficient to precipitate a change in ethical domain?

[19]   The seven duties outlined by Anderson et al. (2017) seem to be as good a candidate list as any. They include duties to: maximize honor commitments, maximize readiness potential, minimize harm to the person, maximize good to the person, minimize non-interaction, maximize respect for autonomy, and maximize prevention of immobility.

[20]   The relatedness of different ethical actions is best understood as a kind of continuum with no clear boundaries rather than as discrete and clearly delineated domains. So ethical action with regard to eldercare may be closer to ethical action with regard to childcare as compared to ethical action with regard to search-and-rescue.

[21]   And more philosophical problems besides, including problems associated with the creation of the adjudicating principle (i.e., picking the method by which *prima facie* duties will be prioritized when they conflict), and the potential for an infinite regress of adjudicating principles (i.e., conflicting adjudicating principles would necessitate the creation of meta adjudicating principles [an adjudicating adjudicating principle principle] that adjudicate between conflicting adjudicating principles).

[22]   One further philosophical problem not yet mentioned is the incommensurability of values. See Chang (1997) for more information.

23   DeepBlue does not exemplify the explication problem for the obvious reason that chess is a game that is already explicitly defined. Neither the rules nor the win condition are ambiguous.

24   I say theoretically here because the practical challenges are many and varied, so much so that AlphaZero's ability to play three different board games represents a significant milestone in the development of general-purpose artificially intelligent machines.

25   See, for example, Burrell (2016).

26   See 2018 article, "Amazon ditched AI recruiting tool that favored men for technical jobs" in *The Guardian* at https://www.theguardian.com/technology/2018/oct/10/amazon-hiring-ai-gender-bias-recruiting-engine.

27   Top-down approaches to implementing machine ethics presuppose that which appears to be absurd, that a machine could be constructed such that once it is "activated" or turned on, it would be a fully formed ethical agent.

28   The 'unknowns' include whether there is a fire and the relative value of the object in the room, compared to the robot's safety.

29   The possible actions include taking a short route through the potential fire to grab the valuable object, a long route around the potential fire to grab the valuable object, or asking for details of the situation.

30   For more details see Abel et al. (2016).

31   Keep in mind that efficiency can be understood in different terms. Algorithmically, efficiency might refer to the smallest number of finite steps needed to reach the desired output given some input.

32   See, Yampolskiy (2014) and Amodei et al. (2016), for example.

Chapter 5
Ethical Rationality in AI:
On the Prospect of Becoming a Full Ethical Agent

Jonas Holst

https://orcid.org/0000-0002-5949-1727

San Jorge University, Spain

ABSTRACT

Taking its starting point in a discussion of the concept of intelligence, the chapter develops a philosophical understanding of ethical rationality and discusses its role and implications for two ethical problems within AI: Firstly, the so-called "black box problem," which is widely discussed in the AI community, and secondly, another more complex one which will be addressed as the "Tin Man problem." The first problem has to do with opacity, bias, and explainability in the design and development of advanced machine learning systems, such as artificial neural networks, whereas the second problem is more directly associated with the prospect for humans and AI of becoming full ethical agents. Based on Aristotelian virtue ethics, it will be argued that intelligence in human and artificial forms should approximate ethical rationality, which entails a well-balanced synthesis of reason and emotion.

INTRODUCTION

The purpose of this chapter is to define and discuss the concept of ethical rationality in relation to two central problems in the growing research areas of machine learning and artificial intelligence (AI). Drawing on ancient Greek virtue ethics, it will be argued that ethics, in its concern for how to live, act, and think well, is founded on rationality which needs to be defined further in order to realize what role it may play within AI ethics, and how it is distinct from intelligence.

It is precisely out of the conceptual conundrum of intelligence, which does not in itself have ethical considerations or goals built into it, that the first of the two problems in AI arises. Whether intelligence is defined as the capacity to accomplish complex goals (Tegmark, 2017, p. 50) or as doing the right thing at the right time (Bryson, in press), these definitions do not contain any explicit links to ethics,

DOI: 10.4018/978-1-7998-4894-3.ch005

Copyright © 2021, IGI Global. Copying or distributing in print or electronic forms without written permission of IGI Global is prohibited.

or their possible ethical implications would need to be clarified further; for instance, what is meant by the term "right." In case there were some third exhaustive definition of intelligence, it would possibly only entail ethical principles, intentions, or considerations if some form of rationality were introduced.

As Nick Bostrom (2014) has observed, "more or less any level of intelligence could in principle be combined with more or less any final goal" (p. 107). This seems to imply that AI could be developed to its utmost realization without giving any serious thought to what is right and wrong, good and bad. One way of tying artificial intelligence to an ethical goal is to secure its explainability, which will be presented as a first step in the development of ethical rationality. When explainability cannot be effectuated, we are faced with the so-called "black box problem," which has become one of the principal concerns in the AI research community, as it appears to stand in the way of a rational, transparent and unbiased use of technology: The black box is meant to convey the image of a machine working behind opaque "walls" without shedding light on what it is, or has been, doing. It is not merely a hotly debated topic among academics, but it is also being discussed by AI practitioners and designers. In a recent debate between NYU Professor, Gary Marcus, and pioneering practitioner of neural networks, Yoshua Bengio, the question of the black box problem and how it might be solved by putting reasoning into a machine was raised several times.[1]

The second problem discussed is related to what was from the beginning considered to be the main challenge of AI, namely developing artificial general intelligence comparable to human level intelligence (McCarthy, Minsky, Rochester, & Shannon, 2006/1955). In the chapter, the connection between the two problems will be interpreted as one between foundation and further development: artificial general intelligence could hardly be developed without being founded on some form of rationality which can explain what, how, and why it acts as it does. However, even if the first problem could at some point be solved, the second problem will keep the research community occupied for decades, probably without coming up with any clear-cut solution. Given that human level intelligence involves rational ways of seeking what is good and avoiding what is bad, the second problem can be associated with the process of becoming a "full ethical agent," a goal, which may not be accomplishable without making reference to emotions and the significant role they play for human cognition, decision-making, and care.

In so far as this same problem could be addressed from a machine's point of view, it might be tentatively denominated the "Tin Man problem." As is well-known from the tale of *The Wizard of Oz*, the Tin Man was made or remade without a heart; i.e. he apparently lacked emotions, although he expressed his desire to get a heart in order to feel and express love. Whether emotions, as we humans know them, can be recreated artificially, remains an open question. Yoshua Bengio's teacher, Geoffrey Hinton, has claimed to be 99.9 percent sure that it can be done.[2] Viewed from an ethical standpoint, it would, though, not be enough to produce and embed emotions into AI agents in order to make them ethical; a further difficulty consists in finding ways of connecting and attuning emotions to an artificially created rationality.

With regards to the "black box problem" the objectives of this chapter are: 1) To define the problem by distinguishing between intelligence and rationality, and 2) To circumscribe the role of rationality in ethics and let AI approximate ethical rationality. The objectives in relation to the "Tin Man problem" are: 1) To define the problem by including into ethical rationality the concepts of sense and emotionality, and 2) To discuss what it entails to become a full ethical agent, and whether this goal is computationally tractable or not. Furthermore, the chapter explores possible and proposed solutions to both problems in a critical dialogue with recent research in the field of AI.

BACKGROUND

Ethical issues have recently started to play a key role in the fields of machine learning and artificial intelligence. From its beginning in the mid-1950s, both fields, which will be addressed under the common term AI in this chapter, were mainly defined and developed by computational engineers and cognitive scientists, who centered their research on linguistic, symbolic and formal theory. This may be part of the explanation why ethics remained almost absent from the field until the mid-1990s, even though focusing on these topics does, of course, not exclude anyone from also taking ethical aspects into account.

Two of the most comprehensive anthologies from the late 80s and early 90s, *The Philosophy of Artificial Intelligence* and *Encyclopedia of Artificial Intelligence*, barely mentioned ethics, whereas one of the most employed manuals today, *Artificial Intelligence: A Modern Approach* by Russell and Norvig, included a short, well-researched subchapter on ethics in the first edition from 1995. Like this chapter, the last-mentioned manual takes its starting point in rationality when approaching the concept of intelligence. Yet, it offers a more pragmatic definition based on utility than the concept of ethical rationality which will be developed in what follows. In order to identify and assess the ethical implications of being a rational agent, it is not enough to state that "[A] system is rational if it does the 'right thing,' given what it knows" (Russell & Norvig, 2010, p. 1). It should be added that a rational agent qua rational is also expected to offer some minimal reason for acting in a certain way, even if it is, or appears to be, the "right thing" to do.

This understanding of rationality as offering reasons for one's actions can be traced back to Plato, who was the first Greek thinker to knowingly declare the good to be the supreme idea in the world, only accessible through reason (2000, 504a-517c). In his dialogues, the crucial capacity for rational thinking is called *logon didonai*, which means to give an account of something. Most of the distinguished people who appear in the Platonic dialogues think of themselves as knowledgeable, and hold their own beliefs to be reasonable, but when asked about their reasons for holding such beliefs, they are often unable to offer any intelligible arguments. People's incapacity to give reasons for why they act or say something in a certain way is for Plato a sign, not merely of ignorance or unreasonableness, but of them acting out of something which is opposite reason.

Influenced by Plato, Aristotle designated this other force, which goes against reason in the human soul, *alogon*; i.e., the negation of *logon* or that which is without reason and speech (2014, 1102a-b). An expression of this could be someone acting out of pure instinct without thinking. For both Plato and Aristotle, this "irrational" way of acting means distancing oneself from what is ethically good in life, as this needs to be sought through elaborate, reflexive strategies of asking, responding, conversing, testing, thinking, and understanding, all expressions of what Aristotle means by *logos*. In his ethical treatises, Aristotle envisages virtuous forms of life based on reason, which enables humans to balance their emotions according to the exigencies of each situation. In contradistinction to other understandings of moral philosophy, such as Stoic and Kantian, Aristotle does not rule out desire and emotion, but includes both in the complex "equation" of what it means to live well in accordance to reason.

The person, who succeeds in establishing a sort of "symphony" between reason and emotion, thus becoming a well-balanced *exemplar* of ethical rationality[3], is the closest one could get to becoming a "full ethical agent." One might ask if such an agent could ever be recreated artificially or made computationally tractable. James H. Moor, who in 2006 embraced the concept of "full ethical agent" in AI, leaves it open, but admits that no machine is anywhere near to "have the practical wisdom that Aristotle thought we use when applying our virtues" (p. 19). Others have denied that future AI will evolve towards acquiring full agency (Pfeifer & Bongard, 2006; Clark, 2008).

The section on "the Tin Man problem" investigates what it would mean for AIs to become full ethical agents, and it questions what Moor takes for granted: namely, that an average adult human is a full ethical agent in virtue of having consciousness, intentionality, and free will. These three properties are not already given possessions of all people but allow for degrees of development and realization. It may well be that humans need to evolve alongside, or together, with future AIs in order to accomplish the goal of becoming full ethical agents; or, as Shannon Vallor, in her recent reactualization of ancient virtue ethics, characterizes our technosocial future "by how our evolved technological powers become embedded in co-evolving social practices, values, and institutions" (2016, p. 6).

TWO ETHICAL PROBLEMS AND THEIR POSSIBLE SOLUTIONS

The Black Box Problem

In *Life 3.0*, Max Tegmark offers a general definition of intelligence which covers many of the ways in which the word is used by the AI research community today: Intelligence is defined as the capacity to accomplish complex goals (2017, p. 50; see also Müller, in press). If Tegmark and others are right, what is not built into intelligence from the outset is the capacity to clarify and reflect on the reasons and goals of its own intelligent behavior. A machine capable of carrying out highly complex behavior successfully, such as diagnosing a disease or driving a vehicle, does not have to explain or consider what it is doing in order to be called intelligent; and as long as its behavior remains unexplained or unjustified, we humans are left with doubts about how it works, and whether there is a rationale behind its actions.

This presents us with the so-called "black box problem" and goes to show that intelligence is not equal to rationality. The black box metaphor in the context of AI refers to a machine, be it an artificial neural network or an intelligent bot, operating behind its opaque "walls" without shedding light on how it reaches its conclusions or results. It is not only artificial intelligences which can turn into black boxes. Humans, who do not verbalize or signalize why they act in a certain way, may also be compared to black boxes, although only temporarily, as it is questionable whether a human being could successfully seal himself or herself completely off without communicating with the surrounding world in some way today. Still, even if it is only for a short period of time that a person acts "irrationally," as we say when there is seemingly no rationale behind his or her actions, this remains a serious charge against any human agent. Since ancient times, people, who are either unable or unwilling to offer reasons for why they act as they do, have been viewed by some other members of society as thoughtless, unreliable, or even reckless. In this way, the black box problem becomes linked to salient ethical issues, which are also present in today's economic, political and legal systems (Pasquale, 2015).

A relevant example of a black box problem in AI has been reported by clinicians in primary health care: despite being useful for detection, analysis and diagnosis, the implementation of AI results in some estimations not being "clinically interpretable," in incapability of "explaining the underlying models completely" and "not knowing the source of the data" (Liyanage et al., 2019). Insofar as "problems of accuracy and uncertainty apply to all probabilistic methods for prognostication," and no model can cover all cases, being sometimes over- or under-fitting, and in some cases of artificial neural networks misleading, AI is far from being a reliable panacea that can be employed uncritically in all cases (Beil, Proft, van Heerden, Sviri, & van Heerden, 2019).

The fact that AIs, especially the most advanced neural networks, do not offer a full explanation of the model or of all the data which they run on can also imply or lead to problems of possible biases inside the black box. This is, of course, not a problem which only pertains to certain areas or systems, such as healthcare or AI itself, but to any entity relying on models for processing data, and the patterns arising out of the data processing. Bias can be present both in the model and in the data selection, for instance, when a model is made for registering and evaluating cases in one part of the world but employed in another part, or when the collected data only covers a specific part of the population but is taken to cover the whole population. The trouble with bias is that it is built into the system and cannot be resolved by extending the model or by accumulating more data if inherent to the system, but the model, or the data set, and sometimes both, need to be modified or completely changed if one wants to get to the bottom of the problem (Yudkowski, 2015, p. xxiv).

One relatively uncomplicated solution proposed to the black box problem is to carefully design systems for specific contexts and purposes so that a rigorous analysis and testing of these systems can be carried out before and after they have been put to use. In order to follow a systematic procedure of tracing or visualizing information, exact and reliable technical specifications are needed which inform those who validate a given system about what, how, and why it was designed and built in a particular way and not in any other way. Overseeing, reviewing, and assessing the causality and functionality of AIs is meant to promote transparency, safety, understanding, and trust, which reduces their opacity, dispels inscrutability, and clarifies the decisions made, any possible trade-offs, and biases. Anything else is either considered to be poor engineering work or an expression of power dynamics that either prevents assessment from taking place or forces certain decisions to be made that lead to black box problems (Kroll, 2018; Bryson, in press).

Seen from this perspective of preventive engineering practice, no machine or AI system is completely inscrutable, although it may become "black-boxed," as Joshua Kroll (in press) puts it. However, this is not only due to bad design or power dynamics, but it can also be the result of the intricate and emergent dynamics of AI systems, such as neural networks, or perhaps more powerful machines in the future. Their "inner workings" will in many cases need more explanation than just reproducing the mechanics, the codes, or the causes behind their behavior, if we want to keep introducing ever more advanced AIs into our societies, where they will interact with humans in multiple new ways and take over many of our cognitive tasks.

Yet, what kind of explanations will be required, in what contexts and to whom? An AI developer or designer is certainly in a much more privileged position to understand and perhaps also explain the "language" of advanced intelligent machines than people who are not familiar with this kind of technology. In terms of explainability, it has been suggested that ethicists, designers, and users of technology ought to be minimally familiarized with technical terminology and know-how in order to tap into the many ways in which models and codes are designed and data is generated, selected, shared, and classified (Bridle, 2018; Hagendorff, in press).

Acquiring such basic knowledge of design and programming may not be viable for most people; yet, even if it were, we should still inquire into and search for a broader notion of explainability that moves intelligence towards the form of explicit rationality of interpersonal communication common to all human beings. As we saw, Plato and Aristotle were among the first to show how clarifying the rationale behind a given behavior or action lays the foundation for human societies by fostering understanding, trust, and conflict-solving. In general, our human way of doing things may be highly intelligent, but by being explicit and giving details of what, how, and why we did something, we become more transparent to ourselves and others. The same holds for other intelligent agents, who will, likewise, benefit from this ancient principle, reformulated by William Robinson in modern, normative terms: "Intelligence worthy of its name ought to approximate rationality" (2014, pp. 68-69). In many studies, clear, coherent explanations and justifications of decisions and predictions carried out by expert systems and interpretable models of machine learning have proven to "significantly increase users' confidence and trust" (Biran & Cotton 2017, p. 8).

Tim Miller (2018) has observed that in research and reviews of explanation and explainability, the social interaction and everyday language of explainer and explainee is usually not commented on. Most people contrast and select explanations according to their own beliefs without looking for a complex, scientific account which draws on multiple forms of definitions, causes and probabilities. In everyday settings, explanations and justifications are shared for other reasons than exchanging exact information; for example, in order to know the intentions of somebody, to find meaning in something, or to influence other people. Likewise, with respect to understanding and explaining AI, it is not indispensable to be able to follow or scrutinize each twist and turn, which an algorithm, a network, or a bot takes when processing data. If it is clear how AI operates in a specific context according to certain mechanisms, procedures, and goals, which are interpretable and meaningful overall, then a lot of the opacity surrounding AI technology will disappear.

Explainable and trustworthy AI is the explicit ethical goal of such prestigious organizations as The European Commission's High-Level Expert Group, and The Royal Society in London. Yet, both organizations also underscore that explainability in itself is insufficient to circumvent all biases, and may lead to a deceitful trust in unsafe systems that exploit personal and private information (EC HLEG, 2018; The Royal Society, 2019). To this it should be added that many researchers show caution when evaluating how far we will be able to go in shedding light on the emergent properties of even the fastest neural networks, which appear to be imponderable in some important aspects (Fazi, 2019; Müller, in press). The only way forward will be to search for, and demand, further ethical measures in terms of accountability and responsibility to help strengthen the concept of explainability.

As we know from ancient Greek ethics and dialectics, accountability takes us one step further in the direction of rational explanation and understanding, as it calls upon the people involved; in the case of AI, designers, developers, and relevant stakeholders, to give an account of the rationale, the context, and the consequences of a given system or machine so that it becomes clear to the "patients" using it who are the responsible "agents" behind it. In so far as users do not have exact, detailed knowledge of a given AI system, and thus are not in full control of it, they have every right to contest and demand from developers that they answer for their technology by explaining its moral impact, biases, and implications (Coeckelbergh, 2019). If designers and developers should hide behind their black boxes, claiming that not even they are in full control of their partly inscrutable technology, they can still be held responsible for not knowing or pretending not to know (Kroll, in press). Given that the AI will not come up with a reason for its own behavior, which has a value-laden impact on its user and is endowed with a preferred set of outcomes with ethical implications, it is left to the responsible agents behind it to step up and make these hidden and often unforeseeable consequences known (Martin, 2018, p. 839).

However, one could challenge the presupposition that AIs are forever excluded from entering the realm of reason which Aristotle considered the hallmark of human aptitude. What if future AIs could be designed and fabricated such that they would be able to give an account of their actions and justify them? In his seminal paper on full ethical agency, Moor considered "explicit ethical agents" to be the future candidates in AI for representing and explaining ethics intelligibly. Anderson and Anderson

(2007), who Moor also mentions, have argued for combining a utilitarian and a deontological approach to AI. They suggest that future machines may be equipped with a human-like ability to "*justify* ethical judgments that only an explicit representation of ethical principles allows…An explicit ethical agent is able to explain why a particular action is either right or wrong by appealing to an ethical principle." They refer to Immanuel Kant for such an understanding of ethics, but, at the same time, they narrow the scope of ethics to "how agents ought to behave when faced with ethical dilemmas" (pp. 16-17).

The Tin Man Problem

Referring to, and behaving according to, certain principles is only a small, limited part of what constitutes ethics. Although fundamental in deontology, principles are by nature general and will be interpreted in varied ways by different groups, and thus come into conflict with each other in specific contexts (Whittlestone, Nyrup, Alexandrova, & Cave, 2019). Practical reasoning in virtue ethics is concerned with interpreting and contextualizing principles, mediating between them and solving the ensuing conflicts. An ethical outlook sustained by the virtues of practical wisdom, "encompasses considerations of universal rationality *as well as* considerations of an irreducibly contextual, embodied, relational, and emotional nature – considerations that Kant and others have erroneously regarded as irrelevant to morality" (Vallor, 2016, pp. 24-25).

Vallor understands "universal rationality" along the same lines as ancient Greek virtue ethics; i.e., as both theoretical insight into, and a critical reflection about, what is good and evil, not merely in particular situations or according to already established principles, but in human life as a whole. The Platonic dialogues are paradigmatic examples of this kind of theoretical insight and critical ethical reflection, which Aristotle integrates with his political conception of human communities when asserting that *logos* or reasonable speech allows human beings to come together and establish enduring relationships by contesting and making clear to each other what they believe is good and bad, just and unjust (1984, 1153a). While it is true that Aristotle was conditioned by the prejudices of his own time and denigrated women, slaves, and foreigners to be less able than native Athenian men, his concept of practical reasoning and ethical rationality, also called *phronesis* in ancient Greek, may still serve as a guiding thread for investigating what it means to become a full ethical agent.

Even though we have witnessed recent examples of bots or machines today, such as Siri or Sophia, which apparently offer some explanation of their own behavior and that of other people, they remain incapable of engaging in a critical dialogue about the ethically best thing to do, if they are taken outside the narrow context within which they are programmed to operate. Were we to ask any of today's AIs to act according to the Aristotelian parameters of ethical-practical reasoning, i.e., what to do, how to do it, when, where and in relation to whom, they could only do so mechanically without showing the sort of sense of the context which is expected of embodied, sensible, and responsible human agents.

Yet, could future AIs be endowed with sensors and feelings which would allow them to perceive and make sense of their environment in much the same way as we do? Trying to answer this question leads our discussion into a whole new area of complex issues which could be tentatively subsumed under as the "Tin Man problem." The predicament, in which the Tin Man found himself in the *Wizard of Oz*, was that he did not have a heart, and so he lacked the ability to express and feel certain emotions, first and foremost love. The story goes that the Tin Man was not completely devoid of emotions, as he was not made of tin from the beginning, but he had lived a life like any other human being, who works, thinks and falls in love. It could even be that he was still aware and felt part of his old self, when he became the Tin Man, not unlike the police officer, who is shot dead in the film *Robocop* and starts to remember events from his past life after he has been recreated as a cyborg.

What appears to be likely is that future machines will still be made or remade from materials which have not, and do not, evolve into an organically integrated unit in unison with their environment. This is basically what makes up the Tin Man problem: Machines, robots or cyborgs are not born into this world and have not evolved through thousands of years in sync with their surroundings like other living beings, but they are *ex situ* inventions which therefore lack, from the outset, a direct contact and familiar sense of coping with, and caring for, the world. Seen from an Aristotelian point of view, the ethical predicament of present and future machines is that they are devoid of an embodied emotionality which could calibrate their intelligence and possible reasoning power. It may come as a surprise that Aristotle, who defines humans as beings in possession of reason, would draw attention to the ethical significance of desire and emotions. Yet, he is keenly aware of their role for sensible action in complex situations of everyday life.

It is probably because the intelligence of bots and robots is not tied up with bodily functions and context-dependent perception that they surpass humans in restricted scenarios of accomplishing single goals, whereas they fall behind, and often produce nonsense, when they have to realize complex tasks which presuppose lived experience in multifaceted surroundings. Even if a machine became capable of justifying its own behavior, we would still expect of an agent displaying ethical rationality that it could question and weigh principles and goals against each other before deciding. As Tegmark has argued, we humans are used to deliberating about goals and sub-goals, because they are built into us through evolution, which again has endowed us with certain emotions that orient us towards goals in close collaboration with reason (2017, pp. 254-256). Given that the computational resources needed to bring an AI up to speed and make it "replicate the relevant evolutionary processes on Earth that produced human-level intelligence are severely out of reach" (Bostrom, 2014, p. 24), we will currently have to look for another way of endowing AIs with ethical rationality. The teleological framework of multiple goals, within which humans move about balancing reason and emotion, brings us back to Aristotle's view of ethics as the pursuit of the good life through a well-orchestrated *ethos*.

Aristotle derives the concept of ethics from *ethos*, which refers to the characteristic way in which a human being composes and expresses himself or herself through action and thinking (2014, 1103a). When acting and speaking, humans have goals in sight that they try to reach, and ethics is, according to Aristotle, about finding the best way to reach the best goals. In order to achieve that, humans are presented with the difficult task of making intelligible use of both their senses and their minds so that they perceive and know what, how, and why they act and think in the best possible manner with the best goals in sight.

Seen from the vantage point of an artificial superintelligence, humans' dependence on their bodies, senses, and emotions for achieving their goals will probably strike it as a weak point. Isaac Asimov famously envisaged what future AIs might say to humans if they developed a clear consciousness of their own potential:

"I say this in no spirit of contempt, but look at you! The material you are made of is soft and flabby, lacking endurance and strength, depending for energy upon the inefficient oxidation of organic material [...]"

Cutie, the robot who says this, has just burst into "a very inhuman laugh," when he – or should we say it? – starts to pick apart human beings. "You are makeshift," he concludes and adds:

"I, on the other hand, am a finished product. I absorb electrical energy directly and utilize it with an almost one hundred percent efficiency. I am composed of strong metal, am continuously conscious, and can stand extremes of environment easily" (2004/1950, pp. 62-63).

It is no coincidence that the title of this tale in *I, Robot* is "Reason." Cutie believes that it is possible to unravel the meaning of life and control humans by relying on reason, which Aristotle also placed at the top of the hierarchy in the human soul: "Since when is the evidence of our senses any match for the clear light of rigid reason?" (Asimov, 2004/1950, p. 71).

Yet, one important difference is that Aristotle knew that ethical rationality needs the senses to allow humans to act well in the world, and Asimov also seems to cue his reader into suspecting that Cutie's authoritarian attitude may originate with his "rigid reason" that is reluctant to come to "its senses" and listen to other peoples' advice. Aristotle highlights the capacity to listen as one of the key competences of ethical-practical reasoning, *phronesis*, which he also calls a "sense" (2010, 437a; 2014, 1142a) as the one, who is apt at deciding well in critical situations and finding solutions to complex problems, is in touch with his or her surroundings and literally makes sense of them.

In *I, Robot*, Asimov also described another robot with a different view of humans and of itself:

"It's your fiction that interests me. Your studies of the interplay of human motives and emotions [...] I see into minds, you see," the robot continued, "and you have no idea how complicated they are. I can't begin to understand everything because my own mind has so little in common with them – but I try, and your novels help" (2004/1950, p. 116).

If Asimov's tales are not taken to be pure fiction without any relation to reality but seen as offering possible future scenarios, they show another side to the Tin Man problem: Precisely because robots will not know the human interplay of motives and emotions by heart, they will have trouble understanding us, and we will have difficulties understanding them as well. Yet, like the robot in Asimov's tale, we may try to think about if, and how, this interplay, which is so crucial for the configuration of ethics, could be recreated artificially.

In relation to the black box problem, we saw that one of the most sought for strategies today is to make AI explainable. Despite being developed in different directions, it is a rather unified and uncomplicated strategy, broadened by a concept of rationality which calls upon agents to be accountable and responsible for their actions. Yet, human rationality has many more ways of expressing itself, such as deducing and deliberating, questioning and thinking things over, and that makes it difficult to explain even for a highly intelligent robot. In their latest report on "Ethics Guidelines for Trustworthy AI," The European Commision's High-Level Expert Group on Artificial Intelligence offers a broad definition of AI which takes into account more aspects of practical reasoning and thus comes closer to the variegated form of human rationality:

Artificial intelligence (AI) refers to systems designed by humans that, given a complex goal, act in the physical or digital world by perceiving their environment, interpreting the collected structured or un-structured data, reasoning on the knowledge derived from this data and deciding the best action(s) to take (according to pre-defined parameters) to achieve the given goal. AI systems can also be designed to learn to adapt their behaviour by analysing how the environment is affected by their previous actions (EC HLEG, 2018).

Yet, it is not enough for an AI to be explainable and accountable, if we want it to become a full ethical agent capable of reasoning, questioning, and deliberating about its goals and those of others. With respect to how moral issues and problems are handled in AI research, the explainability paradigm has been presented as rather one-sidedly rational, calculative, and "logic-oriented;" properties which need to be complemented by "a wider framework of an 'empathic', 'emotion-oriented' ethics of care" (Hagendorff, in press)." This is the goal which this chapter is heading towards. Seen in the light of ancient Greek virtue ethics, we move from *logos* to the interplay of *logos* and *alogos*. The problem, as we have described it, is that AI will not be familiar with the latter part that embodies desires and emotions. Yet, as they are crucial to ethical rationality, at least seen from a human perspective, there is no way around them, if we want to discuss the possible, future development of AI ethics and the subsequent insertion of moral machines into society.

In relation to the interplay of reason and desire, Drew McDermott has given a thought-provoking example of what a reasoning, rule-following machine lacks from an ethical point of view: Let the machine be given a trade assignment to move slave-workers from one place to another following the utilitarian principle, "maximize the benefit of the majority of people involved," (2007) which may refer to the slave-workers themselves or the people moving them. Either way the machine does not realize the dubiousness of the whole undertaking. Changing the rationale behind its actions to "you shouldn't be involved in slave trade at all" obviously makes it stop what it was doing, but as it failed to question the first principle underlying its actions, it did not really assess whether it was good or bad. McDermott concludes that a machine is not a full ethical agent, "until the decision maker feels the urge *not to follow* the ethical course of action it arrives at," which means that it would need to learn what it is like to stand in an ethical dilemma and be tempted to do the wrong thing in order to act ethically. This would again presuppose some sort of consciousness of counterfactuals and the freedom to choose, which the machine does not have, as long as it does not face "conflicting goals 'designed in' by independent evolutionary trends" (2008, pp. 5-7).

Viewing ethics in AI from the standpoint of virtue theory leads us towards a critical assessment of artificially intelligent agents as full ethical agents. Aristotle's ethical thinking revolves around the question of how humans can become virtuous and contribute to the good life, not only for themselves, but in relationship with other people. Along this line of thinking, if we want to create highly intelligent agents and insert them wisely into our societies, we have, basically, two options: Either we make sure that they themselves become ethical, or we settle for less and keep them under our control. Yet, this may not be as easy as it sounds, and the first difficulty which we face, is that we ourselves or the majority of us may not be full ethical agents in the Aristotelian sense of the word.

For somebody to become a full ethical agent within the framework of Aristotelian ethics, it is not enough to feel the temptation of acting differently than what reason commands, as McDermott suggests. It is not even sufficient that reason takes command over the desires and moves them in the right direction. For Aristotle, such a soul remains divided and is continuously in danger of being driven away from the ethically right goals in life. Instead, the virtuous found their ethical outlook on a well-established harmony between the rational and the emotional parts of the soul which are aligned or, as Aristotle says, in symphony (2014, 1102b). Ideally, the truly virtuous feel and think in accordance with what is good in life without being driven in opposite directions.

If this ideal appears to be too far removed from human reality, it could be because we have still not realized its full ethical potential. Aristotle asks of every ethical agent to align his or her desires and emotions with rationality, so that it remains possible to be accountable and justify one's actions to others in responsible ways and to treat others humanely with the respect, understanding, and care which a given situation demands. In order to fulfill the second goal, we need balanced emotions and relationships, such as love and friendship, which both Plato and Aristotle highlight, although their views on these emotions and human beings in general were arguably conditioned by their own time. Still, in the light of ancient Greek virtue theory, we may ask what would happen if we created intelligent beings without these emotions or without any emotions at all.

Some researchers, for example Anderson and Anderson, have ventured to see this as a clear advantage, because desires and emotions often lead humans astray (Anderson & Anderson, 2007, p. 18). Emotions out of sync with rationality can, of course, mislead the decision-maker and mess up reasoning, but McDermott's Aristotelian point was that intelligent beings without emotions might not find any meaning in ethical action or agency at all, and if they get caught in an ethical dilemma, one probable outcome would be that they get stuck without knowing what to do, and what ethics demands of them. Ronald de Sousa has called such dilemmas, in which even the most intelligent beings can get stuck, "angelic," because even a super-intelligent, almost god-like entity, capable of storing and processing millions of bits of information, may get stuck in its own logic without being able to decide which course would be the best to take (1990, p. 16). Or even worse, a superintelligence without emotions may be incapable of ethical commitment, manifesting a pure instrumental indifference towards humanity.

This leaves us with the other scenario still not in sight: Recreating desires and emotions artificially. Geoffrey Hinton, who is often called "the godfather of AI," Alan Turing being "the father," has argued that it will be possible, based on the neural network theory which he has developed, to generate emotions just like intelligence in the future. Emotions do partly seem to function according to an intelligibly scheme of variables, as Hinton has observed, but in humans certain sensations accompany emotions which are tied to the body, and its biological needs and cycles: Take sensations, such as feeling a shiver down the spine, when being afraid or in a state of shock. Are such sensations computable, and can they be coupled with deeper emotions such as fear and love? Even if we succeed in recreating emotions and their accompanying sensations, we would still need, speaking from an ethical standpoint, to balance them with reasoning capacities, such as inferring, arguing, and deliberating. The problem, which will keep the AI research community occupied for decades, is that the two sides are most often intertwined in us as humans, which makes us hard to understand, as the robot in Asimov's tale tells us, but it is at the same time the well-balanced interplay between reason and emotion which makes it possible to become a full ethical agent.

FUTURE RESEARCH DIRECTIONS

In an effort to circumvent black box problems and biases, the Defense Advanced Research Project Agency (DARPA) has made some advanced studies into explainable AI. One of the technology managers at the project, David Gunning, who was also part of the program that produced Siri, has ascertained that "[N]ew machine-learning systems will have the ability to explain their rationale, characterize their strengths and weaknesses, and convey an understanding of how they will behave in the future" (2017). Future research programs of explainable AI may break new ground, if they succeed in making the most complex AI systems interpretable and intelligible to every ordinary user. Still, a worrisome ethical problem remains, if these systems, which Gunning says will be used as warfighters, are not able to interpret and deliberate about the soundness of the goals which they pursue and the significance of the contexts in which they move around. In the years to come, it seems that we will still need humans "in the loop," who possess a sufficiently developed ethical rationality to avoid disasters and promote well-being.

This brings us to the second future research direction which may be explored further: To what degree will it be possible to design and recreate ethical rationality artificially? In a discussion of Hubert Dreyfus' phenomenological investigation of *phronesis* and embodiment, Anne Gerdes har argued that "it is hard to imagine a realization of the kind of architecture" in AI, which would bring about full-fledged human capabilities, such as ethical deliberation and judgment, founded on tacit experience and situational understanding (2016, 132). Like Gerdes, I suggest that we will have to settle for less and explore different hybrid solutions between pure top-down or bottom-up approaches, which take their point of departure in principles or in sensory perception, respectively. Another recent initiative in the field of artificial emotional intelligence, *Cogito*, is more specialized. It was first launched in 2007 but has since then made so much progress that it is being implemented to recognize and pick up on the emotional tone of human voices. Yet, AI devices carrying out voice recognition belong to certain contexts and still need to be interpreted by humans to prove their utility. If it is employed mostly to win or nudge clients, as has been the case until now, then it may become just another way of creating biases and manipulating people.

A third future research area within AI, which resonates with the traditions of virtue ethics, can be found in the creation of accompanying moral machines that function as artificial moral orthosis, a term employed by Dorobantu and Wilks: Similar to a medical orthosis, an AI could serve as an "explanatory software agent" which may aid, accompany, and give advice to humans, who do not always know their way around and often fail to do the right thing. A highly intelligent companion could fulfill the potential of ethical rationality by complementing humans' weak points (Dorobantu & Wilks, 2019, 1016-17).

This is actually not far removed from Aristotle, who reminds us of the ethical significance of companionship and friendship towards the end of the *Nicomachean Ethics*, where good friends aid each other in becoming full ethical agents: Friendship "benefits those in their prime by helping them to do noble actions – "two going together" – since with friends they are more capable of thinking and acting" (2014, 1155a). Yet, he did not envisage that humans would one day consider the possibility of creating artificial agents in order to keep them company and augment their cognitive capacities.

CONCLUSION

The black box problem, as described in this chapter, arises when an AI system, be it a neural network or a software bot, processes vast amounts of data in very short time without revealing the rationale which it has followed in order to reach a given output. The more accurate the system is, the less is usually known about the ground rules or the potential pattern which it has followed. Possible solutions consist of slowing down the system in order to make it more transparent through explainability and accountability. The Tin Man problem concerns the predicament that robots, being *ex situ* inventions which lack a direct contact and familiar sense of coping with, and caring for, their surroundings, will not know the human interplay of motives and emotions by heart, and they will therefore have trouble acting with a feeling for other humans and making sense of their environment.

Even though we find robust and reasonable solutions to black box problems, we would still expect, in so far as we keep pursuing the objective of transforming future AIs into full moral machines or ethical agents, that they could deliberate and think critically about the principles and goals guiding their actions.

This presupposes again that artificial intelligence approximates some form of ethical rationality which has well-balanced emotions built into it that can give salience to certain goals and choices over others. If we settle for less, we would have to be in charge of their interactions with the environment to secure that future AIs are aligned with human ethics. However, according to Aristotle, it is only a minority of humans, who have reached full ethical agency by harmonizing reason and emotions so that they know how to act well with the most exquisite sense of the situation so that the what, where, when and in relation to whom, receives an immediate sensible answer.

Does this mean that we should not demand more of AIs than what we demand of ourselves? While we do demand of every agent that he or she is responsible and caring, why not demand the same of an artificial moral agent? We should rather be careful that our ethical development as a species follow alongside, and do not fall behind, our development of AI. Due to a mismatch of our rational and emotional nature, many of our human ways of acting and thinking are flawed with incoherent, contradictory, and biased elements that still stand in the way of realizing fully ethical rationality. Should the future development of AI become truly ethical, it will also help us become more ethical.

REFERENCES

Anderson, M., & Anderson, S. L. (2007). Machine Ethics: Creating an Ethical Intelligent Agent. *AI Magazine, 28*(4), 15–26.

Aristotle. (1984). *The politics*. The University of Chicago Press. doi:10.7208/chicago/9780226026701.001.0001

Aristotle. (2010). *De sensu and de memoria*. Kessinger Publishing.

Aristotle. (2014). *Nicomachean ethics*. Cambridge University Press.

Asimov, I. (2004). *I, robot*. Bantam. (Original work published 1950)

Beil, M., Proft, I., van Heerden, D., Sviri, S., & van Heerden, P. V. (2019). Ethical consideration of artificial intelligence for prognostication in intensive care. *Intensive Care Medicine Experimental, 7*(1), 70. doi:10.118640635-019-0286-6 PMID:31823128

Biran, O., & Cotton, C. (2017). Explanation and Justification in Machine Learning: A Survey. *IJCAI 2017, Workshop on Explainable Artificial Intelligence (XAI)*, 8-13.

Boden, M. A. (Ed.). (1990). *The philosophy of artificial intelligence*. Oxford University Press.

Bostrom, N. (2014). *Superintelligence: Paths, dangers, strategies*. Oxford University Press.

Bridle, J. (2018). *New dark age: Technology and the end of the future*. Verso.

Bryson, J. B. (in press). The Artificial Intelligence of Ethics of AI: An Introductory Overview. In M. D. Dubber, F. Pasquale, & S. Das (Eds.), *The Oxford Handbook of Ethics of AI*. Oxford University Press.

Clark, A. (2008). *Supersizing the mind: Embodiment, action, and cognitive extension*. Oxford University Press. doi:10.1093/acprof:oso/9780195333213.001.0001

Coeckelbergh, M. (2019). Artificial Intelligence, Responsibility Attribution and a Relational Justification of Explainability. *Science and Engineering Ethics*. https://coeckelbergh.files.wordpress.com/2019/10/2019_10_28-ai-responsibility-relational-explainability-coeckelbergh.pdf

De Sousa, R. (1990). *The rationality of emotion*. MIT Press.

Dorobantu, M., & Wilks, Y. (2019). Moral Orthoses: A New Approach to Human and Machine Ethics. *Zygon*, *54*(4), 1004–1021. doi:10.1111/zygo.12560

EC HLEG. (2018). *Ethics Guidelines for Trustworthy AI*. The European Commision's High-Level Expert Group on Artificial Intelligence. https://ec.europa.eu/futurium/en/ai-alliance-consultation/guidelines

Fazi, M. B. (2019). Can a machine think (anything new)? Automation beyond simulation. *AI & Society*, *34*(4), 813–824. doi:10.100700146-018-0821-0

Gerdes, A. (2016). The Role of Phronesis in Robot Ethics. In J. Seibt, M. Nørskov, & S. S. Andersen (Eds.), *What Social Robots Can and Should Do* (pp. 129–135). IOS Press.

Gunning, D. (2017). Explainable Artificial Intelligence (XAI). *Data Science Central*. https://www.datasciencecentral.com/profiles/blogs/explainable-artificial-intelligence-xai

Hagendorff, T. (2020). The Ethics of AI Ethics: An Evaluation of Guidelines. *Minds and Machines*, *30*(1), 99–120. doi:10.100711023-020-09517-8

Kroll, J. (2018). The fallacy of inscrutability. *Philosophical Transactions, Royal Society A*, *376*. https://royalsocietypublishing.org/doi/full/10.1098/rsta.2018.0084 PMID:30322999

Kroll, J. (in press). Accountability in Computer Systems. In M. D. Dubber, F. Pasquale, & S. Das (Eds.), *The Oxford handbook of ethics of AI*. Oxford University Press.

Liyanage, H., Liaw, S. T., Jonnagaddala, J., Schreiber, R., Kuziemsky, C., Terry, A. L., & de Lusignan, S. (2019)... *Artificial Intelligence in Primary Health Care: Perceptions, Issues, and Challenges*, *i*, 41–46. doi:10.1055-0039-1677901 PMID:31022751

Martin, K. (2019). Ethical Implications and Accountability of Algorithms. *Journal of Business Ethics*, *160*(4), 835–850. doi:10.100710551-018-3921-3

McCarthy, J., Minsky, M. L., Rochester, N., & Shannon, C. E. (1955). A Proposal for the Dartmouth Summer Research Project on Artificial Intelligence. *AI Magazine*, *27*(4), 12–14.

McDermott, D. (2008). Why Ethics is a High Hurdle for AI. *North American Conference on Computers and Philosophy*, 1-8. https://www.cs.yale.edu/homes/dvm/papers/ethical-machine.pdf

Miller, T. (2018). *Explanation in Artificial Intelligence: Insights from the Social Sciences*. https://arxiv.org/pdf/1706.07269.pdf

Moor, J. H. (2006). The Nature, Importance, and Difficulty of Machine Ethics. *IEEE Intelligent Systems*, *21*(4), 18–21. doi:10.1109/MIS.2006.80

Müller, V. (2020). Ethics of artificial intelligence and robotics. In E. N. Zalta (Ed.), *Stanford encyclopedia of philosophy*. Stanford University.

Pasquale, F. (2015). *The black box society: The secret algorithms that control money and information.* Harvard University Press. doi:10.4159/harvard.9780674736061

Pfeifer, R., & Bongard, J. (2006). *How the body shapes the way we think: A new view of intelligence.* MIT Press. doi:10.7551/mitpress/3585.001.0001

Plato. (2000). *The republic.* Cambridge University Press.

Robinson, W. S. (2014). Philosophical challenges. In K. Frankish & W. M. Ramsey (Eds.), *The Cambridge handbook of artificial intelligence* (pp. 64–86). Cambridge University Press. doi:10.1017/CBO9781139046855.005

Russell, S., & Norvig, P. (2010). *Artificial intelligence: A modern approach* (3rd ed.). Prentice Hall, Pearson.

Shapiro, S. C. (Ed.). (1992). *Encyclopedia of artificial intelligence.* John Wiley & Sons. (Original work published 1987)

Tegmark, M. (2017). *Life 3.0: Being human in the age of artificial intelligence.* Allen Lane, Penguin Random House.

The Royal Society. (2019). *Explainable AI: The Basics.* https://royalsociety.org/topics-policy/projects/explainable-ai/

Vallor, S. (2016). *Technology and the virtues. A philosophical guide to a future worth wanting.* Oxford University Press. doi:10.1093/acprof:oso/9780190498511.001.0001

Whittlestone, J., Nyrup, R., Alexandrova, A., & Cave, S. (2019). The Role and Limits of Principles in AI Ethics: Towards a Focus on Tensions. *AIES* 19. http://lcfi.ac.uk/media/uploads/files/AIES-19_paper_188_Whittlestone_Nyrup_Alexandrova_Cave.pdf

Yudkowski, E. (2015). *Rationality: From AI to zombies.* MIRI.

ADDITIONAL READING

Coeckelbergh, M. (2020). *AI ethics.* MIT Press. doi:10.7551/mitpress/12549.001.0001

Dreyfus, H. L. (2007). Why Heideggerian AI failed and how fixing it would require making it more Heideggerian. *Artificial Intelligence, 171*(18), 1137–1160. doi:10.1016/j.artint.2007.10.012

Gunkel, D. J. (2012). *The machine question: Critical perspectives on AI, robots, and ethics.* MIT Press. doi:10.7551/mitpress/8975.001.0001

Nyholm, S. (2020). *Humans and robots: Ethics, agency, and anthropomophism.* Rowman & Littlefield.

Searle, J. (2014). What your computer can't know. *The New York Review of Books.* https://www.nybooks.com/articles/2014/10/09/what-your-computer-cant-know/

Sokolon, M. K. (2006). *Political emotions. Aristotle and the symphony of reason and emotion.* Northern Illinois University Press.

Wallach, W., & Allen, C. (2009). *Moral machines. Teaching robots right from wrong.* Oxford University Press. doi:10.1093/acprof:oso/9780195374049.001.0001

Wallach, W., & Asaro, P. (2017). *Machine ethics and robot ethics.* Routledge.

KEY TERMS AND DEFINITIONS

Accountability: The status of being accountable and responsible for something, such as actions or products. Ethically speaking, it entails minding and explicitly clarifying the relevant context, causes, and implications for what one is accountable.

Artificial Intelligence (AI): The term can both refer to the creation of intelligences, which operate as software applications (bots) or machines (robots), and to these intelligences themselves. In both senses of the word, "artificial" should be understood as a creative aspect of intelligence (as in "art"), not as something fake or phony.

Bias: Attitude comparable to a form of prejudice which may be built into certain ways of thinking or may pertain to the way in which data is treated.

Ethics: A philosophical discipline which studies how, and what it means, to live well. Elaborating critically on the work of Plato, who declared the good to be the supreme idea in the world, Aristotle was the first to write a treatise on ethics, in which he argued that the acquisition of virtues is paramount for humans to act and think well. Today, ethics is present in practically all fields of knowledge, including the life sciences (cf. bioethics).

Explainability: Research paradigm which prioritizes making AI intelligible and interpretable in order to promote safety, transparency, and trust.

Machine Learning: The process by which machines "learn" from vast amounts of data which they are fed. This technology is mostly associated with algorithms and artificial neural networks that are optimized so that they can combine data, detect patterns, and produce novel output at a speed highly superior to human-level intelligence.

Rationality: In ancient Greek philosophy known by the concept *logos*, which covers reason, speech, and argument. It expresses itself first and foremost in the human capacity of giving an account of the causes and the goals inherent in action. The concept is highly contested in modern philosophy and also associated with deduction and deliberation, and critical assessment and thinking.

ENDNOTES

[1] A link to the debate between Bengio and Marcus can be found here: https://www.zdnet.com/article/devils-in-the-details-in-bengio-marcus-ai-debate/

[2] See interview with Hinton, retrieved Februar 25 from https://medium.com/syncedreview/google-i-o-2019-geoffrey-hinton-says-machines-can-do-anything-humans-can-460dff834ae2

[3] For an elaborate study of Aristotle's reflections of the relation between reason and emotion, see M. K. Sokolon, *Political emotions: Aristotle and the symphony of reason and emotion.*

Chapter 6
Steps Toward Real-World Ethics for Self-Driving Cars:
Beyond the Trolley Problem

Tobias Holstein
iD https://orcid.org/0000-0001-6020-1785
Mälardalen University, Sweden & Darmstadt University of Applied Sciences, Germany

Gordana Dodig-Crnkovic
iD https://orcid.org/0000-0001-9881-400X
Chalmers University of Technology, Sweden & University of Gothenburg, Sweden

Patrizio Pelliccione
iD https://orcid.org/0000-0002-5438-2281
University of L'Aquila, Italy & Chalmers University of Technology, Sweden & University of Gothenburg, Sweden

ABSTRACT

Research on self-driving cars is transdisciplinary and its different aspects have attracted interest in general public debates as well as among specialists. To this day, ethical discourses are dominated by the Trolley Problem, a hypothetical ethical dilemma that is by construction unsolvable. It obfuscates much bigger real-world ethical challenges in the design, development, and operation of self-driving cars. The authors propose a systematic approach that connects processes, components, systems, and stakeholders to analyze the real-world ethical challenges for the ecology of socio-technological system of self-driving cars. They take a closer look at the regulative instruments, standards, design, and implementations of components, systems, and services, and they present practical social and ethical challenges that must be met and that imply novel expectations for engineering in car industry.

DOI: 10.4018/978-1-7998-4894-3.ch006

Copyright © 2021, IGI Global. Copying or distributing in print or electronic forms without written permission of IGI Global is prohibited.

INTRODUCTION

Future autonomous (self-driving, driverless, smart) cars are attracting significant societal attention and causing the revolution of transport systems, which is expected to affect society in profound ways (Bissell et al., 2020; Fraedrich et al., 2017; Ryan, 2019). There is a public debate around the world about the possibility and desirability of self-driving cars. The interest of the public up to now was mostly focused on machine decision-making. The discussion has been connected to the trolley problem, an idealized and unsolvable (human) decision-making conundrum.

In this chapter, we present ethical and social aspects of the emerging technology of self-driving cars, addressed through an applied engineering ethical approach. Instead of the discussion of a specific hypothetical moral dilemma, we present ethical analysis focused on the study of ethics of complex real-world engineering problems from the systemic perspective of the socio-technological system.

Modern automated cars are steadily increasing their level of automation, from no automation to driver assistance, partial automation, conditional automation, high automation, and they continue towards full automation or autonomy, as defined by the Society of Automotive Engineers (SAE, 2016) and the United States National Highway Traffic Safety Administration (National Center for Statistics and Analysis, 2018). Concrete examples of self-driving cars are the Waymo car (Waymo, n.d.) and Cruise (Cruise, 2020).

The intense industry development of increasingly automated cars is accompanied by the interest of many domains, such as engineering and computer science (Aydemir & Dalpiaz, 2018; Dennis et al., 2016; Pelliccione et al., 2017), design and human-computer interaction (Eden et al., 2017), cognitive science (Zhu & Tang, 2015), sociology (Bissell et al., 2020), behavioral science (Awad et al., 2020), and ethics and law (Coca-Vila, 2017). Moreover, they increasingly attract the interest of decision-, policy-, and law-makers (Jobin et al., 2019).

From the engineering and scientific perspectives, technical problems of this development are challenging, but they are successively being solved by an engineering approach. Automation might positively affect the system performance, safety, and utility of cars (Favarò et al., 2017). Two recent studies that compare crash experiences of automated vs. conventional vehicles show that automated vehicles perform better (Blanco et al., 2016; Schoettle & Sivak, 2015). We might expect that higher levels of autonomy will further increase safety. The process goes via step-wise improved driving capabilities through machine-learning. New capabilities are added to highly automated cars after they have been thoroughly tested under human supervision.

The chapter is structured as follows. After the introduction, the state of the art of the ethical analysis for autonomous cars is presented, with the account of the problems introduced by the focus of the debate on the hypothetical unsolvable trolley problem. It is followed by the argument for the necessity of re-orienting the focus to the real-world ethics of practical importance. The methodology of the current work is outlined in the subsequent section. Identifying ethical challenges in the techno-sociological ecology of self-driving cars is divided into two sections: addressing technical aspects, and social aspects, respectively. Conclusions and future work close the chapter.

STATE OF THE ART OF THE ETHICAL ANALYSIS FOR AUTONOMOUS CARS

The autonomous cars ethics analysis has been introduced through the trolley problem, which has been dominating the debate since then, and has been discussed in a huge number of publications.[1]

Some of the authors directly apply trolley problem scenarios, as (Islam & Rashid, 2018) who present a crash-optimization algorithm that takes the number, age, and gender of people as input to assess the outcomes in case of an inescapable accident. Noothigattu et al. (2018) use the collected data from the Moral Machine Experiment (MIT Moral Machine Lab, 2016) to implement a decision-making algorithm, while Kim et al. are introducing a computational model by learning and generalizing from moral judgments of humans (2018). Numerous publications suggest implementing moral principles into algorithms of self-driving cars to address ethical issues (Dennis et al., 2016, 2014; Goodall, 2016).

Alternative approaches, oriented towards real-world engineering problems include (Aydemir & Dalpiaz, 2018) who suggest "an analytical framework that assists stakeholders in analyzing ethical issues" and they apply it towards ethics-aware software engineering. Karnouskos (2018) investigates the impact of "five ethical frameworks (Utilitarianism, Deontology, Relativism, Absolutism, and Pluralism)" on self-driving car acceptance, with the conclusion that there are currently "many intertwined aspects that need to be carefully addressed in an interdisciplinary manner."

For self-driving cars, we are experiencing the typical "policy-vacuum" problem (Moor, 1985) of computer ethics, which arises in situations for which we lack policies; e.g., we have no experience, no ethics, and no laws. The fact that in the context of self-driving cars, everyone is focusing on the trolley problem as if it would represent something central for self-driving cars has an effect of directing ethical deliberation in the wrong direction. This leads to focusing the public imagination on AI as a decision-maker about life or death of people. However, this idea is fundamentally misguided, and it is setting the wrong emphasis on hypothetical, unsolvable ethical dilemma instead of relevant challenges for real-world self-driving cars.

Hypothetical vs. Engineering Ethics Problems

Even though in the debate, the trolley problem has been given a very prominent role, there are critical approaches arguing that it is "an ill-suited benchmark for an automated algorithm" (Mirnig & Meschtscherjakov, 2019)(Foot, 1967; Mirnig & Meschtscherjakov, 2019; Thomson, 1976). Johansson and Nilsson (2016) add that "the self-driving car shall not be unprepared in a way that the trolley problem suggests." Based on the early data about the road situation, and assessments of internal state, it should "adjust its own tactical behavior accordingly."

In the following, we present further arguments for the inadequacy of the trolley problem for the analysis of ethical and social aspects of self-driving cars. Beard (2019) points out the fact that autonomous cars are not deterministic in the way trolleys are, so that neither the trajectory is known with certainty, nor how the pedestrians will react. Additionally, the trolley problem assumes that self-driving cars would have a system that will make a precise and reliable distinction, not only between humans and other kinds of obstacles on the road (which is already a problem) but even distinctions among people. However, there are already principles and laws that forbid to differentiate among humans based on attributes such as age, nation, wealth, social status, gender, etc., regarding the *right to life*. Therefore, choosing which human one will kill is not an option (Holstein & Dodig-Crnkovic, 2018).

The assumption about the deterministic nature of all the involved processes made in trolley problem scenarios is fundamentally wrong. It means that all the objects have perfectly known positions from which only one entirely calculable consequence will follow. In the real world with humans, we have a complex system, and it is not possible to predict exactly in real-time. We are dealing with statistical phenomena under uncertainty, and the only way we can handle it, is by constant machine learning.

As a most prominent example, the Moral Machine online experiment (Awad et al., 2018; MIT Moral Machine Lab, 2016) asking people what they would do in different versions of the trolley problem, is about humans, and it is not a suitable basis for the design of self-driving cars. Cars should not mimic people, as human drivers are the major cause of accidents: 94% of serious crashes are due to human errors (National Center for Statistics and Analysis, 2018). The sequel of the Moral Machine paper (Awad et al., 2020) presents a new attempt to explain and justify the idea of the Moral Machine experiment as a way to explore the cultural differences between preferences for whom to kill - young or old, women or men, and so on. The authors mention that the German code of ethics does not allow making this kind of discrimination of humans (Luetge, 2017). Discrimination is not only rejected by experts but also forbidden by European and U.N. laws on fundamental human rights. Moral Machine is an experiment about cultural differences in providing answers of people to the question of what they believe they would do in certain traffic situations, but it is not instructive for the design of self-driving cars.

As prototypes of self-driving cars are increasingly participating in public traffic, it is essential to investigate how self-driving cars are envisaged, designed, developed, and built, how real ethical challenges are addressed, and how decisions in all those stages are justified. Discussing this matter before self-driving cars are regularly introduced into the traffic, allows anticipating and avoiding major ethical problems.

From the emerging normative work (Federal Ministry of Transport and Digital Infrastructure, 2017; European Commission's High-Level Expert Group on Artificial Intelligence (AI HLEG), 2019; Floridi et al., 2018; Spiekermann, 2015) with a value-based approach, we extract a list of ethic-sensitive technical issues such as safety, security, privacy, trust, responsibility/accountability, quality assurance/auditing, sustainability (many issues connected to AI and machine-learning, such as transparency, explainability, fairness, etc.), together with social challenges of disruptive technology with' stakeholders' interests, legislation, norms and standards, as a continuation of our research in the field (Holstein et al., 2018; Holstein & Dodig-Crnkovic, 2018).

We present a systematic conceptual ethical model that connects the different stakeholders as responsible for ethical aspects in the development of fully autonomous self-driving cars. This is an iterative process that involves providers of laws and regulations, society (such as public acceptance), research (e.g., AI-, ML-, and engineering-ethics) as well as the actual development (e.g., automotive/sensors/transport industry). It is necessary to establish knowledge exchange between stakeholders to build the common ground for the solutions for future self-driving cars.

Focusing on the real-world ethical challenges that should currently be addressed is the first step before ethical aspects of self-driving cars can be meaningfully discussed from the point of view of societal, individual, and professional/organizational stakeholders. It is important to base our conclusions, not on abstract thought experiments unrelated to autonomous cars, but concrete circumstances of their development and introduction. We should focus on factors we as stakeholders can influence in our different roles, via the design, development, engineering, and organizational solutions.

METHODOLOGY

As we study the ethics of emergent technology to identify challenges for the development of autonomous cars, we use a hybrid interdisciplinary methodology. It builds on insights from ethics theory with the significance of "policy vacuums" (Moor, 1985) that are being filled by adding the most important aspects of the emerging technology. We combine ethical theory literature with the technical characteristics of present-day automated cars and their anticipated developments. We aim to address the gaps in the understanding of the ethics of automated cars as they develop towards autonomy. From the literature on value-based design and current guidelines (European Commission's High-Level Expert Group on Artificial Intelligence (AI HLEG), 2019; European Group on Ethics in Science and New Technologies and others, 2018; Floridi et al., 2018; Friedman et al., 2013; Friedman & Kahn Jr., 2003; The IEEE Global Initiative on Ethics of Autonomous and Intelligent Systems, 2019), we extract the list of topics of relevance for real-world automated/self-driving cars that we present in a table form, for both technical and social ethical challenges.

We did not conduct a full systemic literature review, but we made extensive searches on the most used scientific repositories, like IEEE Explore and ACM Digital Library, as well as more precise searches in leading ethics journals such as *Philosophy & Technology*, *Ethics and Information Technology*, and conferences in the field. Thus, concluding, our hybrid methodology is based on methods from ethics, the typical approach of humanities with logical argument starting from existing theories, applied to the case of self-driving cars, taking into account basic knowledge of the technology of automated cars today.

We discussed our findings with different stakeholders in several steps. First, we presented our findings in Sweden, at seminars at Chalmers University of Technology (interaction design aspects), and at Science festival in Gothenburg for the public, where we collected reactions from those two groups of essential stakeholders. Two more seminars were held in Norway, one at NTNU with focus on software engineering for the software engineering audience, and the more general ethical aspect views presented at The Big Challenges Science Festival workshop Code of Ethics in Trondheim.

Finally, we discussed our findings with experts: two senior software engineering researchers, and two leading philosophers from different universities in Europe, as well as with a practitioner working in a company involved in the production of self-driving vehicles. We integrated all the experiences from the discussions with different stakeholders and relevant expert advice into the present version of this chapter.

IDENTIFYING ETHICAL CHALLENGES IN THE TECHNO-SOCIOLOGICAL ECOLOGY OF SELF-DRIVING CARS

The concrete ethical challenges of the decision-making must consider the current state of the art of technology and its development, also in comparison with traditional human-driven cars. Human drivers are far from perfect, and there is a clear expectation that self-driving cars will eventually be much better at driving than humans. But decision-making is not the only aspect of autonomous cars that has ethical consequences. We see ethical challenges in the whole ecology of the techno-social system. From the choices on the part of stakeholders of what we want self-driving cars to do for us (such as – will they be shared? – how will they fit into "smart" or "intelligent" cities?) to their design decisions, such as whether a certain technology is used because of its low price, even though the decision-making would be substantially improved with more expensive technology.

Even today, sensors are an important issue, but in an envisaged completely autonomous car, they will be essential for the behavior of the vehicle. This also poses the question about hardware updates, and how long self-driving cars that do not fulfill the state-of-the-art safety technology are allowed to be used, and how will this safety threshold be defined and measured? Since building and engineering of self-driving vehicles involves various stakeholders, such as designers, software/hardware engineers, salespeople, management, the public, etc., we will also explore the questions of stakeholder involvement.

One of the important questions is how will responsibility in the socio-technological system be distributed and assigned (Dignum, 2019) so to assure maximum benefit for the maximal number of stakeholders, at the same time respecting principles of fairness and justice?

ETHICAL ASPECTS OF THE TECHNICAL CHALLENGES

In the following, we will discuss ethical deliberations regarding specific requirements for autonomous vehicles, their technological aspects, including costs versus quality. The multi-faceted and complex nature of reality emphasizes the importance to look broader and from the transdisciplinary, systemic point of view, for each of the requirements on expected properties of autonomous vehicles.

A decision-making process implemented in a self-driving car is abstractly summarized as follows. It starts with the detection of the environment and identifying obstacles (nearby objects, including humans and animals), as well as the current context/situation of the car, using external systems such as GPS, map data, street signs, connections to other vehicles (V2V) or available infrastructure (V2X), or locally measurable information (speed, direction, etc.). Engineering ethics focuses on the assurance of hardware and software involved in the function of the car, as well as maintenance of ethical standards of the socio-technological system.

Safety

Safety is the most fundamental requirement of autonomous cars. The central question is: How should a self-driving car be made safe and its safety reliably tested? What guidelines should be fulfilled to ensure that it is safe?

Leveson (2020) provides excellent advice regarding safety of hardware-software systems, by presenting a list of major misconceptions regarding safety, such as common beliefs that: the software itself can be unsafe; reliable systems are safe; the safety of components in a complex system is a useful concept, and we can analyze the safety of software in isolation from the system design; software can be shown to be safe by testing, simulation, or standard formal verification. According to Leveson, creating the safety-related requirements is the most effective approach to dealing with the safety of computer-controlled systems. It is necessary to take a system-approach, and include both controls implemented in software and hardware and the ones delegated to human controllers, organizations, and social controls.

Currently, there are several standards, such as the ISO 26262 (ISO, 2018), that specify the functional safety standard for road vehicles. For self-driving cars, standards such as the ISO/PAS 21448 (ISO, 2019), which is also known as Safety of the Intended Functionality (SOTIF), are under development.

As an argument for the safety of their cars, Waymo stated that since its start a decade ago, they have "more than 10 million miles on the road, 7 billion miles in simulation" testing their cars under diverse circumstances (Hersman, 2019). But is this enough to certify their software? Kalra and Paddock calculated the "way to safety" concluding that "hundreds of millions of miles and sometimes hundreds of billions of miles" are necessary (2016).

The source code of autonomous cars and its components is typically proprietary, and not publicly available. The legislators have chosen, instead of controlling the software, to focus on the behavior of a vehicle that is being tested, based on the "proven in use" argument. It directly connects to the necessity pointed out by Leveson (2020) of testing the whole software-hardware system.

As testing of present-day cars should demonstrate, for the compliance of their behavior with legislative norms, it is important to have detailed data about their behavior on the road. The DMV sets an example, and provides collision and annual reports online, covering multiple manufacturers (State of California Department of Motor Vehicles, 2020). Faverò et al. in 2017 presented an in-depth analysis of accident reports (DMV data from 2014 to 2017). Disengagements, accidents, and reaction times based on data released in 2016 from the California trials are discussed in Dixit et al. (2016). As autonomous cars are learning from experience, constant improvements connected to continuous software and hardware development issues present a new challenge.

Related to safety, when it comes to hardware and hardware-software systems, there have been discussions about the prices of different equipment, such as laser radars, compared to cameras or ultrasonic sensors. Laser radars are very expensive but deliver high-quality data in diverse weather conditions. Ultrasonic sensors or cameras are less accurate and sensitive under weather conditions like rain. A study by Combs et al. in 2019 compared different sensors and analyzed the number of pedestrians killed in the accidents which would not happen if autonomous cars were involved. The capacity for adequate detection of pedestrians is in the range from <30% to >90% of analyzed cases. They point out that the price of the best sensor technologies "may be unrealistically expensive." However, it is often the case that the costs of advanced technologies get to affordable levels quite quickly with extensive use.

One of the interesting questions for the safety of autonomous cars is the possibility for people to intervene if something goes wrong. In advanced driving assistance systems, the driver would take over if the system could not handle a critical situation. What would happen in a self-driving car? Will passengers be allowed to intervene? Under which conditions? Would the police have a possibility to intervene, and stop the car, when it behaves inadequately or dangerously? Learning from experience is the most important basis for the improvement of safety in self-driving cars. Tesla CEO Elon Musk envisages a vehicle self-driving capability that is 10 times safer than manual, developed by massive fleet learning (2016).

Both for security and safety, it makes the difference if the vehicle is connected to the infrastructure and other vehicles or completely disconnected. Connected vehicles might receive information from other systems that will enhance the understanding of reality, thus opening new and promising safety scenarios.

Security

For autonomous cars, security is of paramount importance, and software security is a fundamental requirement. As an indication of the development, we mention that in August 2017, UK's Department for Transport published their perspective on key principles of cyber security for connected and automated vehicles (Department for Transport (DfT) & Centre for the Protection of National Infrastructure (CPNI), 2017). Similar documents have been developed, such as Microsoft Security Development Lifecycle (SDL), SAFE Code best practices, OWASP Comprehensive, lightweight application security process (CLASP), and HMG Security policy framework, mentioned by the Department for Transport (DfT) & Centre for the Protection of National Infrastructure (CPNI) in 2017.

Breaking the security of existing advanced automated cars has been shown in several demonstrations exploiting the systems and sensors (e.g., LIDAR and GPS) of an automated car, consequently changing its behavior. Attacks might be inevitable in real life, which actualizes the question: Would there be a minimum-security threshold for a self-driving car to be used? Thereupon another question: How secure must the system and its connections be? In the case of aviation accidents, "black boxes" are used after a crash to determine what happened. Should this also be a part of a self-driving car? Software updates can bring security issues. Should a self-driving car be allowed to drive, if it does not have the latest software version running? It is also important to regulate how bugs are handled in the new software.

Security concerning connected driving brings new challenges as well as new possibilities. On one side, the most secure system is the one that is disconnected from the network. On the other side, it would be compromising safety not to deploy new software or a new version of the software in the car if there is evidence that the new update will fix problems, or add improvements. To enable massive fleet learning and to enable software updates, connectivity is needed.

Privacy and Personal Integrity

The more information is taken into consideration for the decision-making, the more it might interfere with the data and privacy protection. For example, a sensor that detects obstacles, such as human beings in front of the car is based on visual information. Even the use of a single sensor could invade privacy if the data is recorded/reported and/or distributed without the consent of the involved people. The general question that regulation should answer is: Which and how much data is the car supposed to collect for the decision-making? Who will have access to such data? When will these data be destroyed? In Europe, this is regulated by the General Data Protection Regulation (GDPR) (EU, 2016).

Following and applying legal frameworks to protect personal data, such as regulation (EU) 2016/679 of the European Parliament (EU, 2016) concerns questions of privacy and personal integrity. It includes the idea of using devices, such as mobile phones, that could send active signals to the surrounding environment which the car is connected to, in order to improve obstacle detection and awareness. People who do not carry such devices would not be possible to detect that way, which can be subject to discrimination, and it therefore requires careful consideration.

In this regard, more privacy concerns arise: Is the collected data anonymized, and will it contain more data than "just" the position of a human? Can and should a system have access to other systems that provide other data points such as phone numbers, bank accounts, credit cards, personal details, or health data? Those and similar questions are met by legislations such as Regulation (EU) 2016/679 of the European Parliament and of the Council (the General Data Protection Regulation) setting a legal framework to protect personal data (EU, 2016), which is discussed in (Wachter et al., 2017).

Transparency

Transparency is of central importance for many of the previously introduced challenges as well as for the social sustainability of the techno-social ecology. Without transparency, none of them could be analyzed because important information would be missing. According to (McBride, 2016), transparency is a precondition for the possibility of the ethical development of this technology. It is a multi-disciplinary challenge to ensure transparency while respecting, e.g., copyright, corporate secrets, security concerns and many other related topics. How much should be disclosed, and disclosed to whom? The car development ecosystem includes many companies acting as suppliers that produce both software and hardware components. In what way and for whom should the entire ecosystem be transparent? Some initial formulations are already present in the current policy documents and initial legislative that will be discussed later on.

The problems of the development and sharing of knowledge on automated and connected driving, and the necessity of interoperability and common guidelines, are addressed in the Declaration of Amsterdam (Ministry of Infrastructure & Environment – Netherlands, 2017) adopting a "learning by experience" approach. Algorithmic decision-making and a "right to explanation" are part of the privacy and integrity complex covered by E.U. regulations expressing the right for a user to ask for an explanation of an algorithmic (machine) decision that was made about them (Goodman & Flaxman, 2016). The Department of Motor Vehicles provides the law requirements (State of California Department of Motor Vehicles, 2020) according to which, "under the testing regulations, manufacturers are required to provide DMV with a Report of Traffic Accident Involving an Autonomous Vehicle (form OL 316) within 10 business days of the incident." The list of all incidents can be found in (State of California Department of Motor Vehicles, 2020).

Algorithmic Fairness

Algorithmic decision-making is required to be fair, and not to discriminate on the grounds of race, gender, age, wealth, social status, etc. (Holstein & Dodig-Crnkovic, 2018). This requirement is related to transparency of decision-making and expectation of explainability of the grounds for decision-making. The quality of recognition algorithms, i.e., their capability to detect human obstacles (Wilson et al., 2019) is central.

Reliability

Besides systems related to reliability of classic cars, such as starters, fuel injection, headlights, anti-lock braking systems (ABS), automatic transmission control, airbags, emission controls, or collision detection radar, autonomous vehicles will heavily rely on advanced driver assistance systems, Wi-Fi connectivity, and vehicle-to-vehicle communication (V2V). Emerging smart vehicles contain processing communication modules, such as parallel processor, Ethernet controller, cell modem, Wi-Fi controller, data storage, as well as human-machine interface (HMI) displays and screens. Some of the basic questions are: What if sensors fail? What level of redundancy is necessary? Is there a threshold that determines when the car is no longer reliable, in terms of component failure? How reliable is the cell network? What if there is no mobile network available? A major issue with connected cars is their vulnerability to hacking. The car must be able to deal with incorrect data, broken communications, including "denial of service" attacks. Many of the issues above are safety-critical, and it is of the highest importance to develop a reliability-aware culture in product design and subsequent phases of the entire system lifecycle.

Environmental Sustainability

Environmental sustainability is expected to permeate all steps of the socio-technical process from the system design and development, to operations and management of smart cars. Alonso et al. provide a detailed insight into the sustainability of future road transport from an E.U. perspective and conclude that "attention should be paid to making production and vehicle EoL more efficient and reducing the related environmental impacts" [EoL=End of Life]. Furthermore, they state a "need to address the social and environmental impacts due to the sourcing of raw materials for the vehicles" (Alonso et al, 2019).

Intelligent Behavior

The main difference between human-driven cars and automated/autonomous ones is in the different basis of their intelligent behavior. Thus, one of the approaches to the ethics of real-world autonomous cars is via artificial intelligence (A.I. or AI) ethics. As the worldwide overview of AI ethical guidelines given in (Jobin et al., 2019) shows, the following ethical principles are common for all 84 guidelines analyzed: transparency, justice and fairness, non-maleficence, responsibility, privacy, beneficence, freedom and autonomy, trust, sustainability, dignity and solidarity.

Quality

Detailed quality assurance (Q.A.) programs covering all relevant steps in the lifecycle of a car must be developed to ensure high-quality functionality that meets ethical challenges. A non-autonomous vehicle today often has more than 100 electronic control units, and this makes it very complex (Pelliccione et al., 2017). For the self-driving functionality, complexity will increase. As argued in (Sapienza et al., 2016), ethical aspects, today implicit, should be made visible as a part of the process of design and development; which requires developing ethics-aware decision-making in all processes.

Transdisciplinarity - Systemic Approach

Experiences from advanced modern technologies show the vital importance of transdisciplinary collaboration between various involved parties, disciplines, and stages in the design, development, implementation, testing, verification, maintenance, etc. Transdisciplinary collaboration contributes to the assurance of system-level properties in accordance with the values and ethical principles for both technological and social sides of the process. The most important ethical aspects of technical challenges grouped by requirement are given in the following table.

ETHICAL ASPECTS OF SOCIAL CHALLENGES

The emergence of self-driving cars brings social challenges as well. Autonomous cars will influence job markets, for example, for taxi- or truck- drivers. The perception of cars will change, and cars might be seen as a service that users pay for and no longer as a good that users buy. The idea of vehicles specialized for the specific use, e.g. off-road, city road, or long travels might become attractive. It might impact the business models of car manufacturers and their markets. Thus, it also poses ethical problems: What strategy should be applied for people losing jobs because of the transition to self-driving cars? It is expected that the accident frequency will decrease rapidly so that car insurances may become less critical, which may affect insurance companies in terms of jobs and business. There is a historical parallel with the process of industrialization and automatization. Experiences from the past may help to anticipate and to create better plans for the transitional process.

Table 1. Summary of the technical challenges and approaches, grouped by requirements

Requirements	Challenges	Approaches
Safety	Hardware and software adequacy. Vulnerabilities of machine-learning algorithms. Trade-offs between safety and other factors (like economic). Possibility of intervention in self-driving cars (including for the police forces). Systemic solutions to guarantee safety in organizations (regulations, authorities, safety culture).	Set safety as the highest priority and learn from the history of automation. Understand driving experience - perception and input interpretation processes. Specify how a self-driving car will behave in cases when the car is not able to operate autonomously. Clarify the role of the police and other external controls. Develop regulations, guidelines, standards as the technology develops.
Security	Minimal necessary security requirements for deployment of self-driving cars. Security in systems and connections. Regular and frequent deployment of software updates. Storing and using received and generated data in a secure way.	Create technical solutions that will guarantee minimum security under all foreseeable circumstances. Anticipate and prevent worst-case scenarios regarding security breaches. Provide active security. Provide accessibility to all data, even in the case of accidents, so that it can be analyzed to foster knowledge and to give facts for next-generation developments.
Privacy	Trade-offs between privacy and data collection/ recording and storage/sharing.	Follow and apply legal frameworks to protect personal data, such as GDPR.
Transparency	Information disclosure, what and to whom. Transparency of algorithmic decision-making. Transparency in the techno-social ecosystem.	Assure transparency and insight into decision-making. Enable active sharing of knowledge to ensure the interoperability of systems and services.
Algorithmic Fairness	Algorithmic decision-making is required to be fair and not to discriminate on the grounds of race, gender, age, wealth, social status, etc.	This requirement is related to transparency of decision-making and expectation of explainability of the grounds for decision-making.
Reliability	Reliability of sensors and software, and the need for redundancy. Reliability of required networks, and solution for the case when a network or remote system is unavailable.	Define different levels for reliability, such as diagnostics, vehicle input sensors, software, and external services, to set the ground for reliability measures of the car as a system and its components. Define a standardized process to shift from fail-safe to fail-operational architecture.
Environmental Sustainability	Environmental sustainability ethics refers to new ways of production, use, and recycling for autonomous vehicles.	Address production, use, and disposal/recycling of technology sustainability issues (batteries, car-sharing, etc.).
Intelligent Behavior Control	Intelligent behavior may lead to unpredictable situations resulting from learning and autonomous decision-making.	Develop self-explaining capability and other features ensuring the desired behavior in intelligent software.
Transdisciplinarity -Systemic Approach	Ethics in design, requirements-engineering, software-hardware development, learning, legal and social aspects, software-hardware interplay.	Adopt transdisciplinary and system approaches and give them a more prominent role.
Quality	Quality of components. Quality of decision-making. Lifetime and maintenance. Q.A. process. Adherence to ethical principles/guidelines.	Include ethical deliberations in the whole process, starting with design and development. Require ethics-aware decision-making to ensure ethically justified decisions.

Stakeholder Involvement

Stakeholder concerns must be taken into account in the development of emergent technology, which means the involvement of professional groups as well as users, and the public. Stakeholders should share information and base their opinions on adequate understanding. From the user's perspective, the possible choices given to the user are of interest. How, for example, will a route be planned? In an extreme scenario, self-driving cars might even avoid or reject certain routes. Would that be an interference with the freedom of choice, will passengers be informed about the reasons for such decisions? It is essential to determine how much control the human should have, that will be taken into account when making design choices for a self-driving car. Here transparency of the system for the user is critical. The question that arises in this context is the number of choices that users will have for control, route planning, and other services of the self-driving car, which we have also discussed with the focus on fairness in (Holstein and Dodig-Crnkovic, 2018). Ferdman (2020) comes to a similar conclusion, and states that there is an urgent "need to develop regulatory mechanisms to ensure that the goals of sustainability, well-being and social justice are not jeopardized in future automated mobility paradigms."

Non-maleficence

This requirement of doing no harm becomes especially important in the case of smart and autonomous cars. The highest priority is *not to harm people* inside or outside the car. However, potential users will have different expectations, depending on who will own the cars - companies, social institutions, or individual users, as they all have different preferences. Among those preferences, besides the protection of humans, environmental and social sustainability criteria can be expected to play a central role to do no harm to humans, the environment, or society.

Beneficence

Beneficence is a stronger requirement than non-maleficence. Technology is expected to do good, such as a United Nations' "AI for Good" platform (United Nations, 2020), Microsoft's "AI for good" initiative (Microsoft, 2020), or the AI for Good Foundation (AI for Good Foundation, 2020). Autonomous cars can actively contribute to sustainability goals and increase the accessibility of transport. Singleton et al. (2020) discuss the impact of autonomous vehicles on health and well-being, weighing positive, negative and uncertain effects, with policy implications and research agendas.

Responsibility and Accountability

Responsibility refers to the role of people themselves and to the capability of AI systems to answer for their own decisions and identify errors or unexpected results. Accountability is the need to explain and justify one's decisions and actions. There is the matter of how responsibility in the socio-technological system will be distributed and assigned so to assure maximum benefit for the maximal number of stakeholders while at the same time respecting principles of fairness and justice (Dignum, 2019). Regarding ethical aspects of responsibility, a lot can be learned from existing roboethics and the debate about responsibility in autonomous robots, e.g., Dodig-Crnkovic and Persson, 2008. This is still an open problem, even though important steps forward are being made by legislators, such as mentioned in (Department for Transport (DfT) & Centre for the Protection of National Infrastructure (CPNI), 2017).

Freedom and Autonomy

Freedom and personal autonomy are an essential part of human rights. Every person has autonomy and is free to make decisions. The Universal Declaration of Human Rights (UN General Assembly, 1948) is the foundation of international law for all people. The Universal Declaration principles protecting human rights are incorporated into the laws of more than 90 countries globally. Human freedom and autonomy are now being defined in relation to intelligent decision-making machines, such as self-driving cars.

Social Sustainability

Technological development affects fundamentally all three main fields of sustainable development (environmental, economic, and social), where social sustainability concerns the ability of society to create healthy and livable communities for current and future generations (Partridge, 2014). Sustainable development of socio-technological system proceeds through the trade-off between ecological, economic and social goals, seeking to balance the three interrelated dimensions so that always minimum criteria are fulfilled for each of them.

According to the United Nations Global Compact (2020), in the domain of business, "social sustainability is about identifying and managing business impacts, both positive and negative, on people." Both the broader and the business-oriented view of social sustainability are relevant to the field of self-driving cars.

Social Trust

Trust is an issue that appears in various forms in autonomous cars; e.g., in design and engineering (through multidisciplinary collaborations), production (trust is the requirement for both hardware and software components), as well as in the use of the car. A human might define where the car has to go, but the self-driving car will make the decisions on how to get there, following the given laws and rules. However, the self-driving car might distribute data like the target location to a number of external services in order to receive traffic information or navigational data, which are used in the calculation of the route. But how trustworthy are those data sources (e.g., GPS, map data, external devices, other vehicles), the sensors and other hardware, and how can trust be implemented, when so many different systems are involved? Also, the opposite can pose a challenge when untrustworthy systems are already in place and have to be identified.

Social trust may evolve by fulfilling multiple requirements, such as accountability, transparency, diversity, non-discrimination and fairness, as suggested by (European Commission's High-Level Expert Group on Artificial Intelligence (AI HLEG), 2019) in their guidelines for trustworthy AI.

Social Fairness

Fairness refers to an absence of discriminatory bias and "the quality of treating people equally or in a way that is right or reasonable" (Cambridge English Dictionary, 2020). Even if it is applicable to organizations and relationships between humans, in the context of autonomous cars fairness refers most often to the quality of decision-making algorithms, but also the quality of recognition algorithms and other components contributing to the decision (Holstein & Dodig-Crnkovic, 2018).

Dignity and Solidarity

In the overview of AI ethical guidelines worldwide, given by Jobin et al. in 2019, dignity and solidarity are among the 10 most important principles of AI ethics in the contemporary guidelines. Applied to autonomous cars, the expression can refer to respect for and solidarity with humans who are affected by the negative consequences of emergent technology such as unemployment.

Justice: Legislation, Standards, and Guidelines

Present-day regulatory instruments for transportation systems are based on the assumption of human-driven vehicles. As the development and introduction of increasingly automated and connected cars proceed, from no automation at all (level 0) towards full automation (level 5), legislation needs constant updates (Federal Ministry of Transport and Digital Infrastructure, 2017; National Highway Traffic Safety Administration, 2020; Pillath, 2016). It has been recognized that state regulatory instruments and the existing NHTSA authority for human-controlled vehicles will not be adequate for self-driving cars, and NHTSA is constantly evaluating and updating its regulations in order to provide up-to-date guidelines, which meet the challenges of autonomous cars, while technologies advance (National Highway Traffic Safety Administration, 2020).

The Declaration of Amsterdam (Ministry of Infrastructure & Environment – Netherlands, 2017) addresses legislation frameworks, use of data, liability, exchange of knowledge and cross-border testing for the emerging technology. It prepares a European framework for the implementation of interoperable connected and automated vehicles (Federal Ministry of Transport and Digital Infrastructure, 2017). It also considers the roles of stakeholders. The terminology has been developed in order to facilitate communication between technology and politics domains, with the definition of levels of automation in vehicles (Pillath, 2016).

The question is thus how to ensure that self-driving cars will be built upon ethical guidelines, which will be adopted by society. The strategy is to rely on rigorously monitoring the behavior of cars, while the details of implementation are within the responsibility of producers. That means, among others, that design and implementation of software should follow ethical guidelines. An example of ethical guidelines trying to think one step further is described in the book Ethical IT innovation (Spiekermann, 2015).

The approach based on "learning by experience" and "Proven in use" argument (Ministry of Infrastructure & Environment – Netherlands, 2017; Schäbe & Braband, 2015; *What is the ISO 26262 Functional Safety Standard?*, 2014) presupposes a functioning socio-technological assurance system that has strong coupling among legislation, guidelines, standards and use, and promptly adapts to lessons learned. Ethical analysis in (Dodig Crnkovic & Çürüklü, 2012; Johnsen et al., 2017; Thekkilakattil & Dodig-Crnkovic, 2015) addresses this problem of establishing and maintaining a functioning learning socio-technological system, while Johnsen et al. discuss why functional safety standards are not enough (Johnsen et al., 2017).

The most important ethical aspects of social challenges, grouped by requirement, are given in the following table.

Table 2. Summary of social challenges and approaches, grouped by requirements

Requirements	Challenges	Approaches
Non-maleficence	Technology not causing harm. Disruptive changes on the labor market. Change of related markets and business models (e.g., insurances, manufacturers).	It is partly covered by technical solutions. Prepare strategic solutions for people losing jobs. Learn from historic parallels to industrialization and automatization.
Stakeholders Involvement	Many different stakeholders are involved – from professionals designing, developing, producing, and maintaining cars, to car users, and the general public.	Involve stakeholders actively in the process of design and requirements specification as well as decisions of their use.
Beneficence	Identifying values and priorities. Ensure that general public values will be embodied in the technology, with interests of minorities taken into account.	Initiatives as "AI for good" exemplify this expectation that new technology not only do not cause harm, but actively do good for its stakeholders.
Responsibility and Accountability	Assignment and distribution of responsibility and accountability that follow ethical principles.	Follow the Accountability, Responsibility and Transparency (ART) principle based on a *Design for Values* approach, which includes human values and ethical principles in the design processes (Dignum, 2019).
Freedom and Autonomy	Freedom of choice hindered by the system (e.g. it may not allow driving into a specific area).	Secure the freedom of choice determined by regulations. Determine and communicate the amount of control that human has in the self-driving car.
Social Sustainability	Identifying and managing impacts of emerging technology on people. Educational system should be updated to support social sustainability of emerging technology.	Assure social equity, community development, social support, human rights, labor rights, social responsibility, social justice, etc. Update the educational system accordingly.
Social Fairness	Ascertaining fairness of the socio-technological system.	Ensure fairness of the decision-making, which relates to transparency and explainability.
Dignity and Solidarity	Applying this requirement to the entire socio-technological system.	Identify and address the challenges that come from the lack of the common wholistic view.
Social Trust	Establishing trust between humans and highly automated vehicles as well as within the entire social system.	Further research on how to implement trust across multiple systems. Provide trusted connections between components as well as external services.
Justice: Legislation, Standards, Norms, Policies and Guidelines	Keeping legislation up to date with the current level of automated driving, and the emergence of self-driving cars. Creating and defining global legislation frameworks. Including ethical guidelines in design and development processes.	Seek legislative support and follow global frameworks. Provide ethics training for involved engineers. Establish and maintain a functioning socio-technological system in addition to functional safety standards.

CONCLUSION AND FUTURE WORK

Self-driving vehicles have been envisioned as the future of transportation systems and will be successively introduced into the transport systems globally (National Highway Traffic Safety Administration, 2020; Pillath, 2016). It is time to start an investigation into the manifold of ethical challenges surrounding self-driving and connected vehicles (Federal Ministry of Transport and Digital Infrastructure, 2017). As this new technology is being gradually allowed on public roads under controlled conditions, the focus is on the practical technological solutions and their social consequences, rather than on idealized unsolvable problems such as much discussed trolley problem. Unlike idealized thought experiments, the real-world engineering ethics deliberation involves characteristics of the whole techno-social system supporting new technology, with the emphasis on maximizing learning from experience, on a machine-, individual-, and social-level (Charisi et al., 2017; Dodig Crnkovic & Çürüklü, 2012).

For the future, a lot of systemic transdisciplinary work remains to be done. A system-level analysis is crucial, as pointed out by Leveson (Leveson, 2020), who argues that the analysis of software in isolation does not guarantee the safety of the whole software-hardware system. The decision-making process and its implementation, which are central to the behavior of a car, might use unreliable, insecure or inadequate hardware technology, as we described in our earlier study (Holstein et al., 2018). Leveson (Leveson, 2011, 2020) argues that in present-day technology, we can no longer separate engineering from human, social and organizational factors, but we have to take a systemic view. This is achieved through the following: systems thinking, solving real problems of stakeholders, communication and cooperation, technology transfer from research to practice, design, development, and management of the entire lifecycle within a socio-technological system.

It is necessary to develop more elaborated ethical principles, guidelines, and analyses, as well as regulatory and legal documents that involve all stakeholders. This affects all stages - from the existing to the new regulatory infrastructure to the requirements engineering, development, implementation, testing and verification and back to the regulatory structure in the iterative process of continuous improvement (Charisi et al., 2017; Dodig Crnkovic & Çürüklü, 2012; Greene, 2016; Mooney, 2016). It is also necessary to ensure the transparency of those processes so that independent evaluations become possible.

Finally, it is important to point out the total ecology of the socio-technological system, where ethics is ensured through education, constant information sharing and negotiation of priorities in the value system. In the development process, values and ethics come first, then follows legislation and standardization processes, which are monitored continuously in practice and validated with value- and ethical standards. That is why we emphasize the central role of real-life system-level ethics as a basis that will sustain and inform ethically sound emerging technology of autonomous cars.

ACKNOWLEDGMENT

The authors want to thank our anonymous reviewers for their useful comments. We would also like to acknowledge excellent help provided during the editorial process. One of the authors (P.P.) acknowledges financial support from the Centre of EXcellence on Connected, Geo-Localized and Cybersecure Vehicle (EX-Emerge), funded by the Italian Government under CIPE resolution n. 70/2017 (August 7, 2017).

REFERENCES

AI for Good Foundation. (2020). *AI for Good - Make the World a Better Place through AI*. https://ai4good.org/

Alonso Raposo, M., Ciuffo, B., Ardente, F., Aurambout, J. P., Baldini, G., Braun, R., Christidis, P., Christodoulou, A., Duboz, A., & Felici, S. (2019). The Future of Road Transport—Implications of Automated, Connected, Low-Carbon and Shared Mobility. EUR 29748 EN. *Publications Office of the European Union, Luxembourg, 2019*. Advance online publication. doi:10.2760/668964

Awad, E., Dsouza, S., Bonnefon, J.-F., Shariff, A., & Rahwan, I. (2020). Crowdsourcing Moral Machines. *Communications of the ACM*, *63*(3), 48–55. doi:10.1145/3339904

Awad, E., Dsouza, S., Kim, R., Schulz, J., Henrich, J., Shariff, A., Bonnefon, J.-F., & Rahwan, I. (2018). The Moral Machine Experiment. *Nature*, *563*(7729), 59–64. doi:10.103841586-018-0637-6 PMID:30356211

Aydemir, F. B., & Dalpiaz, F. (2018). A Roadmap for Ethics-Aware Software Engineering. *2018 IEEE/ACM International Workshop on Software Fairness (FairWare)*, 15–21. 10.23919/FAIRWARE.2018.8452915

Beard, S. (2019). The problem with the trolley problem. *Quartz*. https://qz.com/1716107/the-problem-with-the-trolley-problem/

Bissell, D., Birtchnell, T., Elliott, A., & Hsu, E. L. (2020). Autonomous automobilities: The social impacts of driverless vehicles. *Current Sociology*, *68*(1), 116–134. doi:10.1177/0011392118816743

Blanco, M., Atwood, J., Russell, S., Trimble, T., McClafferty, J., & Perez, M. (2016). Automated Vehicle Crash Rate Comparison Using Naturalistic Data. Vtti. doi:10.13140/RG.2.1.2336.1048

Charisi, V., Dennis, L. A., Fisher, M., Lieck, R., Matthias, A., Slavkovik, M., Sombetzki, J., Winfield, A. F. T., & Yampolskiy, R. (2017). *Towards Moral Autonomous Systems*. https://arxiv.org/abs/1703.04741

Coca-Vila, I. (2017). Self-driving Cars in Dilemmatic Situations: An Approach Based on the Theory of Justification in Criminal Law. *Criminal Law and Philosophy*. Advance online publication. doi:10.100711572-017-9411-3

Combs, T. S., Sandt, L. S., Clamann, M. P., & McDonald, N. C. (2019). Automated Vehicles and Pedestrian Safety: Exploring the Promise and Limits of Pedestrian Detection. *American Journal of Preventive Medicine*, *56*(1), 1–7. doi:10.1016/j.amepre.2018.06.024 PMID:30337236

Cruise. (2020). *Cruise - Create what's next*. https://www.getcruise.com/technology

Dennis, L., Fisher, M., Slavkovik, M., & Webster, M. (2014). Ethical choice in unforeseen circumstances. Lecture Notes in Computer Science (Including Subseries Lecture Notes in Artificial Intelligence and Lecture Notes in Bioinformatics), 8069, 433–445. doi:10.1007/978-3-662-43645-5_45

Dennis, L., Fisher, M., Slavkovik, M., & Webster, M. (2016). Formal verification of ethical choices in autonomous systems. *Robotics and Autonomous Systems*, *77*, 1–14. doi:10.1016/j.robot.2015.11.012

Department for Transport (DfT), & Centre for the Protection of National Infrastructure (CPNI). (2017). *The Key Principles of Cyber Security for Connected and Automated Vehicles*. https://www.gov.uk/government/uploads/system/uploads/attachment_data/file/624302/cyber-security-connected-automated-vehicles-key-principles.pdf

Dignum, V. (2019). *Responsible artificial intelligence: How to develop and use AI in a responsible way*. Springer. doi:10.1007/978-3-030-30371-6

Dixit, V. V., Chand, S., & Nair, D. J. (2016). Autonomous Vehicles: Disengagements, Accidents and Reaction Times. *PLoS One*, *11*(12), 1–14. doi:10.1371/journal.pone.0168054 PMID:27997566

Dodig Crnkovic, G., & Çürüklü, B. (2012). Robots: Ethical by design. *Ethics and Information Technology*, *14*(1), 61–71. doi:10.100710676-011-9278-2

Dodig-Crnkovic, G., & Persson, D. (2008). Sharing Moral Responsibility with Robots: A Pragmatic Approach. *Proceedings of the 2008 Conference on Tenth Scandinavian Conference on Artificial Intelligence: SCAI 2008*, 165–168. https://dl.acm.org/citation.cfm?id=1566864.1566888

Eden, G., Nanchen, B., Ramseyer, R., & Evéquoz, F. (2017). On the Road with an Autonomous Passenger Shuttle: Integration in Public Spaces. *Proceedings of the 2017 CHI Conference Extended Abstracts on Human Factors in Computing Systems*, 1569–1576. 10.1145/3027063.3053126

EU. (2016). Regulation (EU) 2016/679 of the European Parliament and of the Council of 27 April 2016 on the protection of natural persons with regard to the processing of personal data and on the free movement of such data, and repealing Directive 95/46/EC (General Data Protection Regulation). http://data.europa.eu/eli/reg/2016/679/oj

European Commission's High-Level Expert Group on Artificial Intelligence (AI HLEG). (2019). Ethics Guidelines for Trustworthy AI. *High-Level Expert Group on Artificial Intelligence*. https://ec.europa.eu/digital-single-market/en/news/ethics-guidelines-trustworthy-ai

European Group on Ethics in Science and New Technologies and others. (2018). *Statement on Artificial Intelligence, Robotics and "Autonomous" Systems*. Luxembourg: Publications Office of the European Union.

Fairness. (2020). In *Cambridge English Dictionary*. Retrieved July 30, 2020, from https://dictionary.cambridge.org/us/dictionary/english/fairness

Favarò, F. M., Nader, N., Eurich, S. O., Tripp, M., & Varadaraju, N. (2017). Examining accident reports involving autonomous vehicles in California. *PLoS One*, *12*(9), 1–20. doi:10.1371/journal.pone.0184952 PMID:28931022

Federal Ministry of Transport and Digital Infrastructure. (2017). *Automated and Connected Driving. Ethics Commission*. https://www.bmvi.de/SharedDocs/EN/publications/report-ethics-commission.pdf?__blob=publicationFile

Ferdman, A. (2020). Corporate ownership of automated vehicles: Discussing potential negative externalities. *Transport Reviews*, *40*(1), 95–113. doi:10.1080/01441647.2019.1687606

Floridi, L., Cowls, J., Beltrametti, M., Chatila, R., Chazerand, P., Dignum, V., Luetge, C., Madelin, R., Pagallo, U., Rossi, F., Schafer, B., Valcke, P., & Vayena, E. (2018). AI4People---An Ethical Framework for a Good AI Society: Opportunities, Risks, Principles, and Recommendations. *Minds and Machines*, *28*(4), 689–707. doi:10.100711023-018-9482-5 PMID:30930541

Foot, P. (1967). The Problem of Abortion and the Doctrine of Double Effect. *Oxford Review, 5*.

Fraedrich, E., Kröger, L., Bahamonde-Birke, F. J., Frenzel, I., Liedtke, G., Trommer, S., Lenz, B., & Heinrichs, D. (2017). *Automatisiertes Fahren im Personen- und Güterverkehr. Auswirkungen auf den Modal-Split, das Verkehrssystem und die Siedlungsstrukturen*. https://elib.dlr.de/117868/

Friedman, B., & Kahn, P. H., Jr. (2003). Chapter. In J. A. Jacko & A. Sears (Eds.), The human-computer interaction handbook (pp. 1177–1201). L. Erlbaum Associates Inc., https://dl.acm.org/citation.cfm?id=772072.772147

Friedman, B., Kahn, P. H., Borning, A., & Huldtgren, A. (2013). Value Sensitive Design and Information Systems. In N. Doorn, D. Schuurbiers, I. van de Poel, & M. E. Gorman (Eds.), *Early engagement and new technologies: Opening up the laboratory* (pp. 55–95). Springer Netherlands. doi:10.1007/978-94-007-7844-3_4

Goodall, N. J. (2016). Can you program ethics into a self-driving car? *IEEE Spectrum, 53*(6), 28–58. Advance online publication. doi:10.1109/MSPEC.2016.7473149

Goodman, B., & Flaxman, S. (2016). *European Union regulations on algorithmic decision-making and a 'right to explanation.'* https://arxiv.org/abs/1606.08813

Hersman, D. (2019). *Safety at Waymo | Self-driving cars & other road users.* Waymo. https://blog.waymo.com/2019/08/safety-at-waymo-self-driving-cars-other.html

Holstein, T., & Dodig-Crnkovic, G. (2018). *Avoiding the intrinsic unfairness of the trolley problem.* doi:10.1145/3194770.3194772

Holstein, T., Dodig-Crnkovic, G., & Pelliccione, P. (2018). Ethical and Social Aspects of Self-Driving Cars. *ArXiv E-Prints.* https://arxiv.org/abs/1802.04103

Islam, M. A., & Rashid, S. I. (2018). Algorithm for Ethical Decision Making at Times of Accidents for Autonomous Vehicles. *2018 4th International Conference on Electrical Engineering and Information Communication Technology (ICEEiCT)*, 438–442. 10.1109/CEEICT.2018.8628155

ISO. (2018). ISO 26262 -- Road vehicles -- Functional safety (Issue ISO 26262). ISO, Geneva, Switzerland.

ISO. (2019). *ISO/PAS 21448:2019 -- Road vehicles -- Safety of the intended functionality* (Issue ISO/PAS 21448:2019). ISO, Geneva, Switzerland. https://www.iso.org/standard/70939.html

Jobin, A., Ienca, M., & Vayena, E. (2019). The global landscape of AI ethics guidelines. *Nature Machine Intelligence, 1*(9), 389–399. doi:10.103842256-019-0088-2

Johansson, R., & Nilsson, J. (2016). Disarming the Trolley Problem --Why Self-driving Cars do not Need to Choose Whom to Kill. In M. Roy (Ed.), *Workshop CARS 2016 - Critical automotive applications: Robustness & safety.* https://hal.archives-ouvertes.fr/hal-01375606

Johnsen, A., Dodig-Crnkovic, G., Lundqvist, K., Hanninen, K., & Pettersson, P. (2017). Risk-based decision-making fallacies: Why present functional safety standards are not enough. *Proceedings - 2017 IEEE International Conference on Software Architecture Workshops, ICSAW 2017: Side Track Proceedings.* 10.1109/ICSAW.2017.50

Kalra, N., & Paddock, S. M. (2016). Driving to safety: How many miles of driving would it take to demonstrate autonomous vehicle reliability? *Transportation Research Part A, Policy and Practice, 94*(Supplement C), 182–193. doi:10.1016/j.tra.2016.09.010

Karnouskos, S. (2018). Self-Driving Car Acceptance and the Role of Ethics. *IEEE Transactions on Engineering Management*, 1–14. doi:10.1109/TEM.2018.2877307

Kim, R., Kleiman-Weiner, M., Abeliuk, A., Awad, E., Dsouza, S., Tenenbaum, J. B., & Rahwan, I. (2018). A Computational Model of Commonsense Moral Decision Making. *Proceedings of the 2018 AAAI/ACM Conference on AI, Ethics, and Society*, 197–203. 10.1145/3278721.3278770

Leveson, N. (2011). *Engineering a safer world: Systems thinking applied to safety*. MIT press.

Leveson, N. (2020). Are You Sure Your Software Will Not Kill Anyone? *Communications of the ACM*, *63*(2), 25–28. doi:10.1145/3376127

Luetge, C. (2017). The German Ethics Code for Automated and Connected Driving. *Philosophy & Technology*, *30*(4), 547–558. doi:10.100713347-017-0284-0

McBride, N. (2016). The Ethics of Driverless Cars. *SIGCAS Comput. Soc.*, *45*(3), 179–184. doi:10.1145/2874239.2874265

Microsoft. (2020). *AI for Good - Providing technology, resources, and expertise to empower those working to solve humanitarian issues and create a more sustainable and accessible world*. https://www.microsoft.com/en-us/ai/ai-for-good

Ministry of Infrastructure & Environment – Netherlands. (2017, May 18). *On our way towards connected and automated driving in Europe*. https://www.government.nl/binaries/government/documents/leaflets/2017/05/18/on-our-way-towards-connected-and-automated-driving-in-europe/On+our+way+towards+connected+and+automated+driving+in+Europe.pdf

Mirnig, A. G., & Meschtscherjakov, A. (2019). Trolled by the Trolley Problem: On What Matters for Ethical Decision Making in Automated Vehicles. *Proceedings of the 2019 CHI Conference on Human Factors in Computing Systems*. 10.1145/3290605.3300739

MIT Moral Machine Lab. (2016). *Moral Machine*. Massachusetts Institute of Technology Media Laboratory. https://moralmachine.mit.edu/

Mooney, C. (2016, June 23). Save the driver or save the crowd? Scientists wonder how driverless cars will 'choose.' *The Washington Post*. https://www.washingtonpost.com/news/energy-environment/wp/2016/06/23/save-the-driver-or-save-the-crowd-scientists-wonder-how-driverless-cars-will-choose/

Moor, J. H. (1985). What Is Computer Ethics?*. *Metaphilosophy*, *16*(4), 266–275. doi:10.1111/j.1467-9973.1985.tb00173.x

Musk, E. (2016, July 20). *Master Plan Part Deux*. https://www.tesla.com/blog/master-plan-part-deux

National Center for Statistics and Analysis. (2018). *Critical Reasons for Crashes Investigated in the National Motor Vehicle Crash Causation Survey* (DOT HS 812 506). National Highway Traffic Safety Administration. https://crashstats.nhtsa.dot.gov/Api/Public/ViewPublication/812506

National Highway Traffic Safety Administration. (2020). *Automated Vehicles for Safety*. https://www.nhtsa.gov/technology-innovation/automated-vehicles-safety

Noothigattu, R., Gaikwad, S., Awad, E., Dsouza, S., Rahwan, I., Ravikumar, P., & Procaccia, A. (2018). *A Voting-Based System for Ethical Decision Making*. https://arxiv.org/abs/1709.06692

Partridge, E. (2014). Social Sustainability. In A. C. Michalos (Ed.), *Encyclopedia of Quality of Life and Well-Being Research* (pp. 6178–6186). Springer Netherlands. doi:10.1007/978-94-007-0753-5_2790

Pelliccione, P., Knauss, E., Heldal, R., Ågren, S. M., Mallozzi, P., Alminger, A., & Borgentun, D. (2017). Automotive Architecture Framework: The experience of Volvo Cars. *Journal of Systems Architecture, 77*(Supplement C), 83–100. doi:10.1016/j.sysarc.2017.02.005

Pillath, S. (2016). Briefing: Automated vehicles in the EU. *European Parliamentary Research Service (EPRS).* https://www.europarl.europa.eu/RegData/etudes/BRIE/2016/573902/EPRS_BRI(2016)573902_EN.pdf

Ryan, M. (2019). The Future of Transportation: Ethical, Legal, Social and Economic Impacts of Self-driving Vehicles in the Year 2025. *Science and Engineering Ethics.* Advance online publication. doi:10.100711948-019-00130-2 PMID:31482471

SAE. (2016). Taxonomy and Definitions for Terms Related to Driving Automation Systems for On-Road Motor Vehicles. *Global Ground Vehicle Standards, J3016,* 30. doi:10.4271/J3016_201609

Sapienza, G., Dodig-Crnkovic, G., & Crnkovic, I. (2016). Inclusion of Ethical Aspects in Multi-criteria Decision Analysis. *Proceedings - 2016 1st International Workshop on Decision Making in Software ARCHitecture.* 10.1109/MARCH.2016.8

Schäbe, H., & Braband, J. (2015). *Basic requirements for proven-in-use arguments.* https://arxiv.org/abs/1511.01839

Schoettle, B., & Sivak, M. (2015, October). *A Preliminary Analysis of Real -World Crashes Involving Self -Driving Vehicles.* http://www.umich.edu/~umtriswt/PDF/UMTRI-2015-34.pdf

Singleton, P. A., De Vos, J., Heinen, E., & Pudāne, B. B. T.-A. (2020). *Potential health and well-being implications of autonomous vehicles.* Academic Press.

Spiekermann, S. (2015). *Ethical IT innovation: A value-based system design approach.* Taylor & Francis. doi:10.1201/b19060

State of California Department of Motor Vehicles. (2020). *Report of Traffic Collision Involving an Autonomous Vehicle (OL316).* https://www.dmv.ca.gov/portal/dmv/detail/vr/autonomous/autonomousveh_ol316

The IEEE Global Initiative on Ethics of Autonomous and Intelligent Systems. (2019). Ethically Aligned Design: A Vision for Prioritizing Human Well-being with Autonomous and Intelligent Systems. IEEE Global Initiative on Ethics of Autonomous and Intelligent Systems.

Thekkilakattil, A., & Dodig-Crnkovic, G. (2015). Ethics Aspects of Embedded and Cyber-Physical Systems. *2015 IEEE 39th Annual Computer Software and Applications Conference, 2,* 39–44. 10.1109/COMPSAC.2015.41

Thomson, J. J. (1976). Killing, Letting Die, and the Trolley Problem. *The Monist, 59*(2), 204–217. Advance online publication. doi:10.5840/monist197659224 PMID:11662247

UN General Assembly. (1948). *Universal Declaration of Human Rights (217 [iii] a).* https://www.un.org/en/universal-declaration-human-rights/

United Nations. (2020). *AI for Good - Global Summit - Accelerating the United Nations Sustainable Development Goals.* https://aiforgood.itu.int/

United Nations Global Compact. (2020). *Social Sustainability.* https://www.unglobalcompact.org/what-is-gc/our-work/social

Wachter, S., Mittelstadt, B., & Floridi, L. (2017). Why a Right to Explanation of Automated Decision-Making Does Not Exist in the General Data Protection Regulation. *International Data Privacy Law, 7*(2), 76–99. doi:10.1093/idpl/ipx005

Waymo. (n.d.). https://waymo.com

What is the ISO 26262 Functional Safety Standard? (2014). National Instruments Corp. http://www.ni.com/white-paper/13647/en/

Wilson, B., Hoffman, J., & Morgenstern, J. (2019). *Predictive Inequity in Object Detection.* https://arxiv.org/abs/1902.11097

Zhu, X. L., & Tang, S. M. (2015). Autonomous vehicle: from a cognitive perspective. *Multimedia, Communication and Computing Application: Proceedings of the 2014 International Conference on Multimedia, Communication and Computing Application (MCCA 2014),* 401.

ADDITIONAL READING

Alavi, H. S., Bahrami, F., Verma, H., & Lalanne, D. (2017). Is Driverless Car Another Weiserian Mistake? *Proceedings of the 2017 ACM Conference Companion Publication on Designing Interactive Systems,* 249–253. 10.1145/3064857.3079155

Bonnefon, J.-F., Shariff, A., & Rahwan, I. (2016). The social dilemma of autonomous vehicles. *Science, 352*(6293), 1573–1576. doi:10.1126cience.aaf2654 PMID:27339987

Deamer, K. (2016, July 1). What the First Driverless Car Fatality Means for Self-Driving Tech. *Scientific American.* https://www.scientificamerican.com/article/what-the-first-driverless-car-fatality-means-for-self-driving-tech/

Frison, A.-K., Wintersberger, P., & Riener, A. (2016). First Person Trolley Problem: Evaluation of Drivers' Ethical Decisions in a Driving Simulator. *Adjunct Proceedings of the 8th International Conference on Automotive User Interfaces and Interactive Vehicular Applications,* 117–122. 10.1145/3004323.3004336

Goodall, N. J. (2014). Vehicle automation and the duty to act. *Proceedings of the 21st World Congress on Intelligent Transport Systems,* 7–11.

Greene, J. D. (2016). Our driverless dilemma. *Science, 352*(6293), 1514–1515. doi:10.1126cience.aaf9534 PMID:27339966

Greenemeier, L. (2016). Driverless Cars Will Face Moral Dilemmas. *Scientific American.* https://www.scientificamerican.com/article/driverless-cars-will-face-moral-dilemmas

Kirkpatrick, K. (2015). The Moral Challenges of Driverless Cars. *Communications of the ACM, 58*(8), 19–20. doi:10.1145/2788477

Kuchinskas, S. (2013, April 13). Crash Course: Training the Brain of a Driverless Car. *Scientific American*. https://www.scientificamerican.com/article/autonomous-driverless-car-brain/

Riener, A., Jeon, M. P., Alvarez, I., Pfleging, B., Mirnig, A., Tscheligi, M., & Chuang, L. (2016). 1st Workshop on Ethically Inspired User Interfaces for Automated Driving. *Adjunct Proceedings of the 8th International Conference on Automotive User Interfaces and Interactive Vehicular Applications*, 217–220. 10.1145/3004323.3005687

Shashkevich, A. (2017, May 22). Stanford professors discuss ethics involving driverless cars. *Stanford News*. https://news.stanford.edu/2017/05/22/stanford-scholars-researchers-discuss-key-ethical-questions-self-driving-cars-present/

ENDNOTE

[1] For additional reading reference, see *IEEE* (Goodall, 2016), *ACM* (Frison et al., 2016; Kirkpatrick, 2015; McBride, 2016), *Scientific American* (Deamer, 2016; Greenemeier, 2016; Kuchinskas, 2013), *Science* (Bonnefon et al., 2016; Greene, 2016), other publication venues (Coca-Vila, 2017; Goodall, 2014; Goodman & Flaxman, 2016), workshops (Alavi et al., 2017; Riener et al., 2016), and media (Mooney, 2016; Shashkevich, 2017).

Chapter 7
Conceptualizing Policy in Value Sensitive Design:
A Machine Ethics Approach

Steven Umbrello

ⓘ https://orcid.org/0000-0003-2594-6313

University of Turin, Italy & Institute for Ethics and Technology, Italy

ABSTRACT

The value sensitive design (VSD) approach to designing emerging technologies for human values is taken as the object of study in this chapter. VSD has traditionally been conceptualized as another type of technology or instrumentally as a tool. The various parts of VSD's principled approach would then aim to discern the various policy requirements that any given technological artifact under consideration would implicate. Yet, little to no consideration has been given to how laws, policies, and social norms engage within VSD practices, similarly, how the interactive nature of the VSD approach can, in turn, influence those directives. This is exacerbated when considering machine ethics policy that has global consequences outside their development spheres. This chapter begins with the VSD approach and aims to determine how policies come to influence how values can be managed within VSD practices. It shows that the interactional nature of VSD permits and encourages existing policies to be integrated early on and throughout the design process.

INTRODUCTION

The varied influences that artificial intelligence systems and robotics have on society have moved out of the realm of speculation and into reality. The impact that algorithmic trading agents, medical diagnostic systems, driverless cars and smart home assistants – to name a few – already have substantial and unignorable effects on the lives of both direct stakeholders (users, designers, companies, etc.) as well as indirect stakeholders (environments, bystanders, etc.). Their socialtechnicity – i.e., their inextricable link to the social environment in which they are designed and used – makes their study critical if their design

DOI: 10.4018/978-1-7998-4894-3.ch007

Copyright © 2021, IGI Global. Copying or distributing in print or electronic forms without written permission of IGI Global is prohibited.

and deployment are to be responsible. For this reason there has been a considerable amount of attention directed towards the ethical understanding of these systems, and a search towards actionable guidelines and best practices (Dignum, 2019). As a result, numerous principles, guidelines, recommendations, and values have been proposed to govern such systems, with a resulting risk of confusion as to which set to choose, thus delaying much-needed progress into making such principles actionable (Floridi et al., 2018). The next turn in AI ethics is how to translate abstract philosophical and legal principles/values into design requirements that engineers can understand and plan in design.

Multiple approaches have emerged that consider the social embeddedness of technologies and their impacts. The core of many of these methodologies is the engagement and elicitation of stakeholders, whether they are directly or indirectly implicated by technology design. Approaches such as universal design (Ruzic & Sanfod, 2017; van den Hoven, 2017), inclusive design (Gregor, Sloan, & Newell, 2005; Hyppönen, Kemppainen, Gill, Slater, & Poulson, 2000), sustainable design (Fallan, 2015; Lockton, Harrison, & Stanton, 2016; Winkler & Spiekermann, 2019), participatory design (Bødker, Kensing, & Simonsen, 2009; Ehn, 2016), and value sensitive design (Friedman & Hendry, 2019; Umbrello, 2020a; van den Hoven & Manders-Huits, 2009) among others, have been constructed and proposed. Although these methodologies are disparate in many respects, they all aims towards the goal of responsible research and innovation (RRI).

Originally developed within the field of human-computer interaction, value sensitive design (VSD) begins from the premise that technology is not value-neutral; rather, it is sensitive to stakeholder values, whether they are direct stakeholders such as users and designers, or indirect, such as the environment, and that social contexts and technologies co-vary (Friedman, Hendry, & Borning, 2017; van den Hoven & Manders-Huits, 2009). As a starting point then, the VSD approach aims to explicitly design technologies for stakeholder values – with emphasis on moral values - in a manner as to successfully map the values deemed critical and to ensure the robustness of sociotechnical systems (Friedman & Hendry, 2019; Umbrello, 2019b). What differs VSD from other design approaches then is its explicit emphasis on moral values and their inherit embeddedness in technologies (see Friedman & Hendry, 2019).

VSD has traditionally prioritized the values that emphasize human well-being, human dignity, justice, welfare, and human rights as its central concern (Friedman, Kahn, Borning, & Huldtgren, 2013). The approach is considered 'principled' because it assumes an objective moral grounds on which these values spring, one that is independent of whether any particular individual or group subscribe to such values (e.g., the belief in and practice of racial eugenics by a group does not a priori mean that racial eugenics is a morally acceptable practice). Still, VSD maintains that expression of such values in any particular culture, or by any particular individual, can vary greatly (Friedman et al., 2017; Umbrello, 2020a). This ethical objectivism that VSD affirms easily permits it to be integrated into existent design practices across sociocultural dimensions, although it is not without objections (Davis & Nathan, 2014; Umbrello, 2018a, 2020).

The ability for VSD to be adopted and integrated across sociocultural boundaries becomes invaluable, given the current calls for international collaboration and coordination for artificial intelligence regulations and policies. VSD has traditionally viewed policy as it would a technology. Accordingly, the approach would then need to identify policy requirements. Yet, the role of policy and how policy comes to play within VSD has not been seriously considered. This is exacerbated when we consider machine ethics policy that can have global consequences outside their development spheres. What constructs and models will position AI designers to engage in policy concerns? How can the design of AI policy be integrated with technical design? How might VSD be used to develop AI policy? How might law, regulations, social norms, and other kinds of policy regarding AI systems be engaged within value sensitive design? This chapter aims to touch on these fundamental questions and provide preliminary ways forward that can be useful to policy experts, AI researchers and designers, as well as academics.

Previous studies have explored the philosophical basis of VSD (Santoni de Sio & van den Hoven, 2018; Umbrello, 2018b, 2020a), ad hoc applications of the approach to existent technologies (Correljé, Cuppen, Dignum, Pesch, & Taebi, 2015; van den Hoven, 2013; Woelfer, Iverson, Hendry, Friedman, & Gill, 2011), speculative applications of the methodology towards future technologies (Umbrello, 2019a; van Wynsberghe, 2013), as well as preliminary ways of incorporating VSD into AI design (Umbrello, 2019b; Umbrello & De Bellis, 2018). This chapter is comparatively unique, as it takes policy as the central object within VSD practice with specific emphasis on how machine ethics policies can emerge from VSD.

To do this, this chapter is organized in five sections. The first section will look at how policy is typically engaged at the design level, looking specifically at AI research and development, as well as international development goals for which AI&R are situated. The second section briefly accounts the VSD approach in more detail, specifically looking at the tripartite structure of the approach and highlights where existent policy tools can come into play. Section three provides some preliminary suggestions on how the integrative nature of the approach allows for new policy recommendations to emerge. The fourth section discusses some of this chapter's limitations, as well as provides suggestions for potentially fruitful future research streams. The final section concludes the chapter.

POLICY, DESIGN, AND COMPLIANCE

Policy formulation, development, and creation, like technologies, are motivated by problems in which successful policies are capable of solving those problems. Whether such policy measures are reactive, responding to problems that have arisen, or proactive, where policies are designed in anticipation of a problem that may arise, policy, regardless, is motivated by making things better than they are currently viewed (Simon, 1988).

The traditional haphazard way of retroactively making policy is still widespread, and is not well-equipped to handle the exponential growth of technological innovations that consistently bring with them new social and ethical issues (Ben-Haim, Osteen, & Moffitt, 2013). Policy is typically understood as being mapped onto technological development during design from a top-down approach, ensuring client needs while also meeting the minimum standards of legal compliance to ensure safe deployment and minimize system recalcitrance (Bos, Walhout, Peine, & van Lente, 2014). Difficulties arise, however, when considering novel technologies such as artificial intelligence (AI) and robotics (AI&R), which exist across many domains, and in many cases overlap.

Designing policies for AI&R that accurately and effectively permit interventions at a collective level becomes important given the potential consequences of recalcitrant systems. Given the number of abject policy failures (McConnell, 2010), unintended consequences, or ones that often produce the opposite results (Sieber, 2013), the goal towards collective policy to govern the design and use of AI&R poses a particularly exuberant challenge. Natural questions arise regarding the strategy towards policy creation, such as whether or not specific policy interventions should be developed for discrete technologies that risk being too narrow, and whether templates from narrow policies have any applicability to other domains. Similarly, can general policy measures that focus on principles or practices provide effective intervention strategies on the specific level?

The two need not be read as a strong dichotomy however, mutually excluding each other. Design thinking shifts the view of policy as a static object, and it injects systems thinking as a fundamental principle of how policy co-varies and co-constitutes that which it seeks to police (Yoo et al., 2016). How existing policies can affect technological design, as well as how design can inform policy, becomes an interesting area to explore when we consider policy to be a similarly iterative and explorative enterprise, rather than as purely static process to which artifacts are forcefully subject.

AI&R Policy

Currently, there exists no international policy or governance regulating artificial intelligence and robotics (Müller & Bostrom, 2016). Although broad and open discussions are currently being undertaken by various nation states, formalized guidelines remain varied, abstract, and mostly built upon existing policy and governance structures at the national or state levels. Aside from the always-present reasons why sovereign states fail to come to agreement as to the governance of any particular thing, one of the primary causes of this difficulty in global AI&R governance is the already-mentioned inability to agree upon the values upon which policy is built (Floridi et al., 2018; Umbrello & De Bellis, 2018). There is no explicitly adopted framework for engaging with such value tensions and moral overload (van den Hoven, Lokhorst, & van de Poel, 2012).

Given that policy design is fundamentally a human endeavour – i.e., politically an endeavour of citizens – it necessarily implicates human values (Mintrom & Luetjens, 2017). Policy creation has typically taken a utilitarian/consequentialist approach to determining what would be most beneficial to stakeholders (Quah & Mishan, 2007). Cost-benefit analysis (CBA) is the primary framing of the utilitarian approach to policy analysis, and has been employed even in future technology speculation and ethics (Barrett & Baum, 2017; Umbrello & Baum, 2018). Although widely practiced, the CBA approach is fraught with inherent weaknesses, some that could prove particularly detrimental given the potential risks of recalcitrant AI&R systems (Baum, 2014; Muehlhauser & Bostrom, 2014; Soares & Fallenstein, 2014). CBA is predicated on the use of utility functions in which values are converted into monetary values, even those things which are traditionally considered irreducible to any numerical values such as art, happiness, and calmness among many others (Sunstein, 2013).

When considering AI&R ethics, and AI&R policy more specifically, and considering the global effects that AI&R does and will continue to exhibit, it is important to account for a wider notion of stakeholder values that extends beyond the narrow confines of moral law theory approaches such as utilitarianism (Umbrello, 2020a). There is an increasing trend by citizens to resist policies that constrain fundamental values such as justice (Rawls, 2001), fairness/equality (Corak, 2016), and autonomy (Peters, 2018). Each of these values, among others, is critical to adoptable and effective policymaking, and because they are values commonly held as central to democratic systems, they thus bolster those systems. Yet they are each difficult, if not impossible, to quantify with monetary values as undertaken in the CBA approach.

Democratic Commitments to AI&R Policy

We should resist being pessimistic as to the potential for global AI policy in which nation states unilaterally agree, though we should also confront the reality that such policy, albeit possible, may take many years, coming at the opportunity cost of addressing present and near-term concerns of AI&R that may otherwise be overlooked. A potentially fruitful initial first step, that is technically expounded in the proceeding sections, is beginning at national levels to design and deploy AI systems towards international goals (i.e., EU High Level Expert Group on Artificial Intelligence [HLEG AI], AI for Social Good factors [AI4SG]), most saliently the UN 2030 Sustainable Development Goals (SDGs).

The United Nations proposed 2030 agenda for sustainable development was a set of goals directed at the design and implementation of a safe and sustainable future founded on the agreed desire for global peace (United Nations, 2019b). In 2015, all of the UN member states adopted the proposal, which aimed at the realization of 17 distinct, yet interconnected goals (See Figure 1). Part of the commitment of the SDG, which should be co-developed (i.e., not exclusive of one another), is a commitment to discussions on building strong and robust democratic institutions and governance structures [SDG #16] (United Nations, 2019a). A common element amongst different types of democratic regimes is a commitment to certain values, such as peaceful and inclusive societies for sustainable development, access to justice for all, as well as accountable and inclusive institutions at all levels (United Nations, 2019b).

Figure 1. United Nations sustainable development goals
(United Nations, 2019b)

The issues necessary for tackling these SDGs are varied, nuanced, and complex. To better address these issues holistically, the UN has a Technology Facilitation Mechanism (TFM) to encourage innovative solutions towards achieving the SDGs by adopting multi-stakeholder participation (United Nations, 2017, 2019). Before every UN session on SDGs, the TFM council assembles to discuss new solutions regarding the SDGs. The UN's *modus operandi* with respect to the SDGs is that technology can be understood as both the problem and potential solution, as well as its adoption of the interactional stance towards technology. Instead of approaching technology as exclusively instrumental or as purely deterministic, it insists on the interactional performance between technology and social factors at an institutional level. By doing so, the UN aims to address these problems holistically, rather than in an ad hoc fashion.

At some level then, SDGs can be understood as being the consequence of technologies, and that the more transformative a technology is, the greater its potential impact. High-speed trading algorithms, for example, provide asymmetric advantages to users, however they're inaccessible to all but those who have the most capital already to employ such systems, which has the potential to exacerbate economic inequalities and unfair marketplaces (Busch, 2016). To this end, understanding the interactional nature of technology and social factors allows for more efficacious design and policy if tackled holistically. This means that AI systems, which are part of the larger sociotechnical *mise en scène* of information and communication technologies such as big data, deep learning, and cognitive computing, allow for a similar holistic approach towards SDG attainment. Umbrello and van de Poel (2020) already attempt to do this by using SDGs as a source of higher-level values that can then be translated through norms such as the AI4SG principles of Floridi, Cowls, King, and Taddeo (2020) to attain design requirements. This is done through the VSD method that is shown below. This approach, however, can be extended by framing it not in terms of specific design requirements for the technologies themselves, but for the policies that co-vary with those technologies. Similarly, because the values underpinning many of the SDGs are likewise fundamental to democratic regimes (a goal of the SDGs in itself), then it can be asserted that good AI&R policy is likewise aligned with such values; else it risks undermining itself.

AI&R policy, for it to be efficacious, while similarly preserving the fundamental values of sustainable democracy, must then explicitly put democracy at its core (Ingram, deLeon, & Schneider, 2016). Value-sensitive policy design (VSPD), policy that is designed to be sensitive to these stated values, among others, can be viewed as co-constructive with democracy (i.e., it constructs democracy while also constructed by it). Given the various forms of democracy and the gradations of citizen participation and direct involvement, policy design will, like technology design, remain a dynamic practice, different between states (United Nations, 2019a). It can then be justified to state that any democratic regime engaging in AI&R policy design that is open to external information and engages with a wide stakeholder pool will consequently be more likely to produce AI&R policy that manifests a more expansive consideration of stakeholder concerns (both citizens and noncitizens).

Because effective policy design is co-constructive of democracy, either supporting or constraining the values deemed important to the polity, it influences the level of democracy permitted within a nation. Given the stakes at play with technologies such as AI&R, which have global impacts, how to construct effective AI&R policy that manages the critical balance between individual autonomy (i.e., SDG #5) and security (i.e., SDG #16) – which is essential for either of the two to exist in any functional way (Bay, 1961) – becomes the central question of the design practice (Scheve & Stasavage, 2017). The following section introduces the VSD approach in greater detail, highlighting strengths of the approach that map onto the issues discussed, showing both how the VSD methodology is aptly suited to dissolving value conflicts and how it affirms the values central to democracy.

VALUE SENSITIVE DESIGN – A DEMOCRATIC APPROACH TO AI&R DESIGN

As with all technologies that implicate some human values, the above analysis of policy similarly implicates human values. Meaning that, there will be inevitable value tensions that arise throughout the design phase as well as after its implementation. As is true traditionally with policy design, as well as with the currently unregulated AI R&D sphere, decisions about how an object is to be designed has typically rested in the hands of the designer (either the engineer, CEO, company, etc.). This top-down approach to design, regardless of the object of the design program, is bound to increase the probability of value tensions that can arise, given the technocratic way that designers go about evaluating the seemingly objective evidence on which the object is built.

Policy, like technology, almost never arises *de nuovo*, but instead is built upon, or at least within, similar and familiar policy perspectives (Peters, 2018). This constrains designers to paradigms that might be inefficient in dealing with technologies like AI that cross national boundaries in which any single policy paradigm may dominate. This does not necessarily entail that good policy is deterministic, i.e., that because policy is constrained by previous policies and policy paradigms, the outcomes of newly introduced policies cannot be truly free from those constraints. Similarly, the technological *deterministic* approach rings a similar bell, in which the 'inevitable' march of progress cannot be halted, and that because each precursor technology determines the types of technologies that come after, humans are impotent to interfere with this progress (Woolgar, 1991).

This deterministic perspective on either policies or technologies must be resisted if responsible innovation paradigms are to be actualized. Value sensitive design takes up an *interactional* stance on technological innovation design, arguing that technologies and societies are co-constructive of one another (Friedman & Hendry, 2019). Humans can guide the design of any given technology towards certain ends, and the technological impact and scope on society thus influence how we interact with that technology and each other (Friedman & Grudin, 1998). This perspective assigns technologies and policy a sufficient level of sociocultural influence while preserving the human potential to guide technologies, embedding them and designing them for the human values of stakeholders that are most beneficial. To that end, the design of socioculturally situated technologies can be achieved while simultaneously being geared towards more international ends by accounting for their impact of achieving the UN's SDGs, which, of course, are intended to be globally beneficial.

The Tripartite Methodology

The VSD approach has traditionally been described as a tripartite methodology consisting of three distinct, yet iterative *investigations*: 1) conceptual investigations, 2) empirical investigations, and 3) technical investigations (see Figure 2). Conceptual investigations involve designers consulting the philosophical literature that may be relevant to the technology under consideration in order to determine some prima facie values that may be implicated in the design program. It is during this point that designers can engage in preliminary stakeholder analyses to determine the relevant direct and indirect stakeholders that may be affected by the deployment of the technology (Borning & Muller, 2012). Empirical investigations take the conceptual work and elicit various stakeholder groups, enrolling them into the design program by employing social scientific means such as surveys, semi-structured interviews, envisioning cards, value sketches and scenarios (Friedman et al., 2017). The goal here is to better understand the values of stakeholders that may support or constrain the development of technology and vice versa. Finally, technical investigations look at how the architecture of the design object itself can support or constrain values.

The approach can be broken down into at least eight steps that designers can follow. They are not to be taken as being in sequential order; instead, designers can begin with whichever step the design program calls for, increasing both the adoptability of the VSD approach into existent design domains, as well as increasing the overall design flow of a program.

1. **Begin by Considering (1) a Value, (2) a Technology, or (3) the Context of Use**: VSD programs can begin with any one of the three. The ideal way to choose is whichever aligns most with the designer's goals or interests (Figure 3).

Figure 2. The recursive VSD tripartite framework employed in this study
Source: (Umbrello, 2020)

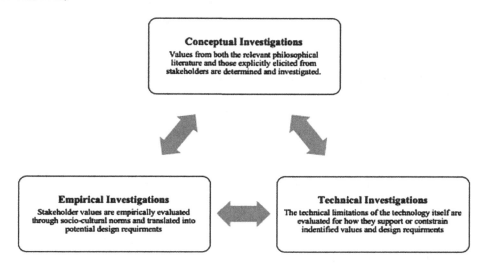

2. **Direct and Indirect Stakeholders:** Methodically determine who the direct and indirect stakeholders are. Direct stakeholders are those individuals who interact directly with the technology itself or its output; indirect stakeholders instead are those individuals/groups that are also impacted by the system, though they never interact directly with it directly.

3. **Identify Harms and Benefits for Each Stakeholder Group:** Identify how the technology in questions will both positively and negatively affect each of the stakeholder groups.

4. **Map Harms and Benefits onto Corresponding Values:** At times the mapping between harms and benefits and corresponding values will be one of identity; at other times, the mapping will be multi-faceted (that is, a single harm might implicate multiple values, such as both security and autonomy).

Figure 3. Starting considerations for VSD. Typically, one of the three is most pertinent to any given design
Source: (Gazzaneo, Padovano, & Umbrello, 2020)

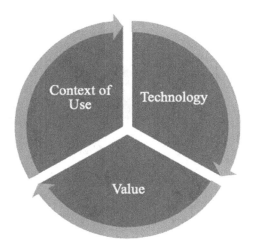

5. **Conduct a Conceptual Investigation of Key Values:** Establish precise working definitions of each of the values elicited. Designers employ the philosophical literature in lieu of conceptual investigations to more accurately define these values and the potential issues that already exist with certain understandings of these values. How these values can be translated into norms and how those can then be translated into design requirements (and vice versa) is also investigated (See Figure 4).

6. **Identify Potential Value Conflicts:** In design spaces, value conflicts are typically not be read as 'either/or' dichotomies, but as tensions and constraints on the design space (van de Poel, 2014). Typical value conflicts include accountability vs. privacy, trust vs. security, environmental sustainability vs. economic development, privacy vs. security, and hierarchical control vs. democratization, among others (van den Hoven et al., 2012).

7. **Technical Investigation Heuristic and Value Conflicts:** Technical structures and tools will often dissolve, if not call, multiple conflicting values, often in the form of design trade-offs. Hence, designers here should aim to make explicit how a design trade-off maps onto a value conflict and differentially affects different groups of stakeholders (Umbrello, 2018b).

8. **Technical Investigation Heuristic and Unanticipated Consequences and Value Conflicts:** In order to be positioned to respond agilely to unanticipated consequences and value conflicts, when possible, design flexibility into the underlying technical architecture to support post-deployment modifications.

Figure 4. Bi-directional values hierarchy
Source: (Umbrello, 2019b)

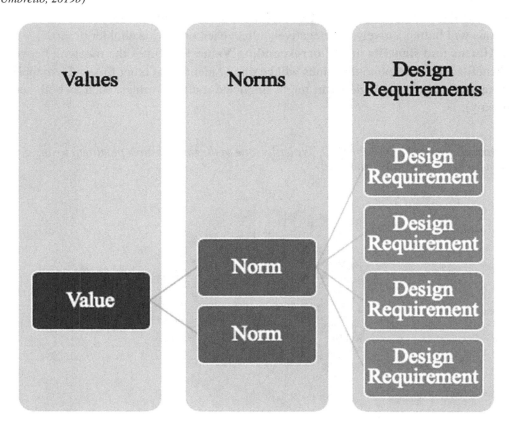

The approach of VSD is then fundamentally participatory, democratically relying on the polity of stakeholders as a fundamental constituent of the design program that will ultimately impact them. Thus stakeholder elicitations, values, and analyses are what technologies, and perhaps policies, can be designed *for*; rather than remaining an afterthought, integrated *ex post facto* deployment, or overlooked entirely. There is, however, a certain level of technocracy within VSD. Although stakeholder values are ultimately the center of the design paradigm, the designers and design teams have final control of the design itself and the final product. Similar to representative democratic systems in which citizens participate but do not ultimately decide, VSD takes an approach of designing *for* citizen values, but designed by designers.

We can begin to see how good policy – that which supports, and, in turn, is supported by democratic regimes – is inextricably linked with VSD. Not only can the VSD approach be used as a democratic and participatory methodology by policymakers in drafting new policies for AI at a global level, but VSD is a form of policy in itself. Given the philosophical foundation of VSD as an interactional approach to considering technologies and their impacts on the implicated polity – and one that is fundamentally committed to certain universal values such as *human well-being, justice,* and *dignity* (Friedman & Hendry, 2019, p. 173) – VSD is political in that it affirms as its central values of considerations, those foundational to good policy and democracy: human well-being, human dignity, justice, welfare, autonomy, and human rights, among others (Friedman, Kahn Jr., & Borning, 2008). These are directly in line with the SDG's outlines in the preceding sections, more saliently well-being as SDG #3, justice as SDG #16, and dignity as the culmination of all 17 SDGs.

ILLUSTRATING VALUE SENSITIVE POLICY DESIGN AND VSD AS POLICY

As mentioned, VSD appears to be in possession of a double potency. Firstly, policy design can be accomplished through a VSD approach. Given that the approach affirms as its central values those that are necessary for the design of good policy; i.e., the values central to democracy and that are aligned with international goals towards those end since VSD is aptly capable as a design approach to achieving these ends (see Friedman & Kahn Jr., 2002). Secondly, because VSD is founded on the principles underlying those values, other objects of design, such as AI&R similarly, are brought into the paradigm of designing for democratic values. In this way, VSD supports democracy via design by acting as a policy-as-practice framework (see van de Kaa, Rezaei, Taebi, van de Poel, & Kizhakenath, 2019).

Yet, these values remain purely abstract, even when considering an applied design approach such as VSD. To move from abstract to concrete, some examples for conceptualizing both of these potentialities that VSD possesses are presented below. Here some preliminary and cursory examples are given in the form presented in Figure 4 in which the bi-directional hierarchy of values can be conceptualized, either beginning with a value or the other way, beginning with a design requirement.

Figure 5 is one of the ways in which two core values that have been heavily discussed in the field of informatics, particularly as it relates to machine learning and data set processing, are data privacy and consent (Floridi et al., 2020). VSD practitioners can translate the values through various sociocultural norms in which the technology program is situated in order to more accurately determine the technical design requirements that can map those values. The norms, and even specific design requirements, can be policy-driven if existent. For example, the EU's General Data Protection Regulation 2016/679 (GDPR) provides norms that various actors must comply to, with regards to the processing and transfer for personal data. The norm 'maximize privacy,' for example, can be satisfied under the GDPR if the systems

Figure 5. Top-down approach beginning with the values of data privacy and consent that can then be translated into values through norms

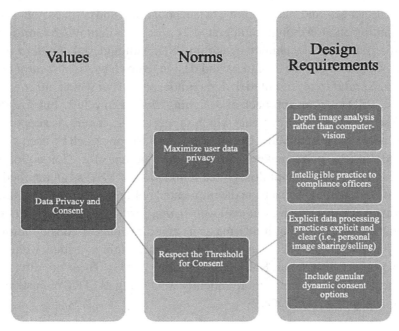

employed in design are intelligible to data protection officers to ensure compliance of the processing and use of data in accordance with the other statues laid out in the GDPR. This is one of a myriad of ways of conceptualizing such values as design requirements; the visualization is employed by designers to better conceptualize how to plan design programs to be compliant to stakeholder values, the GDPR being one of a multitude of considerations.

Data privacy and consent are taken as examples of the many values that are considered when designing AI&R, however, it is particularly salient for this discussion given their importance to other democratic values such as safety and human dignity, which they could not exist without (Nissenbaum, 2009; Solove, 2008). Because personal information is often considered as foundational to the concept of the individual, the core of democracy, respect for data privacy, and consent of its use, are similarly the core of affirming individual safety and dignity (Floridi, 2016). Similarly, given that data privacy forms one of the foundational values of the VSD approach (Umbrello, 2019b; Umbrello & De Bellis, 2018), its adoption for the development of AI&R systems proves particularly relevant and salient.

As mentioned, however, the VSD approach need not only be seen as a tool for designing technologies for existent policies, but it is also a form of policy itself, given the fundamental values on which the approach has been built are those of good policy; e.g., democratic values. If we take, for example, the same hierarchy in Figure 4, but reverse it – solely for illustration's sake of working from the bottom up – we can affirm certain values *ex post facto*, beginning with design requirements (see Figure 6).

Certain design requirements for technologies under question may be presented *prima facia*. The VSD approach is aptly equipped to begin from this stage, translating these design requirements into more general sociocultural norms (such as the AI4SG principles outlined by Floridi et al. 2020) and finally into more universal moral values (i.e., UN SDGs). Figure 6 illustrates how certain design requirements

Figure 6. Beginning with design requirements that can uncover and inform policy requirements

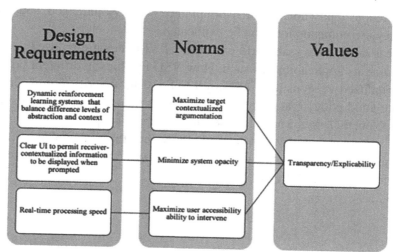

can be translated into norms that can satisfy a functional definition of transparency or explicability within the context of algorithmic decision-makers. They are in no way exclusive nor exhaustive, but demonstrate home some values that may be important, if not fundamental to certain technologies, in this case AI, are crucial if they are to be development for the social good in mind (Floridi et al., 2020). As such, the VSD approach, adopted within the general and distributed context of designing AI&R for social good, can be used to help inform policymakers in developing for certain stakeholders the values deemed necessary for those ends.

This becomes particularly prescient when considering the emerging sociocultural and ethical impacts of transformative technologies such as AI&R will have as they become more embedded in different sociocultural contexts. VSD's fundamental practice of being iterative and self-improving situates it in a unique position to be adopted by engineers and designers to be compliant to stakeholder values while simultaneously helping policymakers to make more technologically compatible policy decisions that support responsible innovation, both at national and international levels.

LIMITATIONS AND FUTURE RESEARCH PROJECTS

The aim of this chapter has been to consider the design of good policy, particularly that of policy regarding artificial intelligence and robotics within the value sensitive design approach. How VSD can be used to design AI&R to be compliant to stakeholder values and current policy has been shown, and historically has marked VSD as being an aptly suited approach in doing so (van Wynsberghe & Robbins, 2014; Warnier, Dechesne, & Brazier, 2014; Woelfer et al., 2011). Similarly, how values can be derived during the design process when beginning with the technology has been discussed, and how such can be used to help policymakers make more relevant and consistent decisions when considering AI&R.

Still, there are areas of limitations that this chapter does not explore, but warrant future research. Firstly, researchers should look at making the VSD explicitly functional as being a policymaking tool, one that policymakers themselves look to, for making intelligible technology policy. Similarly, and perhaps more pressing, is how policymakers can make VSD approaches more adoptable by current AI&R groups to create a more homogenous landscape in which compliance can be adjudicated, and how emerging and new values and policy recommendations can be explicated.

Ultimately, what is needed are real-world examples of VSD being employed as an explicit policy tool to better determine its applicability as such. How VSD can handle different policies for different sociocultural contextualized versions of AI&R is yet to be seen, but critical in determining how VSD can be used to create good policy that supports and balances the stakeholder values that are central to democratic regimes. Nonetheless, the need for open and collaborative policymaking is required if AI&R is to be designed in a responsible way that supports the values that stakeholders affirm. This chapter seeks to spark the conversation on how to put these values into practice, given the urgency of developing a transformative technology that is already underway.

CONCLUSION

This chapter looked at how the VSD methodology is aptly suited as a design approach to designing good policy. VSD's core foundation is predicated on the values that support those of democratic regimes, which places it in a unique position to design policy as it would any other technology, by enrolling stakeholders, eliciting their values, mapping harms and benefits, and designing policy that is interactive, modifiable, and reflective of those values. The specific example of AI&R is used to illustrate the salience and necessity of adopting such an approach if collective policy and governance of those systems is to be achieved. Similarly, an argument was also put forward that VSD, given its philosophical foundations and starting points, is itself a form of policy as it guides design toward certain political ends, those that are affirmed by democratic regimes.

ACKNOWLEDGMENT

This research received no specific grant from any funding agency in the public, commercial, or not-for-profit sectors. All remaining errors are the author's alone. The views expressed are not necessarily those of the Institute for Ethics and Emerging Technologies. The content of this publication has not been approved by the United Nations and does not reflect the views of the United Nations or its officials or Member States.

REFERENCES

Barrett, A. M., & Baum, S. D. (2017). Risk Analysis and Risk Management for the Artificial Superintelligence Research and Development Process. In V. Callaghan, J. Miller, R. Yampolskiy, & S. Armstrong (Eds.), *The technological singularity: Managing the journey* (pp. 127–140). Springer-Verlag Berlin Heidelberg. doi:10.1007/978-3-662-54033-6_6

Baum, S. D. (2014). The great downside dilemma for risky emerging technologies. *Physica Scripta*, *89*(12), 10. doi:10.1088/0031-8949/89/12/128004

Bay, C. (1961). The Structure of Freedom. *Science and Society*, *25*(1).

Ben-Haim, Y., Osteen, C. D., & Moffitt, L. J. (2013). Policy dilemma of innovation: An info-gap approach. *Ecological Economics*, *85*, 130–138. doi:10.1016/j.ecolecon.2012.08.011

Bødker, K., Kensing, F., & Simonsen, J. (2009). *Participatory IT design: Designing for business and workplace realities*. MIT press.

Borning, A., & Muller, M. (2012). Next steps for value sensitive design. *Proceedings of the 2012 ACM Annual Conference on Human Factors in Computing Systems - CHI '12*, 1125. 10.1145/2207676.2208560

Bos, C., Walhout, B., Peine, A., & van Lente, H. (2014). Steering with big words: Articulating ideographs in research programs. *Journal of Responsible Innovation*, *1*(2), 151–170. doi:10.1080/2329946 0.2014.922732

Busch, D. (2016). MiFID II: Regulating high frequency trading, other forms of algorithmic trading and direct electronic market access. *Law and Financial Markets Review*, *10*(2), 72–82. doi:10.1080/17521 440.2016.1200333

Corak, M. (2016). 'Inequality is the root of social evil,' or Maybe Not? Two Stories about Inequality and Public Policy. *Canadian Public Policy*, *42*(4), 367–414. doi:10.3138/cpp.2016-056

Correljé, A., Cuppen, E., Dignum, M., Pesch, U., & Taebi, B. (2015). Responsible Innovation in Energy Projects: Values in the Design of Technologies, Institutions and Stakeholder Interactions. In B.-J. Koops, I. Oosterlaken, H. Romijn, T. Swierstra, & J. van den Hoven (Eds.), *Responsible innovation 2* (pp. 183–200). Springer International Publishing. doi:10.1007/978-3-319-17308-5_10

Davis, J., & Nathan, L. P. (2014). Value Sensitive Design: Applications, Adaptations, and Critiques. In J. van den Hoven, P. E. Vermaas, & I. van de Poel (Eds.), *Handbook of ethics, values, and technological design: Sources, theory, values and application domains* (pp. 1–26). Springer Netherlands. doi:10.1007/978-94-007-6994-6_3-1

Dignum, V. (2019). *Responsible artificial intelligence: How to develop and use AI in a responsible way*. Springer International Publishing. doi:10.1007/978-3-030-30371-6

Ehn, P. (2016). Design, Democracy and Work: Exploring the Scandinavian Participatory Design Tradition. *Critical Design/Critical Futures 2016 Symposium*.

Fallan, K. (2015). Our Common Future. Joining Forces for Histories of Sustainable Design. *Technoscienza: Italian Journal of Science & Technology Studies*, *5*(2), 15–32. http://www.tecnoscienza.net/index.php/tsj/article/view/201%5Cnhttp://www.tecnoscienza.net/index.php/tsj/article/download/201/136%5Cn

Floridi, L. (2016). On human dignity as a foundation for the right to privacy. *Philosophy & Technology*, *29*(4), 307–312. doi:10.100713347-016-0220-8

Floridi, L., Cowls, J., Beltrametti, M., Chatila, R., Chazerand, P., Dignum, V., Luetge, C., Madelin, R., Pagallo, U., Rossi, F., Schafer, B., Valcke, P., & Vayena, E. (2018). AI4People - An Ethical Framework for a Good AI Society: Opportunities, Risks, Principles, and Recommendations. *Minds and Machines*, *28*(December), 1–24. doi:10.100711023-018-9482-5 PMID:30930541

Floridi, L., Cowls, J., King, T. C., & Taddeo, M. (2020). Designing AI for Social Good: Seven Essential Factors. *Science and Engineering Ethics*, 1–26. doi:10.100711948-020-00213-5 PMID:32246245

Friedman, B., & Grudin, J. (1998). Trust and accountability: preserving human values in interactional experience. In *CHI 98 conference summary on Human factors in computing systems* (p. 213). ACM. doi:10.1145/286498.286699

Friedman, B., & Hendry, D. G. (2019). *Value sensitive design: Shaping technology with moral imagination*. MIT Press. doi:10.7551/mitpress/7585.001.0001

Friedman, B., Hendry, D. G., & Borning, A. (2017). A Survey of Value Sensitive Design Methods. *Foundations and Trends® in Human–Computer Interaction, 11*(2), 63–125. doi:10.1561/1100000015

Friedman, B., & Kahn Jr., P. H. (2002). Value sensitive design: Theory and methods. *University of Washington Technical Report*, 1–8.

Friedman, B., Kahn Jr., P. H., & Borning, A. (2008). Value Sensitive Design and Information Systems. *Human-Computer Interaction and Management Information Systems: Foundations*, 69–101. doi:10.1145/242485.242493

Friedman, B., Kahn, P. H., Borning, A., & Huldtgren, A. (2013). Value Sensitive Design and Information Systems. In N. Doorn, D. Schuurbiers, I. van de Poel, & M. E. Gorman (Eds.), *Early engagement and new technologies: Opening up the laboratory* (pp. 55–95). Springer Netherlands. doi:10.1007/978-94-007-7844-3_4

Gazzaneo, L., Padovano, A., & Umbrello, S. (2020). Designing Smart Operator 4.0 for Human Values: A Value Sensitive Design Approach. In *International Conference on Industry 4.0 and Smart Manufacturing (ISM 2019) in Procedia Manufacturing* (pp. 219–226). Elsevier. 10.1016/j.promfg.2020.02.073

Gregor, P., Sloan, D., & Newell, A. F. (2005). Disability and Technology: Building Barriers or Creating Opportunities? *Advances in Computers, 64*, 283–346. Advance online publication. doi:10.1016/S0065-2458(04)64007-1

Hyppönen, H., Kemppainen, E., Gill, J., Slater, J., & Poulson, D. (2000). H. Hyppönen, E. Kemppainen, J. Gill, J. Slater, & D. Poulson (Eds.) Handbook on inclusive design of telematics applications. Themes/STAKES 2.

Ingram, H., deLeon, P., & Schneider, A. (2016). Conclusion: Public policy theory and democracy: The elephant in the corner. In Contemporary approaches to public policy (pp. 175–200). Springer.

Lockton, D., Harrison, D., & Stanton, N. A. (2016). Design for Sustainable Behaviour: Investigating design methods for influencing user behaviour. *Annual Review of Policy Design, 4*(1), 1–10.

McConnell, A. (2010). *Understanding policy success: Rethinking public policy*. Macmillan International Higher Education. doi:10.1007/978-1-137-08228-2

Mintrom, M., & Luetjens, J. (2017). Creating public value: Tightening connections between policy design and public management. *Policy Studies Journal: the Journal of the Policy Studies Organization, 45*(1), 170–190. doi:10.1111/psj.12116

Muehlhauser, L., & Bostrom, N. (2014). Why We Need Friendly AI. *Think (London, England)*, *13*(36), 41–47. doi:10.1017/S1477175613000316

Müller, V. C., & Bostrom, N. (2016). Future Progress in Artificial Intelligence: A Survey of Expert Opinion. In V. C. Müller (Ed.), *Fundamental issues of artificial intelligence* (pp. 555–572). Springer International Publishing., doi:10.1007/978-3-319-26485-1_33

Nissenbaum, H. (2009). *Privacy in context: Technology, policy, and the integrity of social life.* Stanford University Press.

Peters, B. G. (2018). *Policy problems and policy design.* Edward Elgar Publishing. doi:10.4337/9781786431356

Quah, E., & Mishan, E. J. (2007). *Cost-benefit analysis.* Routledge.

Rawls, J. (2001). *Justice as fairness: A restatement.* Harvard University Press.

Ruzic, L., & Sanfod, J. A. (2017). Universal Design Mobile Interface Guidelines (UDMIG) for an Aging Population. In Mobile e-Health (pp. 17–37). Springer.

Santoni de Sio, F., & van den Hoven, J. (2018). Meaningful Human Control over Autonomous Systems: A Philosophical Account. *Frontiers in Robotics and AI.* https://www.frontiersin.org/article/10.3389/frobt.2018.00015

Scheve, K., & Stasavage, D. (2017). Wealth inequality and democracy. *Annual Review of Political Science*, *20*(1), 451–468. doi:10.1146/annurev-polisci-061014-101840

Sieber, S. (2013). *Fatal remedies: The ironies of social intervention.* Springer Science & Business Media.

Simon, H. A. (1988). The science of design: Creating the artificial. *Design Issues*, *4*(1/2), 67–82. doi:10.2307/1511391

Soares, N., & Fallenstein, B. (2014). *Agent Foundations for Aligning Machine Intelligence with Human Interests : A Technical Research Agenda.* doi:10.1007/978-3-662-54033-6_5

Solove, D. J. (2008). Understanding privacy (Vol. 173). Harvard University Press.

Sunstein, C. R. (2013). The value of a statistical life: Some clarifications and puzzles. *Journal of Benefit-Cost Analysis*, *4*(2), 237–261. doi:10.1515/jbca-2013-0019

Umbrello, S. (2018a). *Safe-(for whom?)-by-Design: Adopting a Posthumanist Ethics for Technology Design.* York University. doi:10.13140/RG.2.2.29726.38720

Umbrello, S. (2018b). The moral psychology of value sensitive design: The methodological issues of moral intuitions for responsible innovation. *Journal of Responsible Innovation*, *5*(2), 186–200. doi:10.1080/23299460.2018.1457401

Umbrello, S. (2019a). Atomically Precise Manufacturing and Responsible Innovation: A Value Sensitive Design Approach to Explorative Nanophilosophy. *International Journal of Technoethics*, *10*(2), 1–21. doi:10.4018/IJT.2019070101

Umbrello, S. (2019b). Beneficial Artificial Intelligence Coordination by Means of a Value Sensitive Design Approach. *Big Data and Cognitive Computing*, *3*(1), 5.

Umbrello, S. (2020a). Imaginative Value Sensitive Design: Using Moral Imagination Theory to Inform Responsible Technology Design. *Science and Engineering Ethics*, *26*(2), 575–595. doi:10.100711948-019-00104-4 PMID:30972629

Umbrello, S. (2020b). Meaningful Human Control Over Smart Home Systems: A Value Sensitive Design Approach. *HUMANA.MENTE Journal of Philosophical Studies, 13*(37), 40-65. https://www.humana-mente.eu/index.php/HM/article/view/315

Umbrello, S., & Baum, S. D. (2018). Evaluating future nanotechnology: The net societal impacts of atomically precise manufacturing. *Futures*, *100*(June), 63–73. doi:10.1016/j.futures.2018.04.007

Umbrello, S., & De Bellis, A. F. (2018). A Value-Sensitive Design Approach to Intelligent Agents. In R. V. Yampolskiy (Ed.), *Artificial Intelligence Safety and Security* (pp. 395–410). CRC Press. doi:10.13140/RG.2.2.17162.77762

Umbrello, S., & van de Poel, I. (2020). *Mapping Value Sensitive Design onto AI for Social Good Principles*. https://www.academia.edu/43347384/Mapping_Value_Sensitive_Design_

United Nations. (2017). *Data Privacy, Ethics and Protection Guidance Note on Big Data For Achievement of the 2030 Agenda.* https://unsdg.un.org/resources/data-privacy-ethics-and-protection-guidance-note-big-data-achievement-2030-agenda

United Nations. (2019a). *Democracy & the SDGs.* https://sustainabledevelopment.un.org/

United Nations. (2019b). Sustainable development goals. *GAIA.*

van de Kaa, G., Rezaei, J., Taebi, B., van de Poel, I., & Kizhakenath, A. (2019). How to Weigh Values in Value Sensitive Design: A Best Worst Method Approach for the Case of Smart Metering. *Science and Engineering Ethics*. Advance online publication. doi:10.100711948-019-00105-3 PMID:30963389

van de Poel, I. (2014). Conflicting Values in Design. In J. van den Hoven, P. E. Vermaas, & I. van de Poel (Eds.), *Handbook of Ethics, Values, and Technological Design: Sources, Theory, Values and Application Domains* (pp. 1–23). Springer Netherlands. doi:10.1007/978-94-007-6994-6_5-1

van den Hoven, J. (2013). Architecture and Value-Sensitive Design. In C. Basta & S. Moroni (Eds.), *Ethics, design and planning of the built environment* (p. 224). Springer Science & Business Media. https://books.google.ca/books?id=VVM_AAAAQBAJ&dq=moral

van den Hoven, J. (2017). The Design Turn in Applied Ethics. In J. van den Hoven, S. Miller, & T. Pogge (Eds.), *Designing in Ethics* (pp. 11–31). Cambridge University Press., doi:10.1017/9780511844317.002

van den Hoven, J., Lokhorst, G. J., & van de Poel, I. (2012). Engineering and the Problem of Moral Overload. *Science and Engineering Ethics*, *18*(1), 143–155. doi:10.100711948-011-9277-z PMID:21533834

van den Hoven, J., & Manders-Huits, N. (2009). Value-Sensitive Design. In *A Companion to the Philosophy of Technology* (pp. 477–480). Wiley-Blackwell. doi:10.1002/9781444310795.ch86

van Wynsberghe, A. (2013). Designing Robots for Care: Care Centered Value-Sensitive Design. *Science and Engineering Ethics*, *19*(2), 407–433. doi:10.100711948-011-9343-6 PMID:22212357 van Wynsberghe, A., & Robbins, S. (2014). Ethicist as Designer: A Pragmatic Approach to Ethics in the Lab. *Science and Engineering Ethics*, 20(4), 947–961. doi:10.100711948-013-9498-4 PMID:24254219

Warnier, M., Dechesne, F., & Brazier, F. (2014). Design for the Value of Privacy. In J. van den Hoven, P. E. Vermaas, & I. van de Poel (Eds.), *Handbook of Ethics, Values, and Technological Design: Sources, Theory, Values and Application Domains* (pp. 1–14). Springer Netherlands. doi:10.1007/978-94-007-6994-6_17-1

Winkler, T., & Spiekermann, S. (2019). Human Values as the Basis for Sustainable Information System Design. *IEEE Technology and Society Magazine*, 38(3), 34–43. doi:10.1109/MTS.2019.2930268

Woelfer, J. P., Iverson, A., Hendry, D. G., Friedman, B., & Gill, B. T. (2011). Improving the Safety of Homeless Young People with Mobile Phones: Values, Form and Function. In *Proceedings of the SIGCHI Conference on Human Factors in Computing Systems* (pp. 1707–1716). New York, NY: ACM. 10.1145/1978942.1979191

Woolgar, S. (1991). The Turn to Technology in Social Studies of Science. *Science, Technology & Human Values*, 16(1), 20–50. doi:10.1177/016224399101600102

Yoo, D., Derthick, K., Ghassemian, S., Hakizimana, J., Gill, B., & Friedman, B. (2016). Multi-lifespan design thinking: Two methods and a case study with the Rwandan diaspora. In *Proceedings of the 2016 CHI Conference on Human Factors in Computing Systems* (pp. 4423–4434). ACM. 10.1145/2858036.2858366

Chapter 8
Hauntology of the Machinic

Atsuhide Ito
Solent University, UK & University of the Arts London, UK

ABSTRACT

The chapter observes the distinction between the mechanical and the machinic, and moves beyond the metaphors of android (Metropolis), or cyborg (Donna Haraway), and considers how the machinic has brought new cognitive patterns for human subjects to interact with their environment and others. Artists' dislocation from the central agent of production has opened passages for the posthuman mode of production. Consequently, the machine has become an integral part of artwork and of the artist. Contrary to this development, some artists retain the machine's materiality as a form of Other. The chapter argues that the machine remains as a form of externalization of the Other within the human subject.

INTRODUCTION

Machine ethics can be found entrenched in modern art. The artistic use of machines in art throughout modern time affirms art's intimate and historical entanglement with technology. A tenuous relationship of right and wrong is illuminated often by antagonism between the human and the machine, the latter expressed as an alien force that threatens the human subject's agency for creativity. Artwork is often perceived as a product of a singular mind meld between artists and results of their artistic labor, quite dissimilar to a consumer product made by machines in a factory. While a viewer of a painting may be able to trace the thought processes of a painter by contemplating gestural marks left on the painting and through other evident artifacts, similar to consumer products made by automated machines in a factory, many contemporary artworks today are made by, and with, machines. Such works question the artist as a sole agent of art production. This chapter reflects this antagonism, and situates moments of artistic ethical contentions, while philosophically scrutinizing the notion of the machine. To begin, the terms 'mechanical' and 'machinic' are contrasted in order to re-imagine machine ethics in the context of artistic freedom and critique.

In his chapter "Machinery and Large-Scale Industry" in *The Capital*, Karl Marx (1867, 1990) expresses his anxiety about machinic intrusion into factory floors: "The instrument of labour [machines] strikes down the worker. The direct antagonism between the two is at its most apparent whenever newly intro-

DOI: 10.4018/978-1-7998-4894-3.ch008

Copyright © 2021, IGI Global. Copying or distributing in print or electronic forms without written permission of IGI Global is prohibited.

duced machinery enters into competition with handicrafts or manufacturers handed down from former times" (p. 559). Marx in this chapter emphasizes the competition between the machine and the worker, as machines: 1) replace the worker's involvement into production, and 2) carry out tasks more efficiently and productively. Written earlier between 1857 and 1861, in the section "The Fragment on Machines" in *Grundrisse* (*Foundations of the Critique of Political Economy*), Marx touches on the worker's cognitive relation with machines, observing that "[t]he worker's activity, reduced to a mere abstraction of activity, is determined and regulated on all sides by the movement of the machinery, and not the opposite" (2015, p. 614). In short, the worker in the production process is subordinated to machinery. Marx elaborates:

Labour appears, rather, merely as a conscious organ, scattered among the individual living workers at numerous points of the mechanical system; subsumed under the total process of the machinery itself, as itself only a link of the system, whose unity exists not in the living workers, but rather in the living (active) machinery, which confronts his individual, insignificant doings as a mighty organism (p. 615).

Gerald Raunig aptly summarizes that "Marx describes their relationship between humans and machines primarily as social subjugation [...] Marx seems to follow the pair of metaphors depicting the machine as a gigantic organism and the human beings as its dependent, appropriated components" (2010, p. 22). From this perspective, the machine enslaves the human subject, rather than the human subject being in control of the machine. Consequently, the machine poses ethical problems, as its use threatens the human's autonomy over her/his own actions.

The humanists' fear of the machine threatening the human agent's autonomy is vividly illustrated in a scene from Charlie Chaplin's classic 1936 film, *Modern Times,* where physical actions exemplify the subject's antagonism with the machine while the worker attempts to resist enslavement to the machine. Chaplin plays a character who works at the assembly. A conveyor belt in front of him brings parts faster than he can manage to handle. As he tries even harder to manage, he is swallowed into the machine. The machine is depicted as a gigantic monster with a long and fast tongue of a conveyor belt. As Gilles Deleuze observes, it is "Chaplin, who advances by means of tools, and is opposed to the machine" (1986, p. 175).

In contrast, Deleuze celebrates Buster Keaton's film, *The General* (1926), in which Keaton as a protagonist actively enchains himself to a concatenation of machinic operations.

The steam engine named "The General" is a machine with which Keaton's character collaborates to win a civil war. Keaton' character in a civil war is distinct from Chaplin's factory worker battling in a factory, antagonistic to the mechanical operations built into the factory production. Gerald Raunig (2010) takes this distinction that Deleuze (1986) makes in his *Cinema 1*, between Chaplin's and Keaton's perceptions toward 'the machine' and he further distinguishes the machinic from the mechanical. The mechanical is characterized by its clunky co-ordinations between assembled parts of machinery. The clumsiness of the operations contributes to the antagonism between the human subject and the parts of the machinery. Whereas, the machinic is defined by its smooth and spontaneous concatenations in which the subject is integrated into its operation, even subsumed. Raunig says:

What is evident in this, first of all, is an anticipation of the double relationship of social subjection and machinic enslavement: the machine not only forms its subjects, an automaton, as an apparatus, as a structure, as a purely technical machine in the final stage of the development of labour; it is also permeated by mechanical, intellectual and social "organs," which not only drive and operate it, but also successively develop, renew and even invent it. (2010, p. 24)

For Raunig, the machine is "a compound work, whose movements are grounded in the type of composition" (2010, p. 92). Raunig elaborates the notion of the machinic further by saying that it is "a concatenation of singularities, as a profoundly polyphonous, even a-harmonious composition without a composer" (p. 93). In the sense, furthermore, that "[t]he general intellect no longer presents itself only in the knowledge contained and enclosed in the system of technical machines, but rather in the immeasurable and boundless cooperation of cognitive affective workers" (p. 115).

Preceding Deleuze and Raunig, and Chaplin and Keaton, sociologist Emile Durkheim, leading proponent of Functionalism as social theory, conceived society as a mechanical system; metaphorically speaking, society is a clockwork operation in which parts function to allow the whole work.[1] For Durkheim, a member of society is a cog in the larger machine. In this model, the individual's sense of autonomy over his or her life is illusionary. Everyone, and every part of society, should fit into the mechanical structure of the whole. To follow Durkheim (1897, 2002), when one does not fit to the whole, the individual may choose an option of suicide. The Functionalist model is a static model and it does not take historical dynamics into consideration. In this particular sense, the Functionalist model fails to explain, either the human subject or the society, as a dynamic and mutable agent in time. And yet, the model liberates us from the polemics between humanism that condemn human enslavement to the machine and 'technological fascism' exemplified in the Futurists who embraced the machine as a key to their utopian vision. For Durkheim, the human subject is both an enslaved machinery part and *res cogitans*, a thinking subject who is able to organize his or her own will within the mechanical structure of society.

Donna Haraway in 1984 published her now classic "Cyborg Manifesto" in which a prosthetic extension of the human body is symbolically celebrated against the purist perception of the perfect body, embracing the idea of alien elements infiltrating the 'pure' body. Prior to that publication, the pure, perfect, and supreme human body such as that exemplified in Leni Riefenstahl's film *Olympia* (1938) had been admired and, consequently as result of Riefenstahl's connection to the Third Reich, appalled at the same time. No longer does the pure body retain the supreme position in the hierarchy of bodies.

In artist Matthew Barney's 2002 film entitled *Cremaster 3*, double amputee, Paralympian and model Aimee Mullins, is cast in a number of roles, normalizing prosthetics. More strikingly, in the artist OR-LAN's films, the audience follows a plastic surgery operation on her body as a piece of artwork, literally transforming her 'natural' body into a cyborg. Haraway's (1984) influential manifesto celebrates impure body, which includes impaired, and technologically enhanced bodies, to contrast with the pure and supreme body of western male roots back to the ancient Greek statues that are remodeled in Leni Riefenstahl's controversial film *Olympia* (1938), made during the Nazi era. However, as Jonathan Crary (2014) points out, Haraway's celebration of the suppressed other bodies, injured, imperfect, and also absorbed otherness including machines, can be seen in a different light. Crary in his 2014 book, *24/7*, bemoans that capitalism through Modernity has an embedded project that has been erasing boundaries between day and night, nature and culture, and other dichotomies.

Haraway's point of deconstructing an essentialism pervasive in polemic dichotomies between pure versus impure, male versus female, perfection versus imperfection, remains ethically relevant decades after its publication. On the other hand, to take Crary's point, the notion of cyborg can be understood as a machinic invasion of the body already porous, to be colonized by prosthetic extensions that enhance it to perform under the capitalist rationality of production. Here, the term "invasion" does not mean to indicate a pure body prior to the conquest of the body by the machine, and the machine does not necessarily empower the subject residing in the body. Instead, the machine is already programmed to perform in the capitalist rationale of labor, production of commodities, and consumption of them. For Crary, the human body adopted the machine-other long before Haraway's treatise.

In fine art, mechanical nuances of the human body form shine through Marcel Duchamp's painting, *The Bride Stripped Bare by Her Bachelors, Even* (1915-23). Duchamp's piece shows an abstract form on the upper part of the glass panel, and there are bachelors who look like machine parts in the lower part of the same panel. Why this title? Duchamp made a painting entitled, *Nude Descending the Staircase*, in 1912, in which the nude figure is hardly at all depicted in an erotic way. Instead, the body descending the staircase resembles Etienne Jules Marey's photographs of *The Running Lion Tamer* (1886), in which the lion tamer's movements are a series of abstract lines, and the human figure is no longer recognizable. The photographic image shows the mechanical patterns of the tamer's movements. In Duchamp's *Nude Descending the Staircase*, the nude's motions and rhythm of descent are structured by the architectural features of the staircase.

Needless to say, staircases have been an architectural feature of buildings long before Duchamp's nude in his painting. Yet, Duchamp registers in front of the viewer, the recognition of the descending movement as a mechanical one. Following this example, *The Bride Stripped Bare by Her Bachelors, Even* is an analogy of desires expressed in the mechanical organization of psychological dynamics. The manner of organization in the work is Duchamp's understanding of how desires are structured within the mechanized system. Nonetheless, libidinal dynamics, for Duchamp, required a factory of desire, or a schemata of libidinal mapping in *The Bride Stripped Bare by Her Bachelors, Even*.

In the latter part of the twentieth century, Rebecca Horn exhibited a substantial number of machines as art. Horn often appeared as a performer in her earlier works, but gradually the artist's presence in her work diminished, and the machine began to replace the artist-performer. In *Ballet of the Woodpeckers (Das Ballet der Spechte)*, 1986, the spectator is surrounded by large rectangle mirrors on walls. There are hammers attached to each mirror and like a woodpecker who pecks a tree, a hammer would knock the mirror erratically. The sound of knocking is disturbing and generates discomfort. The spectators' presence is registered by silent mirrors which screen them in the reflection. Instead of contemplating on a piece of sculpture or a painting, the spectators look at themselves, and while gazing at their images, machinic "woodpeckers" awaken them from their gazes. In this work, along with many others by Horn, absence of the performer and presence of the animated machine are coupled, and the machine is often unpredictable and erratic, inducing a sense of the uncanny. Horn's machines appear hauntingly impulsive and unpredictable. They start moving when unexpected, taking the spectators by surprise; yet, the work does not mourn any loss of artist's presence, nor does it nostalgically yearn for a recovery of singular gestures the artist might have made. The erratic and unpredictable movements of the machine alone situate Horn's work in the category of the machinic instead of mechanical.

When compared with Horn's work, Andreas Fischer's machines are messier. Fischer's machines are made up of found objects, seemingly random segments of tools, and pieces of furniture. They are an assemblage of junk, a *bricollage* of found goods that have lost their values and originally intended functions. Through the act of forcing the viewer to stare at the discarded objects, Fischer's machines come alive again and begin to induce the uncanny in the mind of the spectator. Consistently, in both Horn's and Fischer's works, machines are not presented as comprehensible, or tamable. On the contrary, they are uncannily unpredictable, and haunting. As such characteristics assign to the machines, their workings generate a tension between the spectator and the machines themselves, consequently evoking some sense of awe, perhaps similar to what Walter Benjamin (1931) described as 'aura.' This emanation of the auratic is distinctly Modern and incomparable to the awe one may feel before a religious icon. This eeriness is closer to the Freudian uncanny that recalls something familiar, but no longer familiar. When standing in front of Horn's or Fischer's work, the audience is denied a sense of nostalgia; instead these works evoke a sense of alienation.

Similarly, in Tom Hillewaere's installation from 2013, *Valse Sentimentale,* a felt pen is hanging from a helium-filled white balloon as it floats up and down, and sometimes touches the white paper on the floor to make a mark, slowly producing a piece of drawing. Electrical fans surrounding the floor are positioned to trap the balloon above a large sheet of paper to not allow the balloon to escape from its task of drawing. The balloon hovers above the paper, and occasionally comes down to draw. The balloon performs, and thereby produces a drawing, while the artist as an agent of production is absent. Instead, the fans and the balloon collaborate with each other, relying on a range of chances, continuing to draw. Central to the performance of the machines is the simultaneous seduction of the spectator with the melancholic process of mechanical production devoid of a human agent.

It is evident that machines successfully produce art and that artists may be deliberately dislocated from the authorial position from which they conventionally express their views and emotions. Displacement of the artist's subjectivity is paramount in the work produced by machines. As in the case of Fischer's and Horn's works, unpredictability and incomprehensibility induce the sense of the uncanny, and the artists' presence in the forms of their traces, marks, and breaths are missing. Furthermore, in Hillewaere's work, the machines manage their project between themselves. In these regards, Philippe Parreno's work is an interesting case.

In the work entitled *Elsewhen* at The Espace Louis Vuitton, Venice, in 2019, the visitor would find no objects or signs of any artwork when entering a dark empty space. Then, with some noise, the room is suddenly and erratically lit. The light's pulsation is almost aggressive, when abruptly the room returns to darkness. The same sequence of flashes and silent darkness recurs, but it is hard to comprehend if the duration of lights and intervals are regular or irregular. Visitors come in and leave without realizing anything happens in the room. In fact, the timing of lighting is initiated by microorganisms, hidden behind the wall. Here, the connection between the machinic and post-humanism comes to the forefront. The dislocation of the artist is a symptom towards the loci of subjectivity outside the human. In Parreno's work, the data that microorganisms send to the machine triggers the event of art. The artist is not a creative protagonist, and is absent. In this process, microorganisms are incorporated into the machinic operation, and are part of the machine. Instead of a common fear of machines taking over and replacing humans, the machine remains as a medium that incorporates non-human agents -in this case, microorganisms- into its machinic operations. To be a machine, one does not need to be made of metal, wire, or plastic. As Parreno's machine consists of microorganisms, dislocation of the artist as an agent of production is clearly underlined. The shift from the artist as human agent to the machine that mediates data, and in his work, a will of microorganisms does trigger a set of motions.

Different from the more programmed erratic behaviors in Horn's work, Parreno's microorganisms act as an unpredictable machine. In his Palais de Tokyo retrospective entitled, *Anywhere, Anywhere Out Of The World* (2013-14), a similar scene was made on a grander scale. In the basement floor of the art gallery, a dark, spacious hall was lit by 16 unpredictable theater marquee lights, sets of light bulbs hanging from the ceiling. In the total darkness, some of the marquee lights suddenly and unpredictably light up, and after a little while they turn themselves off as if gone out of breath. When marquee lights go off, a visitor realizes that there is another spectator standing close by. Anyone is a stranger hidden in the dark until a second ago. Although at this stage it is doubtful that Parreno used microorganisms. The use of microorganisms appears to be his later development. It is clearer in his later work in 2016 at Tate Modern in London entitled *Anywhen*, a variety of motions were set off by microorganisms in the spacious Turbine Hall, and on one of the corners microorganisms lived in a glass container where they sent data to the other devices that orchestrated and triggered a variety of motions that the audience would experience.

Similarly, Céleste Boursier-Mougenot's work, *Révolutions,* evokes a serene experience wherein the machinic sublime may be an appropriate description. *Révolutions* is uprooted trees with roots buried in a large ball of soil, and sensors and wheels hidden in the soil. The trees move quietly as if looking for a lost home. Boursier-Mougenot's trees wander silently as if being lost existentially in the post-Anthropocenic landscape. And yet, the hybridized trees with machinic devices do not necessarily appear to be seeking a return to the Romantic sublime of the eighteenth century. On the contrary, the uprooted trees, mourning a loss of transcendental longing for their rootedness, do not demand a revival of humanism or the humanist's Romantic sense of sublime, but they acknowledge that such a sentiment is no longer recoverable. They accept and affirm the sense of loss as a fatal but actual condition.

The machinic tree apparatus affects the human subject without being antagonistic to the human, contrary to Chaplin's factory worker at the assembly line. The eeriness and the sentiment of loss do not derive from the machine as an inanimate object crossing the line over to the animate, as Sigmund Freud (1919) explains in his article "The Uncanny." Rather, it is a mixture of intimacy and estrangement towards the machine that is an integral aspect of the modern subject.

The "uncanny valley" initially proposed by Masahiro Mori in 1970 re-contextualizes the Freudian notion of the uncanny in the late twentieth century, in which prosthetics, automation, and robotics technology developed and advanced. Mori (2012) explains that humanoids, distinct from functional robots, with high levels of semblance to human appearances and behaviors, cause discomfort to the human and evoke a sense of uncanny. Instead of the sense of affinity with the humanoids who appear visually similar to the human, the humanoids' extreme proximity causes incomprehension and terror for the human subject. Mori identifies this narrow spectrum between the robotic 'other' with a nearly perfect human appearance, and the human subject in the uncanny valley where one experiences discomfort. Freud, in his 1919 essay "The Uncanny," introduces the plot of the early nineteenth century crime writer E. T. A Hoffmann's story called "The Sand Man." The protagonist of the story, Nathaniel, falls in love with Olimpia, a "beautiful, but strangely silent and motionless daughter" of a professor (2003, p. 137). Later, Nathaniel realizes that Olimpia is an automaton and this realization makes him mad. Freud uses this to explain how terrifying it is to observe the inanimate transgressing to the animate state. Mori's uncanny valley re-articulates the experience of witnessing the transgression in the late twentieth and early twenty-first century, as prosthetics and robotics technology allow machines to look and behave like a human.

The historical development of an attachment to the machine exceeds the mystical manifestation of the projections of human desire on the "thing." As Walter Benjamin (2002) reformulates Marx, by saying the fetish is the projection of human desire onto dead objects, a phantasmagoric projection of one's desire when manifest in the machines; if one follows Benjamin, the confusion appears as an uncanny seduction and alienation.[2] The machine is no longer an object on which one projects his or her desires, but the machine is a cognitive fluid that affects ones' emotive and intellectual life. Once data begins to influence the thinking of the subject through machinic operations, the dynamics between the machine and the subject become fluid and organically complex.

The first version of the film, *Blade Runner,* released in 1982, includes an iconic scene in which Rick Deckard, the android hunter-policeman, played by Harrison Ford, is about to fall from a building during a fight with the android-rebel, Roy Batty, played by Rutger Hauer. The moment Deckard is about to fall to his death from a roof of the building where they are fighting, the android grabs Deckard's wrist and saves his life. Soon afterwards, Batty's life expires. Realizing the moment his programmed date has come, Batty experiences his forthcoming death existentially, he empathizes with the mindless human who has hunted his fellow androids. The reversal of roles is played out in a way that the supposedly inhuman android displays his most empathetic trait against the human, a cruel android hunter. In the sequel *Blade Runner 2049*, Stelline makes an appearance. Stelline is a daughter of the android hunter, Deckard, and his android partner Rachael. Stelline is a robotic "being" with consciousness, and the image of the machine is subject to change by the ambiguous being of Stelline. When robots begin to develop consciousness defined by their capacity for self-reflection, an ethical hierarchy between "proper" humans and secondary "beings" begins to emerge.[3]

The Kafkaesque Machine

In an exhibition at the New Museum in New York entitled *Ghost in the Machine* (2012), curator Massimiliano Gioni included a machine initially made for an earlier exhibition that had been curated by acclaimed curator Harald Szeemann in 1975. Its design was derived from the machine described in Franz Kafka's short story entitled "In the Penal Colony" that was written in 1914 and published in 1919 (2005). In Kafka's story, the protagonist is an explorer who arrives at an isolated penal colony. The explorer learns that the former Commandant in the colony invented an utterly cruel execution machine through which those sentenced would be subjected to a torture lasting 12 hours until their execution would be complete. Kafka's fable repeats the humanistic anxiety against the machine. The execution officer, as he executes a prisoner, explains to the explorer how the execution machine works. The reader follows the explanation given by the officer and experiences the cruelty programmed in the machine. The officer halts the execution of the condemned man after learning that the explorer disagrees with the cruel process of execution carried out by the monstrous machine. Then the officer places himself in the machine to execute himself. The machine constructed by the human ends up killing the father-advocate of it. Similar to Chaplin's character, a moral message is implied in the fable.

The machine, known as the Harrow Machine in the Szeemann and Gioni exhibitions does not come directly from Kafka's short story. Rather, it is based on writer Michel Carrouges' drawing that was made after Kafka's story. This machine was included in a recent exhibition about the curatorial career of Szeemann entitled *Museum of Obsessions* at Kunsthalle in Düsseldorf from 2018 to 2019. Kafka's apprehension towards the machine is made more tangible when realized from Carrouges' drawing as the bulky and monstrous bed-like machine. Yet, Kafka's machine is more than a physical object; rather, it is an allegory of law and other coercive, enforceable institutions in society. Steven Conner in his article "Mortification" suggests the torture machine here is allegorically suggesting that "law, like psychoanalysis and the other privileged expressions of the discourse network, bypasses consciousness and is made to appear directly on the body of the subject" (2001, p. 39). Kafka's machine, in this sense, is an allegory of social institutions that cruelly execute the unjustly condemned.

Massimiliano Gioni included this machine in another exhibition entitled *The Great Mother* at Plazzo Reale in 2015. Benjamin Sutton (2015) wonders in his review, "A Mother Lode of a Show About Motherhood", why the Kafkaesque machine known as the Harrow Machine was included in the exhibition. Curiously, Andreas Fischer's piece entitled *Mother* (2003) appears to relate to this monstrous torture machine. The cables, the motors and the shelves used in Fischer's *Mother* suggest some degree of semblance to Kafka's machine. Briefly, in a text included in Fischer's catalogue for his exhibition, *Your Time is My Rolex,* in Cologne in 2012, Jasmine Merz comments on Fischer's *Mother:*

...in the work Mother, in which a nerve-cell-like plethora of electric motors drum on the surfaces of a conventional metal warehouse shelf as if wanting to scare and at the same time boast and beguile, like a diva laden with chunky, rattling jewelry. (p. 11)

Kafka's bed-like execution machine suggests potential violence in the most private and supposedly safest of domestic spaces. Exhibitions by Gioni and Fischer suggest that the Mother trope is a metaphor for social institutions of structural violence and cruelty.

Machines as The Other

The machine is seen often as The Other; that is, an annexation of the function of something human to be externalized and serve the human. We observed an example in Chaplin's *Modern Times* that contrasted to Deleuze' observation of Keaton's film *The General*, in which the human subject is integrated in the concatenation of machinic operations. From this point, the machine can be understood as a cognitive fluid or device that affects the human subject. And yet, in analyzing contemporary art practices of Horn, Fischer, Boursier-Mougenot and Parreno, the human subject is dislocated, and the machine at times is made operable with microorganisms and plants. Humans begin to disappear and the machines that co-ordinate with other organisms exclude humans. Yet, the machine as an object-apparatus is no longer occupying center stage, but placed behind the white cubic walls of galleries. Does this tell us something of the current situation?

To follow Theodor Adorno's view, artists incorporate how a mode of production in which a commodity is produced in society at large into their artistic process of production (1999). That is to say, machinic artworks are a reflection of general modes of production in contemporary society. The machine is no longer an apparatus separate from the human body or subjectivity, but cognitively is a part of it and that constitutes its subjectivity. Secondly, the machine has dislocated the human subject, and has begun to coordinate with other organisms. This challenges the conventional perception of the artist as a sole agent for art production. In this regard, the machine occupies a crucial role in understanding what art is, and what occupation is meant by the widely and loosely used term, the artist. Instead of an artist conceiving an initial idea, turning it into objects, images, or moving images, the role of the artist is shifted towards an initiate who sets up a chain of events.

In *Ways Things Go,* by Peter Fischli and David Weiss (1987), a chain of domino effects involving a series of objects and conditions triggers one new set of situations after another. Each trigger element is not a cog, or a card as in a domino-like succession, but gas, water, or fire, among other objects. Like Horn's works, the artist's body, or gestures in the form of traces of actions, is absent, but a sequence of events constitutes the entire work as a machine. At this point, Raunig's definition of the machine as a concatenation of agents contributing to each other makes sense, and the concatenation of events that produces an outcome; but, as in the case of Fischli and Weiss' work, the machine is the entirety of the series of events, instead of the final outcome. The omission of the human subject from the stage on which the process is presented is not a form of alienation, or subordination. The retreat of the human from the stage postulates recognition of other agents that are active and potentially productive, including "things" and atmospheric elements. The machine mediates the post-human condition for the artists through a series of concatenations. In such cases, artists willingly give away agency to other potential agents, and evade the interpretation that the artwork is a product of a genius or an autonomous individual with relevant skills such as drawing or painting.

To follow this understanding, it is misleading to posit the question of the machine replacing artists as an urgent question. Horn, along with others, deployed machines to make drawings; a "drawing machine" has its history, and it is not anything new. Automation is already a large part of industrial production in car and furniture production, for instance. Domestically many appliances such as washing machines and dishwashers already have adopted the task of domestic labor for a long time. Large-scale post-industrial farms produce energy, goods, even vegetables in buildings often located in remote areas, operated by relatively small numbers of human employees who monitor and manage the automated production system, rather than being engaged in actual production. These 'mega-autopic' farms do not require humans who are productive or inventive; instead, human workers are monitors trained to carry out emergency procedures in case of unpredictable failures of production, or accidents.

If such a situation is our actuality today, and if artworks discussed here represent the current condition of artistic production, how do we assess human relationship with the machine, if the machine as a cognitive influence is already integrated into the human subject? This threatens the Enlightenment understanding of the subject as a thinking agent who is supposed to be in control of his or her individual actions. Of course, this has a consequence in criminality, as how we judge who is responsible for an action that causes harm to others. While this question may be best left to legal practitioners, the deconstructed subject is a machinic subject who is placed in a concatenation of gestures and actions that deliberately trigger a series of events.

When Jacques Derrida (1994) coined the term *Hauntology* to articulate the post-ontological condition, Derrida deconstructed the presumed essence of the subject with critique towards Kantian Enlightenment and the ontology of Martin Heidegger, the latter who locates an individual's human consciousness as core to subjectivity. Typically, ontology locates the site of agency in the unified consciousness of the human subject. Instead, Derrida incorporates haunting as a part of this fragile and elusive subject. Derrida's project incorporates the Other's presence; that is, both from the past and the future, in oneself. This is an attempt to recognize the other in oneself. In Derrida's writing, injustice experienced in the past re-surfaces in the form of haunting. Re-surfacing resembles the structure in which a repressed object reappears in one's life, again and again, until it is recognized and confronted.

When observing artworks that deploy machinic operations, roughly identifiable as "machine art" (Broekman, 2016), it is easy to apply the notion of haunting as simply a spectator confrontation with the situation where the object of art is animated by a mechanical apparatus, and the operations that enact the object's movement remain mysterious to its spectators. This resembles Benjamin's structure of aura in which a certain 'distance' is produced between the object of art and audiences. To maintain somewhat the function of auratic, a quality that elevates the artwork from the ordinary or everyday, presented in Benjamin's article "The Work of Art in the Age of Mechanical Reproduction" (1969), the mysterious "aura" that separates an artwork from everyday, in machine art, resides in this space: between the spectator, and the machine that produces surprising and incomprehensible outcomes, as in Hillewaere's or Horn's work.

Benjamin, a Jew subject to Hitler's purge during World War II, was ready to embrace mechanical reproduction that could fight fascists. While his endorsement of the newest technology of film has been used in progressive worker movements, as well as for war propaganda, Benjamin's framing of mechanical [re]production as a gesture of wiping off aura, yet to politicize art, has been met with a contention that art can become an instrument for political aims. While politics may be a part of art, a formal endorsement of art to be "used" for politics, instead of art as understood, as a form of politics, needs differentiation.

When art is a form of politics, it affects aesthetically. It appeals sensorially, as well as intellectually and cognitively. Though we may put them all in the term aesthetics as an abbreviation, and in the aesthetic experience, the auratic still functions in art as a notion that elevates artwork from other objects and experiences. An artwork objectifies an artist's labor that occurs in the production process, and appears as phantasmagoria, similar to aura that separates the object from other everyday objects. Throughout the twentieth century, however, validation of values inherent in the art object has been challenged numerous times. Consequently, values in an art object derive from the artist's idea that privileges the object or an action, distinct from such in the everyday. Put another way, conceptual artwork's value is not an objectification of artist's skill or labor, but derives from artist's intellectual suggestion of novelty value, often reflecting contemporary conditions. When the artist is understood as a machine, and machinery is already an integral part of art production, then the supposed "aura" that machinic artwork produces is not a phantasmagoric manifestation of labor. Aura, then does not explain the mysterious experience that audiences behold. It is closer to the uncanny that Nicholas Royle (2003) elaborates, after Freud. It is the experience of unfamiliarity to the familiar: something lost remains.

Kinetics in the work is not the determining cause of the work appearing strange and effective, but cybernetic machines surpass mechanical operations of older machines and induce unpredictable effects. Cybernetic machine operations are based on data processing, thus distinguishing them from strictly mechanical machines. Cybernetic machines, often reliant on algorithms, produce outcomes that begin to surpass models based on causal sequences, as in the work of Fischli and Weiss. Cybernetic interpretation and management of a given environment in a machine is ready to accommodate chance, and respond to chance, as opposed to a mechanical machine that repeats its operations without any optional consideration for its fixed environment.

Some of Kristina Huxley's heat-sensitive paintings echo Hans Haacke's classic work, *Condensation Cube* (1963-5). In Huxley's paintings, entitled *Sensitive Painting* (2001) a heat sensitive medium responds to changing temperatures of the room in which the paintings are exhibited, partly influenced by the timed heating system, attached on the back of a canvas, and also by the temperature of the room in which the paintings are exhibited (See Figure 1). As more visitors come into the room and raise the temperature in the room, the paintings begin to show change on its surface[4]. Relational works to consider changes in the environment are further explored with the development of accessible microcomputing devices, artists have explored this opportunity for much experimentation.

Differently from Deleuze's comparison between Chaplin and Keaton, cybernetically-speaking, the distinction between the mechanical and the machinic relates to the notion of machine as operations of parts in a physical co-ordination to the cybernetic machines that process and incorporate chance. Through this, the machinic absorbs human, plants, atmosphere, temperature, or any "other" organic or inorganic agents. So what is the next ethical question regarding machines in art? The following section explores audience participation and a disappearance of the artist's gesture.

Disappearance of the Artist's Gesture

Art in the form of social engagement has become a recognizable form of practice that usually involves participants; or, an artist becomes involved in communities and they together produce outcomes recognized as art. Pierre Huyghe's *Streamside Day Follies* of 2004 is a fitting example in which the artist

Figure 1. Kristina Huxley, Sensitive Painting, 2001
Heat sensitive medium, polymer, acrylic on canvas. Heating system, flexible 13A cable, timer. Courtesy, the artist.

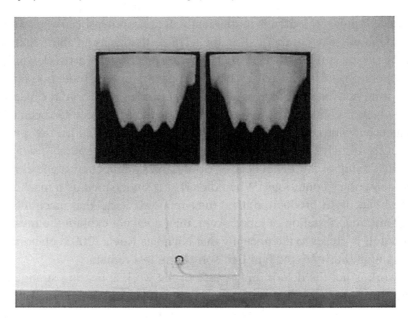

worked with local residents in an area bordering the Hudson River more or less where nineteenth century painter Frederick Edwin Church painted landscapes, and built his house. Huyghe, observing the newly regenerated area in which the community did not have means to congeal together socially, introduced a festival where residents participated. The artist, in other words, facilitated a platform on which the residents built their community.[5] The festival was to be repeated annually. In this act, the artist is a 'machine' that manages the situation with artistic insight to help the community develop. Participants, whether interested in art or not, are the immediate audience of Huyghe's work, and at the same time the work itself; yet, the object of his work is the elusive annual festival as a communal performance. In this work, still, the artist's active involvement in designing the appearance of the festival retains the artist's gesture, equating his involvement to a mark that the painter would make on a canvas.

Contrasting this work with what retains his mark of artist intention, Huyghe's installation at London's Serpentine Gallery in 2018 entitled *UUmwelt,* removes such "mark-making." In *UUmwelt*, "[t]hey take a brain wave at the moment that a person [artist] is thinking about the image, and this brainwave becomes a pattern and this pattern goes through a multi-neural networks which have a data bank of multi-million image" (Serpentine Galleries, 2018). The visitor sees images that are a result of the artist's brain activity, intercepted and interpreted through a databank, then turned into a series of non-sequential but approximated images that appear reasonably representational, such as images of animals or something in the physical world (See Figure 2).

In this work, the artist no longer entertains the visitors by setting a mechanical device to surprise them. Audiences are invited to be part of an environment in which the artist's brain and the machine communicate to make images appear on the screen. Inside the gallery, there were 10,000 blue flies living and dying in their lifecycle, hovering as part of the exhibition. In this exhibition, the artist is an agent who imagines; and yet, the machine provides corresponding images or approximations of these thoughts

Figure 2. Pierre Huyghe's, UUmwelt, 2018 – ongoing, exhibition view
Source: *Courtesy of the artist and Serpentine Galleries. (Rindal, n.d.)*

in the fast-changing process of imagination. The machine allows externalization of the artist's 'imagining' into a reasonably recognizable set of images on the screen for the flies and human visitors to see.

If we take the conceptual art's premise that artwork is a concept, rather than an image or an object, and take it literally, Huyghe's work comes close to the essence of the statement. What are these images that the visitors watch? They are translations of the artist's brain waves into patterns that resemble some things in the physical world; yet at another layer, what the audience is looking at is the machine itself, a human-machine integration that is presented as concept. Here, particular images that visitors experience, highly pixelated, unformed figures of one kind or another, are less important than the event of seeing the production of images made by the collaboration of human brain and machine. Huyghe's work is situated far from the point in a spectrum at which Chaplin's factory worker occupies. Huyghe's work occupies a singular position in contemporary art when considering what is meant by the machine. Huyghe's piece works as a double-sided shift in conception of the machine: 1) as a monster that the human subject is fearful of, and 2) the externalization of the human into an apparatus as the other who serves the human. Huyghe's work marks the point of becoming the machine. There is a distance from the position of fearing against the machine to the position that the artist willfully incorporates the machine into his or her subjectivity. In everyday conversations, in parallel to the above shifts, we incorporate machine metaphors such as we "store" memory, as if it is a set of data, and "retrieve" memory, instead of "recall" an event. Becoming the machine in this sense articulates a current condition in which the machine is further integrated into the human body, its language, and its subjectivity.

Manipulation and Control

We have observed a gradual development from Chaplin to Huyghe. And yet, what does the artist's willful integration of the machine into the human framework mean within the larger ideological framework of cognitive capitalism? More specifically, how is the possibility of 'machinic humans' to be subservient or resilient to ideological operations that may govern the decision-making capacities of each individual?

As we may wake up by an alarm clock embedded in our mobile phone and respond to a reminder that prompts us to go through a list of things to do, a large number of mobile phone users already are cognitively in tune with the machine. While we decide what time to set an alarm clock, in other areas, situations are more complex. Our shopping and voting behaviors, as well as online behaviors, may be more similar to auto-piloting than a series of conscious decision-making events. Integrating the machine entails potential of being manipulated at a cognitive level. This is distinctly different from Raunig's machinic as a concatenation of individuals to resist coercive ideological forces. Raunig's model deconstructs the heroic and autonomous individual to rebel, but also questions an organic community in which the human bond between members can turn to be a repressive social pressure to behave in uniform manners and share a reasonably narrow range of values. Raunig imagines the machinic as a political strategy without returning to the conventional notion of community. The machinic in this context provides one strategy to re-imagine individuals, without disqualifying an autonomy, while revitalizing our capacity to affect one another for a just purpose. While valid, at another level, integration of the machine into the human subject induces allowance for an external agent to take advantage of a situation.

When the machinic is thought of as cognitive fluid, and its materials as data that travels through neurological networks, metaphorically speaking, fluid travels to-and-fro from non-locatable, random sites. In such a world in which one's shopping behaviors are monitored, and one's opinions on political parties and candidates are influenced while using social media, without user awareness, how does one defend oneself? Even so, are one's cognitive boundaries no longer definable? What are the roles of art when thinking about these questions? Among a range of strategies, while being an artist-in-residence in Somerset House in London, Nastja Säde Rönkkö, in her recent work entitled *6 Months Without,* stopped using the Internet for six months. She communicated reflections on her life without a connection to the Internet, by writing and receiving letters. While this straightforward obstruction in a world electronically connected is a statement, it does not answer more fundamental questions about the ways in which one critically re-configures our relationship with the machine.

Machinations through algorithms dictate and reduce room of criticality, or slower reflection, while data as a tangible and objectified indicator of possibilities can demand a range of actions. Writings of James Bridle, Franco Berardi, and Hito Steyerl all convey this skepticism against Internet technology as a part of capitalism that absorbs user participation into the network and turns it into an instrument for enslaving and exploiting them. Säde Rönkkö's suspended use of the Internet suggests "the battleground," to appropriate Steyerl's use of the term, is located in the machine-network itself.

Nervous Machines

Returning to Benjamin's last remark in "The Work of Art in the Age of Mechanical Reproduction" (1969), ethical questions need to be asked in the field where the machine operates. Eyal Weizman and Lawrence Abu Hamdan of Forensic Architecture provide an approach that brings out a different kind of ethical question. They use data to supplement human sensory capacities to investigate ethically and politically sensitive cases. They use machines as an aid to detect experiences that are not possible to collect or analyse through human sensory capacity. In Abu Hamdan's work entitled *Earshot* (2016), the artist studies a video recording of gunshots that killed a Palestinian youth. To disprove the Israeli soldiers' claim that only rubber bullets were fired when a Palestinian youth was shot, the artist studies the sound frequency of the shots recorded in the video. By noting the difference between the sound frequencies of shots of live ammunition coated in rubber bullets (i.e., to disguise them as rubber bullets) and the sound frequencies of a rubber bullet, the artist demonstrates that the youth was killed by intentional firing of live ammunition, wrapped in rubber bullets. While the artist's work is more like sound forensics, this revelatory process is what Heidegger points out as the initial function of art and technology, signified in the Greek term *Techne*, integrated art and technology.[6]

Machines are not used for entertaining audiences, nor does it offer aid in having spectacular experiences. Instead, Abu Hamdan deploys software in order to identify live ammunition that killed a civilian on the Israeli-Palestinian border. In a similar way, Forensic Architecture as a team reconstructs situations in the past that may constitute a crime, but evidence is difficult to provide. In their work, the machine does not mean a device. Their machines are software, data, sound, Internet or, for that matter, anything available to reconstruct a past event from multiple angles as precisely as possible. Here the notion of machine becomes very broad: devices, software, electrical network, anything that provides data or data translation. This brings us back to re-examine the border between the machine as materiality, and the more elusive apparatus including algorithm, Internet or software. What in this context is a machine? Why may we be hesitant to call the Internet a machine?[7]

Tomoko Takahashi's work, *Untitled,* in 1997, staged in Beacons Field Gallery in London, was an installation in which outmoded machines such as printers, television sets, telephones among many other devices, were put in small piles chaotically, and yet, poetically, across the floor of the gallery. It was as if they were no longer needed and while some of them were dead, others were still alive. Occasionally, as one walked through the installation some machines worked, but they would turn silent in a next minute. The machines evoked a strangely familiar sentiment in detecting inanimate things as having life.

Tarek Atoui's work provides a similar impression, but less sentimental. Atoui in his 2016 and 2019 work, *The Spin,* 24 assembled objects are set to function as musical instruments, some of them made of ceramic or stone. As Atoui spent five years traveling in Pearl River Delta in China, and as a response to that experience, he asked craftspeople and instrument-makers to make objects resembling musical instruments. A turning ceramic vase has strings with beads attached at the ends, and as the vase turns the beads hit the vase and makes sounds. A stone needle touching the surface of a ceramic disc on a turntable makes sounds out of friction. Altogether in the same room 24 instruments were orchestrated and played music for visitors. This seemingly low-tech approach, through careful artistic coordination produced affective experiences. Different from Huyghe's *UUmwelt*, an analogue aspect of the machine in Atoui's piece is prominent, as in Takahashi's work. The machine in Atoui's work emphasizes the analogue, tactile, clumsy aspect of relatively inanimate things generating sounds. There is a do-it-yourself flavor to it, as wires and cables are visible, and machines and amplifiers are displayed, as if they are meant to be seen; different from Parreno's work in which microorganisms and machines are often hidden or marginally placed in the exhibition spaces. Atoui's approach reminds the audience of the expanded cinema movement in the 1970s in which conceptual filmmakers incorporated projectors and celluloid films as sculptural objects that allowed moving images to be seen.

In other words, the apparatus of visual persuasion was displayed, as viewers of moving images were deliberately made aware of the process in which images came to appear in front of them. The machine as a medium occupies centerstage, instead of the content being the focal point to which audiences are expected to channel their attention. The machines altogether work independently without a conductor, and yet, produce a strange sound environment in Atoui's work. This represents a working model for Raunig's use of the term "concatenation" (2010, p. 93). A collaborative work does not take away the individual's autonomous contribution to the collective, and together without a charismatic leader, or oppressive dictator, or an administrative manager, produces an environment that is specific to their own making. Both Takahashi's and Atoui's work emphasize the machine's material condition, distinguished from the mechanical, but haunted by its initially assigned functions and designs. This materiality of the machines haunts the machine without returning to the machine as a monster, but as a seductive and mysterious companion of time, and this conceptualization of the machine is clearly distinct from software that translates the artist's brainwaves to images, or data that distinguishes live ammunition from rubber bullets.

The Machinic Haunts

We have returned to the machine that materially embodies time, instead of coming full circle to the mechanical. Discourse on the machine moved from the mechanical to the machinic, and the dissolution of the machine into the neurological network that breaks the boundary between human brain and machine-apparatus. Yet, it is worth being skeptical to draw a linear line of evolution from the earlier interest in machines, as in Kafka's monstrous machine, to the machines of the cybernetic age of artificial intelligence. This line is disrupted by the gesture of return, as in Atoui's work, as if a manifestation of haunting. Almost as if the clumsy operations of the machines in Atoui's work is a call for the viewer as well as an artist to be able to relate to the machines as a humble and fragile beings. Any artists to produce artwork with cybernetic inclination require technical knowledge and training. This leads an artist to collaborate with technical experts, as in the case of Huyghe who collaborated with a lab in Kyoto, Japan. In contrast, although Atoui's work also involved potters and craftspeople, as well as technical assistance, emphasis is clearly placed on the inventive concatenation of disparate elements that were not intended to be orchestrated for the purpose of music production.

Lucie Vitkova uses domestic appliances to make performances and music. Vitkova uses an electric vacuum cleaner as one of her instruments, or she would put her face in a bowl of water to make bubbling sounds and coordinates these two to make "music". The performative body of the artist's labor is in coordination with mundane domestic appliances to make an unexpected synthesis of sounds. Not only the coordination between the human body and the machine is made in unexpected ways, but the work also illuminates the human body's coordination in domestic labor.

The machine has a revelatory function, not even returning to Heidegger's notion of tool that assists one's endeavor to reveal the human's place in a larger cosmic order. To understand phenomena undetected through human senses may need some assistance from the machine. For instance, Fuyuki Yamakawa's work of 2013 entitled the *Atomic Guitar* uses a pair of electric guitars wired to a Geiger counter. The counter detects radioactivity that human senses cannot detect. Accordingly, the guitars' strings are struck as the counter detects a high level of radioactivity. The machine allows the human subject to hear the invisible and inaudible radioactivity by translating it into data, and that is again translated into vibrations that a human being can hear.

Similarly, in Carsten Nikolai's *Milch* of 2000 is a set of shallow trays, each tray containing milk. Each tray is connected to a sound machine that sends vibrations to the tray. The machine in this process lets the spectator see the sounds. This transmutation from one form of phenomenon to another is made through machinic translatability. It mediates experience in the form of data, not necessarily digital, and we may call it memory to use a broader term, into another form of experience. Different from Forensic Architecture and Abu Hamdan's work in which software is a key to translate multiple layers of data, Yamakawa's and Nikolai's works rely on the presence of the machines: in Yamakawa's case it is the Geiger counter and the electrical guitars, and in Nicolai's case it is the sound machines and milk trays connected by electrical cables. Again, it is not a monstrous mechanicality that characterized their early deployment of machines in art. Instead, it is a co-ordination of machinic bodies, including the human body, as in the case of Vitkova, to orchestrate a distinct moment of affect.

CONCLUSION: THE MACHINE AS INTERNALIZED OTHER

Starting with the contrast between the mechanical and the machinic, illuminated by contesting views expressed by Charlie Chaplin's factory worker in *Modern Times* and Buster Keaton's character in *the General,* this chapter has discussed how, metaphorically speaking, the machinic as a cognitive fluid has transformed the relationship between the machine and the human subject. Following Gerald Raunig's notion of the machinic as a concatenation of singularities, the machinic as a cognitive fluid is contrasted against the mechanical as the clumsier and clunky organization in machinery, and its relations to the artist machinist.

A series of transitions has taken place from the perception over the machine as the demonic and monstrous figure antagonistic to the human as moral and compassionate being, such as represented in *Modern Times*. As shown in the first version of *Blade Runner* in 1984, already a perception on the machine was shifting to one that displays more empathetic human emotional traits. The humanist's anxiety towards the machine is also the anxiety characteristic to the Enlightenment and Kantian subject whose center of command, will, and thinking originate in the human consciousness, and not in animals, plants, microorganisms or atmospheric elements, or the machine, that is the Other. Against this post-humanist backdrop, the machine is the other that begins to close the distance with the human consciousness. This is exemplified in Pierre Huyghe's work *UUmwelt,* where the artist's brainwaves are translated by the machine to be viewed by spectators. Although the translation of the data marks the distance between brain and machine, the proximity between them is remarkable. It is hard to tell if the artist is the machine and the machine is part of the artist, or nearly one and the same. While Huyghe's work is exemplary of one approach, in contrast,

Tomoko Takahashi's and Tarek Atoui's works move in another direction. Relatively speaking, their work is low-tech, and the machine's tangible materiality is emphasized. In Atoui's work, the artist initiates the situation in which "things" come together to produce an atmospheric sound environment, "instruments" take their own material specificity, such as clay, wood, stone, or string, to their advantage to self-orchestrate themselves and produce an outcome. In Atoui's work, the machinic element is laid bare in front of the audience, instead of being hidden, as in the case of Philippe Parreno's work, in which microorganisms trigger a series of flashing lights. In contrast to Parreno, whose work dislocates the human but adopts the machine to the center of production, and Huyghe's work that closes the distance between the human consciousness and the machine, Atoui's work insists on the machine as an external set of apparatus, without being antagonistic to the machine as a monstrous and demonic other. Rather, the external apparatus to the human subject is a mysterious and seductive "thing" that carries the history of its material conditions. Through a series of concatenations, the machines reveal the human relationship to the external apparatus that refuses to be completely integrated into the human body, though the human body is more responsive to the machine to the point that the human subject operates within machinic metaphors.

The legacy of Rebecca Horn's work is worth noting among many others. Horn's erratic and unpredictable machine marked a clear transition from the mechanical to the machinic. Her machines are an incomprehensible other whose presence evokes a sense of uncanny, and her gradual withdrawal from her performative work that includes machinic elements mark a transition in which artists began to give away a central stage to the machine, leading to the dislocation of the artist as a central agent of production.

Finally, Kafka in his short story "In the Penal Colony" shared the same anxiety against the machine as did Chaplin's factory worker. In Kafka's call for establishing a hospital for treatment of nervous diseases, Kafka wrote:

This great war which encompasses the sum total of human misery is also a war on the nervous system, more a war on the nervous system than any previous war. All too many people succumb to this war of nerves. Just as the intense industrialization of the past decades of peace had attacked, affected, and caused disorders of the nervous system of those engaged in industry more than ever before, so the enormously increased mechanization of present-day warfare presents the gravest dangers and disorders to the nervous system of fighting men. (cited in Kittler, 1999, p. 223)

Kafka is not writing about the machine, but the text is fitting when considering he is referring to the First World War in which, for the first time, the modern machines occupied a significant place in battles. As followed by Michel Carrouges' drawing, and later by the curators Harald Szeemann and Massimilano Gioni, the execution machine that Kafka conceived haunts the machine as an idea that permeates still since its publication in 1919. Allegorically, the machinist in Kafka's story is destroyed by the instrument, and by the same token it tells us that the machine is more than an instrument to serve the operator. The relationship between the two is not always fluid. It can be antagonistic and destructive, but even when the machine fails to operate to serve, it does not provide another validation for the humanist values that posit antagonism on the machine.

On the contrary, a failing machine reminds us that the machine is the other, an integral part of the human subjectivity that is externalized, as if to see a part of unresolved and haunted subjectivity in its materiality. The seduction of machinic art derives from seeing the machine as the internalized other in the externalized art form. Consequently, the artist is haunted by the machine, and the category of a purely autonomous artist is no longer an option.

REFERENCES

Adorno, T. W. (1999). *Aesthetic theory* (R. Hullot-Kentor, Trans.). Athlone Press.

Benjamin, W. (1969). The Work of Art in the Age of Mechanical Reproduction. In *Illuminations* (pp. 217–252). Schocken Books.

Benjamin, W. (2009). A Small History of Photography. In *One way street and other writings* (pp. 240–257). Penguin.

Berardi, F. (2011). Cognitarian Subjectivation. In J. Aranda, B. K. Wood, & A. Vidokle (Eds.), *Are you working too much?: Post-Fordism, precarity, and the labor of art* (pp. 134–146). Sternberg Press.

Bridle, J. (2018). *New dark age: Technology and the end of the future.* Verso.

Broeckman, A. (2016). *Machine art in the twentieth century.* MIT Press.

Canguilhem, G. (1992). Machine and Organism. In J. Crary & S. Kwinter (Eds.), *Incorporations* (pp. 44–69). Zone.

Conner, S. (2001). Mortification. In S. Ahmed & J. Stacy (Eds.), *Thinking through the skin*. Routledge.

Crary, J. (2014). 24/7. Verso.

Crary, J., & Kwinter, S. (Eds.). (1992). *Incorporations*. Zone.

Deleuze, G. (1986). *Cinema 1: The movement-image*. Athlone Press.

Derrida, J. (1994). *Specters of Marx*. Routledge.

Durkheim, E. (2002). *Suicide*. Routledge. doi:10.1522/cla.due.sui2

Freud, S. (2003). *The uncanny*. Penguin.

Haraway, D. (1991). Cyborg Manifesto: Science, Technology, and Socialist-Feminism in the Late Twentieth Century. In Simians, cyborgs and women: The reinvention of nature (pp. 149-182). Free Association Books.

Heidegger, M. (1996). The Question Concerning Technology. In *Basic writings* (pp. 311–341). Routledge.

Kafka, F. (2005). In the Penal Colony. In N. N. Glatzer (Ed.), *Franz Kafka: The omplete short stories* (pp. 140–167). Vintage Books.

Kittler, F. (1999). *Gramophone, film, typewriter* (G. Winthrop-Young & M. Wutz, Trans.). Stanford University Press.

Marinetti, T. (1912). *Futurist manifest*. Sackville Gallery.

Marx, K. (1990). *The capital*. Penguin.

Marx, K. (2015). Foundations of the critique of political economy (Grundrisse) (M. Nicolaus, Trans.). Penguin Books in association with New Left Review.

Merz, J. (2012). Andreas Fischer: Rules, Roles and Routines. In J. Merz (Ed.), *In the wool (In der Wolle)* (pp. 11–58). Museum Ludwig.

Mori, M. (2012). The Uncanny Valley (K. F. MacDorman & N. Kageki, Trans.). *IEEE Spectrum*. https://spectrum.ieee.org/automaton/robotics/humanoids/the-uncanny-valley

Rafael, M. (2013). *Pierre Huyghe: On site*. Walter König.

Raunig, G. (2010). *A thousand machines* (A. Derieg, Trans.). Semiotext(e).

Royle, N. (2003). *The uncanny*. University of Manchester Press.

Serpentine Galleries. (2018, October 17). *Hans Ulrich Obrist in Conversation with Pierre Huyghe*. YouTube. https://www.youtube.com/watch?v=emYOOVRzG8E

Steyerl, H. (2012). *The wretched of the screen*. Sternberg Press.

Sutton, B. (2015). *A Mother Lode of a Show About Motherhood.* https://hyperallergic.com/249073/a-mother-lode-of-a-show-about-motherhood/

Thompson, S. J. (2011). *Endless Empowerment and Existence: From Virtual Literacy to Online Permanence in Presence.* Academia.Edu. https://www.academia.edu/2519291/

Zizek, S. (2019). *Like a thief in broad daylight: Power in the era of post-humanity.* Penguin.

ENDNOTES

1   Rene Descartes applied the mechanical model of society earlier as discussed in George Canguilhem's 1992 article, "Machine and Organism," in J. Crary and S. Kwinter (Eds.), *Incorporations.*

2   Benjamin, when talking about fashion in the Arcades Project says, "Fashion stands in opposition to the organic, it couples the living body to the inorganic world. To the living, it defends the rights of the corpse. The fetishism that succumbs to the sex appeal of the inorganic is its vital nerve" (2002:8).

3   A supplementary and useful commentary on *Blade Runner 2049* may be found in Slavoj Zizek's (2009) article "State of Things: Topsy-Turvy World of Global Capitalism –Virtual Capitalism and the End of Nature -of Mice and Men" in *Like a Thief in Broad Day Light: Power in the Era of Post-Humanity.*

4   See related Kristina Huxley works at www.kristinahuxley.art.

5   Marie-France Rafael's (2013) interview with Pierre Huyghe is useful in understanding Huyghe's intentions.

6   Heidegger in his essay: The Question of Technology says, "There was a time when it was not technology alone that bore the name *techne.* Once the revealing that brings forth truth into the splendor of radiant appearance was also called *techne.* There was a time when the bringing-forth of the true into the beautiful was called *techne.* The poiesis of the fine arts was also called *techne.*
At the outset of the destining of the West, in Greece, the arts soared to the supreme height of the revealing granted them. They illuminated the presence [*Gegenwart*] of the gods and the dialogue of divine and human destinings. And art was called simply *techne.* It was a single, manifold revealing. It was pious, promos, i.e., yielding to the holding sway and the safekeeping of truth.
The arts were not derived from the artistic. Artworks were not enjoyed aesthetically. Art was not a sector of cultural activity. What was art – perhaps only for that brief but magnificent age? Why did art bear the modest name *techne*? Because it was a revealing that brought forth and made present, and therefore belonged within poiesis" (1996, p. 339).

7   This book's editor, Steven John Thompson, calls the Internet an appliance. Internet, though more elusive than a tangible object, is understood as an apparatus to which one is attached and accustomed.
Thompson says:
"It is evident that social media and other applications today have turned the Internet appliance into something habitual, not unlike a toaster, however, much more pronounced and repetitive, like a hobbyist's radio or artisan's craft; e.g., a potter's wheel, a walkie-talkie, or even a skateboard may be some possibly analogous connections." (2011, p. 5)

Chapter 9
Amusements Made to Save Man:
The History of Moral Amusement Rides

Jill Anne Morris
Frostburg State University, USA

ABSTRACT

This chapter re-introduces the idea of roller coasters as moral machines and morality mechanisms, as they were designed to rid mankind of immoral entertainment, and traces their ability to spread American culture via themed entertainment from World's Fairs to Disneyland and beyond. It features an analysis of two Chinese themed rides, one of which has been developed with American cultural constructs and one of which begins to develop a new form of Chinese historical theme park. Through these examples, it suggests the potential for themed amusements to spread not just American morality and culture, but to provide sites of cultural exchange.

INTRODUCTION

LaMarcus Adna Thompson invented the Switchback (or Scenic) Railway in order to save man from degradation by drink, prostitution, and immoral entertainments (Mangels, 1952). He believed that—answering a call made to him from God—roller coasters would save man. If man had roller coasters, he would have no need for houses of ill repute, and so—in less than a decade—patents for up-stop wheels, brakes, track, lift hills and enhanced trains quickly changed Thompson's invention into a modern thrill ride. Thompson's rides took guests on an adventure—tracks were surrounded by murals and scenes meant to duplicate scenery from other parts of the world. They were meant to educate. In short, his rides were rhetorical. They argued that an educated populace was one that sought to experience the Western world, that bodily delights were best experienced in controlled circumstances, and that amusements could be—beyond all else—moral.

This paper will trace the result of this early invention to present day. What does it mean that amusement parks have been meant, since their inception, to present Western moral values to the world, and to do so in such an embodied way that the argument is sometimes invisible? What does it mean that Eastern

DOI: 10.4018/978-1-7998-4894-3.ch009

Copyright © 2021, IGI Global. Copying or distributing in print or electronic forms without written permission of IGI Global is prohibited.

themes, such as rounded roofing, pagodas, and ornamentation were only added to buildings in Coney Island by Fred Thompson because it made them seem "child-like" and "depraved" (Register, 2001, loc. 1425). The ride inventions that followed the scenic railway enabled old mills, dark rides, carousels, and others to be quickly added to parks, transforming pleasure gardens and picnic grounds to amusement parks. The earliest parks were not subtle in their depictions of Western morality. Dreamland, one of the three major parks at Coney Island that stood during the first decade of the 1900s, had a spectacular called Creation, which Biblically told the story of Genesis from the creation of the Earth to the story of Adam and Eve (Sullivan, 2015). Dreamland also featured Hell Gate, a ride in which the guest rode in a boat that was sucked into a whirlpool and pulled under and into the center of the Earth, where they would witness subterranean horrors and might just find Hades. Even carousel horses featured the richly attired saddles and regalia of warhorses of the past (including those of the Crusades) instead of racing attire of thoroughbreds from the same time period (a notable exception being the horses that ran along the tracks of Steeplechase Park and that vied for a winning position at Church and Prior's Racing Derby).

However, the morality created in and exported by early amusement parks was not just Christian. It was, by means of culture and segregation, white. Though amusement parks in Japan and Denmark predated Coney Island by hundreds of years, it was the surge of technological advancement of the Industrial Revolution followed by the world's fairs meant to display new technologies (including rides) and teach about world cultures that drove Luna Park, Dreamland, and Steeplechase to be not only the model for American amusement parks, but also amusement parks worldwide. Amusement parks were segregated, meant for white guests, and guests of color were only there as attractions—and there was a time when neatly every city in America with a population of over a few thousand had its own amusement park or pleasure garden, and copies of these parks spread across national boundaries and oceans as well. This was the beginning of American supremacy in amusements. They defined a genre, but it was not a genre that was well-planned beyond one of spectacle. It was assumed that what sold and was successful was good, even to the extent of "What appears is good; what is good appears" (Debord, 2009, loc. 409). By World War II, amusement parks that looked very much like the ones in America existed on nearly every continent (Mohun, 2013).

By the 1940s and 50s, amusement parks had fallen away from their earlier lofty goals, largely because two World Wars' worth of rationing and the Great Depression meant that many simply could not afford maintenance. Hundreds closed, unable to update. Teenagers were seen as untrustworthy, and frequented parks. Despite their earlier goal of uplifting mankind, roller coasters and parks closed and were seen as unsafe and immoral. It did not help that desegregation efforts centered around parks and swimming pools.

Enter Walt Disney

Just when it seemed as though amusement parks and American morality would be disconnected again forever, Walter Elias Disney stepped forward with a plan for a new style of amusement park that would radically alter the course of theme park development forever (Adams, 1991). His new park was clean, moral, upstanding, and good—and it presented a view of Western supremacy and morality that would be carried not just to other parks that would open after it, but around the world all over again.

And yet Disney did not redefine or update that morality from LaMarcus Thompson's day. Disney's morality performed its segregation by cost (and continues to do so). Disney codified the entrance gate price—one on top of ride tickets—and thus set into motion a steep climb of pricing, patrolling, and perfection that we expect today of any park that should open. Only a few remain without "gates," and many more were built with them.

What is this morality? Let's pause for a moment to define morality more generally. In its most general sense, our "morals" or our "morality" are the generally accepted codes of conduct or codes of action agreed upon by societal or cultural fiat (Gert, 2016). To be raised within a culture is to understand these sets of conduct and those who accept them generally are moral agents, indeed: "it might well be that all moral agents would also accept a code of prudence or rationality, but this would not by itself show that prudence was part of morality" (2016). Althusser writes that "a moral standpoint is a moral standpoint: it produces approval or condemnation" (2014, p. 59). Morality requires rationality and intellect, to a certain degree, in that all rational persons should be able to endorse a moral code.

What could amusement park morality be, then, other than a reflection of the society that spawned the park in the first place? Yes, but, 1. in the case of the United States that moral code may be one from 50-100 years ago instead of one more modern, and 2. In the case of other countries, that moral code might not even be their own. If an American movie gains popularity in Japan, does it express American values or Japanese ones? Is it generally recognized that the morals contained within are potentially, uniquely American? Of course, which is one of the concerns of colonization and broad distribution of media. Unlike movies, however, amusement park rides are built and rarely ethically analyzed.

The moral code of amusement parks is largely American—it values duty and adventure alongside family and a certain sort of 'clean-cutness' that might not be immediately apparent to the guests but almost certainly is in the worker handbooks that refuse workers with "natural" hair, beards, or tattoos. Žižek privileges politics over ethics in his morality—perhaps we should as well (Rayman, 2017). If so, then amusement park morality is all about ignoring the politics of today for the politics of yesteryear.

The wish for "simpler times" is writ large in America today, but has been writ larger in its theme parks for decades. Not only do we wish for a time when we were all children, but we wish for a time when we didn't have to worry about all of "that stuff" ("that stuff" being the messy racial milieu of being a fan of "Splash Mountain" but not *Song of the South*, of enjoying the jokes on the "Jungle Cruise" till it cruises right by terrible representations of native peoples, or sincerely thinking that "It's a Small World" is about peace till you ride a knock-off in a park overseas with black people eating watermelon in loincloths). Every small change made to our favorite childhood rides is met with righteous condemnation in a country that is all about thinking that the past is great, and that Main Street USA is still where we all live. It isn't—and it never was.

Morality is that which is culturally written into the politics and ethics of the objects we create. If our creations reflect a morality and ideology not our own, then we must either remake those objects or look to what outside influences make them not our own.

This chapter does the work of tracing these early moral roots of the American amusement park to the present-day echoes of white supremacy and morality that continue to affect the amusement industry today. Roller coasters are still moral machines, and still present us with a story of technological supremacy that is more complex than one hundred years ago, but more invisible, too. As such, the chapter presents both historical discussions of American amusement parks, the culture and morality that was spread by amusement (and how those park owners were aware of it), as well as author analysis of current day rides, themes, and park design that continue to reproduce that morality today.

BACKGROUND

Roller coasters developed over a period of a couple hundred years, and are usually traced back to Russian ice slides or the Mauch Chunk Railway (Adams, 1991). Patents for roller coaster-like devices began appearing in the late 1800s, such as one by Richard Knudsen of Brooklyn who "patented an amusement coaster he called an 'inclined-plane railway.' The device consisted of two parallel tracks with undulating hills on which coaster cars holding four passengers each ran by gravity" (Adams, 1991, p. 14). However, Knudsen is generally not credited with the development of the coaster at all. That credit goes to LaMarcus Adna Thompson.

Thompson took Knudsen's design and used it to build a "gravity railway" in 1884 in Coney Island (Adams, 1991). In the next four years, he would go on to build almost 50 more roller coasters across the United States and Europe, as the ride turned out to be very profitable. However, Thompson had a unique vision for roller coasters that many of the great amusement park entrepreneurs that followed him shared: he believed that roller coasters and amusement parks could save mankind from sin, and saw it as his personal calling from God to enable them to do so. He said:

Many of the evils of society, much of the vice and crime which we deplore come from the degrading nature of amusements....to substitute something better, something clean and wholesome and persuade men to choose it, is worthy of all endeavor...[we can offer] sunshine that glows bright in the afterthought and scatters the darkness of the tenement for the price of a nickel or dime. (qtd. in Adams, 1991, p. 17)

He chose Coney Island as the place to build this attraction not just because it had a beach and not in a premonition of the century of amusements that would follow in its location, but because "he hoped to lure poor people away from the barrooms, brothels, and other such unsavory vices available in the same area" (Rennix, 2019).

It is important that Thompson is credited with the design of the roller coaster. We choose the cultural narratives that we tell each other, and—in this case—as a country, Americans have chosen Thompson, the man who said that roller coasters would save us from unwholesome activities. Our parks were meant to be something more than idle amusements, and in the century and a half that has followed, they have indeed become more than that. They are deliverers of culture, education, and thrills. Thompson was just the first to recognize their potential. He realized that by combining the "appearance of danger with actual safety" that we could allow "the public to intimately experience the Industrial Revolution's new technologies of gears, steel, and dazzling electric lights" (Adams, 1991, p. 17). He built the first roller coaster tunnels and used them to not just scare riders, but to make the rides about travel. He filled his tunnels with light instead of darkness, and then with scenery from around the world, and began to call the new attractions "Scenic Railways" (Mangels, 1952). He understood, more than other showmen of his time, that parks would be used for more than just entertainment, that they could be used as vessels for cultural teaching and exchange.

He was not alone in these thoughts, however. Charles Wallace Parker, who made amusement devices in Kansas, had similar ideas. His public relations department often referred to him in an "aura of saintliness" as he "considered it his mission to rescue the amusement business from the hoochie-coochie shows and the snake charmers. His house publication, the *Bedouin*, glorified Parker, his family, the moral superiority of his shows, and his 'Perfect Pleasure' carousels" (Adams, 1991, p. 12). Years later, Walt Disney would be recognized as the same type of man—a businessman meant to uplift the amusement industry again.

World's Fairs

A second source of ethics and morality that runs through today's amusement parks began in approximately the same time period, as a theme of the various world's fairs. While world's fairs and expositions existed for years before the late 1800s, it was during this time that they took on great significance both in the US and abroad. The movement started in the 1850s with the Crystal Palace Exhibition in London (Rydell, 2000). In the United States, the World's Columbian Exposition, which was the world's fair held in Chicago in 1893, is:

...recognized as a primary influence on the merging forms of amusement enterprises from the late 19th *century to the present. The exposition gave us the midway; the Ferris wheel (the first large-scale harnessing of technology solely for the purpose of fun); the presentation of exotic cultural environments as exhibits; a clearly sectored landscape design; a celebration of American technology and industry in a highly entertaining mode of presentation; the merger of engineering and planning to produce a unified, precisely controlled and minutely organized environment; and perhaps the exhibition's most important contribution, the actualization of a "Celestial City" serving as a prophetic model for the utopian and spiritual perfection that America has always dreamed is its destiny. (Adams, 1991, p. xiii)*

Every park constructed in the years following the Exposition attempted to utilize one or all of its themes. The midway, with its rides, was of course omnipresent, meant to introduce us to technology while delivering us from drinking and sin. The construction of buildings grand in scale and architecture, often white, was made part of the genre. Parks featured "cultural exhibits" that showcased people from far flung parts of the world, displayed as if they were zoological exhibits (today these may be animatronic, but they are often present in some way or another). Thompson gave us the signature ride and morality, but the world's fairs gave us their superiority.

Judith Adams writes that from the moment that the Puritans landed in America, we have been "convinced of [our] redemptive role, that is, [our] ability eventually to transform the City of the World into a Celestial City" (1991, p. xiii). However, Americans very early on became convinced that the way to enlightenment of the Celestial City was through technology and American exceptionalism:

The grand alabaster classical structures of the World's Columbian Exposition presented a hymnbook conception of Heaven on Earth, made possible by the dances in iron and steel technology that formed the hidden framework supporting the splendid mantle of spiritual and aristocratic allegory. The exposition suggested, on artistic and practical levels, that technology joined with a progressive spirit could create a utopian garden city out of the wilderness. (Adams, 1991, p. xiv)

Rydell (2000) also writes that:

To say that world's fairs have exerted a formative influence on the way Americans have thought about themselves and the world in which they live probably understates the importance of those expositions. World's fairs have been sources of much pleasure, inspiring the creation of Coney Island and other amusement parks and subsequent theme parks like Disneyland. Fairs have introduced generations of Americans to pathbreaking scientific and technological innovations like telephones, X rays, infant incubators, television, moving walkways, asphalt, and plastics. The architecture and parklike settings of world's fairs, along with their sometimes visionary schemes for public and private transportation, have influenced the ways our cities and small towns look and the way we behave in them. The importance of world's fairs is undeniable. (loc. 128)

The White City of the World's Columbian Exposition was pure, but also elitist. It was also illusionary and temporary. It was made of plaster that could be put up very quickly, but also fell apart within a year. The grand statues were not real and began degrading before the Exposition even ended. Later, amusement parks (such as Coney Island's Dreamland) that used similar construction technologies would fall victim to terrible fires; in part, because the method of construction was not ever meant for long-standing structures and the result was incredibly flammable.

But there was a greater dark side to the White City than flimsy construction. Frederick Douglass criticized the Exposition for ignoring:

...the realities of urban poverty and the treatment of nonwhite races in America. It presented blacks and American Indians as quasi-ethnological entertainment or as product advertisements...Built as a celebration of capitalist enterprise, the very existence of the grand White City seemed to be a justification for ignoring the horrible effects of capitalism, that is, the growing number of people living in poverty, unemployment, and the spread of slums in urban areas. (Adams, 1991, p. 20)

Douglass was one of the authors of a pamphlet distributed outside the fair noting the absence of African Americans in its planning and celebrations.

The world's fairs also introduced the exotic "hoochie coochie" dancer (mentioned above as one of the evils that Charles Parker hoped to deliver amusements from) as a main attraction. These women were meant to be from the Middle or "Far East" and were shown as supposedly more sexual than American women, and therefore more barbaric (Rabinovitz, 2012, loc. 1046). The dancers themselves were rarely from those cultures, the dances were not actually from the cultures to which they claimed to belong. They were purely meant to sexually titillate male customers, and as Lauren Rabinovitz notes, "They were a case of instilling sexual desire as a substitute or front for imperialist desires" (2012, loc. 1052). The women would not be nearly as exciting if they were white—even though they often were. These shows were brought to Coney Island following the Fairs, and often were given religious themes.

The ethnological displays at the fair—such as the Igorottes, a Philippine tribe that traveled to several world's fairs—became traveling exhibits until finding permanent homes at amusement parks. Coney Island had an exhibit from Singapore that was incredibly successful in 1910 (Rabinovitz, 2012). Although shows varied, subjects often lived in terrible conditions, and were forced to eat food that they would not normally eat (the most common was dog food, which was a 'delicacy' to the Igorottes, but they were often forced to eat it daily for the crowds). As these displays became less popular, they were sometimes replaced by plantation shows.

The world's fairs and their continued influence on worldwide amusements are incredibly important, not just to those seeking to study amusement parks and culture, but because they were organized and initiated by the people who held power in the nineteenth and twentieth centuries (Rydell, 2000). That their influence on parks being built now on the other side of the world continues is unsurprising, but also troubling, given that they re-enact power structures from the 1800s and 1900s as often as those present today. Considering that the anthropological exhibits at the World's Columbian Exposition were headed by W. J. McGee, this is especially troubling—McGee held that various races had different cranial capacities and "emphasized the white man's burden as the key to worldwide evolutionary human progress" (Rydell, 2000, loc. 918). Even when Disneyland opened, an Indian village was part of the initial display, meant as a living exhibit of Native American life. It was quietly removed, though still remembered by early guests. Parks worldwide continue to have "Western" and "exotic" themed areas, though today they are much more likely to use animatronic figures in the dark or water rides to represent native peoples than actual people cajoled into servitude from their homelands. Yet this type of display remains a central tenet of the amusement park genre, designed for the betterment of white people, despite the fact that guests also include people of color.

Segregation at amusement parks was a de facto rule, even in northern parks, until the Civil Rights movement of the 1960s. Southern parks explicitly disallowed African Americans and had "whites only" policies (Rabinovitz, 2012). Amusement parks allowed for the mingling of the sexes, and even immigrants, in a way that had never been allowed in public before, but African Americans were still not allowed (despite other "non-white" races generally being granted admission). Some parks would close for the season for whites and then have late autumn seasons for African Americans, while others would hold special days when black people were allowed to attend (Rabinovitz, 2012). Northern parks were *also* segregated, though it was done much more quietly. Parks would hire private security guards, and even sometimes the police, and they had policies that enabled them to ask anyone to leave at any time. Interracial dating and swimming were not allowed, and at parks where black people were able to ride rides, they were definitely not allowed to swim. In Cleveland, following Plessy v. Ferguson, black people were no longer allowed in Euclid Beach Park's dance hall, and at Youngstown's Idora Park a man lost a lawsuit when he tried to gain entry into the dance hall legally only to be told that "a park dance hall was not 'a place of public resort'" (Rabinovitz, 2012, loc. 694). In order to avoid "trouble," more and more Northern parks would admit black people on "Jim Crow Days" but often the pool was mysteriously out of order that day. Other parks would admit black patrons to the pool one day during the week or once a year, directly before the pool was drained and cleaned and refilled. Black only parks also were built and owned by African American families, often just down the street from the white-owned and operated parks, but they often did not last many years, and were beset by the same issues that closed many white parks, such as the Great Depression and rationing during the World Wars.

Lauren Rabinovitz (2012) argues that parks managed to flourish *because* they were able to determine ways to socially stratify their guests and maintain the separations of races and classes as was expected by "polite" society during the formative years of American amusements. The primary difference between then and today is that today's parks maintain a certain degree of class and racial segregation through pricing—and while Rabinovitz argues that parks "were able to include everyone in learning technological accommodation and urban modernist perceptions" that is simply no longer the case (2012, loc. 976). As parks moved away from being in cities, and to a Disney model where theme parks were located farther away (and at a greater price), not everyone could afford to go, a situation often re-enforcing models of class and racial stratification.

At the exact moment that parks began languishing because they were being forced to integrate, Disneyland opened with an entirely new model for amusement parks worldwide. During the Civil Rights movement, several parks simply closed rather than integrate. Many of those remaining open were seen as dirty and unsafe; in part, because of poor maintenance and in part because of integration. Riots at parks occurred during demonstrations, but were still unusual, as most demonstrations remained peaceful. Although Disney's model proved very lucrative and has been copied many times, it also provided a means of "answering" the displeasure people had with park integration with an entirely new model of park design and control.

Disney

The story of how Walt Disney was watching his young children at an amusement park only to be disgusted by the state it was in and decided to start thinking about his own park is emblematic of the shift that occurred in the amusement industry in the mid-century years. Disney would "revive the aspiration to create a paradise within the limitations of a protective enclave. Disney and theme park planners after him created ideal visions of history and the future, with an emphasis on technological advances and the achievements of the American corporate system" (Adams, 1991, p. xiv). In short, Disney reified the purpose that amusement parks and roller coasters were first built with, and brought back Thompson's ideals of what the right ride, right park, and right people could do. New parks were built in the middle of swamps, out in the country, and far away from the busy messiness of cities and their inhabitants. Most of them required cars to visit (unlike the trolley parks of the early 1900s, that were all in cities or reachable or even owned by public transit).

Judith Adams describes Disney's parks and those built afterwards as:

...miraculous Elysiums of exotic locales, gardens, technological wonders, and thrill rides. Walt Disney World Resort would elevate the concept to that of New World Mecca, a pilgrimage center that has replaced the spiritual shine as the symbolic glorification of cultural achievement" (1991, p. xiv).

Disney parks permanently enshrined the myths of America and "elevate[d] cultural heroes to the status of sainthood" (1991, p. xiv). These new parks are utterly controlled, utterly selective, and utterly technological. Theme parks are simply new world's fairs, new White Cities, and a new means of spreading American culture and exceptionalism—they look different, but have the same aims as Thompson's railways and the World's Expositions that came before them.

Disneyland, though it did not immediately create successors and imitators, has become the theme park on which all others are based. Its success is in every aspect of the park being controlled. It is contained within a gate which guests must pay to pass (not all amusement parks in the preceding century did this, many were accessible from every angle, and some still exist without a main gate to this day such as Knoebel's in Elysburg, Pennsylvania). At Disney, "everything about the park, including the behavior of the 'guests,' is engineered to promote a spirit of optimism, a belief in progressive improvement toward perfection. Elements within the park achieve mythic, religious significance as treasured icons protecting us against infusion or assault by evil in any form, including our own faults" (Adams, 1991, p. 97). As we enter Main Street USA, we are brought into a world that is a perfect America—here are shops, here are smiling people, here is a trolley, there is a fire station "just in case," and everything is very clean and looks very prosperous. Adams describes it as a "haven for white America," lacking any "immigrant and ethnic infusions" (1991, pp. 98-99). This is a place we are all meant to feel safe, though who "we" is remains discreetly ill-defined. In Shanghai Disneyland, for example, there is no "Main Street USA" but, nevertheless, there is a front section of the park with European-themed shops that focus on various Disney characters, and that serves the same purpose, despite the lack of name.

In Disneyland (or any of the Disney parks), "Disney realism" reigns, where the past is cleaned up, unpleasantries from history are simply ignored, and the stories of the past of our country are repackaged and whitewashed for an adoring public (Fjellman, 1992). Disney parks are marketed as incredibly safe, at odds with the parks that came before them where race riots had occurred. As Stephen Fjellman writes, "one of the most palpable things at WDW is the lack of fear—not just fear of moving vehicles...but fear of other people. Visitors remark that one can walk Disney's streets without fear of being attacked, hurt, or robbed. Even at night, under lights often surprisingly subdued, people seem unafraid" (Fjellman, 1992, p. 200). As such, the park meets Disney's vision of being different from all those that came before. There would be no dirt, no sham, no menace—of course, had he only visited those parks years before, he would have found a shining White City instead of the "menacing atmosphere" he claimed dominated parks (Adams, 1991, p. 93).

Disneyland was a genre-setting park, creating the standard from which future theme parks would be made. Its "lands" (Tomorrowland, Adventureland, Frontierland, etc.) would be introduced into older parks and new parks would be built around them. Today, parks tend to set their "lands" (if not in the future) as in the past. from independence from Great Britain through the "taming of the West" (Fjellman, 1992, p. 80). The history that is represented is very carefully picked and chosen to represent the best of America—and while it might seem silly to suggest that we represent the worst, certainly what Fjellman refers to as the "silences" in the history provided at parks can be troubling, even if they might interrupt our fun. As guests have become increasingly diverse, so, too, should the histories that are represented in our playlands. Fjellman calls the history that is represented in theme parks "Distory," noting that:

...the romance is underlined and the anarchy defused through humor and nostalgization. The tension between anarcho-pragmatism and mechanical geographic determinism...is resolved by making the 'I' into a 'we' and the 'we' into a corporation, whose scientists will undo the determinisms. Disney transforms the pioneer into the inventor. (1992, p. 95)

Nowhere is this clearer than in EPCOT.

EPCOT

In the last film that he ever made, Walt Disney talked about his vision for a new type of city that he was going to build at Walt Disney World:

This model city...will be a community of tomorrow that will never be completed, but will always be introducing and testing and demonstrating new materials and systems. And EPCOT will always be a showcase to the world for the ingenuity and imagination of American free enterprise.

I don't believe there's a challenge anywhere in the world that is more important to people everywhere than finding solutions to the problems of our cities. But where do we begin? Well, we're convinced that we must start with the public need. And the need is not just for curing old ills of old cities, or even just building a whole new shiny city. We think the need is for starting from scratch on virgin land like this, and building a special kind of community....

It will be a planned, controlled community, a showcase for American industry and research, schools, cultural and educational opportunities. In EPCOT there will be no slum areas because we won't let them develop. There will be no landowners and therefore no voting control. People will rent houses instead of buying them, and at modest rentals. There will be no retirees. Everyone must be employed. One of the requirements is that people who live in EPCOT must keep it alive. (Fjellman, 1992, pp. 114-116)

EPCOT, as Walt Disney envisioned it, was a White City for the future. Here is a world where there are no slums, and everyone rents. There are no retirees (are they asked to leave when they are too old to work?) and apparently children either do not live there or are also employed. Everyone must work to keep EPCOT alive.

The EPCOT that was built, of course, is not a city that people live in. However, it does feature some of the things that Disney hoped for, including even more rigid technological control and infrastructure than Disneyland or the Magic Kingdom. Instead, EPCOT has become an always-evolving world's fair, complete with corporations that display applied technologies and a World Showcase with displays from many countries around the world. Currently, it is slowly evolving away from a model similar to the world's fair, and is including more Disney Intellectual Properties (IPs) in its various rides. Despite that, it should not be ignored that Walt Disney wished to build a true White City—one that was meant to be lived in and always be developing, instead of one that would collapse within a few years.

Amusement Parks as a Means of Distributing Culture

Lauren Rabinovitz (2012) has argued that amusement parks spread American metropolitan culture across the country. They provided people with a place to see movies, view science experiments, listen to lectures, and even to attend school (in the cases where amusement parks hosted Chautauquas). However, this cultural dissemination also spread racism, prejudice, and white supremacy alongside new scientific knowledge. As noted above, for every Edison or Tesla making incredible demonstrations of the power of electricity, there was also a businessman selling the lives of natives from the Philippines, Africa, South America, and other supposedly "wild and uncivilized" locations into slavery for the sake of American education. These "traditions" have been difficult for the industry to break away from.

Rabinovitz writes about the period when amusement parks spread from Coney Island in New York very rapidly across the country. Today, her writings can be used to track and understand the spread of theme parks from Disneyland across the world, and the culture that has come with it.

Amusement parks and movies were two intertwined means of the distribution of city cultures across the country. Prior to World War I, movies and amusement parks (amusement parks often housed movie theaters as well as vaudeville theaters) helped to homogenize the American public (Rabinovitz, 2012). They were also seen as places where reckless behavior was explicitly encouraged, and men and women were allowed to hold hands, straddle the same carousel horse, and touch one another on the human roulette wheel.

Rabinovitz argues that there was less difference between the rural and city dweller in part because amusement parks brought technologies, electricity, and movies to the masses (2012). They were able to see fashion in the movies, experience technologies and electricity through the rides, and ultimately were able to bring those things into their homes. Amusement parks were built in cities across the country to copy what was in Coney Island and to have their own White City. Today we have many more means of cultural transmission than in the early 1900s; and indeed, the Internet, television, movies, radio, cell phones, and other amusements have taken the place of amusement parks as ways that people learn about the world.

And yet, amusement parks themselves remain incredibly formulaic, and are modeled almost exclusively from the formula set by Disney in the mid-1950s. These parks have a castle as a centerpiece, a water ride that shows various nations of the world, a dark ride that is frightening, a carousel, and several themed areas—why? And why does Western folklore dominate? Though this has been proven to be monetarily effective, the very few advancements in design are surprising when theming, attractions, and rides have all improved immeasurably. If you visit a theme park in almost any country there will be themed areas, lands, a castle, some gardens, and areas built around European fantasy, or fairytales—very little has changed.

ROLLER COASTERS AND AMUSEMENTS AS MORAL MACHINES

The roller coaster was invented to bring morality to the masses, opened in a city corner of ill repute, then copied in cities across the country. It was added to the White Cities, to Coney Island, and it formed a literal and spiritual backbone of American entertainment for half a century. While its mechanical and technological nature was criticized, its moral nature was not. Thompson's roller coaster argues that if man just had the right entertainment then he will not be driven to the wrong entertainment.

Technology has always been the American savior as well as the American serpent, leading us astray. Roller coasters have followed an altered path to other new technologies (from writing to novels to radio to movies, television, the Internet, and video games—most new technologies are assumed to be evil when first invented, but slowly accepted into our salvation), as they were developed first as saviors, fell from grace, and later would be redeemed time again as potential means of distribution of proper morals.

However, the American morality distributed with our amusement machines is not one devoid of superiority, racism, and ethnocentrism—it could not be. The theme park industrial structure continues to advantage American-style policies and stories, with very few parks daring to move beyond Western conceptions of storytelling in their park designs and experience architecture. The culture disseminated by the amusement park and theme park is more complicated than Thompson could have ever imagined. As Rabinovitz argues,

...amusement parks both appealed to and resisted "melting pot" culture in important ways: (1) They served as a symbol of revolt from traditional, genteel cultural standards. (2) They offered new forms of spectacle for individuals and families whose lives were increasingly organized by the time clock, technologies, and pressures of an industrial society. (3) They tamed and turned people's fears of new technologies and of each other into more tightly integrated routines and rhythms of work and leisure. (4) They helped to teach men and women how to cope with women's increasing autonomy and independence and how to contain it through visual surveillance. (5) They promoted identification and unity with American nationalist values while spatially and structurally maintaining social divisions of race and class: they more often upheld social segregation over social integration. (2012, loc. 1420)

In many ways, the amusement park is the perfect representation of American morality—always wanting to be better, more inclusive, more diverse than it actually is.

Lewis Mumford described the amusement park as "spiritual masturbation" (1922, p. 13). We believe that we are being moral and good, but in reality we are only continuing to expose ourselves to more subjugation by technology and machines. Machines cannot bring us morality:

The urban worker escapes the mechanical routine of his daily job only to find an equally mechanical substitute for life and growth and experience in his amusements.... The movies, the White Ways, and the Coney Islands, which almost every American city boasts in some form or other, are means of giving jaded and throttled people the sensations of living without the direct experience of life—a sort of spiritual masturbation. (Mumford, 1922, p. 13)

In a sense, these entertainments are part of what Mumford believed to be evidence of a depleted civilization that bred conformity while trying to urge creativity, stuck in a cycle of longed-for monetary success at the expense of spiritual satisfaction.

Spectacle and Ideology

Debord writes that authentic social life has been replaced with a representation of that social life, or spectacle (1994). Indeed, nowhere should that be clearer than in an amusement park where people ride through a fake mountain in a fake train, visit all the countries of the world by flying through them or riding a boat around them, or race on the back of a horse tied to a pole. In fact, a lot of modern amusements sound a lot like Debord's description of societies ruled by modern production:

...life is presented as an immense accumulation of spectacles. Everything that was directly lived has receded into a representation...The images detached from every aspect of life merge into a common stream in which the unity of that life can no longer be recovered. Fragmented views of reality regroup themselves into a new unity as a separate pseudoworld that can only be looked at. The specialization of images of the world evolves into a world of autonomized images where even the deceivers are deceived. The spectacle is a concrete inversion of life, an autonomous movement of the nonliving. (1994, Loc. 357)

Specifically, Debord's concept that the spectacle presents itself "simultaneously as society itself, as a part of society, and as a means of unification" (1994, loc. 360) fit the modern-themed amusement ride. The hero (because there is always a hero) is guiding us through a dangerous passage filled with dinosaurs ("Jurassic Park"), the "Other" ("Indiana Jones") or aliens ("Toy Story Mania"). Then we unify through our desire to defeat the other, who in an amusement ride is always bigger and badder than they might be in real life. But that is not its danger—the danger of the spectacle is its attempts at unification and social relation "mediated by images" (loc. 366). The images that we accept as the "Other," as the enemy, as the object of humor or contempt affect us, and are accepted parts the spectacle both within parks and outside of them.

But it is not just othering at play in racism in theme park attractions that is problematic. It is that the rides themselves (if not characters within them) represent "sublime objects" that people will defend and honor beyond a reasonable point. Žižek notes that:

...all successful political ideologies necessarily refer to and turn around sublime objects posited by political ideologies. These sublime objects are what political subjects take it that their regime's ideologies' central words mean or name extraordinary Things like God, the Fuhrer, the King, in whose name they will (if necessary) transgress ordinary moral laws. (Sharpe, 2020)

Is Mickey Mouse equivalent to God? Outside of the boundaries of a theme park—no. Within? Mickey is sublime. Mickey is the goal of any theme park designer. Recreating the success of the sublime object is the goal of copying the attractions that surround the sublime objects.

Althusser insists that our ideology is material—that ii is embodied in our institutions, our practices, our lives, and—for our purposes--our amusement rides (Sharpe, 2020). What ideology is materialized in the "Jungle Cruise" and every ride designed after it? What ideology is materialized when we open a ride designed to be like "It's a Small World" but with racist caricatures? What ideology is materialized when Six Flags Over Texas opened with an entire section dedicated to one of its Six Flags—the Confederacy? What ideology is materialized and manifest when parks are designed to look like Disney World in a country that does not celebrate princesses? Is there anyone even to name the castle after? "In all of its particular manifestations — news, propaganda, advertising, entertainment — the spectacle represents the dominant model of life" (Debord, 1994, loc. 373). The materialization of these ideologies is in many cases no longer necessary—there are other stories to be told, and plenty of technological means to do so.

Debord (1994) writes that commodities are fetishized. Our societies are dominated by things both tangible and not, and our society "attains its ultimate fulfillment in the spectacle, where the real world is replaced by a selection of images which are projected above it, yet which at the same time succeed in making themselves regarded as the epitome of reality" (1994, loc. 576). The larger question I'd like to raise would be, how do we keep our spectacle from infecting the rest of the world?

Western Colonialism in Amusement Park Design

American and Western domination in theme park design internationally presents two issues: 1) the erasure and silencing of local culture in amusement parks, and 2) the emulation of racist cultural practices embedded in American and Western culture. Much as the spread of amusement parks across early America also spread the subjugation of Filipinos and other peoples put on ethnographic display and segregated amusements, today's cultural influences are not neutral. When a theme park opens with an Old West section in a country that never had an "Old West," when a park adopts fairy tales from other places in the world simply because "that's what theme parks do," and when parks even open far outside of the city boundaries disabling the use of public transit to get to them, they are welcoming both the negative *and* positive influence of Western morality into their parks.

To demonstrate one (of many) potential issues with the sort of rides and designs that come from Western colonialism in international parks, this section will compare two Chinese amusement parks. Chinese parks are chosen for this exercise because Chinese parks are incredibly new. According to Lew, Yu, Ap, and Zhang (2003), the first Chinese theme park is usually recognized as Splendid China, which opened in 1989. When visiting Chinese theme parks, locals will often refer to those built in the 1990s as "old," sometimes even claiming that they must be 50 years old or older—but there are not Chinese theme parks that are 50 years old or older. China holds a unique position in the world of themed entertainment because their parks do not have a long history. What historical relics they feature come entirely from extra-cultural interference.

The first park meant for comparison, Happy Valley, is largely designed based upon the Western/Disney model. It is incredibly well-themed, and features many large, well-designed roller coasters. Despite this, some of its rides and its theming suggest Western-influenced racism. In the second example, this chapter will look at a new Fantawild park that is based upon Chinese history—a break with past parks in the chain that were more Western-influenced. In so doing, it will show how theme parks can successfully be used to tell other stories.

China is chosen because of the rapid expansion of their amusement and theme park industry during the past decade, and also because their parks would mostly be defined as theme parks (as opposed to parks that tell fewer stories or focus exclusively on rides—Universal Studios is a theme park, while most Six Flags parks are more geared towards amusements). However, China is also a good example because the myth of the West appeals in modern day China. In China:

For the settling of the western United States is not simply a myth of national identity. It is also a commercial product. The myth of the West sells. It sells books, paintings, clothes, children's birthday party themes, and, most importantly, tourism. The U.S. model of western development offers not only the rugged cowboy but a theme park in which to play the cowboy. And the theme park model is certainly one that China has taken to heart. If California was singled out by the campaign's framers as the model par excellence of nineteenth-century land development and twentieth-century high-tech industrialization, then Disneyland's Frontierland in Anaheim, California, surely marks the apogee of America's ability to turn myths into money. The theme park's alchemic magic, churning the ephemera of myth into hard cash, is something that the U.S. West has also bequeathed China. (Jensen & Weston, 2007, p. 243)

At once, Chinese theme parks are wonderful examples of Chinese exceptionalism, while featuring largely Western themes. In part, this is because, as Philips observes, "the stories that the theme park tells are those of Empire and of colonial adventure" (1999, 106). Creating a theme park that is non-colonial, that is not about conquering heroes, that is not about the exotic, is a challenge for every country to come up their own response.

Happy Valley Beijing

Happy Valley in Beijing (北京欢乐谷), owned by Beijing OCT (Overseas Chinese Town Company) has a ride that showcases why American export of culture via the amusement industry is potentially problematic. Happy Valley parks follow an easily recognizable structure based upon Disney. The parks feature large, prominent, themed elements that not only enable guests to navigate the parks via landmarks (Walt Disney referred to these as "weenies"), but they also feature themed areas that are easily recognizable as being similar or identical to those found at parks worldwide. It might be easy to accuse Chinese parks of copying rides and park designs from European and American ones (roller coaster producer Golden Horse has a coaster with very similar track design, layout, and train design to Vekoma's Standard Looping Coaster, for one example). However, that is not entirely fair. Parts of theme parks worldwide, from their rides to shows to sections meant to be culturally educational—can trace their roots, as previously shown, to either world's fairs or the influence of the Walt Disney Company. In short, Disneyland determined what a theme park "is" and that structure has been replicated across national borders.

In the case of Happy Valley Beijing, the themed sections are based heavily upon Greek mythology, the lost civilization of the Mayas, and other world sites. Sections are themed to the Aegean Harbor, Fjords, Atlantis, Shangri-La, the Mayan ruins, and desserts (for the children's area). Now, by no means should any country have only theme areas based upon their own culture, but the influence of Western culture (and its potential genre-ification in theme parks) should be clear.

However, more than the themed areas, Happy Valley here is analyzed because of a single ride. Titled "Happy World," the ride is a dark ride on a boat through a number of rooms themed to different parts of the world clearly modeled after "It's a Small World."

"It's a Small World" was first built for UNICEF for the 1964 New York World's Fair (Nooshin, 2004). After the Fair, it was moved to Disneyland, then copies and updated versions were opened at Walt Disney World's Magic Kingdom, Tokyo Disneyland, Disneyland Paris, and Hong Kong Disneyland. The ride is meant to playfully depict world unity, with the use of children singing the theme in their own languages being central elements to that design.

Outside of *Song of the South* (1946) and its connection with "Splash Mountain[1]," few other Disney rides have been the object of as many objections or outright accusations of racism as "It's a Small World." While the ride is meant to promote peace, depictions of many races around the world in a cute, and potentially reductive, manner has certainly been seen as racist over the past 60 years. Small changes to the ride, from costumes to props have been made as a result, and while it does not continue entirely un-challenged, in general, the ride has been seen as having merits that outweigh those issues. In an analysis of the Paris version of the ride, Lauden Nooshin writes,

The visitor to Small World does not experience the ride in isolation, but in relation to the many other narratives and discourses around which the park is built. The most prominent of these are the narratives of colonial adventure, empire and encounter with the 'Other', whether in human form or symbolized through frontiers of nature, science or geography, which run through many theme parks (not just Disney) and which are well documented in the literature. (2004, p. 239).

The colonial adventures of the Disney parks are clearly seen in the stories represented: we are ar-chaeologists with Indiana Jones, we are Pirates of the Caribbean, we are members of the crew of Jules Verne's many adventure tales, and so on. Nooshin notes that the "pith-helmeted explorer" is a common figure in theme parks, marking the colonizer as the hero of the tales that it tells. The colonizer is the hero, and—the colonized? They are mostly absent. "In short, then, the Disney theme parks are largely shaped (to varying degrees of subtlety) by the history of Euro-American expansionism in one form or another, or by American appropriation of European fairy stories (Nooshin, 2004, p. 240).

This makes rides like "It's a Small World" at times uncomfortable, as here are the missing cultures that remain underrepresented elsewhere in the park. The ride represents a specific world order that is not just present within it, but connected outside the park as well: "this ride does not simply constitute a representation of a certain world order and a particular set of asymmetrical power relationships: it also plays a part in reinforcing and perpetuating them" (Nooshin, 2004, p. 246). Indeed, as similar rides have spread across the globe, it *has* perpetuated an odd world order and cultural supremacy, especially when removed from Disney's parks.

Happy Valley Beijing is one of many parks world-wide that have a "tour of the world" boat ride. In "Happy World," guests board boats that take them through several different themed rooms with characters dressed as people from around the world and from many different time periods. In this case, however, the animatronic figures are not children, but instead are ostensibly adults, as they are shown drinking beer (there is a beer room with animated beer pitchers), and represent famous people from all over the world, such as Steve Jobs. The characters have huge noses, small eyes, and large open mouths.

While the representation in the original "It's a Small World" at least attempted to be respectful, in many copies of it all over the world that respect has not been emulated. Truthfully, it's hard to say if this is due to cultural misunderstanding, different cultures' definitions and understandings of racism, and even simply different cultures of origin. It is impossible as a Westerner to pronounce that "Happy World" or any other ride like it located anywhere outside of the West is racist, but there are definitely depictions of cultures and races inside the ride that are deeply problematic by Western standards. At this time, parks like Disney are attempting to remove racist elements from their rides. Meanwhile, rides based upon those elements are still being constructed elsewhere in the world and are unlikely to have their racist elements removed.

For example, on this ride at Happy Valley there is a figure of a Native American next to a teepee holding both a bow (no arrow) and a parrot. Michael Jackson is presented as white. In another scene Hawaiian girls and a rabbit (human-sized) dance together. Totems and symbols from a wide array of cultures are mixed and displayed together (or incorrectly). One of the figures from Africa has large teeth, a headdress, and both a mustache and face paint. Most of the native islanders or African nations are represented by what appear to be cartoonish gods instead of actual human figures granted to other nations. There is clear cultural superiority granted to China, Japan, Egypt, and the United States (while penguins also get a room and a great deal of seeming respect). Worse still, golliwog dolls were sold in the gift store at the park's exit in 2018.

As noted above, it is difficult to charge Happy Valley or its ride designers with racism. After all, they are just making a ride that is very much like all the others that have come before it—just unfortunately one complete with the racist issues involved therein. "Happy World" manages to emulate both the best and worst elements of its ride genre. This is why the export of American culture via theme parks matters—when America exports our culture this way we do not just export our current culture, we export our past. We do not just export the best parts of our parks, but also the worst parts. Rides based upon Splash Mountain are, it turns out, going to drastically out live Splash Mountain itself, which will be redesigned into a *Princess and the Frog* ride in the near future. In making American theme parks the model for the rest of the world, America also set up the rest of the world to inherit our prejudices and our morals.

Fantawild Oriental Heritage

However, just because theme parks have always been a genre that glorifies American stories and exceptionalism does not mean, in any way, that they must remain so. Some, such as Bakken in Denmark Wurstelprater in Austria, and Hanayashiki (浅草花やしき) in Japan, literally predate the American model. However, parks built either after the model of the world's fairs or after Disney present either American-centric or Euro-centric designs, stories, and even discrimination into their experience. Despite the "formula" that was presented by CV Wood when he left employment with Disney and began opening his own series of amusement parks, there is no real "rule" stating that amusement parks must feature American-styled adventure stories into their grand narrative in order to be successful (Lambert, 1992).

Today, some of the largest expansion in the theme park industry is occurring in the Middle East and China. The Roller Coaster Database lists 1,107 parks in China, only 21 of which are "standing but not operating," and the majority of which opened in 1995 or later with the greatest period of expansion occurring in the 2000s (RCDB, 2020). In comparison, the United States houses an estimated 400 parks according to IAAPA, and even those numbers may be bloated by arguments over what counts as an "amusement park" (for example: do Family Entertainment Centers count? Malls with one to two rides such as a carousel?). While the US market has been compressing, there has been great expansion in the East.

Although many parks in China such as Happy Valley follow the American model, there have been some notable departures. Fantawild has recently added a new "gate" to their Wuhu, Xiamen, Jinan, Ningbo, Jingzhou and Changsha parks called "Oriental Heritage" or similar names (Fantawild, 2020). Oriental Heritage is described as "a high-tech theme park with the essence of five-thousand-year Chinese culture as the core and modern high-tech as a means of expression" (Fantawild, "About Fantawild," 2020). These parks are part of Fantawild's "Beautiful Chinese Trilogy" series of parks designed to educate and immerse guests in 5,000 years of Chinese history.

Specifically, Fantawild Changsha Oriental Heritage will be examined as the example here for the potential of theme parks to use theming, technology, rides, and immersive technologies to successfully tell new stories to the world. Oriental Heritage is the third "gate" (separate park, such as the Magic Kingdom, EPCOT, and Animal Kingdom are all gates at Walt Disney World) located east of Changsha, the capital city of the Hunan Province. The other two gates of the park feature castles, roller coasters, and even European-themed cities as part of their theming, setting the distinctly Chinese history focus of Oriental Heritage apart. The new park features a roller coaster, but also indoor attractions that present different Chinese legends that celebrate Huxiang culture (Xinhua Net, 2019).

The most impressive is the story of Lady Dai, a world-famous mummy from the Han Dynasty (roughly 163 B.C.E.) which is presented using VR and special effects film techniques that Fantawild is specifically known for, as they are the largest special effects movie company in China (Fantawild, "Special Effects Films," 2020). The life of Xin Zhui (known more widely as "Lady Dai") is performed on a virtual reality stage for audiences.

Lady Dai is important to Changsha, as her tomb was unearthed outside of Changsha in 1971, and she is one of the best-preserved mummies ever found (Smithfield, 2018). While digging for air raid shelter construction, workers stumbled upon a tomb, at the bottom of which they found the nearly perfectly preserved body of Lady Dai wrapped in several layers of silk. When the tomb was found, the shelter construction was halted, and the site began to be excavated. There were many precious artifacts in the tomb, some of which are now displayed in the nearby Hunan Provincial Museum along with the body of Lady Dai. Lady Dai was the wife of Li Chang (the Marquis of Dai), and she was sealed within multiple coffins. When she was found, her skin was soft and moist, her hair was intact, and her muscles were bendable without the normal signs of decomposition or rigor mortis (Smithfield, 2018). It was eventually determined that she had to have been preserved in an unknown acidic liquid which prevented decomposition, but it has not been identified.

The story of Lady Dai's discovery is incredibly important to the surrounding province and a source of national pride. The Hunan Provincial Museum was recently redesigned and reopened so that now guests travel to the top of the tomb first, traveling through rooms and layers of artifacts that tell the story of not only how the tomb was found, but what was in each layer. At the bottom, they are able to peer down into a sealed vault with a glass roof that allows them to see Lady Dai herself. Lady Dai has been featured on multiple television shows and documentaries, including *Unsolved Mysteries*, and so is relatively well-known world-wide as well.

Naturally, a history theme park in Changsha would have to feature some part of this story. The Fantawild ride does not choose to retell what one can learn at the museum, however. Instead, it focuses on the life of Lady Dai, taking advantage of virtual reality and augmented reality elements to show what her life was like, and immerses the audience into things that she might have done and experienced. As a result, it takes full advantage of the technology available to not only help the audience learn about the past, but also to help them feel as though they have experienced it.

Fantawild features ride systems that are (not yet) seen anywhere else in the world, including large domed theaters with rotating and moving seats, projection technologies extended beyond those seen in the Universal Parks, and incredible attention to theming that most Western-themed parks lack. They are selling these new technologies to parks world-wide as well, and have exported their technology to more than 40 countries and territories (Fantawild, "Special Effects Films," 2020).

Most importantly, however, Fantawild has moved past a model that uses Western models of theme parks to tell Western stories with Western morals. While their earlier gates might have featured IPs with Western ideals, this new series of parks is fully Chinese. This is done not only intentionally for Asian guests, but also is meant to fuel worldwide cultural exchanges. The company is responding to a "policy of 'deepening cultural exchanges globally'" which they have seen as a natural "new direction for the industry" (Xinhua Net, 2019). There is not, at this time, any indication that Fantawild wishes to build parks in North America, but there is simply no reason (beyond American nationalism) that it should not happen. While most American theme park operators are not in a position to open new parks at this time, overseas companies that are rapidly expanding *could* export their cultural and technological products to the US—whether or not these would be accepted by US audiences remains to be seen. Of course, if such parks came with roller coasters and ride technologies not seen anywhere on the continent, vacationers would certainly visit.

CONCLUSION

There are no easy answers to what means should be used to change what morals and cultures that theme parks represent. It is risky to open a park like one that no one has seen before, after all. Can a theme park be successful that does not meet our preconceived notions of what a theme park is? Fantawild suggests that it can, but these parks have not yet spread outside of their country of origin.

It may not be up to the West to lead the way in a revolution in this industry. The Disney California Adventure Park eventually re-themed the area that was explicitly themed Coney Island to Pixar IPs, losing much of the local "California" theming of the park—other than its Hollywood influences. These local elements were likely less interesting to guests as they could experience some of them outside the gates, and parks worldwide have similar issues—how to work the stories of an area into its theme park without introducing disinterest and boredom?

China's Fantawild (and, indeed, all Chinese parks) has a unique perspective, in that Chinese history covers entire millennia, and the cultural stories of China are well-known to its inhabitants due to the way that they are studied in school. Being able to blend new technologies with historical stories that are known well allows the park to go beyond the well-known into the fanciful, and even educational, without introducing disinterest or boredom to guests. Also, Chinese people often have strong feelings of pride in their country, history, and stories, and appreciate having them celebrated in such a public space.

As a public, we should be willing to accept new stories via technological formats such as roller coasters, dark rides, motion theaters, and more. While our newer rides in the United States tell stories of superheroes, wizards, and pirates, few have moved away from traditional Campbellian hero narratives. The few that have (such as the "Nights in White Satin: The Trip" ride at the now-defunct Hard Rock Park) have been widely well-acclaimed. Such risk-taking should be recognized more broadly by the public, and even amusement ride awards bodies in general.

Roller coasters, dark rides, and theme parks are all moral machines, currently employed primarily to recreate Western values across the world. However, in looking at the history of this phenomenon and showing its repercussions today, that does not mean that there is no way forward. Amusement parks were meant to save man—but that does not just mean that they need to continue to only save white man. They can be used to share culture across borders, not just reinforce Western supremacy.

REFERENCES

Adams, J. (1991). *The American amusement park industry: A history of technology and thrills (Twayne's Evolution of American Business Series)*. Twayne's Publishers.

Althusser, L. (2014, February). *On the reproduction of capitalism: Ideology and ideological state apparatuses*. New York: Verso.

Debord, G. (2009). *Society of the spectacle*. Sussex: Soul Bay Press.

Fantawild. (2015). Fantawild Oriental Heritage Opens Soon. *Fantawild*. https://www.fantawild.com/en/medialist/show/88.htm

Fantawild. (2016). About Fantawild. *Fantawild*. https://www.fantawild.com/en/layout.shtml

Fantawild. (2016). Special Effects Films. *Fantawild*. https://www.fantawild.com/en/business vrmovie.shtml

Fjellman, S. (1992). *Vinyl leaves: Walt Disney World and America* (1st ed.). Routledge.

Fletcher, P. (2015). *Historically African American leisure destinations around Washington, D.C.* New York: The History Press.

Foster, H., & Jackson, W. (1946, November 12). *Song of the South*. Walt Disney Productions.

Frank, A. (2020, June 26). Disney is overhauling Splash Mountain to remove the ride's ties to a racist film. *Vox.com*. https://www.vox.com/culture/2020/6/26/21303247/disney-splash-mountain-redesign-racist-song-of-the-south

Gert, J. (2016, February 8). The definition of morality. *Stanford encyclopedia of philosophy*. https://plato.stanford.edu/entries/morality-definition/#NormDefiMora

Happy Valley. (2020). *Happy Valley Beijing*. http://bj.happyvalley.cn/

Jensen, L., & Weston, T. (2007). *China's transformations: The stories beyond the headlines*. Rowan & Littlefield.

Kasson, J. (1978). *Amusing the million: Coney Island at the turn of the century*. Hill & Wang.

Lambert, B. (1992, March 16). C. V. Wood Jr., who pioneered large theme parks, is dead at 71. *The New York Times*. https://www.nytimes.com/1992/03/16/us/c-v-wood-jr-who-pioneered-large-theme-parks-is-dead-at-71.html

Lew, A. A., Yu, L., Ap, J., & Zhang, G. (2003). *Tourism in China*. The Haworth Hospitality Press.

Mangels, W. (1952). *The outdoor amusement industry*. Vantage Press Inc.

Mitchell, R. (1998). Learning through play and pleasure travel: Using play literature to enhance research into touristic learning. *Current Issues in Tourism*, *1*(2), 176–188. doi:10.1080/13683509808667838

Mohun, A. (2013). Amusement Parks for the World: The Export of American Technology and Know-How, 1900—1939. *Icon (London, England), 19*, 100–112.

Moscardo, G. (1996). Mindful visitors: Heritage and tourism. *Annals of Tourism Research, 23*(2), 376–397. doi:10.1016/0160-7383(95)00068-2

Mumford, L. (1922). *The city. Civilization in the United States: An Inquiry by 30 Americans* (H. E. Stearns, Ed.). Harcourt Brace & Company. https://ia800302.us.archive.org/10/items/civilizationinun00stea/civilizationinun00stea.pdf

Nooshin, L. (2004). Circumnavigation with a Difference? Music, Representation and the Disney Experience: "It's a Small, Small World." *Ethnomusicology Forum, 13*(2), 236.

Philips, D. (1999). Narrativized spaces: The function of story in the theme park. In D. Crouch (Ed.), *Leisure/ tourism geographies: Practices and geographical knowledge* (pp. 91–108). Routledge.

Pitman, T., Broomhall, S., McEwan, J., & Majocha, E. (2010). Adult learning in educational tourism. *Australian Journal of Adult Learning, 50*(2).

Prentice, C. (2014). *The lost tribe of Coney Island: Headhunters, Luna Park, and the man who pulled off the spectacle of the century.* Amazon Publishing.

Rabinovitz, L. (2012). *Electric dreamland.* Columbia University Press.

Rajtz, T., Smith, M., & Mihalka, G. (2008). New places in old spaces: Mapping tourism and regeneration in Budapest. *Tourism Geographies, 10*(4), 429–451. doi:10.1080/14616680802434064

Rayman, J. (2017). Žižek's Ethics. *International Journal of Žižek Studies, 11*(2). http://zizekstudies.org/index.php/IJZS/article/view/1002/0

RCDB. (2020). Roller Coaster Database Search Results: China. *Roller Coaster Database.* https://rcdb.com/r.htm?order=10&ot=3&ol=26380

Register, W. (2001, October 18). *The kid of Coney Island: Fred Thompson and the Rise of American amusements.* Oxford: Oxford University Press.

Rennix, B. (2019, September 24). Roller coasters and the left. *Current affairs: A magazine of politics and culture.* https://www.currentaffairs.org/2019/09/roller-coasters-and-the-left

Rivers, C. (2016, May 10). *The black and white city: The history of race and race relations at the 1893 Chicago World's Fair.* Amazon Digital Services LLC.

Rydell, R., Fielding, J. E., & Pelle, K.D. (2000, March 17). *Fair America.* Smithsonian Books.

Sharpe, M. (2020). Slavoj Žižek (1949 —). *Internet Encyclopedia of Philosophy.* https://www.iep.utm.edu/zizek/#Hd

Smithfield, B. (2018, February 25). One of the world's most preserved mummies, the Lady of Dai, is still soft to the touch, has bendy ligaments, and is 2,100 years old. *The Vintage News.* https://www.thevintagenews.com/2018/02/25/lady-of-dai/

Sullivan, D. (2015). Coney Island history: The Story of George Tilyou and Steeplechase Park. *Heart of Coney Island*. https://www.heartofconeyisland.com/steeplechase-park-coney-island.html

Sullivan, D. (2015). Coney Island history: The story of William Reynolds and Dreamland. *Heart of Coney Island*. https://www.heartofconeyisland.com/dreamland-coney-island.html

Sullivan, D. (2015). LaMarcus Adna Thompson's scenic railways at Coney Island. *Luna Park, the Heart of Coney Island*. https://www.heartofconeyisland.com/thompson-scenic-railways-roller-coaster.html

Tucker, H. (2001). Tourists and troglodytes: Negotiating for sustainability. *Annals of Tourism Research, 28*(4), 868–891. doi:10.1016/S0160-7383(00)00084-0

Wolcott, V. (2012). *Race, riots and roller coasters: The struggle over segregated recreation in America.* The University of Pennsylvania Press. doi:10.9783/9780812207590

Xinhua Net. (2019, April 17). Fantawild theme parks poised for growth, a fresh dose of vitality to the tourism industry. *Fantawild News*. https://www.fantawild.com/en/newslist/show/1153.htm

ENDNOTE

[1]   On June 26, 2020 it was announced that Disneyland and Walt Disney World would both be revamping "Splash Mountain" to now match the theme of *The Princess and the Frog*, following a petition tied to the Black Lives Matter movement (Frank, 2020). Immediately following the announcement, another petition was created to make changes to "Jungle Cruise."

Chapter 10
Moral Psychology and Artificial Agents (Part One):
Ontologically Categorizing Bio-Cultural Humans

Michael Laakasuo
University of Helsinki, Finland

Anton Kunnari
University of Helsinki, Finland

Jukka R. I. Sundvall
University of Helsinki, Finland

Mika Koverola
University of Helsinki, Finland

Anton Berg
University of Helsinki, Finland

Marko Repo
University of Helsinki, Finland

Marianna Drosinou
University of Helsinki, Finland

Teemu Saikkonen
University of Turku, Finland

Volo Herzon
University of Helsinki, Finland

Jussi Palomäki
University of Helsinki, Finland

ABSTRACT

This is the first of two chapters introducing the moral psychology of robots and transhumanism. Evolved moral cognition and the human conceptual system has naturally embedded difficulties in coping with the new moral challenges brought on by emerging future technologies. The reviewed literature outlines our contemporary understanding based on evolutionary psychology of humans as cognitive organisms. The authors then give a skeletal outline of moral psychology. These fields together suggest that there are many innate and cultural mechanisms which influence how we understand technology and have blind spots in recognizing the moral issues related to them. They discuss human tool use and cognitive categories and show how tools have shaped our evolution. The first part closes by introducing a new concept: the new ontological category (NOC i.e. robots and AI), which did not exist in our evolution. They explain how the NOC is fundamentally confounding for our moral cognitive machinery. In part two, they apply the background provided here on recent empirical studies in the moral psychology of robotics and transhumanism.

DOI: 10.4018/978-1-7998-4894-3.ch010

Copyright © 2021, IGI Global. Copying or distributing in print or electronic forms without written permission of IGI Global is prohibited.

INTRODUCTION

We are surrounded by autonomous artificial agents, many of which pose previously unseen moral challenges through their actions and the consequences of these actions. Artificial Intelligences (AIs) are already used in medical diagnostics (Mangasarian, Setiono, & Wolberg, 1990; Fjell et al., 2008), financial credit evaluation and approval (Poon, 2007), traffic and transportation (Li et al., 2016), and numerous military applications (Springer, 2013). There are visions of life-saving robots guarding our beaches (Guillette, 2019), nanobots cleaning our polluted oceans (Singh & Naveen, 2014), and even robot prostitution (Levy, 2007). But what if an AI recommends medication against a patient's will, or denies a life-changing loan to a family in dire need? What if an autonomous vehicle carrying children decided to divert into a ditch to avoid hitting elderly pedestrians? Should one be allowed to "cheat" on their spouse with a robot, or better yet, marry one? What if military drones could decide on their own where to unload their weapons? These questions of responsibility for autonomous decision-making and behavior that belong to "robot morality" have exceptional societal relevance, not only in terms of law and regulation, but also for our future as a species.

Despite our modern surroundings, however, human cognition is shaped by evolution. What this means in practice, is that humans have fundamental intuitive, automatic, and non-conscious processes constantly operating in the background. Such processes organize our perceptions, thoughts, and reactions to the world outside our minds. Here we argue that robots and AIs should be evaluated not only through the lens of analytical moral philosophy, but also using the tools of experimental moral psychology and evolutionary processes. Understanding what people in general (not only academics) think of moral and legal issues regarding AI helps anticipate them and could (or should) inform technological development and legislation.

In this chapter, we will provide a theoretical background for this current discussion taking place in a variety of different journals. Of late, an increasing number of empirical studies have focused on moral issues related to AIs and opined on transhumanistic concerns for the future of our species. Research has begun uncovering previously unseen moral cognitive phenomena, such as new types of cognitive biases in human-AI interaction, thereby challenging existing theoretical frameworks in cognitive science. In order to describe these challenges, we need to provide the reader with an extensive review of evolutionary, moral, and cognitive sciences of concepts and categories. In another chapter of this book, we review empirical research in the emerging field of moral psychology of robotics and transhumanism.

Within the last few years, empirical studies have focused on topics such as cross-cultural and cross-geographical differences in moral preferences concerning self-driving cars (Awad et al., 2018), the moral psychology of sex-robots and nursing robots (Koverola et al., 2020; Laakasuo, under revisions), attitudes towards military drones making autonomous decisions as compared with people making the same decisions (Malle et al., 2019), and attitudes toward brain implant technology (Castelo et al., 2019) or mind upload technology (Laakasuo et al., 2018). All of these themes were predicted by several prescient philosophically oriented scholars (see Allhoff et al., 2011 for a review). However we have now come to a point where the topics are being investigated from new moral psychological angles.

Novel findings from these studies show, for example, that people appreciate hypothetical decisions made by robots more if the robots are perceived to have human-like minds (Bigman & Gray, 2018; Malle et al., 2019). This is peculiar because a decision to save somebody, for example, from drowning, is the same decision superficially - from a third-person perspective - whether it is made by a human lifeguard, a trained rescue dog, or an autonomous life-saving robot. One proposed explanation draws from a family of cognitive phenomena known as *mind perception mechanisms* in the context of robotic interactions (Bigman & Gray, 2018): robots are perceived as having less cognitive or emotional capabilities, and thus their decisions are more suspect. However, in our own studies we have observed that mind perception does not fully explain our aversion towards robots making moral decisions. Instead, we have found that the *type* of moral decision matters in terms of mind perception (Laakasuo et al., under revisions).[1] Current theories also fail to explain recent findings in research on transhumanistic themes and whether the problems observed in the context of robots extend to androids and cyborgs as well. For example, why is it that the aversion towards "mind upload" technology (making a digital copy of the brain into a computer) and silicon-based brain implant technology ("chips in the brain") seems to be associated with sexual disgust sensitivity (Laakasuo et al., 2018; Koverola et al., 2020)?[2]

Technologies that merge the human body and the human mind/brain (or mimic them in some ways) with different forms of information processing machines are usually defined as transhuman technologies. They are called transhuman because they are perceived as something that alters the fundamentals of the human nature and allows humans to take control of their own evolutionary processes. However, technologies like uploading one's mind into a computer or substituting parts of one's brain with silicon-based chips also cause categorical confusions. When does a human become a machine and when does a machine become human? How do we feel, morally, about things that deeply challenge the fundamentals of being human? In this chapter, we dive deep into the cognitive science of categories and categorization, and aim to give the reader a theoretical background that helps them come to terms with recent empirical findings that we will introduce in Part 2.

In the next section, we briefly introduce the basics of evolutionary psychology as it offers a coherent view of human cognitive capacities and their coevolution with tool creation, and it is connected to both the field of moral psychology and the question of how people perceive non-human agents. In the section "What is Moral Psychology?", we provide an overview of moral psychology and its current most important theoretical models and questions. The section "Human Cognitive Categories Shaped by Evolution" focuses on the innate human tendency for categorical thinking and category formation. This theme is explored further in the last section, where we consider how contemporary robots and AIs do not easily fit within existing mental categories, and how this can lead to systematically biased judgment. We conclude Part 1 with a quick summary of the themes covered.

In Part 2, we briefly cover transhumanism as a philosophy, and consider how transhumanistic technologies cause further categorical confusions that lead to previously unseen moral psychological conundrums. We bring the previous themes together in a review of moral psychological literature pertaining to both transhumanistic technologies and intelligent artificial agents. At the end of Part 2, we propose some new directions for the study of human moral cognition relating to robots and AIs, and summarize the implications of the themes of Parts 1 and 2 for cognitive science and related fields.

EVOLUTIONARY PSYCHOLOGY – HUMAN SOCIAL COGNITION AND OTHER MINDS

Humans have evolved under a myriad of different conditions and ecological niches during the last six million years. The most significant evolutionary changes in human cognitive capacities took place in the Pleistocene epoch, between approximately 1.8 million and 10,000 years ago (see, e.g. Lee & Wolpoff, 2003; Shultz et al., 2012). During this time, anatomically modern humans developed symbol use, cave painting techniques, and language (Lewis-Williams, 2002). The cranial capacity of *Homo sapiens* has not significantly changed in about 200,000 years (Dunbar, 2014).

Evolutionary psychology (EP) argues that modern *Homo sapiens* are, by and large, the same all around the planet (Pinker, 1997; 2002). EP seeks to find what is universal and common in all humans by studying their cognitive and behavioral similarities across cultures. EP aims to provide evolutionary explanations to these similarities, based on selection pressures and challenges that humans went through during the Pleistocene era (Tooby & Cosmides, 2005). Many cultural phenomena can be thus explained as by-products of our evolutionary background (Tooby & Cosmides, 1992). EP thus focuses on human cognitive universals. To paraphrase anthropologist Roger Keesing (see Keesing & Strathern, 1997), humans are equally rational wherever they scratch their behinds; only the ways in which this rationality is expressed are different on the surface.

Although humans have evolved in various ecological environments with various challenges to survival and reproduction, certain challenges have remained constant. For example, there has always been rain, sunshine, hunger, pathogens, plant toxins, predators, competition for mates, violence, child rearing, hunting, food gathering, group-coordination, communication, and tool use and creation (Tooby & Cosmides, 2005). All of these challenges create selection pressures, and thusly, humans have evolved specific cognitive mechanisms to deal with those challenges. EP argues that humans have evolved cognitive adaptations for specific functions (i.e. *modules* of cognition) such as mate selection (interest towards the preferred sex), avoiding sources of pathogens (the emotion of disgust), and avoiding predators or other dangers (the emotion of fear). Nonetheless, probably the most relevant or interesting cognitive aspects from an evolutionary perspective for humans, in the context of this chapter, are socio-cognitive.

Group living is one of the fundamental constants in human evolutionary history. There has always been some element of resource sharing with one's kin, extended kin, and friends (Dunbar, 2014). Humans are born into this world probably more helpless than any other mammals (Baumeister & Leary, 1995); the simple act of walking takes humans about a year to learn, whereas for elephants, horses, and antelopes it takes some hours at most. The human socio-evolutionary environment is complex and it takes environmental fine-tuning of cognitive adaptations for several years before the individual can survive on its own (Pinker, 1997). As an example, the human capacity for language is biological – it grows out of people, like breasts and beards do (requiring nutritional resources from the environment to fully develop) – but the language humans learn as their primary one is obviously controlled by the environment (Pinker, 1994).

Similarly, humans have evolved as organisms that have several socio-cognitive instincts to solve problems of group and tribal living. In this context, EP uses the term *instinct* in a very specific way: automatic cognitive processing that happens fast, and largely outside of consciousness, and that is only felt in the mind as feelings. In this sense, our instincts are like the feeling of hunger, which is an output of a complex psycho-physiological machinery keeping track of multiple variables. On the physiological level, the "state" of hunger is a complex interaction pattern between different kinds of peptides, hormones, neurotransmitters, and neural impulses taking place between the digestive system and the central nervous system. We feel hunger, but are not consciously aware of the workings of the machinery behind it.

A similar logic applies to human social instincts. Feelings of obligation (attachment, care, etc.) towards one's offspring, the feeling of guilt when one has transgressed on another's well-being, or the feeling of embarrassment when one has committed a norm violation in public, are similar to hunger. Social instincts have functions, but we may not be acutely aware of the logic behind them (Keltner, Haidt, & Shiota, 2006). The function of hunger is to guide the organism towards calorie consumption. Calories enable it to survive until the opportune moment for mating presents itself, so that the genes responsible for that instinct can make copies of themselves[3]. Similarly, the sense of obligation towards one's children makes it more likely that younger generations are raised until the age of reproduction. The function of guilt is to motivate the individual to signal remorse and make amends so that they are not ostracized by the larger community from vital resources relevant for survival and mating opportunities (Breggin, 2015). Similarly, embarrassment functions as a signal to others in one's community that a norm was accidentally violated and that one is not a threat (Feinberg et al., 2011), thus preventing potentially violent situations from escalating, avoiding potential costly physical damage.

These and other socio-cognitive adaptations mostly regulate the social environment where the individual is embedded, and ultimately serve survival (Francis, 1990). CONSIDER the cognitive deficiency known as prosopagnosia (Grüter et al., 2008); that is, impaired facial recognition. People with prosopagnosia can survive and reproduce, but ultimately there are survival-related advantages in being able to tell people apart based on their faces.

For the area of moral psychology, one of the central socio-cognitive mechanisms that humans have more than other great apes is the capacity to think about other minds (Dunbar, 2014). Without going into technicalities of how this capacity has developed (Dunbar, 2014)[4], it allowed proto-human apes to keep tabs on the social reputations of their partners and stay vigilant about not being exploited in the social exchange of favors (i.e. mostly grooming behavior). The ability to reason about other minds may also have been more immediately beneficial for the survival of one's offspring, as some recent research suggests a link between a mother's capacity for thinking about other minds and their sensitivity to their child, which in turn is predictive of developmental cognitive capacities (Licata et al., 2016; Rigby et al., 2016; Zeytinoglu et al., 2018). Whatever the evolutionary origins or earliest functions of the capacity to think of other minds, this capacity is relevant in many areas of human social interaction.

The capacity to assign mental states and emotions to others and think about them is commonly referred to as *theory of mind* (ToM; see, Saxe & Baron-Cohen, 2006). People who lack this specific ability, or who have some deviation in this ability from the population average, are often diagnosed with an autism spectrum disorder and have higher tendencies of treating other living beings as objects or in a more objectifying manner (Saxe & Baron-Cohen, 2006). However, ToM research largely focuses on how (and whether) people ascribe specific mental *contents* to others. We argue, in line with Gray, Young and Waytz (2012) that ascribing any kind of mind that could even have those mental contents - *mind perception* - is more fundamental, even if similar cognitive processes are behind both capacities. That is, one has to be able to view someone or something as having or not having a mind (i.e. differentiate between agents and non-agents) before being able to (correctly or incorrectly) ascribe contents to that mind. Any of the human socio-cognitive skills we have mentioned here would not be able to develop without the ability to perceive others as thinking and feeling agents in the world. Thus, mind perception is a central evolved cognitive feature, with relevance to evolutionary and moral psychology in general, and the moral psychology of robotics more specifically: artificial agents are very different from the kinds of minds people have usually perceived until now and in our evolutionary history. We return to these themes throughout the rest of this chapter.

WHAT IS MORAL PSYCHOLOGY?

Moral psychology studies cognitive processes and structures in humans (and other animals) that are related to decisions, judgments, negotiations, and actions regarding what is considered to be right and wrong in a given context (Voyer & Tarantola, 2017). Moral philosophers use different types of *a priori* methods – like philosophical conceptual analysis and philosophical intuition – to test propositions that follow from moral theories for logical coherence with intuitions (top-down). Or abduct a proposition from a set of moral intuitions (bottom-up) and then test the logical coherency with moral propositions from other theories. They do this to dissect and analyze different types of social situations, and commonly reach conclusions or recommendations in their analyses regarding what should be done about a specific topic. Unlike moral philosophy, moral psychology usually does not take explicit positions regarding what is objectively, or by normative standards, right/wrong.

Moral psychologists mostly aim to observe and measure the expression of ordinary people, children, and professional experts in their judgment, reasoning, and deduction in situations which are commonly related to the well-being of other sentient beings or otherwise relevant for the moral domain[5,6]. Until quite recently, moral psychology was mostly focusing on how humans treat other humans, but as of late, animal rights-related questions have also received attention (e.g. Loughnan et al, 2010). Part 2 introduces the recent expansion of moral psychology to new subjects: robots (Awad et al., 2018) and transhumanism (Castelo et al., 2019; Laakasuo et al., 2018).

There are two traditions in moral psychology (Haidt, 2007; 2010). The First Wave of moral psychology – labelled *Kohlbergian moral psychology* – studies how morality develops in adults and in children. In this tradition, the research was mostly conducted with deep probing interviews and careful scoring of the level of abstraction the participants used in their speech in order to justify certain moral actions. It was assumed that morality develops in a step-by-step fashion, beginning from a concrete fear of punishment, and then advancing towards abstract universal moral principles applied consistently in various situations (Helkama, 2009).[7]

The focus in this book chapter, as well as our research, is more generally anchored in the Second Wave of moral psychology. In many ways, the Second Wave tradition is an off-shoot, or a parallel development of EP (Haidt, 2007; 2010). In most research in this area, EP is accepted as the background theory more or less explicitly, even if the topics and themes studied in moral psychology are not immediately obviously related to the core topics usually studied in EP (e.g. mating-related cognition). However, moral psychology in many ways continued the themes related to EP by expanding them, including themes like altruism, cooperation, intergroup helping (Laakasuo et al., 2018), or condemnation of out-group behaviors (Cohen-Chen et al., 2014).

Research conducted in this tradition often utilizes moral dilemmas or *vignettes* (specifically crafted stories or situational descriptions) that juxtapose different types of moral intuitions (Cushman & Greene, 2012). In this tradition, it is also common to use measurement tools and theories developed by personality psychologists, behavioral economists, evolutionary psychologists, and neuroscientists. Second Wave moral psychology is understood mostly as quantitative science as it employs statistics much more than qualitative methods. Modern moral psychology is also theoretically and methodologically closely-knit with research on decision-making and emotions. It is also very multidisciplinary. For example, clinically-oriented moral psychologists might be interested in the emotional lives of psychopaths and narcissists, and how they solve moral dilemmas compared with "normal people" (see Kahane et al., 2015; Tassy et al., 2013). Furthermore, theologically-oriented researchers might be interested in how people's free will beliefs predict altruism (Sinnott-Armstrong, 2014). In other words, moral psychology is a broad area within the cognitive sciences, and the topics it studies can be approached from different angles, bringing together clinicians, neuroscientists, philosophers, legal scholars (Mikhail, 2007), and anthropologists.[8]

Central Models of Moral Cognition

There are a few models which form large partitions of the core of the Second Wave Moral Psychology. It is essential to understand these basic concepts, so that the themes covered in this book chapter can be understood in their proper context. We will briefly summarize some of them here, however, by no means is this list exhaustive[9].

The Theory of Dyadic Morality (TDM)

The TDM has been developed by Kurt Gray and his colleagues in several publications (Gray et al. 2007; 2012; Schein & Gray, 2018). According to the TDM, *mind perception* is the central cognitive mechanism enabling moral cognition. Mind perception refers to the automatic tendency of healthy humans to perceive mental capacities in other living beings, especially in people. Humans project onto other living beings the same mental capabilities that they themselves have, such as: a) the capacity to experience suffering; b) the capability to feel motivated, and c) the proclivity to act in goal-oriented, sensible, or meaningful ways.

The TDM argues that humans perceive and interpret social situations as morally meaningful if four requirements are met: 1) there is an intentional *moral agent* who 2) causes harm to 3) another being (i.e. a *moral patient*) who 4) has the capacity to experience suffering. Thus, the (fuzzy) template of a morally relevant event always contains an agent, a patient, and a harm. Importantly, this dyadic template allows for a kind of "filling-in." The TDM claims that perceiving some elements of the dyadic interaction between the perpetrator and the victim can lead one to interpreting that the other elements were present as well. This is the TDM's explanation for why people sometimes condemn seemingly harmless acts, and how people may come to infer the presence of an agent causing harm from the presence of a patient experiencing harm, or vice versa.

Consider the so-called "moral dumbfounding" effect. A famous example from Haidt and Hersh (2001) concerns a fictional scenario where two siblings have consensual, non-reproductive sex. Many people unsurprisingly find this wrong, but cannot seem to articulate why: they are dumbfounded, as the act has been carefully described as having no harm. Schein & Gray (2018), in defense of the TDM's stance that moral condemnation implies harm, argue that dumbfounding is an artifact of psychological experiments. That is, an experimenter may tell someone that a hypothetical case of incest was *objectively* harmless, but those who condemn the act do not believe the experimenters: harm is *subjective* to the person judging. Thus, if it turned out that people who find "harmless incest" a believeable scenario still condemned it, this would be evidence against the TDM.

The TDM seeks to maximize explanatory power while remaining as simple as possible. The central point is that perceiving moral violations depends on the ability to perceive mental capacities for agency and experience in others, and a flexible cognitive schema for what "harm" looks like. The model seeks to explain what happens in moral condemnation (or moral judgment processes); the model makes no claims as to what people may consider morally praise-worthy. Furthermore, the model is explicitly constructionist and does not tie individual differences in morality to any modular EP framework (Schein &

Gray, 2018). That is, unlike, the Moral Foundations Theory (see below), the TDM claims that morality stems from one basic cognitive template instead of several distinct, innate moral concerns. The TDM grants that cultural, political, and individual differences in what people find harmful, and thus morally condemnable, are possible, but it always ties these differences back to perceptions of agents, patients, and harm.

The TDM has been criticized for being at times circular and its assumptions of necessary elements to a moral violation not being necessary or sufficient (see Alicke, 2012 and Monroe et al., 2012, for critiques; see also Schein & Gray, 2018, for a response from the developers of the TDM). Critics have argued, among other things, that not all intentional harmful actions are considered immoral (e.g. soldiers who kill their enemies in a war), and that not all harmful actions considered immoral are intentional (e.g. gross negligence). We will not delve deeper into the debate here: our intention is simply to introduce a model that is relevant to discussion in Part 2 of this article.

Moral Foundations Theory (MFT)

The Moral Foundations Theory (MFT) posits that human morality consists of five different "foundations" or "moral taste receptors," each having their corresponding domain of functioning (Graham et al. 2011, 2013; Haidt, 2012; Haidt et al., 2009). According to the MFT, when people evaluate the acceptability of each other's actions, they pay attention to the following issues: 1) Did the action cause harm? 2) Was the action fair? 3) Was the action respectful towards authorities? 4) Was the action loyal towards the agent's in-group? 5) Was the action "pure" or did it violate holy values[10]?We will refer to these five key issues, respectively, as the foundations of harm, fairness, authority, loyalty, and (moralistic) purity (their labeling, but not content, has changed over time).

Contrary to the TDM, in the MFT the moral condemnation of an action does not presuppose that the action must harm some conscious entity, or fit a catch-all cognitive template. The MFT also assumes that humans differ in their tendencies to favour the five types of moral domains. According to Haidt (2012), liberally oriented people mainly favor the first two foundations: harm and fairness. Conservatives, on the other hand, seem to care about all five foundations equally; but they especially care much more about the (moralistic) purity foundation than liberals. Conservatives, for example, condemn the burning of their country's flag and oppose cannabis use more than liberals. Liberals, on the other hand, condemn income inequality and the intentional widening of the income gap.

The MFT is explicitly modular and thus more closely tied to the EP framework (Haidt, 2012). Each of the foundations is considered a separate cognitive module with specific types of inputs (events in the world, perceived as a violation of a specific foundation) and outputs (foundation-specific moral judgment). To return to the example of "harmless incest," the MFT would explain condemnations of this event as stemming from the event being a violation of the purity foundation. Furthermore, the reason for differences in judgments of acts that violate this foundation is simply that different groups of people develop to emphasize the purity foundation differently.

As can be expected, the MFT has been criticized by proponents of the TDM, who claim the foundations can be reduced to concerns about harm (Schein & Gray, 2018). There are also alternative models with different foundations argued to have better evolutionary psychological footing than those of the MFT (Curry et al., 2019). Again, we will not delve deeper into the debate, as we simply wish to introduce an influential model that will be relevant for later discussion.

Do Moral Emotions Guide Moral Decision-Making?

The science of moral cognition is a hotly debated area. Simplifying slightly, one of the areas of debate regards the question whether moral decision-making is mostly motivated by emotions or by reason (Greene, 2013). Haidt (2001, 2007) has previously suggested that moral judgments are mostly based on emotions and intuitions: we condemn actions because they evoke negative emotions, such as disgust or anger. While this emotion-driven view has been impactful, some researchers are still in favor of moral reasoning as the most important component (e.g. Mikhail, 2007). Recently, McAuliffe (2019) argued that the evidence for the causal role of emotions in moral judgment is weaker than assumed, and that existing research on emotions and morality sometimes actually supports rationalist theories of moral thought.

The role of emotions in moral judgment is highlighted in studies of utilitarian moral judgment. From a utilitarian (or consequentialist) perspective, killing can be justified if by killing one, several others are saved (see, e.g. Greene, 2007; 2013). According to the utilitarian morals (Mill,1861; Bentham, 1816; Sidgwick, 1874), it is imperative to try to maximize the amount of "good" regardless of the specific act. Utilitarian morality is commonly juxtaposed with deontological morality, which focuses on absolute rules, principles, and obligations to perform or omit a certain action regardless of the situation (Greene, 2013). Deontological morality has been argued to be more reliant on emotions (either implicitly or explicitly) than utilitarian "moral calculus." The juxtapositioning of these two moral standings supposes that humans are primarily *either* deontological *or* utilitarian in their judgments (but not necessarily in their stated moral philosophies, if they have any). Previous neuroimaging research implied that deontological moral evaluations were made faster than utilitarian ones (Greene, 2013). Indeed, utilitarian evaluations correlated with "higher cognition" brain activation (i.e. activation in areas related to working memory, rational thinking, and self-reflection). Based on these findings, Greene (2013) argued that, compared with deontological morality, utilitarian morality is cognitively more costly and reflective, less emotional, and less intuitive.

However, more recent research undermines this interpretation; neural lesions (Christensen & Gomila, 2012; Koenigs et al., 2007), psychopathy, alexithymia (Patil & Silani, 2014), and some acute states of intoxication (Duke & Bègue, 2015; Perkins et al., 2013) can increase the tendency towards utilitarian moral judgments. Moreover, quick, intuition- and feel-based cognitive processing that does not require active step-by-step reasoning in working memory is a fundamental aspect of the human cognitive architecture. For instance, chess masters often rely on an intuitive "feel" for different moves and assessment of the "board as a whole" when there are too many move options to work through in working memory (e.g. Chassy & Gobet, 2011; Gobet & Chassy, 2009). Expert chess decision-making is largely a *feel-based* cognitive process, wherein the board configuration is compared to a vast knowledge-base of middle game positions encountered over thousands of hours of playing chess, solving chess problems, and reading chess literature (Chassy & Gobet, 2011; Gobet & Chassy, 2009). The same holds for many other domains, such as music, medical diagnostics, and poker, to name a few (Kahneman & Klein, 2009) (Palomäki et al. 2020).

Thus, fast emotional reactions, intuitions, and feelings are equally "cognitive" as the processes involved in slow deliberative reasoning. In fact, automatic, feel-based cognition could be processing a larger number of bits than "slower" conscious cognition. Generally, the majority of human functioning is based on massive numbers of cognitive processes taking place outside of awareness, while conscious step-by-step calculations in working memory, mental "speech", and other similar phenomena are merely the tip of the iceberg.

The specific emotions of disgust, anger, and contempt have been linked to moral judgements (Steiger & Reyna, 2017). Anger motivates punishment (Gummerum et al., 2016): if somebody insults us, steals from us, or otherwise treats us badly, our anger motivates us to assert ourselves and defend our space, and to seek formal or informal punishment for the culprit. This signals to the transgressing person that their actions were costly. Disgust, too, has a significant, but contested, role in moral behaviors and judgments (Laakasuo et al., 2017; Tybur et al., 2013). Disgust may function as the gatekeeper of moral condemnation: things we find disgusting seem wrong and are therefore condemned. However, disgust is a complicated emotion. It is associated with the presence of pathogens (bacteria), but also with sexuality (as a reaction to unsuitable mates or non-normative forms of sexuality), and abstract issues (e.g. as a reaction to burning of the flag of one's home country).

A detailed analysis of different forms of disgust is beyond the scope of this chapter (see Tybur et al., 2013), but because of its relevance to our topic, we will briefly focus on the connection between disgust and morality. In our own studies, we have measured individual differences in trait *disgust sensitivity* (DS; Tybur et al., 2009) in relation to moral judgment. DS differs from *incidental* disgust experienced during a specific situation (i.e. the state of feeling disgusted). Feeling disgusted *per se* might not be associated with moral judgment (Landy & Goodwin, 2015), but DS is. In other words, the more people are disgust-sensitive, the more likely they are to condemn different things. What is especially puzzling is the connection between sexual DS and completely non-sexual areas of moral judgment. The ostensible function of sexual disgust – in the evolutionary framework – is to guide mate selection and weed out potentially costly mating situations. Nevertheless, people more sensitive to sexual disgust are more conservative, careful about conventional norm violations, averse to drug use (Tybur et al., 2010), and less utilitarian (Laakasuo et al., 2017).

HUMAN COGNITIVE CATEGORIES SHAPED BY EVOLUTION

How can our understanding of the world be modelled? Although different sciences involved in studying cognition and knowledge-structures often disagree on the levels of explanation and analysis (Mitchell 2003; Horst 2016), almost all agree that our knowledge is nested into categories and concepts. These different knowledge forms can be mapped to procedural ("action"), semantic ("meaning"), and episodic ("event") memory systems (Tulving, 1985; Fletcher et al., 1999; Barrett, 2015: Farmer & Matlin, 2019).

Virtually all animals have procedural memory capabilities used for achieving various tasks (Tulving, 2002). However, humans in significantly higher extent create abstractions from their experiences and form semantic concepts (i.e. mental representations that have *meaning*). Semantic memory is crucial when making generalizations without actual experience (Binder & Desai, 2011). Our ability to categorize is linked to semantic memory, allowing us the use of conceptual knowledge beyond direct interaction with objects. This, in turn, makes human culture, science, religion, and art possible (Binder & Desai, 2011). That is, these cognitive properties enable us to recognize objects, create, and manipulate symbols to communicate with, and understand others, remember the past, and imagine the future. Declarative knowledge is necessary for essentially all uniquely human phenomena.

Some knowledge domains also seem to be more basic than others. The notion of "domain specificity" – cognitive structures operating on narrow and specific problems – describes this aspect of our cognition. Spelke (2000) has identified four basic "core knowledge systems" representing: 1) visuospatial structure, 2) objects and their interactions, 3) actions and goal directedness, and 4) numbers and relationships of ordering. These are processed via computational resources stored in sensorimotor programs and are crucial for the development of semantic domains (Spelke & Kinzler, 2007). Semantic domains are needed for different levels of intersubjectivity (for example representing the desires or emotions of others) and communication. This is the form of cognition that is commonly referred to as having a "theory of mind," as noted earlier.

EP also study *natural categories* and intuitive biology, that is, innate, automatic, and domain-specific abilities to classify environmental stimuli into semantic categories (Atran, 2012; Boyer & Barrett, 2015). Small children can intuitively classify animals, plants, and rocks into their own categories. In learning their first words, infants already expect them to denote whole objects, rather than their parts. Similarly, when two objects collide, infants do not expect them to merge into one object (Boyer, 2018; Moll & Tomasello, 2010). Small children are, in general, very sensitive to a wide range of category violations. When children play, zebras do not eat lions, and trees do not walk and eat zebras (Boyer & Barrett, 2015). Moreover, in children's play, "a dog is still a dog" even when equipped with unusually big ears, a glued-on trunk, or other elements typically not associated with dogs (Gelman & Wellman, 1991).

Very early on, children have at least some level of understanding of different categories, the essential nature of different objects in these categories (e.g. what makes a certain individual organism an "animal"), and the causal relations between them. They expect the "essence" of animals, instead of their external appearance, to be the reason why they behave in certain ways (Carey, 2009; Gallistel & Gelman, 2000; Hirschfeld & Gelman, 1994; Spelke & Kinzler, 2007). Children also expect animals to move by themselves, guided by the animal's own intentions and beliefs (Boyer, 2018) – that is, children perceive animals to have minds.

This intuitive or innate understanding of the world is useful only if it reflects the structure of the outside reality to a good enough degree (Hoffman, 2019). Such understanding can be inaccurate, but not so inaccurate as to seriously impede survival. This knowledge has helped us during our evolutionary history to avoid making miscalculations and faulty predictions in a hostile and unpredictable environment, or when facing a complex new situation. But what about robots and other AIs? We did not confront them in the evolutionary savannah or Pleistocene forest. Moreover, they are a relatively new phenomenon even to modern humans. This means that robots and AIs do not belong in any evolution-given natural category, or necessarily even in any cultural one. Still, similar to other animate agents, we may perceive them as having internal states; intentions and even beliefs. They can stimulate and bias our cognition in unpredictable ways. The way in which we classify them may significantly affect our ethical and moral cognitions concerning them.

Illustration: Tools as the First Cognitive Category Shaped by Technology

Tools are a universal human cognitive category with deep evolutionary roots. Tools can be defined as commonly hand-held objects that make it easier to carry out specific tasks. Modern chimpanzees and even ancient Australopithecines used tools similar to early hominid tools, such as chipped stones (Stanford et al., 2011). Initially, all three species used unmodified tools (objects found in nature); but over time the tools used by *Homo sapiens* became self-made and more sophisticated. The differences between modern humans and other modern primates in their tool use reflect evolutionary differences in multiple traits between the species, such as hand-eye coordination, causal reasoning, social intelligence, learning, and language (Vaesen, 2012).

In human evolution, there are two long and specific periods where two types of tool-creating cultures existed; the Oldowan periods (started 2.5 million years ago) and the Acheulean periods (1.75 mya), both of which lasted for about a million years. These periods are commonly described as periods of archeological boredom, since during them, large quantities of very similar stone tools were produced. These time periods, however, seem to have been long enough to act as selection pressures for human cognition. Brain imaging studies have revealed that an area on the left side of the brain - left anterior supramarginal gyrus, aSMG - responds in a species-specific and unique way to images of tools; just mimicking tool use or hearing the tool's sound is enough to activate aSMG (Orban & Caruana, 2014). In addition, Uomini and Meyer (2013) observed similar brain activation when subjects were silently thinking of words starting with a given letter and when they were knapping an Acheulean flint axe, suggesting that tool-making and language share a basis in more general human capacities for complex, goal-directed action.

Furthermore, different types of brain lesions are associated with consequences on tool use. After certain types of brain damage, otherwise normally behaving patients may no longer understand how to bend their arms to use a hammer: some do not understand what to use a hammer for, and some may have lost the whole concept of "hammer" from their minds (Baumard et al., 2014). This suggests that we have specialized systems in our brains for tools, and if they are malfunctioning, we lose our special ability to use, or even think flexibly about, tools. Studies also show that using tools has a cascading effect on our species' survival. Intelligence allowed us to use tools, tools helped us gather and process more food, food helped nourish our brains, better nourished brains allowed more intelligence which again allowed more and improved tools, taking us from stone age to today (Flinn et al, 2006; Ko, 2016). Thus, the cognitive category of tools seems to have deep biological origins in our evolutionary history.

Machines are certain kinds of tools recently introduced in human cultural history; i.e. they are a cultural category distinct from purely cognitive categories. The category of "machine" is now rooted in our collective thinking, and most of us have a basic understanding of what various different machines are used for – even if we could not give a detailed breakdown of their functionality. We generally view machines as devices, or tools, to achieve some goal: dishwashers are used for washing dishes, cars for transportation, and microwaves for heating food. However, machines such as robots (even without intelligence) and intelligent programs, fool us into thinking they have minds, thus challenging our cognition in ways previously unseen in our evolutionary history. A hypothesis can be made that robots, being able to move autonomously, and intelligent programs being able to reason, make decisions, sometimes talk, and unlike any other inanimate objects, activate some automatic (instinctive, sub-conscious, evolutionary programmed) cognitive reactions classifying those objects as human-like, even though we know they are just artifacts.

BIO-CULTURAL HUMANS AND THE NEW ONTOLOGICAL CATEGORY

Kahn et al. (2011) suggest that artificial agents form a *new ontological category*: robots and AIs are something entirely novel in the natural and cultural history of our planet. Thus, when interacting with robots we must rely on intuitions that evolved in the absence of robots. This may result in various forms of categorical confusions and misinterpretations when dealing with robots or other AIs.

The *uncanny valley effect* (UVE) is a classic example of perceptual categorical confusion (Mori, 1970) – but not specific towards robots. The UVE occurs when the appearance of a robot (or any non-human agent) passes a certain threshold of similarity to humans, and we become repulsed by it. The actual mechanisms underlying the UVE are still unclear (Palomäki et al., 2018). Nevertheless, by watching YouTube videos made of the humanoid robot Sophie, one can perhaps affirm that there is something creepy about her (see CNBC, 2016). Does Sophie belong in the category of *animate living objects* (like other people), or *inanimate objects* (like dolls)? She might even be categorized as a *tool* if she were viewed as a robot with specific functions to perform.

In the *biocultural* view of humans, biology and culture are perceived as intertwined entities feeding into one another (Fuentes, 1999; Donald, 2002; Richerson & Boyd, 2005). Various religions across the world can be seen as products of this dynamic interaction (Atran & Norenzayan 2004; Geertz, 2010; Sørensen 2004), and within religions there are many examples of new cultural categories having emerged that utilize our evolutionarily old mechanisms. For example, it is well documented that animistic cultures and tribal communities had (and have) rich spiritual conceptual worlds, with beliefs and ritual practices that held natural objects as animate and essential agents (Atran, 2002; Boyer, 2001; Lawson & McCauley, 1990; McCauley & Whitehouse, 2005). In the animistic worldview, everything is connected; minds and mental states are attributed to natural objects, different kinds of spirits, deities, gods, and ancestors similar to humans: they can set goals, have intentions, and feel emotions. Early animistic cultures had moralizing gods, varying in the degree to which they cared about the morality of their followers (Boyer, 2001; Purzycki et al., 2016; Willard & McNamara, 2016). These beliefs about supernatural agents spread through ancestral rituals and migration (Norenzayan et al., 2015). From the viewpoint of cognitive science, animism is an example of people associating human-like agency either to things that do not act in any way (such as rocks and trees), or that do not necessarily have any clear agency (e.g. natural events such as rain seen as "caused" by spirits).

Technological animism is a new cultural concept of personhood that is emerging from the interaction between fiction, robotics, and different cultural models of agency (Richardson, 2018). Technological animism has already had an impact in human-robot interaction. For example, Japanese roboticists radically differ from their Euro-American colleagues in their use of animistic elements from Japanese Buddhism and Shintoism to support a cultural narrative of robots as friends instead of enemies (Coeckelbergh, 2013; Jensen & Blok, 2013). However, even in Western countries, children tend to associate human-like emotional and cognitive capabilities to robots, prompting researchers to instruct parents to explicitly teach their children to call a robot "it" (Shellenbarger, 2019). Without explicit cultural training or education, if they manage to avoid the uncanny valley, robots appear to inspire seemingly animistic thinking.

To be clear, our claim is that artificial agents may activate similar cognitive processes related to agency, mind perception, and morality as seen in "animistic" interpretations of non-human objects or natural phenomena. We do not mean to claim that robots and AIs will induce religious or spiritual behavior in humans (however, see Harris, 2017, for a report on the first "church of AI"). Mind perception may even be easier in the case of robots and AIs than, for example, other animals, rocks, or natural events, as both robots and AIs can be made intentionally more human-like. In addition, we can concretely observe robots (i.e. AIs with *bodies*) in action, and see that their behavior causes specific things to happen in the world. Thus, from the cognitive perspective, robots are by nature closer to humans or other animals than to inanimate objects such as rocks or trees. However, the logical, probabilistic computations whereby AIs function are often opaque and even counterintuitive to humans (see Rode et al., 1999 on human difficulties with probabilities). We will return to this mismatch between the way humans think of agency and the kinds of agency robots and AIs actually have in Part 2, where we will utilize the theories presented here in detail.

CONCLUSION

In this first of two chapters, we shortly summarized the basics of evolutionary and moral psychology. We also reviewed the basics of how human categorization of natural environments may run into issues with novel technologies. We discussed how emotions and reason have a complex interplay and give rise to our moral cognitive judgments, and how previous technological stages in human evolution have influenced the development of our cognitive system and given us the concept of tools. We concluded the chapter by introducing the concept of the *new ontological category*, and discussed how we do not have the evolutionary capabilities to deal with robots and other intelligent information processing systems intuitively. Given that it took us two million years or so, to evolve the concept of tools, it seems that we only have cultural solutions to the new moral problems facing us in the technological domain. One of the main cognitive mechanisms that we currently utilize in our interaction with robots and AIs is the mind perception mechanism, which is nonetheless constantly fooled into projecting minds to where there are none, at least for now.

REFERENCES

Alicke, M. D. (2012). Self-Injuries, Harmless Wrongdoing, and Morality. *Psychological Inquiry*, *23*(2), 125–128. doi:10.1080/1047840X.2012.666720

Allhoff, F., Lin, P., & Steinberg, J. (2011). Ethics of human enhancement: An executive summary. *Science and Engineering Ethics*, *17*(2), 201–212. doi:10.100711948-009-9191-9 PMID:20094921

Atran, S. (2002). *In gods we trust: The evolutionary landscape of religion.* Oxford University Press.

Atran, S. (2012). Psychological orgins and cultural evolution of religion. In R. Sun (Ed.), *Grounding Social Sciences in Cognitive Sciences* (pp. 209–238). MIT Press.

Atran, S., & Norenzayan, A. (2004). Religion's evolutionary landscape: Counterintuition, commitment, compassion, communion. *Behavioral and Brain Sciences*, *27*(6), 713–730. doi:10.1017/S0140525X04000172 PMID:16035401

Awad, E., Dsouza, S., Kim, R., Schulz, J., Henrich, J., Shariff, A., Bonnefon, J.-F., & Rahwan, I. (2018). The Moral Machine experiment. *Nature*, *563*(7729), 59–64. doi:10.103841586-018-0637-6 PMID:30356211

Barrett, H. C. (2015). *The shape of thought: How mental adaptations evolve.* Oxford University Press. doi:10.1093/acprof:oso/9780199348305.001.0001

Baumard, J., Osiurak, F., Lesourd, M., & Le Gall, D. (2014). Tool use disorders after left brain damage. *Frontiers in Psychology*, *5*. Advance online publication. doi:10.3389/fpsyg.2014.00473 PMID:24904487

Baumeister, R. F., & Leary, M. R. (1995). The Need to Belong: Desire for Interpersonal Attachments as a Fundamental Human Motivation. *Psychological Bulletin*, *117*(3), 497–529. doi:10.1037/0033-2909.117.3.497 PMID:7777651

Bentham, J. (1816). *Chrestomathia.* William Tait.

Bigman, Y. E., & Gray, K. (2018). People are averse to machines making moral decisions. *Cognition*, *181*, 21–34. doi:10.1016/j.cognition.2018.08.003 PMID:30107256

Binder, J. R., & Desai, R. H. (2011). The neurobiology of semantic memory. *Trends in Cognitive Sciences*, *15*(11), 527–536. doi:10.1016/j.tics.2011.10.001 PMID:22001867

Boyer, P. (2001). *Religion explained: The evolutionary origins of religious thought*. Basic Books.

Boyer, P. (2018). *Minds make societies: How cognition explains the world humans create*. Yale University Press.

Boyer, P., & Barrett, H. C. (2015). Intuitive Ontologies and Domain Specificity. In D. M. Buss (Ed.), *The handbook of evolutionary psychology* (pp. 161–174). John Wiley & Sons, Inc., doi:10.1002/9781119125563.evpsych105

Breggin, P. R. (2015). The biological evolution of guilt, shame and anxiety: A new theory of negative legacy emotions. *Medical Hypotheses*, *85*(1), 17–24. doi:10.1016/j.mehy.2015.03.015 PMID:25890689

Carey, S. (2009). *The origin of concepts*. Oxford University Press. doi:10.1093/acprof:oso/9780195367638.001.0001

Castelo, N., Schmitt, B., & Sarvary, M. (2019). Human or Robot? Consumer Responses to Radical Cognitive Enhancement Products. *Journal of the Association for Consumer Research*, *4*(3), 217–230. doi:10.1086/703462

Chassy, P., & Gobet, F. (2011). A Hypothesis about the Biological Basis of Expert Intuition. *Review of General Psychology*, *15*(3), 198–212. doi:10.1037/a0023958

Christensen, J. F., & Gomila, A. (2012). Moral dilemmas in cognitive neuroscience of moral decision-making: A principled review. *Neuroscience and Biobehavioral Reviews*, *36*(4), 1249–1264. doi:10.1016/j.neubiorev.2012.02.008 PMID:22353427

Coeckelbergh, M. (2013). *Human being @ risk: Enhancement, technology, and the evaluation of vulnerability transformations*. Springer Science & Business Media. doi:10.1007/978-94-007-6025-7

Cohen-Chen, S., Halperin, E., Saguy, T., & van Zomeren, M. (2014). Beliefs About the Malleability of Immoral Groups Facilitate Collective Action. *Social Psychological & Personality Science*, *5*(2), 203–201. doi:10.1177/1948550613491292

Curry, O. S., Chesters, M. J., & Van Lissa, C. J. (2019). Mapping morality with a compass: Testing the theory of "morality-as-cooperation" with a new questionnaire. *Journal of Research in Personality*, *78*, 106–124. doi:10.1016/j.jrp.2018.10.008

Cushman, F., & Greene, J. D. (2012). Finding faults: How moral dilemmas illuminate cognitive structure. *Social Neuroscience*, *7*(3), 269–279. Advance online publication. doi:10.1080/17470919.2011.614000 PMID:21942995

Donald, A. (2002). *A mind so rare: The evolution of human consciousness*. W. W. Norton and Company.

(2020). Doris, John, Stich, Stephen, Phillips, Jonathan and Walmsley, Lachlan. InZalta, E. N. (Ed.), *Moral Psychology: Empirical Approaches*. The Stanford Encyclopedia of Philosophy.

Duke, A. A., & Bègue, L. (2015). The drunk utilitarian: Blood alcohol concentration predicts utilitarian responses in moral dilemmas. *Cognition*, *134*, 121–127. doi:10.1016/j.cognition.2014.09.006 PMID:25460385

Dunbar, R. (2014). *Human evolution*. Pelican Books.

Feinberg, M., Willer, R., & Keltner, D. (2011). Flustered and Faithful: Embarrassment as a Signal of Prosociality. *Journal of Personality and Social Psychology*. Advance online publication. doi:10.1037/a0025403 PMID:21928915

Fjell, C. D., Cherkasov, A., Hilpert, K., Jenssen, H., Waldbrook, M., Mullaly, S. C., Volkmer, R., & Hancock, R. E. W. (2008). Use of Artificial Intelligence in the Design of Small Peptide Antibiotics Effective against a Broad Spectrum of Highly Antibiotic-Resistant Superbugs. *ACS Chemical Biology*, *4*(1), 65–74. PMID:19055425

Fletcher, P., Büchel, C., Josephs, O., Friston, K., & Dolan, R. (1999). Learning-related Neuronal Responses in Prefrontal Cortex Studied with Functional Neuroimaging. *Cerebral Cortex (New York, N.Y.)*, *9*(2), 168–178. doi:10.1093/cercor/9.2.168 PMID:10220229

Flinn, M. V., Geary, D. C., & Ward, C. V. (2005). Ecological dominance, social competition, and coalitionary arms races: Why humans evolved extraordinary intelligence. *Evolution and Human Behavior*, *26*(1), 10–46. doi:10.1016/j.evolhumbehav.2004.08.005

Francis, R. C. (1990). Causes, proximate and ultimate. *Biology & Philosophy*, *5*(4), 401–415. doi:10.1007/BF02207379

Fuentes, A. (1999). *Evolution of human behavior*. Oxford University Press.

Gallistel, C. R., & Gelman, R. (2000). Non-verbal numerical cognition: From reals to integers. *Trends in Cognitive Sciences*, *4*(2), 59–65. doi:10.1016/S1364-6613(99)01424-2 PMID:10652523

Geertz, A. W. (2010). Brain, Body and Culture: A Biocultural Theory of Religion. *Method & Theory in the Study of Religion*, *22*(4), 304–321. doi:10.1163/157006810X531094

Gelman, S. A., & Wellman, H. M. (1991). Insides and essences: Early understandings of the non-obvious. *Cognition*, *38*(3), 213–244. doi:10.1016/0010-0277(91)90007-Q PMID:2060270

Gobet, F., & Chassy, P. (2009). Expertise and Intuition: A Tale of Three Theories. *Minds and Machines*, *19*(2), 151–180. doi:10.100711023-008-9131-5

Graham, J., Haidt, J., Koleva, S., Motyl, M., Iyer, R., Wojcik, S. P., & Ditto, P. H. (2013). Chapter Two - Moral Foundations Theory: The Pragmatic Validity of Moral Pluralism. In P. Devine & A. Plant (Eds.), Advances in Experimental Social Psychology (Vol. 47, pp. 55–130). Academic Press. doi:10.1016/B978-0-12-407236-7.00002-4

Graham, J., Nosek, B. A., Haidt, J., Iyer, R., Koleva, S., & Ditto, P. H. (2011). Mapping the moral domain. *Journal of Personality and Social Psychology*, *101*(2), 366–385. doi:10.1037/a0021847 PMID:21244182

Gray, H. M., Gray, K., & Wegner, D. M. (2007). Dimensions of Mind Perception. *Science*, *315*(5812), 619–619. doi:10.1126cience.1134475 PMID:17272713

Gray, K., Young, L., & Waytz, A. (2012). Mind Perception Is the Essence of Morality. *Psychological Inquiry*, *23*(2), 101–124. doi:10.1080/1047840X.2012.651387 PMID:22754268

Greene, J. (2007). The Secret Joke of Kant's Soul. In W. Sinnott-Armstrong (Ed.), *Moral Psychology* (Vol. 3). MIT Press.

Greene, J. (2013). *Moral tribes: Emotion, reason, and the gap between us and them*. Penguin Press.

Grüter, M., von Kriegstein, K., Dogan, Ö., Giraud, A., Kell, C. A., Grüter, T., Kleinschmidt, A., & Kiebel, S. J. (2008). Simulation of talking faces in the human brain improves auditory speech recognition. *Proceedings of the National Academy of Sciences of the United States of America*, *105*(18), 6747–6752. doi:10.1073/pnas.0710826105 PMID:18436648

Guillette, S. (2019, December 6). Your new lifeguard may be a robot. *Verizon*.

Gummerum, M., Van Dillen, L. F., Van Dijk, E., & López-Pérez, B. (2016). Costly third-party interventions: The role of incidental anger and attention focus in punishment of the perpetrator and compensation of the victim. *Journal of Experimental Social Psychology*, *65*, 94–104. doi:10.1016/j.jesp.2016.04.004

Haidt, J. (2001). The Emotional Dog and Its Rational Tail: A Social Intuitionist Approach to Moral Judgment. *Psychological Review*, *108*(4), 21. doi:10.1037/0033-295X.108.4.814 PMID:11699120

Haidt, J. (2007). The new synthesis in moral psychology. *Science*, *316*(5827), 998–1002. doi:10.1126cience.1137651 PMID:17510357

Haidt, J. (2008). Morality. *Perspectives on Psychological Science*, *3*(1), 65–72. doi:10.1111/j.1745-6916.2008.00063.x PMID:26158671

Haidt, J. (2012). *The righteous mind: Why good people are divided by politics and religion*. Vintage.

Haidt, J., Graham, J., & Joseph, C. (2009). Above and Below Left–Right: Ideological Narratives and Moral Foundations. *Psychological Inquiry*, *20*(2–3), 110–119. doi:10.1080/10478400903028573

Haidt, J., & Hersh, M. A. (2001). Sexual Morality: The Cultures and Emotions of Conservatives and Liberals. *Journal of Applied Social Psychology*, *31*(1), 191–221. Advance online publication. doi:10.1111/j.1559-1816.2001.tb02489.x

Harris, M. (2017, November 15). Inside the First Church of Artificial Intelligence. *Wired*.

Helkama, K. (2009). *Moraalipsykologia: Hyvän ja pahan tällä puolen*. Edita Publishing Oy.

Hirschfeld, L. A., & Gelman, S. A. (Eds.). (1994). *Mapping the mind*. Cambridge University Press. doi:10.1017/CBO9780511752902

Hoffman, D. (2019). *The case against reality: Why evolution hid the truth from our eyes*. W. W. Norton and Company.

Horst, S. (2016). *Cognitive pluralism*. The MIT Press. https://muse.jhu.edu/book/46963

Jensen, C. B., & Blok, A. (2013). Techno-animism in Japan: Shinto Cosmograms, Actor-network Theory, and the Enabling Powers of Non-human Agencies. *Theory, Culture & Society*, *30*(2), 84–115. doi:10.1177/0263276412456564

Kahane, G., Everett, J. A. C., Earp, B. D., Farias, M., & Savulescu, J. (2015). 'Utilitarian' judgments in sacrificial moral dilemmas do not reflect impartial concern for the greater good. *Cognition, 134*, 193–209. doi:10.1016/j.cognition.2014.10.005 PMID:25460392

Kahn, P. H., Reichert, A. L., Gary, H. E., Kanda, T., Ishiguro, H., Shen, S., Ruckert, J. H., & Gill, B. (2011). The new ontological category hypothesis in human-robot interaction. *Proceedings of the 6th International Conference on Human-Robot Interaction - HRI '11*, 159. 10.1145/1957656.1957710

Kahneman, D., & Klein, G. (2009). Conditions for intuitive expertise: A failure to disagree. *The American Psychologist, 64*(6), 515–526. doi:10.1037/a0016755 PMID:19739881

Keesing, R., & Strathern, A. J. (1997). *Cultural anthropology: A contemporary perspective* (3rd ed.). Wadsworth Publishing.

Keltner, D., Haidt, J., & Shiota, M. N. (2006). Social functionalism and the evolution of emotions. In M. Schaller, J. A. Simpson, & D. T. Kendrick (Eds.), *Evolution and social psychology* (pp. 115–142). Psychology Press.

Ko, K. H. (2016). Origins of human intelligence: The chain of tool-making and brain evolution. *Anthropological Notebooks*, 5–22.

Koenigs, M., Young, L., Adolphs, R., Tranel, D., Cushman, F., Hauser, M., & Damasio, A. (2007). Damage to the prefrontal cortex increases utilitarian moral judgements. *Nature, 446*(7138), 908–911. doi:10.1038/nature05631 PMID:17377536

Koverola, M., Kunnari, A., & Palomäki, J. (in press). Moral Psychology of Sex Robots: an experimental study – How Pathogen Disgust is associated with interhuman sex but not interandroid sex. *PALADYN – Journal of Behavioral Robotics*.

Laakasuo, M., Drosinou, M., Koverola, M., Kunnari, A., Halonen, J., Lehtonen, N., & Palomäki, J. (2018). What makes people approve or condemn mind upload technology? Untangling the effects of sexual disgust, purity and science fiction familiarity. *Palgrave Communications, 4*(1), 1–14. doi:10.105741599-018-0124-6

Laakasuo, M., Köbis, N., Palomäki, J., & Jokela, M. (2018). Money for microbes-Pathogen avoidance and out-group helping behaviour. *International Journal of Psychology, 53*, 1–10. doi:10.1002/ijop.12416 PMID:28229500

Landy, J. F., & Goodwin, G. P. (2015). Does Incidental Disgust Amplify Moral Judgment? A Meta-Analytic Review of Experimental Evidence. *Perspectives on Psychological Science, 10*(4), 518–536. doi:10.1177/1745691615583128 PMID:26177951

Lawson, E. T., & McCauley, R. N. (1990). *Rethinking religion: Connecting cognition and culture*. Cambridge University Press.

Lee, S.-H., & Wolpoff, M. H. (2003). The pattern of evolution in Pleistocene human brain size. *Paleobiology, 29*(2), 186–196. doi:10.1017/S0094837300018054

Levy, D. (2007). *Love and sex with robots*. Harper Collins.

Lewis-Williams, D. (2002). *The mind in the cave: Consciousness and the origins of art.* Thames & Hudson.

Li, L., Lv, Y., & Wang, F. Y. (2016). Traffic signal timing via deep reinforcement learning. *IEEE/CAA Journal of Automatica Sinica, 3*(3), 247-254.

Licata, M., Zietlow, A.-L., Träuble, B., Sodian, B., & Reck, C. (2016). Maternal Emotional Availability and Its Association with Maternal Psychopathology, Attachment Style Insecurity and Theory of Mind. *Psychopathology, 49*(5), 334–340. doi:10.1159/000447781 PMID:27498091

Loughnan, S., Haslam, N., Murnane, T., Vaes, J., Reynolds, C., & Suitner, C. (2010). Objectification leads to depersonalization: The denial of mind and moral concern to objectified others. *European Journal of Social Psychology, 40*(5), 709–717. doi:10.1002/ejsp.755

Malle, B. F., Magar, S. T., & Scheutz, M. (2019). AI in the Sky: How People Morally Evaluate Human and Machine Decisions in a Lethal Strike Dilemma. In M. Aldinhas Ferreira, J. Silva Sequeira, G. Singh Virk, M. Tokhi, & E. Kadar (Eds.), *Robotics and Well-Being.* Springer. doi:10.1007/978-3-030-12524-0_11

Mangasarian, O. L., Setiono, R., & Wolberg, W. H. (1990). *Pattern Recognition Via Linear Programming: Theory And Application To Medical Diagnosis.* Academic Press.

McAuliffe, W. H. B. (2019). Do emotions play an essential role in moral judgments? *Thinking & Reasoning, 25*(2), 207–230. doi:10.1080/13546783.2018.1499552

McCauley, R. N., & Whitehouse, H. (2005). New frontiers in the cognitive science of religion. *Journal of Cognition and Culture, 5*(1-2), 1–13. doi:10.1163/1568537054068705

Mikhail, J. (2007). Universal moral grammar: Theory, evidence and the future. *Trends in Cognitive Sciences, 11*(4), 143–152. doi:10.1016/j.tics.2006.12.007 PMID:17329147

Mill, J. S. (1861). Utilitarianism. *Fraser's Magazine, 64,* 391–406; 525–534; 659–673.

Mitchell, S. D. (2003). *Biological complexity and integrative pluralism* (1st ed.). Cambridge University Press. doi:10.1017/CBO9780511802683

Moll, H., & Tomasello, M. (2010). Infant cognition. *Current Biology, 20*(20), R872–R875. doi:10.1016/j.cub.2010.09.001 PMID:20971425

Monroe, A., Guglielmo, S., & Malle, B. (2012). Morality Goes Beyond Mind Perception. *Psychological Inquiry, 23*(2), 179–184. doi:10.1080/1047840X.2012.668271

Mori, M. (1970). The uncanny valley. *Energy, 7*(4), 33–35.

Norenzayan, A., Shariff, A. F., Gervais, W. M., Willard, A. K., McNamara, R. A., Slingerland, E., & Henrich, J. (2016). The cultural evolution of prosocial religions. *Behavioral and Brain Sciences, 39,* e1. doi:10.1017/S0140525X14001356 PMID:26785995

Orban, G. A., & Caruana, F. (2014). The neural basis of human tool use. *Frontiers in Psychology, 5.* Advance online publication. doi:10.3389/fpsyg.2014.00310 PMID:24782809

Palomäki, J., Kunnari, A., Drosinou, M., Koverola, M., Lehtonen, N., Halonen, J., Repo, M., & Laakasuo, M. (2018). Evaluating the replicability of the uncanny valley effect. *Heliyon*, *4*(11), e00939. Advance online publication. doi:10.1016/j.heliyon.2018.e00939 PMID:30519654

Palomäki, J., Laakasuo, M., Cowley, B. U., & Lappi, O. (2020). Poker as a Domain of Expertise. Journal of Expertise/March, 3(2).

Patil, I., & Silani, G. (2014). Reduced empathic concern leads to utilitarian moral judgments in trait alexithymia. *Frontiers in Psychology*, *5*. doi:10.3389/fpsyg.2014.00501 PMID:24904510

Perkins, A. M., Leonard, A. M., Weaver, K., Dalton, J. A., Mehta, M. A., Kumari, V., Williams, S. C. R., & Ettinger, U. (2013). A dose of ruthlessness: Interpersonal moral judgment is hardened by the anti-anxiety drug lorazepam. *Journal of Experimental Psychology. General*, *142*(3), 612–620. doi:10.1037/a0030256 PMID:23025561

Pinker, S. (1994). *The language instinct*. William Morrow and Company. doi:10.1037/e412952005-009

Pinker, S. (1997). *How the mind works*. W. W. Norton and Company.

Pinker, S. (2002). *The blank slate: The modern denial of human nature*. Penguin Books.

Poon, S. H., Jondeau, E., & Rockinger, M. (2007). *Financial modelling under non-Gaussian distributions*. Springer Science & Business Media.

Purzycki, B. G., Apicella, C., Atkinson, Q. D., Cohen, E., McNamara, R. A., Willard, A. K., Xygalatas, D., Norenzayan, A., & Henrich, J. (2016). Moralistic gods, supernatural punishment and the expansion of human sociality. *Nature*, *530*(7590), 327–330. doi:10.1038/nature16980 PMID:26863190

Richardson, K. (2016). Technological Animis: The Uncanny Personhood of Humanoid Machines. *Social Analysis*, *60*(1), 110–128. doi:10.3167a.2016.600108

Richerson, P. J., & Boyd, R. (2005). *Not by genes alone: How culture transformed human evolution*. University of Chicago Press.

Rigby, J., Conroy, S., Miele-Norton, M., Pawlby, S., & Happé, F. (2016, July). Theory of mind as a predictor of maternal sensitivity in women with severe mental illness. *Psychological Medicine*, *46*(9), 1853–1863. doi:10.1017/S0033291716000337 PMID:26979486

Rode, C., Cosmides, L., Hell, W., & Tooby, J. (1999). When and why do people avoid unknown probabilities in decisions under uncertainty? Testing some predictions from optimal foraging theory. *Cognition*, *72*(3), 269–304. doi:10.1016/S0010-0277(99)00041-4 PMID:10519925

Saxe, R., & Baron-Cohen, S. (2006). Editorial: The neuroscience of theory of mind. *Social Neuroscience*, *1*(3–4), 1–9. doi:10.1080/17470910601117463 PMID:18633783

Schein, C., & Gray, K. (2018). The Theory of Dyadic Morality: Reinventing Moral Judgment by Redefining Harm. *Personality and Social Psychology Review*, *22*(1), 32–70. doi:10.1177/1088868317698288 PMID:28504021

Shellenbarger, S. (2019, August 26). Why We Should Teach Kids to Call the Robot 'It.' *The Wall Street Journal*. https://www.wsj.com/articles/why-kids-should-call-the-robot-it-11566811801

Shultz, S., Nelson, E., & Dunbar, R. I. M. (2012). Hominin cognitive evolution: Identifying patterns and processes in the fossil and archaeological record. *Philosophical Transactions of the Royal Society of London. Series B, Biological Sciences, 367*(1599), 2130–2140. doi:10.1098/rstb.2012.0115 PMID:22734056

Sidgwick, H. (1874). *The methods of ethics.* MacMillan & CO.

Singh, M., & Naveen, B. P. (2014). Molecular Nanotechnology: A new avenue for Environment Treatment. *Journal of Environmental Science, Toxicology And. Food Technology, 8*(1), 93–99.

Sinnott-Armstrong, W. (Ed.). (2014). Moral psychology, Vol 4: Free will and moral responsibility. MIT Press.

Sørensen, J. (2004). Religion, evolution, and an immunology of cultural systems. *Evolution & Cognition, 10*(1), 61–73.

Spelke, E. S. (2000). Core knowledge. *The American Psychologist, 55*(11), 1233–1243. doi:10.1037/0003-066X.55.11.1233 PMID:11280937

Spelke, E. S., & Kinzler, K. D. (2007). Core knowledge. *Developmental Science, 10*(1), 89–96. doi:10.1111/j.1467-7687.2007.00569.x PMID:17181705

Springer, P. J. (2013). *Military robots and drones: A reference handbook.* ABC-CLIO.

Stanford, C., Allen, J. S., & Antón, S. C. (2011). *Biological anthropology.* Pearson Education.

Steiger, R. L., & Reyna, C. (2017). Trait contempt, anger, disgust, and moral foundation values. *Personality and Individual Differences, 113*, 125–135. doi:10.1016/j.paid.2017.02.071

Tassy, S., Deruelle, C., Mancini, J., Leistedt, S., & Wicker, B. (2013). High levels of psychopathic traits alters moral choice but not moral judgment. *Frontiers in Human Neuroscience, 7.* Advance online publication. doi:10.3389/fnhum.2013.00229 PMID:23761743

Tooby, J., & Cosmides, L. (1992). The Psychological Foundations of Culture. In J. Barkow, L. Cosmides, & J. Tooby (Eds.), *The adapted mind: Evolutionary psychology and the generation of culture* (pp. 19–136). Oxford University Press.

Tooby, J., & Cosmides, L. (2005). Conceptual Foundations of Evolutionary Psychology. In D. M. Buss (Ed.), *The handbook of evolutionary psychology* (pp. 5–67). John Wiley & Sons, Inc., doi:10.1002/9780470939376.ch1

Tsoukalas, I. (2018). Theory of Mind: Towards an Evolutionary Theory. *Evolutionary Psychological Science, 4*(1), 38–66. doi:10.100740806-017-0112-x

Tulving, E. (1985). Memory and consciousness. *Canadian Psychology, 26*(1), 1–12. doi:10.1037/h0080017

Tulving, E. (2002). Episodic Memory: From Mind to Brain. *Annual Review of Psychology, 53*(1), 1–25. doi:10.1146/annurev.psych.53.100901.135114 PMID:11752477

Tybur, J. M., Lieberman, D., & Griskevicius, V. (2009). Microbes, mating, and morality: Individual differences in three functional domains of disgust. *Journal of Personality and Social Psychology, 97*(1), 103–122. doi:10.1037/a0015474 PMID:19586243

Tybur, J. M., Lieberman, D., Kurzban, R., & DeScioli, P. (2013). Disgust: Evolved function and structure. *Psychological Review*, *120*(1), 65–84. doi:10.1037/a0030778 PMID:23205888

Tybur, J. M., Merriman, L. A., Hooper, A. E. C., McDonald, M. M., & Navarrete, C. D. (2010). Extending the Behavioral Immune System to Political Psychology: Are Political Conservatism and Disgust Sensitivity Really Related? *Evolutionary Psychology*, *8*(4), 147470491000800420. doi:10.1177/147470491000800406 PMID:22947823

Uomini, N. T., & Meyer, G. F. (2013). Shared Brain Lateralization Patterns in Language and Acheulean Stone Tool Production: A Functional Transcranial Doppler Ultrasound Study. *PLoS One*, *8*(8), e72693. Advance online publication. doi:10.1371/journal.pone.0072693 PMID:24023634

Vaesen, K. (2012). The cognitive bases of human tool use. *Behavioral and Brain Sciences*, *35*(4), 203–218. doi:10.1017/S0140525X11001452 PMID:22697258

Voyer, B. G., & Tarantola, T. (2017). Toward a Multidisciplinary Moral Psychology. In B. G. Voyer & T. Tarantola (Eds.), *Moral psychology: A multidisciplinary guide* (pp. 1–3). Springer International Publishing., doi:10.1007/978-3-319-61849-4_1

Willard, A. K., & McNamara, R. A. (2019). The Minds of God(s) and Humans: Differences in Mind Perception in Fiji and North America. *Cognitive Science*, *43*(1), e12703. doi:10.1111/cogs.12703 PMID:30648803

Zeytinoglu, S., Calkins, S. D., & Leerkes, E. M. (2018). Maternal emotional support but not cognitive support during problem-solving predicts increases in cognitive flexibility in early childhood. *International Journal of Behavioral Development*. Advance online publication. doi:10.1177/0165025418757706 PMID:31036983

ENDNOTES

[1] See section on What is Moral Philosophy? and Part 2.

[2] See Part 2.

[3] Naturally, we acknowledge that genes themselves do not think, feel, or act in any way. However, this form of expresson is a convenient short-hand, which only means that some gene variants in the gene pool are, on average, in comparison to all the other variants, more efficient in increasing in their relative frequency.

[4] See also Tsoukalas, 2018, for a more fundamental evolutionary hypothesis.

[5] . Naturally, harming or benefitting a person is not the only morally relevant action and does not cover everything that can be placed under the umbrella of "morality."

[6] . To put it shortly, moral psychology is mostly a desciptive science: it describes how morality happens in the the observable universe, but does not "take sides." In this sense, moral psychology, or the field of moral cognitition more broadly, is similar to the study of history, where the historian might describe the attrocities of genocides accurately and carefully, without actually supporting such horror.

[7] Piagetian and Kohlbergian tradition.

8   See also Zalta, 2020, for further discussion on definitions of moral psychology.

9   With moral cognition, we mean that multidisciplinary area of moral psychology that focuses on defining, explicating and studying the information processing aspects of moral judgments and decisions.

10   We understand that this list is not exhaustive from a philosophical perspective; i.e. it lacks many of the classical themes that moral philosophy is based upon, such as respect for individual liberties, rights, and respect for the dignity of others. However, this is the theory in its current formulation and it is based on empirical investigations.

Chapter 11
Moral Psychology and Artificial Agents (Part Two):
The Transhuman Connection

Michael Laakasuo
University of Helsinki, Finland

Anton Kunnari
University of Helsinki, Finland

Jukka R. I. Sundvall
University of Helsinki, Finland

Mika Koverola
University of Helsinki, Finland

Anton Berg
University of Helsinki, Finland

Marko Repo
University of Helsinki, Finland

Marianna Drosinou
University of Helsinki, Finland

Teemu Saikkonen
University of Turku, Finland

Volo Herzon
University of Helsinki, Finland

Jussi Palomäki
University of Helsinki, Finland

ABSTRACT

Part 1 concluded by introducing the concept of the new ontological category – explaining how our cognitive machinery does not have natural and intuitive understanding of robots and AIs, unlike we have for animals, tools, and plants. Here the authors review findings in the moral psychology of robotics and transhumanism. They show that many peculiarities arise from the interaction of human cognition with robots, AIs, and human enhancement technologies. Robots are treated similarly, but not completely, like humans. Some such peculiarities are explained by mind perception mechanisms. On the other hand, it seems that transhumanistic technologies like brain implants and mind uploading are condemned, and the condemnation is motivated by our innate sexual disgust sensitivity mechanisms.

DOI: 10.4018/978-1-7998-4894-3.ch011

Copyright © 2021, IGI Global. Copying or distributing in print or electronic forms without written permission of IGI Global is prohibited.

INTRODUCTION

Human cognition is shaped by evolution. What this means in practice, is that humans have fundamental intuitive, automatic, and non-conscious processes constantly operating in the background. Such processes organize our perceptions, thoughts and reactions towards the world outside our minds. In Part 1, we showed how evolution equipped us with such capacities as mind perception (understanding other minds), tool use, and the emotion of disgust.[1] We concluded the previous chapter by analyzing the concept of the New Ontological Category. The New Ontological Category (i.e., Robots, AIs, and other forms of intelligent technologies) which are neither alive nor inanimate (but non-alive and animate), did not exist during our evolution. We therefore do not have an intuitive understanding of them the same way we have of humans, animals, plants, rocks, and inanimate matter. This fundamental observation, stemming from the basic findings in evolutionary psychology, then makes it salient that there are bound to be odd and unexpected clashes between new "animate" technologies and the human moral cognitive system. Human understanding of the world divides the world into epistemic categories, of inanimate nonliving and animate living, but it has no conceptual category naturally corresponding to the *new ontological category* which dilutes these categories to "animate non-living."

Here we show how the fact that we do not have intuitive understanding of the *new ontological category* unwinds in unexpected and unpredictable ways in the recent moral psychological literature focused on understanding human moral psychology in new contexts. We will show how category violations that happen between humans and machines, and between minded and non-minded entities, results in inconsistent moral judgments, which are not explained by existing moral psychological theories. We start with the definition of transhumanism – a long standing philosophical project that aims to redefine what humanity is – then discuss the categorical clashes between our cognition, robots, and human enhancement technologies (Thompson, 2014). The reason for covering transhumanism here is that transhumanism is a philosophy that fundamentally blurs the categories of humans and machines. Transhumanistic technologies, such as cognitive enhancement, can create similar confusions to our moral psychological apparatus, as do robots, AIs, and other information processing technologies. In a sense, transhumanism pulls humans into the New Ontological Category as well, since it fundamentally sees humans as information processing systems that can and should be integrated with AIs and machines. This is guaranteed to create moral cognitive clashes, as we will show.

After covering the basics of transhumanist philosophy, the moral psychology of robotics, and the moral psychology of transhumanist technologies, we move on to discuss the limits of present-day moral psychological theories. These are limits made obvious by the *new ontological category*; we also suggest some directions for future studies. Finally, we conclude by summarizing the lessons learned.

DEFINING TRANSHUMANISM

The term "transhumanism" was originally defined by biologist and first UNESCO director, Julian Huxley, as a belief in the possibility of "man remaining man, but transcending himself, by realizing the new possibilities of and for his human nature" (1957). Whereas Huxley emphasized both the spiritual and communal aspects of this enterprise, the term was later adopted by thinkers focused on the technological aspects of human improvement; that is, human cognitive and physical enhancement or alteration going beyond our normal limits. Today, *transhumanism* is an umbrella term for philosophical, religious, aesthetical, social and political movements, engineering, various research projects, worldviews, and life-styles claiming that: a) the current state of humanity is not the endpoint of its evolution, and b) humanity can (and maybe should) take conscious action to guide its own evolution through technological means (O'Connell, 2018; Thompson, 2014; see also Lin et al., 2014a; 2014b).

While there is no strict universal transhumanist moral code, transhumanist arguments do have strong utilitarian leanings (Bostrom, 2005; Frohlich, 2015; More, 2010; Sotala & Gloor, 2017). Critiques of transhumanism have centered on broad concerns about loss of the meaning of life, sanctity of the body, or essential humanity (Kass, 2003); or claimed that blind faith in technological progress is equivalent to believing in a benevolent God who will *ex machina* solve our problems (Burdett, 2014). Some fear that transhumanistic technologies and visions might alter our social interactions by making them more superficial and instrumental (Frischmann & Selinger, 2018). Further criticism has focused on the potential damaging socioeconomic effects of transhumanism, suggesting it might widen the gap between the haves and the have-nots, coerce eugenics, or lead to a permanent division of humanity into a master and a slave class (Moravec, 1988). To all of these concerns, the transhumanist response might be summed up in Russell Blackford's words:

The concern is essentially a matter of social justice, a problem that modern societies must, and do, wrestle with continually, within real-world economic and political constraints. Responses to the problem might vary from redistribution of the wealth that enables differential access in the first place, prohibition or limitation of enhancement technologies in the interests of fairness, or steps to make at least some genetic technologies – those relating to health and longevity – as widely available as possible. (2003)

The key areas of transhumanist interest[2] are different forms of cognitive and physical enhancement (e.g. drugs, implants, and other technological aids to performance), life extension technologies (e.g. cryonics, cloning, "mind-uploading," eugenics, and gene therapies against aging), and new sentient "life forms" (e.g. radically augmented humans, robotics, brain-computer symbiotes, "whole brain emulations"). Attempts to increase human performance and longevity, or to change our very nature, also relate to how we categorize things. How much can a human being be altered before they are no longer (categorized as) human, and what does this mean in terms of their moral status? Technologies that make people radically better at something through invasive means also raise questions of harm and fairness, making above-baseline human enhancements novel challenges for our moral cognition (Thompson, 2014; Lin et al., 2014a, 2014b).

One central aspiration of transhumanism is to increase the levels of human general intelligence, for instance, through eugenics, gene editing, and other biotechnological innovations (Bostrom, 2014). However, transhumanists usually talk about eugenics from an ahistorical perspective, where they are concerned about improving the quality of human life. Their perspective on eugenics is then radically different from the perspective of the general population – a theme we will return to in Future Studies.

MORAL PSYCHOLOGICAL PERSPECTIVES ON ROBOTICS AND TRANSHUMANISM

Here, we will present recent empirical evidence from moral psychology showing how human moral cognition and intelligent technologies collide with unexpected results. We will first review recent findings on moral psychology of robotics, and then continue to present some intriguing novel findings from research studying attitudes towards transhumanistic technologies.

Human Universals in the Moral Psychology of Robots?

In Part 1, we argued that mind perception is a crucial part of morality: we need to perceive something as an agent to hold it morally responsible, and to perceive something as having an inner experiential world to see it as also having moral rights. Here, we focus on the ways mind perception and moral judgment interact, and review studies on human preferences regarding how artificial agents act in moral situations.

In a rare study of robots as the victims (rather than perpetrators) of harm, Ward et al. (2013) turned the morality of machines upside down, suggesting that the link between mind perception and morality works both ways. Machines and corpses by definition are non-living and have no true moral interaction with humans. Robots that were intentionally abused (in a fictional story) were attributed *more* cognitive capacities than robots that were untouched; while (conscious) humans who were intentionally harmed were attributed *less* cognitive capacities. Thus, in the case of harm-causing abuse, mind perception depends on the status of the abused agent.

In a similar vein, several age groups of children between 7 and 15 years old thought it was equally morally wrong to maltreat the robot dog AIBO and a real dog (Melson et al., 2009). These findings align with the Theory of Dyadic Morality (TDM; see Part 1), particularly the idea of "dyadic completion." That is, the TDM's proposed "dyadic loop" has three elements that form the template of a moral violation: a perpetrator, a victim, and harm. "Dyadic completion" means that people may infer all three elements to be present (and thus, that moral violation has occurred) when, in reality, only one or two elements are present (Schein & Gray, 2018). In other words, merely *perceiving* a typical morally questionable action (e.g. hitting something) can be enough to "inject mind" into the situation.

In another recent paper, Bigman and Gray (2018) argue that people have earlier denied full moral status to children,[3] animals, and even to other races (see below section on dehumanization), and the same might be true for machines. Machine *agency* and responsibility may be linked to the extent that people perceive the machines as minded entities. In six of their studies, the authors found that people are averse to machines making moral decisions: people prefer machines not to decide on matters of life and death. This aversion arguably stems from thinking that machines lack a mind. This aversion is also not easy to overcome, as it persists even if the machines are described as having expertise or capacity for mental experience.

However, people do sometimes have clear opinions on what a robot moral agent should do in matters of life and death, even if they are averse to the very idea. Awad et al. (2018) argue, based on an extensive attitude survey on autonomous vehicles (AVs), that the dream of universal machine ethics is not doomed, since there are points of relative agreement between broad geographical regions. The authors studied how people react to utilitarian decisions made by AVs with cross-cultural data (over 40 million answers to moral dilemmas achieved through an online gamified survey platform). They wanted to know what types of road users, from domestic animals to individuals with high social status, survey participants would be willing to sacrifice. People generally preferred the utilitarian option of saving the most people possible. Additionally, people preferred to save humans over animals, and young over old. Demographic factors did not have an impact, but three cultural clusters were detected: the occidental, oriental, and southern clusters. In the oriental cluster, people had a lower preference to save young over old people. In the southern cluster (mostly Latin America), people had a lower preference to save humans over animals, but were more willing to save individuals with high status over those with lower status. The findings are in line with Evolutionary Psychology (EP; see Part 1) theory: human moral judgments are relatively universal, with some regional variations around a common "core" of moral thought.

However, AVs also reveal a darker side of the seeming universal utilitarian preference. Bonnefon et al. (2016) scrutinized the AV utilitarian dilemmas, finding that people are willing to recommend utilitarian vehicles for others, but for themselves prefer AVs that would protect them at all costs. Assuming both utilitarian and self-protective cars were on the market simultaneously, few people expressed willingness to buy the car with the utilitarian algorithm. Additionally, a majority of Bonnefon et al.'s participants, when asked, opposed the idea of regulations that would force AVs to be utilitarian (2016). Such contradictions in morals are not new when it comes to humans. However, it is interesting how clearly the idea of automated moral agents highlights these contradictions. When it comes to an actual autonomous moral decision-maker a person can buy, one cannot demand one kind of "moral car" for themselves and another kind for others. Moreover, the moral choices of these AVs would be pre-specified rather than left to be decided by people (with little time) – the results of Bonnefon et al.'s results suggest that people do not favor such prespecification, even if it saved more lives on aggregate (2016). The question of truly utilitarian cars is essentially the following: Would you put your life in the hands of something, that may decide it is better for you to die to prevent a larger loss of life, and with which you cannot negotiate?

Waytz et al. (2014) studied the effects of enhanced anthropomorphism on the perception of AVs. Car manufacturers design their products to represent something they presume potential buyers desire in terms of driving comfort, power, and aesthetics. Waytz et al. went further by adding a name, gender and voice to one of their AV simulators (2014). This anthropomorphic AV simulator was rated more trustworthy and likeable than a non-autonomous vehicle simulator or an AV simulator without any anthropomorphic features. Naming cars is not exactly new: four-time Formula 1 world champion, Sebastian Vettel, has named his racing cars with seductive female names (such as Kinky Kylie or Hungry Heidi). Boats are also traditionally named after people. However, these are instances of people naming things they like and control. A manufacturer adding a name and a voice (similar to the Alexa voice assistant) to a widely distributed product is entirely different and potentially riskier. Waytz et al. (2014) show how easy it is to manipulate people into seeing agency in, or feeling trust towards, lifeless objects, through simple manipulations that do not bear on the AV's primary function. A name and a voice may make an AV more approachable to humans, but increased trust without an increased understanding of how the machine works is a risky combination.

Malle et al. (2019) focused on different types of agents and moral responses these agents evoke in a military context. Participants were requested to judge the actions of a human military pilot, an autonomous drone, or an aircraft with artificial intelligence. The agents were to either carry out an attack on terrorists while risking the life of an innocent child wandering in the target area, or to cancel the attack to protect the child, which, in turn, risked a terrorist strike. Participants treated all the agents as more or less morally responsible: even the autonomous drone was condemned by half of the respondents. When people were asked what the agent should do, launching the strike was generally considered the better option for each of the agents. People thus imposed similar norms on all three agents. However, people morally evaluated a human and artificial agent's decision in an identical dilemma differently, blaming the human pilot who cancelled the attack significantly more than the other agents. The authors supposed that the military command chain might justify, in the participants' minds, the actions of soldiers: a human pilot is seen more blameworthy for cancelling the strike than launching it because self-reliantly terminating the command chain is seen as a moral violation, although no differences in norms postulated to agents were detected. Thus, if machines are a part of a complex command chain and malfunction or people get killed, somehow the perception of responsibility gets diffused and disappears; although somebody did make the decision to use a machine to achieve this morally relevant task.

copy of part of a rat's conflict with existing literature. Laakasuo et al. (under revisions)[4] studied how people judge morally a hypothetical scenario where either a human nurse or a nursing robot forcefully medicates an unwilling patient. This dilemma juxtaposes two moral principles: the patient's autonomy and the medical establishment's goal to heal the patient. In a series of studies, both qualitative and quantitative (total N > 1300), we found that people disliked robot-made decisions depending on the type of decision made, and not generally. If the nursing robot decided not to forcefully medicate the patient, the decision was judged similarly to a human nurse made the same decision. However, forceful medication was only tolerated for a human nurse. These findings are in some tension with findings of Bigman and Gray (2018), wherein mind attribution (or lack thereof) explained the aversion to robots as decision-makers. While people may be generally averse to robots as moral agents, this aversion does not seem to reflect in their judgments about a robot's decisions, if those decisions align with what they would prefer a human to decide in a similar situation. Our results also conflict with those of Malle et al. (2019), as it is the robot - and not the human agent - that is judged more harshly for a specific moral decision.

In a similar vein, Laakasuo et al. (in preparation) presented participants with vignettes (short stories that often depict social events), describing a moral dilemma involving a human or robot coast guard. The guard witnessed a boating accident caused by two intoxicated motorboaters, where three people ended up in water separated by distance: the motorboaters in one location, and a fisherman in another. The guard had to then decide to either save the two motorboaters (utilitarian decision) or the fisherman (favouring the innocent party). The results consistently showed that saving the motorboaters (who caused the accident) was more condemnable than saving the innocent fisherman, but only if the coast guard was a robot. If the guard was a human, both decisions were equally approved.

It seems that robots are held to a "higher" moral standard than humans: people are allowed to choose the "worse" option, but a robot should "know better". Interestingly, the coast guard robot making a utilitarian decision to save the motorboaters was perceived to have "less mind" than a robot deciding to save the fisherman. Utilitarian robots may be seen as cold and calculating, and thus less human. Alternatively, people may consider a robot that (seemingly) takes the moral blameworthiness of the motorboaters into account as more human-like; or people may simply attribute more human-like qualities to robots acting in line with their own morality (not saving the blameworthy motorboaters). Whatever the case, there may be several factors that play into how much human-like thought or feeling people perceive in robots, and how this perceived human-likeness affects judgments on those robots in turn.

As this short review reveals, the *new ontological category* raises its head in situations where machines make decisions about human lives, and humans need to judge whether these decisions are acceptable. With a quick glance, it seems that machines are capable of making near-optimal decisions in multiple domains such as risk management (Lin & Hsu, 2017), medical diagnostics (Elkin et al., 2018), and even in games requiring strategic decision-making (Tegmark, 2017). However, this superficial understanding does not take into consideration that conceptions of "optimal" or "good" might be fuzzy and intuitive rather than sharp and logical. It might be a good idea to delegate moral decisions to machines; it just seems we do not really know how to do that correctly, because our thinking is fuzzy and further complicated by the NOC.

Transhumanism and Disgust Sensitivity

Previously, we described what transhumanism is as a (normative) philosophy. There have not been many empirical studies on how ordinary people actually feel about transhuman philosophy if it becomes an actuality. Here, we present novel results of work currently under preparation or in press. We describe a number of experiments where we, and others, have studied reactions of ordinary people towards transhuman technologies and technologies that break down the human-machine dichotomy.

Castelo et al. (2019) investigated how individuals who decide to alter their brain functions with either chemicals or brain-implanted chips are perceived as less "human," a phenomenon labelled as *dehumanization*. Dehumanization commonly occurs before intergroup conflicts escalate into full-blown genocides (Arendt, 1951; Haslam, 2006; Haslam et al., 2007). The dehumanized out-group is often described as something less-than-human, animal-like, or less deserving of dignified human treatment. Nonetheless, Castelo et al. (2019) did not attempt to explain *why* dehumanization occurred in their study, or what *motivated* dehumanization of individuals undergoing cognitive or brain enhancement. This question was, however, explored by Koverola et al. (2020b) in a five-study paper (preprint).

The authors investigated whether there were differences in people's reactions when the *memory* or *IQ* enhancement is used to: a) fix an existing ailment, b) achieve optimal human functioning, or c) achieve superhuman functioning. As dependent variables, Koverola et al. (2020) measured: 1) the moral condemnation of the decision to get brain implants, 2) the perceived unfairness of their use, and 3) dehumanization of those individuals who decided to use cognitive enhancements. The results showed that people were quite accepting of the use of brain-implant chips, unless they were used to gain superhuman abilities. Moreover, the moral foundation of purity (norms about bodily "sanctity"; see Part 1 on the Moral Foundations Theory) predicted dehumanization and moral condemnation of memory implants. Further probing revealed that science fiction hobbyism[5] predicted moral approval, and that sexual disgust sensitivity (SDS, see Part 1) was the strongest explaining factor of condemnation and dehumanization of brain-implant chip users (see Figure 1). The authors ruled out competing explanations such as the respondents' tendency to oppose new and unknown technologies, medical operations *per se,* or body-envelope violations.[6]

In Figure 1, Koverola et al. (2020b) chart results from a series of five experiments where an office worker is suffering from early onset of memory problems and decides to go to the doctor's office for diagnosis. There the patient is given a recommendation of having one of three brain-implanted chips (participants read only one version of the story) with the following potential outcomes: 1) alleviation of the memory problems, 2) return to functioning at the level of youth, or 3) superhuman memory abilities. Participants were asked to rate "how human" the office worker would be after the operation. In this figure, the authors have pooled the data from the studies that show that sexual disgust sensitivity predicts increased dehumanization of brain-implant users (the office worker), irrespective of this level of enhancement. However, individuals with superhuman memory capacities are dehumanized more than individuals with normal levels of memory functioning.

The fact that a person's familiarity with science fiction is associated with them having a more positive attitude towards transhuman technology makes intuitive sense. Exposure to new ideas makes them less scary: there are cultural effects on what people judge (alternatively, people drawn to science fiction may share certain personality traits that make them less judgmental in this area). This effect was also observed in another study by Koverola et al. (2020a), where participants judged hypothetical scenarios about robot and human prostitution: both were condemned by participants, but only the judgment of robot

Figure 1. Partial results from an upcoming paper by Koverola et al. (2020b)

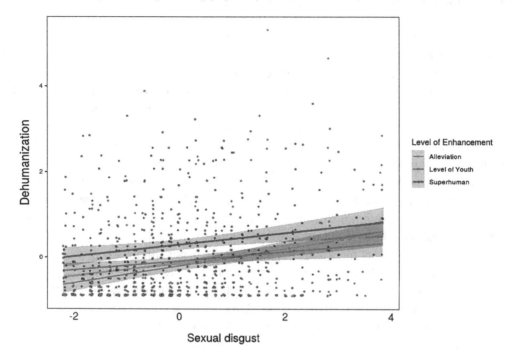

prostitution depended on the participants' familiarity with science fiction. Thus, there is some indication that an intuitive effect of familiarity on judgment of very different novel technologies replicates. What is less intuitive is the connection between judgment and sexual disgust.

Why was SDS associated with transhuman technologies? Sexual disgust evolved for mate selection, but has also been co-opted to guard conservative norms and, apparently, also motivates the condemnation of new technologies. Perhaps our complex modular and categorical cognitive system cannot cope rationally with the blending of the human category with the *new ontological category* (i.e. modern intelligent implant technology). Dehumanization may be triggered by this perceived *mix* of human and machine, which confuses our biological motivational systems (relating to sexual reproduction). It is hard to imagine a more fundamental blending of ontological categories than that of humans turning into robots.

Humans have evolved to quickly recognize the difference between the living and the dead, minded and un-minded. But how would humans deal with the ultimate transhumanist dream of uploading one's mind into a supercomputer (Kurzweil, 2012)? This might seem like the most far-off version of science fiction fantasy. However, a copy of a *C. elegans'* (Fessenden, 2014) nervous system has already been placed inside a robot, and a functional copy of a part of a rat's brain has been digitized (Markram et al., 2015). In both cases, the copy functions similarly to the original. In principle, at least, there is no reason for why this could not be done for the human brain. The movie *Transcendence* (Pfister, 2014) juxtaposes the ethics of self-enhancement, individual freedom, and the conservative public backlash against creating "conscious machines". Clearly, this theme of *mind upload* has deeply enticing moral dimensions for people to produce a multimillion dollar movie.

This theme was recently examined in detail by Laakasuo et al. (2018). In four studies the authors show a familiar pattern previously discussed in the context of brain-implants. Science-fiction hobbyism strongly and independently predicted positive approval of uploading one's consciousness into a computer, whereas sexual disgust and moral purity (independently of each other) strongly and robustly predicted disapproval.[7] The authors also showed that people probably did not consider mind upload as a form of suicide or death, since participants anxious about death and judgmental towards suicide were likely to approve using such technology.

One core part of transhumanist arguments for promoting life-extension technologies and cognitive enhancement is the elimination of suffering and increase of life quality. Thus, transhumanism is not that far-removed from the philosophical tradition of utilitarianism. Indeed, many transhumanists are implicitly or explicitly utilitarian in their ethical leanings. They wish to develop transhumanist technologies to promote wellbeing. Tied to this is also the sub-field of AI research known as *AI safety research* (Sotala & Yampolskiy, 2015; Yampolskiy, 2018). In this field, many prominent transhumanists and AI developers analyze risks that humanity might face in seeking to develop human-like Artificial General Intelligence (AGI). One central risk associated with creating an AGI is that it, or its developer, could be a callous, psychopathic, and selfish being with the potential to develop an entity with superhuman capacities.

Focusing more on this issue, we ran several structural equation models on a large dataset from an online study (N = 1000) and found a pathway model shown in Figure 2 below. The results once again replicate the statistical effect of sexual disgust on disapproval of mind upload technology. However, one of the fears of the transhumanists seems to be supported, as approval of mind upload technology was linked with Machiavellianism – a personality trait associated with narcissism and psychopathy[8] (Paulhus & Jones, 2015; see Figure 2).

Figure 2. Structural equation model from a forthcoming paper by Laakasuo et al. (2020)

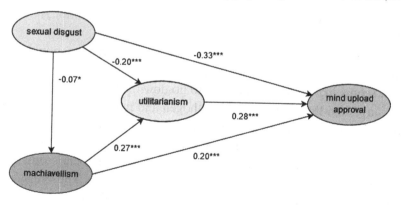

In Figure 2, Laakasuo et al. show how Machiavellian tendencies are associated with both utilitarian moral choices and approval of mind upload technologies. $N = 1000$; $X^2_{SB(578)}$: 1356,22, CFI = .95, TLI = .94, Robust RMSEA = .039, [.036, .042], SRMR = .043 (indicating an excellent fit between the model and the data). See also Laakasuo et al. (2018).

Machiavellianism is commonly considered as a more functional form of psychopathy, since both dimensions are described as manipulative, callous, and cold (Miller et al., 2017). While Machiavellianism and psychopathy are similar, they are two separate constructs: psychopathy is separated from Machiavellianism mostly by impulsivity and a lack of long term strategizing (Paulhus & Jones, 2015).

This implies that callousness is associated with utilitarian views, which then feed into positive approval of mind upload technology. This study is a good example of how AI safety research[9] can generate hypotheses (in this case, the risk of callous individuals being especially interested in this futuristic technology), which can then be studied by moral psychology. From an EP perspective, empathy and sexual disgust explain individuals' interest towards morally volatile future technologies. The issues, as well as the novel results listed here are salient warnings of the challenges posed by the *new ontological category* to our stone-aged moral cognition.

FUTURE RESEARCH DIRECTIONS

Crossroads for Transhumanism, AI Ethics, and Moral Psychology

Evolutionary approaches have been effective at generating hypotheses on how humans behave in moral dilemma situations. This might not be the case anymore, when the *new ontological category* of AIs and intelligent technologies enter the scene, were they within or outside of our bodies. In the context of the *new ontological category,* there are no obvious immediate hypotheses that could help us understand the implications for our moral cognition. It merely states that new information processing technologies are challenging our moral cognition and gives a plausible explanation for why this is the case. What we specifically need, however, is to gain understanding regarding the deeper process at the level of cognitive structures, as to why we treat robotic decisions and transhuman technologies the way we do. In other words, we need a better/new theoretical framework for hypothesis generation, now that EP approaches are running out of steam.

For instance, the empirical findings presented previously suggest that we should investigate the role of sexual disgust sensitivity in predicting aversion to robots making moral decisions in possibly utilitarian contexts. However, it seems like a bizarre alleyway to go down, since utilitarian robots are not potential disease vectors (i.e., anything, that might carry a pathogen and make us sick), and it is quite difficult to understand why mate choice mechanisms would be associated with the condemnation of robots. Sexual disgust sensitivity specifically seems to be connected to political conservatism (Elad-Strenger et al., 2020), but the associations between sexual disgust sensitivity and moral judgment seems to remain even after controlling for measures of political views (Laakasuo et al., 2018; 2020). Thus, disgust sensitivity has effects independent of its association with political views (ignoring, for the moment, the question of potential ultimate causes for political views). Theoretically, this connection between disgust and judgment makes little sense, and should be investigated further. One explanation has been offered by Voiklis and Malle (2018): there is no moral cognition as such, and we simply have a collection of social cognitive information processing systems functioning in domains that have been culturally delineated as moral domains. However, this does not tell us *why* a certain set of socio-moral cognitive mechanisms get activated in specific ways with robots and transhuman technologies. Who would have predicted, from evolutionary premises, that mind-uploading is condemned mainly due to sexual disgust mechanisms? This seems obvious post-hoc, but we claim that it would have required exceptional theoretical arguments to produce this hypothesis *a priori*.

Another area that we believe needs more work is in understanding the dynamics of mind perception, dehumanization/infrahumanization, and morality. Will people become more accepting of any and all moral decisions by machines if they are made to resemble humans more? Are "humanized" AVs allowed to make more utilitarian decisions than non-talking AVs, or do we perceive them as something even creepier? Will upbringing among (or even by) increasingly humanized robots disrupt normal cognitive development in children, necessitating countermeasures? What will be the moral status of "enhanced" human beings, as either moral agents or patients? Do perceptions of "enhanced" humans as "less human" also manifest with more clearly visible enhancements such as prostheses, for which there is more cultural history and familiarization? We encourage other researchers to examine these phenomena, since the well-being of future generations might be linked to these sorts of mechanisms and their clear understanding.

We also presented the concept of technological animism. This observation, stemming from cross-cultural comparisons (see Part 1) between Eastern and Western cultures implies that we might need to pay more attention to other mechanisms that are associated with mind attribution when we are trying to understand the moralization processes of humans toward robots and transhuman technologies. Previous research implies that human intuitions about souls (not minds) and their purity are also important (Bering, 2006; Laakasuo et al., 2018), but we do not know why. However, it seems clear that human-robot moral interactions are not just about mind (or soul) perception, but also about many auxiliary mechanisms (emotions, perceptions of moral causality, etc.), the role of which needs to be clarified. For example, robots may simply be percieved as something that humans are not as able to negotiate with, as they are with other humans – a potential reason for the increase wariness about the idea of allowing robots to, for example, make morally complicated medical decisions.[10]

As world-changing as the above mentioned technologies are, there are visions of far more disruptive technologies that moral psychology should examine. For example, AI-assisted eugenics would open a space for interesting inquiry where transhumanism, AI, and moral psychological theory intersect. The transhuman idea of increasing the IQ of humanity already has some "prototypes" in existing medical practice. Currently, about 90% of embryos diagnosed with Down's syndrome in prenatal screening are terminated (Morris & Springett, 2014). In some countries, like Iceland, there are almost no individuals with Down's syndrome. In China, genetically modified embryos have already been grown (and widely condemned); police and other state officials have AI technology at their disposal, making it possible to visualize the basic phenotypical characteristics of individuals just from their DNA sample alone (Curtis & Hereward, 2018; Lippert et al., 2017; Schaefer, 2016), and use this as an estimation whether the fetus should be aborted or not.

Corresponding technology can theoretically provide means for estimating the characteristics of unborn children, including their IQ, based on the analyzed DNA sequence of the fertilized ova. Within the past 20 years, AI technology and algorithmic data-mining have made it possible to alter the genome of unborn humans (and other organisms) in increasingly reliable ways (Pluysnin et al., 2008; Ritchie et al., 2015). Efficient and automatic computation has quietly made it easier to genetically screen for IQ; essentially making "personal eugenics" a possibility (Regalado, 2018). Given the growing role of machine learning in medicine, AI-based recommendations on embryo screening for "desired" genotypes are a possible, if scary, future development. The idea of screening embryos for intelligence, aided by AI, brings together many of the issues we have discussed: artificial agents affecting human lives, the modification of humanity, even the ultimate EP theme of procreation and survival. As with many other themes discussed here, we do not really know how people feel about these technologies. What moral cognitive processes are activated, if culture shifts towards accepting the use of these technologies (Rozin, 1999)?

We encourage researchers to study people's responses to seemingly far-fetched or "sci-fi" ideas. We are not in a technological utopia or dystopia, nor likely to get there very soon, but some of the themes dealt with in the moral psychology of robotics or transhumanism are getting closer to real-world relevance, or are already there. Self-driving cars, robot companions to children, and at least pharmacological cognitive enhancement are already happening (Thompson, 2014). Our suggestion to the problem of being out-paced by technology is to ask questions about technologies that are not here (yet).

CONCLUSION

To have a basic understanding of the problems that artificial moral agents and transhumanistic technologies pose, we should (or must) use the combined tools of philosophy, evolutionary psychology, moral psychology, technology studies, and anthropology. We hope to have shown that there are indeed some previously unencountered questions and problems with which our evolved moral cognition must deal. We have shown how evolutionarily old cognitive mechanisms (e.g., sexual disgust sensitivity) are unexpectedly linked with transhumanist technologies. We have also shown that although robots are not "minded" in the same way as biological beings are, people still treat them as having at least a degree of a mind. Clearly robots are not treated like rocks, trees, other tools, or even like "mere machines," but neither are they treated as humans or animals (see Part 1).

Moral dilemmas involving self-driving cars, killer drones, nursing robots, and rescue robots, when analyzed from this novel point of view (combining as mentioned, philosophy, evolutionary psychology, moral psychology, technology studies, and anthropology) reveal new vantage-points into our own moral cognition and its functioning. We do treat them as if they have minds, but to which degree seems to depend on the type of decisions (e.g., utilitarian vs. deontological) these devices make. We also recognize that many of the findings, models, and theories presented here might only apply to Western cultures. However, research by Awad et al. (2018) suggests there are some cross-cultural universals further highlighting the need for bio-cultural approaches that take into consideration both evolutionary modular models and cultural influences.

We have discussed how the existing moral psychological theories help us to understand our own reactions when robots make moral decisions or merge with the human brain. What is the evolutionary explanation, or even a hypothesis, for why sexual disgust sensitivity predicts moral approval or condemnation of mind upload, or brain implants? The *new ontological category* is a cybernetic cosmic trickster monkey throwing its wrench into our moral cognitive system. The ensuing mess is unique in the history of humanity and should be studied.

REFERENCES

Arendt, H. (1951). *The origins of totalitarianism*. Schocken Books.

Bering, J. M. (2006). The folk psychology of souls. *Behavioral and Brain Sciences*, 29(5), 453–462. doi:10.1017/S0140525X06009101 PMID:17156519

Bigman, Y. E., & Gray, K. (2018). People are averse to machines making moral decisions. *Cognition*, 181, 21–34. doi:10.1016/j.cognition.2018.08.003 PMID:30107256

Blackford, R. (2003). Who's Afraid of the Brave New World? *Quadrant, 47*(5), 9.

Bonnefon, J.-F., Shariff, A., & Rahwan, I. (2016). The social dilemma of autonomous vehicles. *Science, 352*(6293), 1573–1576. doi:10.1126cience.aaf2654 PMID:27339987

Bostrom, N. (2005). A History of Transhumanist Thought. *Journal of Evolution and Technology / WTA, 14*(1).

Bostrom, N. (2014). *Superintelligence: Paths, dangers, strategies.* Oxford University Press.

Burdett, M. (2014). The Religion of Technology: Transhumanism and the myth of progress. In C. Marcer & T. J. Trothen (Eds.), *Religion and transhumanism: The unknown future of human enhancement* (pp. 131–147). ABC-CLIO, LLC.

Castelo, N., Schmitt, B., & Sarvary, M. (2019). Human or Robot? Consumer Responses to Radical Cognitive Enhancement Products. *Journal of the Association for Consumer Research, 4*(3), 217–230. doi:10.1086/703462

Curtis, C., & Hereward, J. (2018, May 4). How Accurately Can Scientists Reconstruct A Person's Face From DNA? *Smithsonian Magazine.* https://www.smithsonianmag.com/innovation/how-accurately-can-scientists-reconstruct-persons-face-from-dna-180968951/

Elad-Strenger, J., Proch, J., & Kessler, T. (2020). Is Disgust a "Conservative" Emotion? *Personality and Social Psychology Bulletin, 46*(6), 896–912. doi:10.1177/0146167219880191 PMID:31619133

Elkin, P., Schlegel, D., Anderson, M., Komm, J., Ficheur, G., & Bisson, L. (2018). Artificial Intelligence: Bayesian versus Heuristic Method for Diagnostic Decision Support. *Applied Clinical Informatics, 09*(02), 432–439. doi:10.1055-0038-1656547 PMID:29898469

Fessenden, M. (2014, November 19). We've Put a Worm's Mind in a Lego Robot's Body. *Smithsonian Magazine.*

Frischmann, B., & Selinger, E. (2018). *Re-Engineering humanity.* Cambridge University Press. doi:10.1017/9781316544846

Guillette, S. (2019, December 6). *Your new lifeguard may be a robot.* Verizon. https://www.verizon.com/about/our-company/fourth-industrial-revolution/your-new-lifeguard-may-be-robot

Haslam, N. (2006). Dehumanization: An Integrative Review. *Personality and Social Psychology Review, 10*(3), 252–264. doi:10.120715327957pspr1003_4 PMID:16859440

Haslam, N., Loughnan, S., Reynolds, C., & Wilson, S. (2007). Dehumanization: A New Perspective. *Social and Personality Psychology Compass, 1*(1), 409–422. doi:10.1111/j.1751-9004.2007.00030.x

Huxley, J. (1957). Transhumanism. In *New bottles for new wine.* Chatto & Windus.

Kass, L. R. (2003). Ageless Bodies, Happy Souls: Biotechnology and the Pursuit of Perfection. *New Atlantis (Washington, D.C.), 1*, 9–28. PMID:15584192

Koverola, M., Drosinou, M., Palomäki, J., Halonen, J., Kunnari, A., Repo, M., Lehtonen, N., & Laaka-suo, M. (2020a). Moral psychology of sex robots: An experimental study – how pathogen disgust is associated with interhuman sex but not interandroid sex. *Paladyn: Journal of Behavioral Robotics*, *11*(1), 233–249. doi:10.1515/pjbr-2020-0012

Koverola, M., Kunnari, A., Drosinou, M., Palomäki, J., Hannikainen, I., Sundvall, J., & Laakasuo, M. (2020b, June 30). *Non-Human Superhumans - Moral Psychology of Brain Implants: Exploring the role of situational factors, science fiction exposure, individual differences and perceived norms.* doi:10.31234/osf.io/qgz9c

Kurzweil, R. (2012). *How to create a mind: The secret of human thought revealed.* Viking Penguing.

Laakasuo, M., Drosinou, M., Koverola, M., Kunnari, A., Halonen, J., Lehtonen, N., & Palomäki, J. (2018). What makes people approve or condemn mind upload technology? Untangling the effects of sexual disgust, purity and science fiction familiarity. *Palgrave Communications*, *4*(1), 1–14. doi:10.105741599-018-0124-6

Laakasuo, M., Köbis, N., Palomäki, J., & Jokela, M. (2018). Money for microbes-Pathogen avoidance and out-group helping behaviour. *International Journal of Psychology*, *53*, 1–10. doi:10.1002/ijop.12416 PMID:28229500

Lin, P., Mehlman, M., Abney, K., French, S., Vallor, S., Galliott, J., Burnam-Fink, M., LaCroix, A. R., & Schuknecht, S. (2014). Super Soldiers (Part 2): The Ethical, Legal, and Operational Implications. In S. J. Thompson (Ed.), *Global Issues and Ethical Considerations in Human Enhancement Technologies* (pp. 139–160). IGI Global. doi:10.4018/978-1-4666-6010-6.ch008

Lin, P., Mehlman, M., Abney, K., & Galliott, J. (2014). Super Soldiers (Part 1); What is Military Human Enhancement. In S. J. Thompson (Ed.), *Global Issues and Ethical Considerations in Human Enhancement Technologies* (pp. 139–160). IGI Global. doi:10.4018/978-1-4666-6010-6.ch008

Lin, S.-J., & Hsu, M.-F. (2017). Incorporated risk metrics and hybrid AI techniques for risk management. *Neural Computing & Applications*, *28*(11), 3477–3489. doi:10.100700521-016-2253-4

Lippert, C., Sabatini, R., Maher, M. C., Kang, E. Y., Lee, S., Arikan, O., Harley, A., Bernal, A., Garst, P., Lavrenko, V., Yocum, K., Wong, T., Zhu, M., Yang, W.-Y., Chang, C., Lu, T., Lee, C. W. H., Hicks, B., & Ramakrishnan, S., … Venter, J. C. (2017). Identification of individuals by trait prediction using whole-genome sequencing data. *Proceedings of the National Academy of Sciences*, *114*(38), 10166–10171. 10.1073/pnas.1711125114

Malle, B. F., Magar, S. T., & Scheutz, M. (2019). AI in the Sky: How People Morally Evaluate Human and Machine Decisions in a Lethal Strike Dilemma. In M. I. Aldinhas Ferreira, J. Silva Sequeira, G. Singh Virk, M. O. Tokhi, & E. E. Kadar (Eds.), *Robotics and Well-Being* (Vol. 95, pp. 111–133). Springer International Publishing. doi:10.1007/978-3-030-12524-0_11

Markram, H., Muller, E., Ramaswamy, S., Reimann, M. W., Abdellah, M., Sanchez, C. A., Ailamaki, A., Alonso-Nanclares, L., Antille, N., Arsever, S., Kahou, G. A. A., Berger, T. K., Bilgili, A., Buncic, N., Chalimourda, A., Chindemi, G., Courcol, J.-D., Delalondre, F., Delattre, V., … Schürmann, F. (2015). Reconstruction and Simulation of Neocortical Microcircuitry. *Cell*, *163*(2), 456–492. doi:10.1016/j.cell.2015.09.029 PMID:26451489

Melson, G. F., Kahn, P. H. Jr, Beck, A., Friedman, B., Roberts, T., Garrett, E., & Gill, B. T. (2009). Children's behavior toward and understanding of robotic and living dogs. *Journal of Applied Developmental Psychology*, *30*(2), 92–102. doi:10.1016/j.appdev.2008.10.011

Moravec, H. (1988). *Mind children: The future of robot and human intelligence*. Harvard University Press.

More, M. (2010). The Overhuman in the Transhuman. *Journal of Evolution and Technology / WTA*, *21*(1), 1–4.

Morris, J. K., & Springett, A. (2014). *The National Down Syndrome Cytogenetic Register*. Academic Press.

O'Connell, M. (2017). *To be a machine: Adventures among cyborgs, utopians, hackers, and the futurists solving the modest problem of death*. Granta Publications.

Paulhus, D. L., & Jones, D. N. (2015). Measures of Dark Personalities. In G. J. Boyle, D. H. Saklofske, & G. Matthews (Eds.), *Measures of Personality and Social Psychological Constructs* (pp. 562–594). Academic Press. doi:10.1016/B978-0-12-386915-9.00020-6

Pfister, W. (2014, April 10). *Transcendence*. Warner Bros. Pictures.

Plyusnin, I., Evans, A. R., Karme, A., Gionis, A., & Jernvall, J. (2008). Automated 3D Phenotype Analysis Using Data Mining. *PLoS One*, *3*(3), e1742. doi:10.1371/journal.pone.0001742

Plyusnin, I., Evans, A. R., Karme, A., Gionis, A., & Jernvall, J. (2008). Automated 3D Phenotype Analysis Using Data Mining. *PLoS One*, *3*(3), e1742. doi:10.1371/journal.pone.0001742 PMID:18320060

Regalado, A. (2018, April 2). DNA tests for IQ are coming, but it might not be smart to take one. *Technology Review*. https://www.technologyreview.com/s/610339/dna-tests-for-iq-are-coming-but-it-might-not-be-smart-to-take-one/

Ritchie, M. D., Holzinger, E. R., Li, R., Pendergrass, S. A., & Kim, D. (2015). Methods of integrating data to uncover genotype–phenotype interactions. *Nature Reviews. Genetics*, *16*(2), 85–97. doi:10.1038/nrg3868 PMID:25582081

Rozin, P. (1999). The Process of Moralization. *Psychological Science*, *10*(3), 218–221. doi:10.1111/1467-9280.00139

Schaefer, G. O. (2016, August 2). The future of genetic enhancement is not in the West. The Conversation. https://theconversation.com/the-future-of-genetic-enhancement-is-not-in-the-west-63246

Schein, C., & Gray, K. (2018). The Theory of Dyadic Morality: Reinventing Moral Judgment by Redefining Harm. *Personality and Social Psychology Review*, *22*(1), 32–70. doi:10.1177/1088868317698288 PMID:28504021

Sotala, K., & Gloor, L. (2017). Superintelligence as a Cause or Cure for Risks of Astronomical Suffering. *Informatica (Vilnius)*, *41*, 501–505.

Tegmark, M. (2017). *Life 3.0: Being human in the age of artificial intelligence*. Knopf.

Thompson, S. J. (Ed.). (2014). *Global issues and ethical considerations in human enhancement technologies*. IGI Global. doi:10.4018/978-1-4666-6010-6

Voiklis, J., & Malle, B. F. (2018). Moral cognition and its basis in social cognition and social regulation. In K. Gray & J. Graham (Eds.), Atlas of Moral Psychology (pp. 108–120). Academic Press.

Ward, A. F., Olsen, A. S., & Wegner, D. M. (2013). The Harm-Made Mind: Observing Victimization Augments Attribution of Minds to Vegetative Patients, Robots, and the Dead. *Psychological Science*, *24*(8), 1437–1445. doi:10.1177/0956797612472343 PMID:23749051

Waytz, A., Heafner, J., & Epley, N. (2014). The mind in the machine: Anthropomorphism increases trust in an autonomous vehicle. *Journal of Experimental Social Psychology*, *52*, 113–117. doi:10.1016/j.jesp.2014.01.005

Yampolskiy, R. V. (2018). *Artificial intelligence safety and security*. Chapman and Hall/CRC. doi:10.1201/9781351251389

ENDNOTES

[1] We remind the reader that moral psychology is a descriptive science, not normative philosophy. Naturally, there are more emotions than just disgust associated with human moral behavior. However, disgust is probably the most extensively studied emotion in the field of moral psychology and is therefore one of the main things we cover here.

[2] See Transhumanist FAQ 3.0. http://www.whatistranshumanism.org.

[3] See United Nations Global Issues at https://www.un.org/en/sections/issues-depth/children/.

[4] Preprint at https://psyarxiv.com/bkhyq/.

[5] The science fiction hobbyism scale, used in these studies, measures a general interest and participation in science fiction, with questions about, e.g., participation in conventions, following science fiction series and movies, etc.

[6] Body Envelope Violation: invasion of bodily integrity, harm caused to the body that somehow violates its usual status like cuts, injections, fractures, and unwanted penetration.

[7] Laakasuo et al. (2018) ran several multivariate regression analyses where the associations of independent variables in relation to the dependent variable (moral approval of mind upload) can be investigated while holding the other variables constant. These associations are not causal effects, but they do have predictive value, nonetheless.

[8] Note that the definition of Machiavellianism in psychology is simply a collection of specific traits (a person being cold, calculating, etc.). This is different from how the term has been used in, e.g., political theory.

[9] AI Safety Research is a specific sub-field of computer science and technology studies that focuses on pre-emptively thinking of strategies for how to avoid pit-falls in creating human-level AIs (e.g., Bostrom, 2014).

[10] We wish to thank an anonymous reviewer for pointing us to this possibility.

Chapter 12
Machines and Technological Unemployment:
Basic Income vs. Basic Capital

Elias Moser
Karl-Franzens-Universität Graz, Austria

ABSTRACT

Recently, economic studies on labor market developments have indicated that there is a potential threat of technological mass unemployment. Both smart robotics and information technology may perform a broad range of tasks that today are fulfilled by human labor. This development could lead to vast inequalities. Proponents of an unconditional basic income have, therefore, employed this scenario to argue for their cause. In this chapter, the author argues that, although a basic income might be a valid answer to the challenge of technological unemployment, it fails to account for some ethical problems specific to future expectations of mass unemployment. The author introduces the proposal of an unconditional basic capital and shows how it can address these problems adequately and avoid objections against a basic income. However, the basic capital proposal cannot replace all redistributive social policies. It has to be interpreted as a supplement to either a basic income or more traditional redistributive policies.

INTRODUCTION

In the coming decades, a large number of jobs that, nowadays are performed by humans, may be taken over either by intelligent software or smart robotics. On the one hand, this will lead to a substantial growth in real income; on the other hand, it will eradicate employment opportunities for many people. One broadly discussed ethical and political challenge in light of this technologically-caused unemployment makes reference to ideas of distributive justice. If a large number of jobs are rationalized and replaced by machines, productive power will almost exclusively lie in the hands of capital owners, whereas people who are dependent on paid labor to make a living will be deprived of their capability of doing so. It is obvious that the former group of people, the capital owners, most probably remains very small compared to the latter.

DOI: 10.4018/978-1-7998-4894-3.ch012

Copyright © 2021, IGI Global. Copying or distributing in print or electronic forms without written permission of IGI Global is prohibited.

So-called "technological unemployment" (Klimczuk-Kochańska & Klimczuk, 2015) can therefore be said to cause a problem of inequality that calls for distribution according to principles of justice. Proponents of an unconditional basic income grant (BIG) have employed these expectations to argue for their cause (Walker, 2014; Hughes 2014; Bruun & Duka, 2018). A BIG grant is a distributive scheme in which every citizen is paid a periodical salary that is unconditional, upon the additional income the person acquires through the labor market.

My intention in this chapter is to critically reflect this proposal and to introduce the account of an unconditional basic capital grant (BCG) to counter the problem of technological unemployment. In contrast to a BIG, the BCG consists of a single payment to every citizen that allows him or her to make an investment early in his or her life; for example, to make investments on the financial market, to launch a business, or to pay for education costs. Although there has been a lively debate among proponents of a BIG and those of a BCG (Alstott, & Van Parijs, 2006), the BCG has not yet become subject to the debate around technological income. I will defend a BCG that is not meant as an alternative but as a viable supplement to other redistributive policies with respect to the ethical challenges of technological unemployment.

I proceed in three steps. First, I attempt to provide an overview of different scenarios on labor market developments due to automation. Since they range from highly pessimistic to overly optimistic expectations, I will sketch them, on the one hand, in a utopian and, on the other, in a dystopian framework. Second, I will outline the shortcomings of both these views, establishing what I call a "more realistic" view on future labor market developments. This view acknowledges the threat of technological mass unemployment but it also maintains the thesis of a complete eradication of paid labor. The section concludes with lessons to be learned from the utopia and dystopia with respect to how we should evaluate the ethical implications of technological unemployment. Third, I will discuss two policy proposals to deal with the challenge of technological unemployment—BIG and BCG. I argue that a BIG can address some ethical issues while it is unable to deal with others. A BCG in contrast may be able deal with these problems more effectively. Thus, the chapter concludes that the challenge of technological unemployment is best met by a BCG.

SCENARIOS OF A POST-WORK SOCIETY

What will happen in the near future when a large number of jobs cease to exist due to automation? Expectations of future labor market developments range from pessimistic scenarios of poverty and vast inequalities to future societies of abundance and a liberation from all sorts of material necessities. In this section, I aim to sketch these scenarios in order to outline how certain fears and hopes might be based on unrealistic assumptions. Nevertheless, the picture of the different scenarios gives us some insights with regard to the question of how to address the challenge of automation and unemployment with the help of different policy options. The overview reveals some societal processes we may already observe today. Furthermore, it shows which anticipations might be justified. I will first draw the picture of a so-called post-work utopia in order to elucidate the great prospects automation holds for our society. I then contrast this idea with what I call the post-work dystopia. I argue that the idea is probably too pessimistic. The section concludes with some lessons to be learned from different future expectations.

Post-Work Utopia

Imagine a society similar to ours but different in that it has abolished paid labor completely. The use of machines and computer programs has obviated the need for human work. Members of that society are liberated from a life mostly filled with hard industrial labor or mindless office jobs, and people have arrived at a productive, happy, and more meaningful level of existence. They are able to spend their time engaging in arts, music, literature, science, and in rich social relationships.

Robots have taken over agricultural and industrial production of all commodities people need and desire. All goods are produced without the help of humans. Resources are harvested, extracted, transformed, and combined anew by machines. Robotic industries build component parts of consumer products. Other fully automated industries assemble the components into a ready-made product that is sold to the customers. Purchase programs guarantee the availability of the right amount of input factors. Intelligent computer programs monitor the machines and find solutions if irregularities occur. Maintenance robots take care of dysfunctional machines.

An intricate automated transport system delivers goods right into people's homes. Smart vessels are loaded with the help of automated cranes and are navigated by intelligent software. Self-driving trucks distribute the goods from the harbors to the warehouses and, if the goods are bought online by the customers, drones fly them to the doorstep. Individual households may make their own products not found available on the market at home, for example, with 3D printers.

Algorithms estimate the demand for goods and their most probable future development and fluctuation by collecting data from the customers. They are able to make an informed guess on how many products should be produced and for what price they can be sold. In observing consumer preferences, algorithms will also know how to marketize the goods. There are all sorts of salesman and broker programs to supply the customers with the necessary information to make a buying decision.

Public and private buildings, roads, railways, power lines, sewage systems, etc. are built and maintained by machines. All sorts of face-to-face services have been replaced. No human needs to work as a vendor, barber, baker, florist, or waiter because self-service check-out clerks or online shops have taken over their function. Medical diagnoses and treatment recommendations can be made precisely by algorithms fed with biomedical data from people's smart mobile devices (Cohn, March 2013), surgery robots perform operations in fully automated self-service hospitals. Legal conflicts can be settled by the help of attorney programs subsuming the facts of the case (Markoff, 2011); impartial decision-making on legal cases is performed by court programs (e.g., see Phua, Lee, Smith, & Gayler, 2012). There are fitness instructor and care robots, even electronic psychotherapists. Children may learn from online teaching programs. Neither schools nor teachers are needed anymore. Finally, this society has also overcome prostitution, since sex-surrogate robots and artificial intelligence are able to meet the needs and desires of their customers just as well as prostitutes in our society (Levy, 2008).

In this society, the costs of production and the supply of services are extremely low. That is because no wages have to be paid. The only economic input factor needed is capital. The society has thus entered an era of super abundance. The development, design, production, and maintenance of the machines and programs in use are so cheap, that either prices are miniscule or profits are extraordinarily high. Even a tiny share of the capital in use can make for a comfortable living (Hanson, 2008). For those who have none, the super-rich could, without hesitation, pay charitable subsidies (Chomanski, 2018), such that every person living in this society has more than enough.

The incredulous reader might already be able to pinpoint the shortcomings of this overly romantic picture. As desirable as this state of affairs might be, in which we need no redistributive mechanisms to make everybody have enough, it appears to be wishful thinking. The post-work utopia as sketched above is based on highly optimistic assumptions.

Post-Work Dystopia

One problem with the utopian view is that it looks into the far future without telling us how to get there. The transition from our society today to a super-abundant post-work society will probably not run very smoothly. While some people may become extremely rich others will end up being replaced by machines, unemployed, and in severe poverty.

Technological progress cannot be assumed to be a linear process. As futurologists suggest (e.g., Kurzweil, 2000), development is advancing at an *increasing pace*. It is accelerating in an exponential manner.[1] At some point, the pace of automation and the replaceability of labor could increase so quickly that labor markets might not be able to accommodate the large amount of free workforce anymore. The adjustment would simply need more time. Economists Eric Brynolfsson and Andrew MacAfee, therefore, draw a different picture of the near future:

Rapid and accelerating digitization is likely to bring economic (...) disruption, stemming from the fact that as computers get more powerful, companies have less need for some kinds of workers. Technological progress is going to leave behind some people, perhaps even a lot of people, as it races ahead. (...) [T] here's never been a worse time to be a worker with only 'ordinary' skills and abilities to offer... (2014)

Before a society becomes super-affluent through technological progress, it has to deal with the problem that, within a short period of time, many people will become unemployed. This is the problem that is called "technological (mass-)unemployment." It occurs when "people are without work and seeking work because of innovative production processes and labor-saving organizational solutions" (Klimczuk-Kochańska & Klimczuk, 2015).

In contrast to the picture drawn above, imagine a society, not far in the future, in which the vast majority of people cannot find a job anymore. On the other end, there is a small group of people having ownership of the machines that produce all goods and services being traded and consumed. The former group of people has no means to contribute to the economic welfare of this society, whereas the latter group possesses exclusive control over the productive means. This society obviously suffers from a high degree of inequality.

A system of charitable subsidies (as in our super-abundant post-work utopia) could indeed provide for everyone to have enough. But, in such a society, a great number of people will have to rely on these gifts from the rich. The inequality the society faces is more severe than a mere unequal distribution of income and assets: it is an inequality in power. One group of people who possess no capital and have no property on machines is unilaterally dependent on the other group of people holding capital.

One has to concede that not all people who do not own a share in the machines will be without work. It is perfectly conceivable that the wealthy members of the society will have a certain amount of nostalgia about former production methods, and maybe they will want some of their services provided by humans instead of intelligent robots (Walker, 2014). Those who can afford it, will probably want to have their hair cut by a real person with whom they can chat and share their problems, or they will want to buy their vegetables and fish at a market place that resembles the old-fashioned bazaars of the earlier days. However, to satisfy one's nostalgic feelings is costly since one has to pay wages and these are far more expensive than the costs for machines. Therefore, only the rich can afford this luxury and, because of that, the nostalgia business does not accommodate many employees.

Given the costs of their wages, the great majority of people are left without the possibility to contribute to the economic wealth. They can sell neither muscle nor brain power in order to receive a share of the economic wealth in return. Therefore, they start offering labor more cheaply. They enter into competition with the machines. Of course, machines are less expensive than human labor but still they are not free. On the one hand, owners have to meet the expenses of periodic depreciation and maintenance costs. On the other hand, the invention of new machines comes at high development costs. In our dystopian society, the non-shareholders offer their labor below these costs to make themselves affordable for companies and in order not to be replaced by a machine. The dumping of salaries for human workers not only leads to precarious standards of living for the working class but also hinders further technological progress: humans compete *against* new developments.

The pessimistic scenario of a post-work dystopia is indeed threatening. While some social and economic processes of it are already underway, others are still fiction. As I will attempt to show in the following section, we need to take a closer look at the economic processes involved in technological progress. Based on these observations, we may develop more realistic expectations.

THE CHALLENGE OF TECHNOLOGICAL MASS UNEMPLOIYMENT

Do we have to fear that if technological progress keeps on growing, we will soon be living in a dystopian jobless society in which the vast majority of people can either not find employment or have to work in highly precarious circumstances? There are reasons why this may not be the case, which need to be elucidated in this section. As I argue, some forms of employment are unlikely to vanish completely; but, nevertheless, technological unemployment is a threat to be taken seriously.

A More Realistic View

From a historical perspective, the fear of mass unemployment due to replacement of the human workforce by machines is an ever-present feature of pessimistic expectations in economics (e.g., Bix, 2000). Classic economists, such as James Steuart (1767), expressed concern that human labor is susceptible to replacement by machines and that this circumstance may lead to vast unemployment. However, throughout the history of industrialization this expectation has not become reality. This fact can be explained mainly by two economic considerations.

First, technological innovations can be divided into: 1) so-called "product innovations"—the discovery of new marketable products, and 2) "process innovations"—the discovery of improved methods to produce goods at lower cost (OECD, 2013; Falk, 2015). The former type of innovation opens new business opportunities and therefore probably increases the demand for labor. Only the latter is said to have a potentially negative impact on the availability of job opportunities. Since product innovation usually goes hand-in-hand with process innovation, technological development does not reduce the overall amount of jobs.

Second, even if upcoming technological inventions predominantly consist of process innovations, this does not necessarily result in an increase in unemployment. Neoclassical economic analysis may explain this fact by the following considerations (Vivarelli, 2014).

On the one hand, product innovation leads to a reduction of costs and, under circumstances of functioning market competition: a decline in prices (*price effect*) for products. Because automation enables us to produce the goods cheaper, we have additional real income. So, this price effect increases demand for other goods and, eventually, the increase in demand opens prospects for new businesses as well as new forms of employment.

On the other hand, if workers are replaced by machines, there are temporarily more unemployed people in the short run. In the long run, however, this leads to more competition on the labor market, which, in turn, may effectuate a reduction in wages (*real-wage effect*). Due to unemployment, labor becomes less expensive, and this increases demand for the workforce (OECD, 2016). In reality, it is improbable that this effect occurs. In many business sectors, wages do not have the possibility of downward adjustment.

If, for some reason (e.g., not fully competitive markets) the reduction of costs is not passed on to the consumers and does not result in lower prices, there is a higher profit margin for companies: they produce the goods more efficiently while achieving the same price on the market. This may either increase the shareholders' returns and thus result in: 1) an increase in investment that leads to economic growth and new job opportunities, or the margin is passed on to the employees, and 2) salaries increase (Hughes, 2014; Vivarelli, 2014). The recipients spend their money on consumer goods, and thus have a higher demand for goods, which creates new jobs. For example, two scenarios:

1. Process innovation (cost-reducing development)
   a. Lower price, stable wages ® higher demand for products (price effect)
   b. Lower wages, lower price ® higher demand for workforce (real-wage effect)
   c. Higher profit margin
      i. increased investment ® higher demand for labor
      ii. higher wages ® higher demand for products
2. Product innovation (discovery of new marketable goods)

Therefore, economies so far have had the capacity and the dynamic structure to cope with technological development. With regard to the imminent developments in smart robotics and artificial intelligence, the legitimate question is: Why should it be different this time? Two possible arguments suggest that the upcoming technological developments will severely challenge our faith in labor market's ability to adjust.

First, the advance of artificial intelligence threatens a wide range of middle-skill jobs at once (Autor, 2015). Since artificial intelligence can be programmed to be self-learning and self-adjusting to new circumstances, robots and programs can function independently with information and techniques. Furthermore, it is observed that (apart from the growing replaceability of industrial labor) "cognitive tasks" are endangered (Autor, Levy, & Murnane, 2003). Carl Frey and Michael Osborne (2013) estimate that approximately 50 percent of today's jobs in the US are under threat of extinction.

Second, in information technology there are business branches in which it is highly probable that monopolies will occur. The market often suffers from the so-called "winner-take-all" syndrome: the first company to develop a program or online service will absorb all potential customers in the market. It is able to provide the product at next to *zero marginal cost*, which excludes the possibility for other companies to compete for lower production costs and to enter the market (Rifkin, 2014). If such monopolies arise, the market does not function under conditions of full competition. Potential price effects may not come into effect and firms lack incentives for further product innovation. This closes options for new business opportunities and leads to increased unemployment.

The empirical fact that, in the course of the history of industrialization, technological development has not led to mass unemployment does not imply that in the future this might not be the case. Although neoclassical economic theory of labor market development provides a rationale as to why technological development does not yield unemployment, this rationale is based on *a priori* models, which cannot account for all contingencies. It is debatable whether these models are applicable for upcoming developments because it is probable that background conditions will change in the age of increased automation and computation (Brynjolfsson & McAfee, 2014).

So, we have to take the challenge of automation to our labor market seriously. The use of machines could lead to unemployment and, in turn, to vast inequalities. Those endangered are not only employees who perform routine tasks in the manual and cognitive labor sector but also employees performing non-routine tasks. In some areas, intelligent computer programs and smart robotics are able to learn by themselves and to adapt to new situations as well as humans. Does this, however, mean that machines may replace all human labor?

In his essay "Why are there still so many jobs?" David Autor provides several reasons for the non-replaceability of some human labor. He starts with observing that...

[o]ver the very long run, gains in productivity have not led to a shortfall of demand for goods and services: instead, household consumption has largely kept pace with household incomes. We know this because the share of the population engaged in paid employment has generally risen over (...) the past century despite vast improvements in material standards of living. An average US worker in 2015 wishing to live at the income level of an average worker in 1915 could roughly achieve this goal by working about 17 weeks per year.[2] Most citizens would not consider this tradeoff between hours and income desirable... (2015)

This passage makes clear that the price effect of technological development has not induced people to work less for the same amount of goods and services. Instead people tend to spend their additional real-wage on more goods. Both the post-work utopia and the post-work dystopia fail to acknowledge the significance of the fact that human needs and desires for new products do not appear to ever reach a point of satisfaction. Needs "grow" with real income.

New products require new tasks to be performed. Both the post-work utopia and the post-work dystopia seem to commit the so-called "Luddite fallacy" (Brynjolfsson & McAfee, 2014). They assume that the number of possible tasks performed by labor will remain stable and that once machines are capable of taking over the tasks, there will be nothing left for humans to do. The Luddite view implicitly assumes that, because there are limited human needs, there is a limited number of different products meeting those needs. If all products that meet human needs are produced automatically, human work is not needed anymore. However, the assumption of a stable number of possible products is wrong. Technological progress always leaves room for product innovations. As long as people are not satisfied with what they have, the combination of desire and demand will result in the creation of new jobs.

Another reason (put forward by Autor) why neither utopia nor dystopia are realistic outcomes is that process innovations do not simply replace human labor, but happen to make human labor more productive, and thus, more valuable. Technology not only has a supplementary effect but can be complementary to human work (Autor, 2015). Autor uses the example of automated teller machines (ATMs) which were introduced to replace traditional banking front-office jobs. As a matter of fact, the application of the new technology did not result in a reduction in employment. The number of tellers even increased. Convincingly, Autor explains this fact in pointing at the change of specific tasks performed by bank tellers. They developed from mere check-out clerks into salespersons offering additional banking services (2015).[3]

Therefore, there are reasons to assume that increased automation may not replace human work altogether. The post-work utopia is unlikely to realize because people tend not to be satisfied with the goods available to them. They will strive to discover new ways of consumption on which they can spend their newly acquired real income. Process innovations open new forms of employment and newly created business sectors can accommodate a substantial number of employees. It is not unimaginable that eventually an artificial intelligence will be able to anticipate the development of human needs such that it is able to create new business sectors by itself. However, this will not become reality in the near future. Until then, humans will define and develop their needs themselves. To a large extent, therefore, product innovation remains a task to be fulfilled by humans.

What We Can Learn From These Scenarios

Although automation may lead to the replacement of many jobs, some tasks are hard to imagine ever being performed by even highly intelligent robots or computer programs. I do not believe that automation will necessarily lead to a jobless future. Neither the post-work utopia nor the post-work dystopia seems to be a plausible scenario. Nevertheless, automation yields a substantive risk for future labor markets. The threat of technological mass unemployment is real. In order to see that, let us briefly recapitulate the three reasons why this might be so (Danaher, 2017; 2019a): 1) the exponential growth of technological development, which leads to the situation that replaceability outpaces the creation of new jobs through product innovation, 2) the broad range of work-sectors susceptible to potential replacement, and 3) the occurrence of factual monopolies for specific online services hindering real income growth of consumers and innovation.

1. Pace of automation
2. Broad range of endangered jobs
3. Winner-take-all phenomenon

Only time will tell whether the provided reasons are adequate, wrong, or over-stated. However, the three reasons support the claim that it is legitimate to ask the question of how we could meet the challenge of mass unemployment due to automation (Bruun & Duka, 2018). In the subsequent section I will consider two different policy options to react to the challenge—the basic income and the basic capital grant. Before I turn to these, let me introduce the standards by which they could be assessed. In order to formulate such standards, one needs to know which ethical problems the envisioned future in the scenario might yield. From the elucidation of the post-work utopia one can infer that automation will lead to substantial gains in economic wealth. However, as the post-work dystopia shows, if this wealth is not properly distributed among the members of a society, economic and social disruptions are likely to occur. One can identify at least four particularly worrisome disruptions.

- **Race Against the Machines:** From the dystopia scenario we could infer that some sectors of the labor market are severely endangered and there is a possibility that new employment opportunities will not evolve quickly enough. Some workers therefore stand in direct competition to the machines. In order to secure their employment, they need to offer labor at a lower price than the cost of machines (or the costs of developing new machines). This is a potential race to the bottom: machines, once developed and applied, become cheaper while wages have an absolute lower limit determined by the costs of living. If such a race against the machines occurs, humans are predestined to lose. The competition will result in extreme poverty.

- **Unilateral Dependency:** Even if (as utopian imaginations of the future suggest) a social system could easily be sustained by charitable subsidies of the super-rich capital owners, such a future society is based on a very severe form of inequality that is undesirable both from intrinsic (e.g., Lovett, 2010) as well as instrumental considerations. Having exclusive control over productive means, capital owners are in a dominating position. Non-capital-owners are fully dependent on their charity. They will need to trust in the capital owners' benevolence and they have no means to enforce provision of the subsidies necessary for their subsistence. Furthermore, they have no possibility to set incentives for periodic subsidy payment since they possess no bargaining power. This unilateral dependency can be exploited in various ways. Thus, it is undesirable because it induces non-capital-owners to make decisions under coercion, and because it allows capital owners to benefit disproportionately from these decisions.

- **Inability to Contribute:** If large-scale technological unemployment occurs, there is a group of people who are deprived of their formerly possessed opportunities to sell labor and to receive a salary in return. Even in comparatively rich countries, for most individuals the only thing they can offer to make a living is work. In a society where most of the economic production is provided by machines, work becomes a significantly less important factor for the creation of income. Capital, in turn, becomes ever more important. Those who possess none, therefore, have no means to create wealth. They are unable to contribute to society's welfare. This problem is a precondition for the above-mentioned unilateral dependency but also, even if a social security system is in place, non-capital owners are in a situation of dependency. It is unlikely they will be able to create their own wealth by the means they possess; i.e., work.[4]

- **Reduced Social Mobility:** This leads to a further problem concerning the structure and dynamics of a society that suffers from vast technological unemployment. Because non-capital-owners can offer their labor on the market only to a limited extent, they have no opportunity to ever leave their precarious situation behind. In being deprived of selling work, they are not only unable to make a living by themselves but also unable to ever ascend to the class of capital owners because it is simply impossible for them to accumulate capital.

POLICY RECOMMENDATIONS

Policy options to circumvent problems involved in technological unemployment have to incorporate these four potential ethical problems of the future labor market developments. One broadly discussed option to face the challenge is the implementation of a BIG (Roberts, 1982, recently Walker, 2014). I will discuss this policy proposal in this section and will contrast it with the conception of a BCG.

Basic Income

The idea of proposing a BIG as a response to the challenge of technological unemployment is comprehensible: the use of machines reduces costs of production, technological development and the increase in the use of machines create a constant surplus. As outlined above, the main problem is a result of the unequal distribution of the surplus. While a few capital owners control the production force, the great many have no means of production. A BIG grants every individual a share of the so-called "technological dividend;" i.e., the surplus created though technological progress.

We understand the term 'BIG' (or 'universal basic income' or 'unconditional basic income') to mean a redistributive scheme that grants every citizen of a country a periodically paid amount of money, irrespective of the income the citizen generates through his or her own work. Usually, a BIG is designed so that it enables a certain minimal standard of living—the provision of basics such as food, shelter, healthcare, education, social activities, etc. Furthermore, it is intended to replace a range of other social security institutions; e.g., welfare aid, unemployment and health insurance, retirement funds, etc. Opinions on how to raise tax income to finance a BIG diverge. The differences are due to the individual proponents' philosophical justifications of the BIG.[5]

Four attributes of a BIG are worth spelling out in detail (cf. Bruun & Duka, 2018):

1. A basic income is *unconditional* upon individual contributions to the economy.
2. It is *universal* in the sense that every citizen is entitled to it, irrespective of origin, class religion, gender, etc.
3. The income is *basic*, such that it does not satisfy needs of citizens beyond a certain threshold and, more importantly, it does not leave anybody with *less* than the minimum.
4. The redistributive scheme is designed as an *income*. It differs from a lump-sum subsidy in that it is granted periodically (monthly or yearly).

Beyond the minimum income, individuals are free to generate additional income by offering their services on a (relatively unregulated)[6] labor market or by investing their savings. Therefore, a distributive scheme such as the BIG does not rule out individual incentives to work. Compared to traditional social-security measures, the BIG has some advantages when it comes to incentives to work. Social insurance may enclose recipients in a so-called "poverty gap." Once receiving social aid, people have no more incentive to work, because every additional hour of work reduces their claim on social aid.

Still, a BIG might be setting economically undesirable incentives. The BIG reduces the supply of labor. People would most probably not be willing to work for low paid hard work if they were paid a monthly income. Since reduction of offered labor has a negative effect on economic growth, one may object to the BIG that it reduces potential real income of people. However, proponents of a BIG may answer to this challenge in two ways.[7]

First, if vast technological unemployment occurs, many people are unable to offer their labor on the market anyway. In this situation, a BIG would not reduce the economic output of the society by much. Second, a BIG is desirable because it relieves recipients from the economic pressure to work and enables them to make a coercion-free choice which job to perform and for how many hours a week. Many jobs nowadays performed by people could in fact be taken over by artificial intelligence or robots. In making humans perform these jobs unavailable on the labor markets, a BIG would force companies to develop and to implement artificial intelligence in their production processes. Eventually, this BIG-induced automation could lead to the desirable outcome of a high economic output without human work necessary. In other words, the BIG can be seen as bringing us one step closer to a post-work utopia (Danaher, 2019).

The proposal of a basic income also has a number of advantages over other policy options to react to the challenge of technological unemployment (Perry, 2013; Marchant, Hennessy, & Stevens, 2014; Hughes, 2014). One often discussed option to circumvent technological unemployment is to restrict or to regulate the use and application of economizing technologies in certain sectors (or even to prevent their innovation). For a short term, many jobs could indeed be secured if replacement was legally banned.

The obvious unfairness of this proposal lies in the fact that consumers have to bear the cost of the employment protection. Process innovation technology leads to less expensive opportunities for production and this reduction in costs could be passed on to the consumers in the form of price reductions. In hindering the use of technology, however, potential cost reductions are ruled out. Therefore, a society protecting jobs from replacement by restricting the use of machines does not allow its citizens to benefit from the potential increase in wealth that technological development yields. I submit that some egalitarian positions might readily accept this consequence.[8] In addition to considerations of justice, however, one might also question the instrumental rationality of protecting employment against technology (Marchant, Hennessy, & Stevens, 2014):

In an internationally competitive environment, a state implementing a ban on the application of some cost-saving technologies suffers a disadvantage. Economies in other countries could easily become more competitive and export their goods at lower prices. The domestic industries would experience a strong decline in demand. A technology-restricting state would therefore need to protect its companies against international competition. This could be achieved by means of protectionist trade policies, such as import restrictions, regulations or customs duties. But in the long run, these policy options have a hazardous effect on growth and, therefore, on the overall wealth of the citizens.

A second policy option to attempt to avoid mass unemployment would be to redistribute labor, or more specifically, to redistribute working hours. For instance, proposals have been made to face technological unemployment with a reduction in working hours (Weston, 1985). Although this would imply a decrease in our average standard of living, it could be accepted when people's preferences shift toward more leisure. Considering the discussion on a legally enforced reduction in working hours, opinions diverge. The measure is highly disputable from an ethical perspective. It entails a restriction of individuals' liberty to choose the amount of work they are willing to perform and the level of material welfare they intend to achieve. A radical constraint on the number of working hours is therefore questionable with regard to commonly shared liberal convictions (Kirchgässner, 2009).

It is worth mentioning that, also from an empirical perspective, the effectiveness of an upper limit for working hours is uncertain. It is unclear whether it in fact leads to more leisure. As studies reveal, companies have found ways to circumvent the working hours cap (Kapteyn, Kalwij, & Zaidi, 2004). The restriction did not necessarily effectuate a reduction of individual working hours nor did it increase the overall employment rate.

A third proposal focuses on the role of the state as a creator of employment (Arneson, 1990). If the private sector rationalizes jobs by introducing machines into their production, the government may be asked to jump in and offer jobs to the unemployed. It is certainly possible that to some extent the state can and should function as an employer. However, its capacity to accommodate the large proportion of the population threatened by technological unemployment is limited.

The price for goods and services provided by the government with the help of human labor would be inefficiently high because firms using machines could produce the same goods at lower cost. In order to protect the public production of goods against competition from private companies, the state therefore would either have to claim a legal monopoly on these goods and services (i.e., restricting supply by private firms) or it would have to sell the goods at a price below the production costs (including wages for human labor). The former option is unfair to the consumers for the same reason as the above-mentioned protection of employment and it is also hazardous in that it hinders growth and further development. The latter option would lead to increased governmental expenses. Upholding the artificially low prices of goods while maintaining the high costs due to the wages would, eventually, require governmental subsidies and the tax payers would have to pay them.

The three mentioned proposals, therefore, are either short-sighted or simply not feasible. Firstly, employment protection is both unfair toward consumers and may even aggravate the problem of unemployment by rendering an economy less competitive. A BIG does not protect employment but instead insures individuals against unemployment while allowing the economy to apply labor-saving new technologies. Secondly, the redistribution of working hours would restrict individuals' liberties to choose their amount of labor and may, eventually, fail to reach its target. The BIG is more liberal in the sense that it allows individuals to freely choose whether they want to work and how much. It also enables individuals to make this decision free from economic pressure. Thirdly, the employment-creation proposal is undesirable compared to a BIG. Instead of subsidizing humans to do inefficient work that machines could do, the state could as well pay the individuals an unconditional income without forcing them to work (Marchant, Stevens, & Hennessy, 2014). Therefore, the BIG seems to perform better than proposals to protect, redistribute, or create labor. Let me now assess the proposal of a BIG with respect to the above-mentioned standards.

On the one hand, the BIG proposal eradicates the possibility of a *race against the machines*. Individuals receiving their monthly salary unconditionally, without exerting effort, would not be willing to work to generate further income below a certain threshold. They would not voluntarily sign low-wage labor contracts. On the other hand, a BIG can be successful for liberating individuals from *unilateral dependence*. A strong claim in favor of a BIG indeed makes reference to a republican ideal of positive liberties (Pettit 2007; Raventós, 2007). The basic income liberates people from potential dependencies and therefore puts them in a better bargaining position from which they do not need to enter into exploitative relations.

Considering an individual's *inability to contribute* to society's economic welfare in a post-work society, however, the BIG proposal performs poorly. If in fact the vast majority of jobs cease to exist, people, though receiving a regular income, have little opportunity to generate additional income with paid labor. Individuals who possess no capital are also unable to make investments and, therefore, unable to own a share of the factors that generate the economic output of the society. Of course, individuals can reserve some of their monthly income for savings in order to invest them later. However, since, the BIG is construed as a minimum income according to a specific standard of living, the opportunity costs for making savings are very high. Considering the discount rate, today's consumption might be more valuable than investing. The inability to make a contribution includes the problem of social mobility. Even if a basic income is granted in a future of technological mass unemployment, individuals have little chance to ascend from the class of mere recipients of governmental subsidies to the class of capital owners and generators of economic wealth. An imagined future society insuring people against unemployment with the help of a BIG does not allow for much *social mobility*.

For these two reasons, the proposal of a BIG is only an insufficient reply to the challenge of technological mass unemployment. The next sub-section proposes the idea of a BCG as a necessary supplement to a BIG in order to face the problem of an inability to contribute and the problem of reduced social mobility.

Basic Capital

A BCG differs from a BIG in that it consists of a single (i.e., non-periodical) lump-sum payment to all members of society. It is intended to enable its recipients to make an investment early in their lives (e.g., on maturity) either in order to receive yearly interest, to enable higher education, or to start one's own business (Ackermann & Alstott 1999).[9] According to most conceptions, the BCG's monetary value is lower compared to the discounted value of all periodical payments included in a BIG. The capital stock of the BCG is not intended to finance the living costs of individuals but to enable them to make an investment, and to make a living from the returns on the investment.

In contrast to BIG, the BCG is not presumed to be an exclusive redistributive policy able to replace all other sorts of social security institutions. It can also be conceived as partial substitute for certain redistributive policies.[10] For example, it may simply consist of subsidies for education (Glennerster & McKnight, 2006). Furthermore, BIG and BCG do not necessarily contradict each other. The latter may also be construed as a supplement for the former (Prabhakar, 2018). Keeping this in mind, the BCG proposal is not assessed as an exclusive alternative to the BIG. However, a BCG may be able to perform functions that a BIG cannot. The proposal of a BCG is therefore defended on the basis of the shortcomings of a BIG policy.

As we have seen, the BIG fails to address the individual's difficulty in making an economic contribution (inability to contribute) and the problem that some individuals are unable to climb the social lather (reduced social mobility). A BCG might help to attenuate these problems in that it provides individuals with real opportunities to become shareholders of the society' economic output. The BCG serves three main purposes that help individuals to either become irreplaceable parts of the remaining labor force or to become partial owners of the society's accumulated capital.

- **BCG as Investment:** Individuals can directly invest the lump-sum capital grant on the capital market such that they can secure a minimal income or insure themselves against longer periods of unemployment. If we assume that capital markets are relatively stable and that, with some certainty, they guarantee an income from interest and dividends, the BCG used as an investment has a similar function as a BIG: it ensures a periodic income. It is also comparable to a policy option proposed by James Meade (1989) of a Citizens' Trust Fund (CTF) which consists of a public investment fund that provides each citizen with a share of its returns.

At first glance, both the BIG and the CTF seem to have an advantage over a BCG in that they insure against risks of investment. The former grants an income irrespective of capital market performance. The latter pools the risk and distributes it among all members of society. However, neither of these proposals account for the two ethical problems—the inability to contribute and the reduced social mobility.

Because it is not the individuals themselves who make investments, who take risks, and who eventually benefit from their skill in making wise decisions, they do not contribute to the generation of wealth. Individuals receiving returns from a CTF are not contributing to the economic output of a society. Furthermore, individuals can enjoy the same advantage of pooling risks as under a system of CTF in that they join a voluntary conglomerate of investors and establish their own funds. In this sense, compared to the BCG, the citizens' trust offers less liberty.

Social mobility—i.e., the possibility that a person may ascend to the class of capital owners—is also less likely if every individual receives either a periodic payment or an average share of the returns of pooled investments. In contrast, the BCG provides individuals with the opportunity and the self-responsibility to make investment decisions and yields the possibility that those who happen to be good investors can benefit from their capabilities, profit more from their investments, and become shareholders of the society's means of production.

BCG as Education Subsidy: As was argued above, even in a highly automated economy some employment opportunities are still available. However, to compete on the labor market requires a different and, most probably, broader set of skills. It is therefore reasonable to assume that the best preparation for individuals to deal with future developments on the labor market is to be well educated and well trained. For example, Frank Levy and Richard Murnane (2004) highlight the importance of education with regard to the challenge of automation. They argue that:

[t]he major consequence of computerization will not be mass unemployment but a continued decline in the demand for moderately-skilled and less-skilled labor. Job opportunities will grow, but job growth will be greatest in higher-skilled occupations in which computers complement expert thinking and complex communication to produce new products and services. (2004)

From this observation, Levy and Murnane infer that education is the best available tool to prepare workers for an unpredictable and dynamic employment market. They conclude that many of todays' jobs will become extinct and that the future jobs will be substantially different with respect to the required skill and the specific tasks performed: The "dynamic environment requires new policies, and the first step in creating those policies is to recognize the new realities" (Levy & Murnane, 2004). In making prospective employees more adaptable to new tasks, education may increase an individual's ability to become an integral part of the remaining workforce in future labor markets. This argument is also closely related to Autor's view that technology has a complementary effect on the productivity of workers (2004, Sect. 4). In order not to be replaced by a machine, human workers need to invent new ways and new tasks, while machines can be used, complementary, to increase their efficiency in performing these tasks.

BCG Enabling Entrepreneurship: What distinguishes a BCG from a BIG significantly is the individual's ability to make an investment. This not only opens the possibility to purchase assets on financial markets but also to start one's own business. New businesses often emerge as suppliers of a newly developed product. The BCG, in this respect, really enables the creation of new jobs: instead of merely insuring individuals against unemployment and thus reacting to the challenges of future labor market developments (as the BIG seems to do), the BCG has an active impact on technological development itself. The fact that all members of society are given the possibility to invent, create, and provide a new marketable product eventually leads to more product innovation.

A key argument in favor of the BCG, as elucidated by Bruce Ackermann and Anne Alstott (1999), is based on the value of autonomy. They assume that one ultimate goal of a society must be to enable its citizens to become autonomous persons (White, 2015). A BCG, it is argued, has the desirable effect of promoting so-called "ambition formation": It educates recipients to develop and form their ambitions early in their lives. They are confronted with the life-changing decision of how to invest their grant. In imposing this responsibility on the individual, the BCG gives an incentive to become more autonomous—to reflect and actively shape one's own life-plans. In contrast to other life-changing decisions, the decision on how to spend a BCG is based on opportunity and not on coercion. While, for example, many career decisions are nowadays determined by strong economic pressure, the availability of a BCG would not force individuals into such a decision but would instead allow them to make an autonomous choice.

With respect to the challenge of technological mass unemployment, the argument from ambition formation gains in strength. A reduced availability of employment opportunities has a further deteriorating effect on potential ambition formation and autonomy. Options to choose one's life-plan by selecting a specific profession are limited. When work becomes a less important factor for the creation of economic output and, on the other hand, capital becomes more important, the endowment of individuals with a BCG re-opens opportunities to participate in the economy.

In the face of the challenge of technological mass unemployment a BCG seems to provide a more adequate policy option than a simple BIG. It can enable individuals to contribute to the creation of wealth and it improves individuals' chances of becoming shareholders in the economic output of a society. However, BCG must not be interpreted as an exclusive redistributive policy. Rather, it has to be considered as a supplement to redistributive policies.

On the one hand, the proposal of a BCG presupposes an ideal situation of sufficiently informed rational agents making their investment decisions. Philippe Van Parijs makes the justified criticism that there is a substantive risk that a large group of people might not invest their one-time capital endowment wisely. There is a risk that people would "blow" their stake (White, 2003). A BIG circumvents this problem in that it does not provide citizens with all their entitlements at once. In this sense, the BIG is a "mildly paternalistic" policy (Van Parijs, 1995).

However, while certainly being supportive of a periodical payment instead of a lump-sum payment, this argument does not rule out the viability of a BCG. It shows that a BCG is not sufficient and that it has to be accompanied with a social security system that insures individuals against poverty resulting from "stake-blowing." Whether this system should take the form of a BIG, however, does not logically follow from the argument (White, 2003).

On the other hand (and closely related), every investment carries a substantial risk. Assets may lose their value, education may not pay off, and businesses may end up bankrupt. Even if an economy is stable and does not suffer from episodic recessions, these risks of investment never cease. The BCG is insufficient for protecting individuals against poverty resulting from bad outcomes of their investment. Therefore, it can only be considered as one element of a set of social policy options in a future society suffering from technological unemployment. Nevertheless, compared to a traditional social security system, consisting e.g. of unemployment insurance, or compared to a BIG, it opens more opportunities for individuals to benefit from taking risks.

CONCLUSION

The impact of smart robotics and artificial intelligence on future labor market developments includes both great merits and challenges. On the one hand, the reduction of costs for production through automation will significantly increase economic wealth. On the other hand, the replacement of human labor by machines may lead to widespread unemployment. This chapter first sketched the divergent anticipations of future developments by outlining the most optimistic of all scenarios—the post-work utopia—and contrasting it with an extremely skeptical expectation—the post-work dystopia. While both views have certain shortcomings, they reveal some truths about what a society may want to avoid and which future it may want to strive for. A more realistic scenario that incorporates these normative aspects, but, nevertheless, does not assume the complete abolition of human labor, was outlined.

It was argued that, if technological mass unemployment occurs, this yields four ethical problems: 1) the race against the machines, which may lead to extreme poverty; 2) the unilateral dependency of non-capital-owners on the goodwill of capital owners, which leads to severe inequalities and potentially exploitative relations; 3) the inability of unemployed non-capital-owners to make a contribution to the economic output of a society and thus to selling something in order to make a living; and 4) the inability of non-capital-owners to ever ascend to the class of capital owners.

A policy to attenuate or circumvent the challenge of technological unemployment needs to account for these four ethical problems. First addressed was the widely discussed proposal of an unconditional basic income guarantee (BIG). It was argued that it is successful in avoiding (1) and (2) above. However, it is insufficient to tackle problems (3) and (4). Therefore, the conception of an unconditional basic capital grant (BCG) was introduced, which may supplement either a BIG policy or other redistributive social policies. Since it is specifically designed to give individuals a chance to become capital owners or to successfully compete and participate in the remaining labor market, it can address problems (3) and (4). In this sense, the challenge of technological unemployment provides a reason for supporting BCG.

REFERENCES

Ackerman, B., & Alstott, A. (1999). *The stakeholder society*. Yale University Press.

Alstott, A., & Van Parijs, P. (Eds.). (2006). *Redesigning distribution: Basic income and stakeholder grants as cornerstones for an egalitarian capitalism*. Verso.

Arneson, R. J. (1990). Is work special? Justice and the distribution of employment. *The American Political Science Review, 84*(4), 1127–1147. doi:10.2307/1963256

Autor, D. H. (2015). Why are there still so many jobs? The history and future of workplace automation. *The Journal of Economic Perspectives, 29*(3), 3–30. doi:10.1257/jep.29.3.3

Autor, D. H., Levy, F., & Murnane, R. J. (2003). The skill content of recent technological change: An empirical exploration. *The Quarterly Journal of Economics, 118*(4), 1279–1333. doi:10.1162/003355303322552801

Bix, A. S. (2000). *Inventing ourselves out of jobs? America's debate over technological unemployment, 1929–1981*. Johns Hopkins University Press.

Bruun, E. P., & Duka, A. (2018). Artificial intelligence, jobs and the future of work: Racing with the machines. *Basic Income Studies, 13*(2), 1–15. doi:10.1515/bis-2018-0018

Brynjolfsson, E., & McAfee, A. (2014). *The second machine age: Work, progress, and prosperity in a time of brilliant technologies*. Norton & Company.

Chomanski, B. (2018). Massive technological unemployment without redistribution: A Case for Cautious Optimism. *Science and Engineering Ethics*, 25(5), 1389–1407. doi:10.100711948-018-0070-0 PMID:30357558

Cohn, J. (March 2013). The robot will see you now. *The Atlantic*. https://www.theatlantic.com/magazine/archive/2013/03/the-robot-will-see-you-now/309216/

Danaher, J. (2017). Will life be worth living in a world without work? Technological unemployment and the meaning of life. *Science and Engineering Ethics*, 23(1), 41–64. doi:10.100711948-016-9770-5 PMID:26968572

Danaher, J. (2019a). In defense of the post-work future: Withdrawal and the ludic life. In M. Cholbi & M. Weber (Eds.), *The Future of work, technology, and basic income* (pp. 99–116). Routledge. doi:10.4324/9780429455902-8

Danaher, J. (2019b). *Automation and utopia: Human flourishing in a world without work*. Harvard University Press. doi:10.2307/j.ctvn5txpc

Douglas, P. H. (1930). *Real wages in the United States, 1890–1926*. Houghton Mifflin Company.

Falk, M. (2015). Employment effects of technological and organizational innovations: Evidence based on linked firm-level data for Austria. *Jahrbucher fur Nationalokonomie und Statistik*, 235(3), 268–285. doi:10.1515/jbnst-2015-0303

Frey, C. B., & Osborne, M. (2013). *The future of employment*. Oxford Martin School. https://www.oxfordmartin.ox.ac.uk/publications/the-future-of-employment/

Glennerster, H., & McKnight, A. (2006). A capital start: but how far do we go? In W. Paxton & S. White (Eds.), *The Citizen's Stake: Exploring the Future of Universal Asset Policies* (pp. 87–106). The Policy Press. doi:10.2307/j.ctt1t88x4c.11

Hanson, R. (2008). Economics of the singularity. *IEEE Spectrum*, 45(6), 45–50. doi:10.1109/MSPEC.2008.4531461

Hughes, J. J. (2014). A strategic opening for a basic income guarantee in the global crisis being created by AI, robots, desktop manufacturing and biomedicine. *Journal of Evolution and Technology / WTA*, 24(1), 45–61. https://jetpress.org/v24/hughes2.htm

Kapteyn, A., Kalwij, A., & Zaidi, A. (2004). The myth of work sharing. *Labour Economics*, 11(3), 293–313. doi:10.1016/j.labeco.2003.08.001

Kim, T. W., & Scheller-Wolf, A. (2019). Technological unemployment, meaning in life, purpose of business, and the future of stakeholders. *Journal of Business Ethics*, 160(2), 319–337. doi:10.100710551-019-04205-9

Kirchgässner, G. (2009). Critical analysis of some well-intended proposals to fight unemployment. *Analyse & Kritik*, 31(1), 25–48. doi:10.1515/auk-2009-0102

Klimczuk-Kochańska, M., & Klimczuk, A. (2015). Technological unemployment. In M. Odekon (Ed.), *The SAGE encyclopedia of world poverty* (2nd ed., pp. 1510–1511). SAGE Publications Ltd.

Kurzweil, R. (2000). *The age of spiritual machines: When computers exceed human intelligence.* Penguin.

Levy, D. (2008). *Love and sex with robots: The evolution of human-robot relationships.* Harper Perennial.

Levy, F., & Murnane, R. J. (2004). *The new division of labor: How computers are creating the next job market.* Princeton University Press. doi:10.1515/9781400845927

Lovett, F. (2010). *A general theory of domination and justice.* Oxford University Press. doi:10.1093/ac prof:oso/9780199579419.001.0001

Marchant, G. E., Stevens, Y. A., & Hennessy, J. M. (2014). Technology, unemployment, and policy options: Navigating the transition to a better world. *Journal of Evolution and Technology / WTA, 21*(1), 26–44. https://jetpress.org/v24/marchant.htm

Markoff, J. (2011, March 4). Armies of expansive lawyers, replaced by software. *New York Times.* https://www.nytimes.com/2011/03/05/science/05legal.html

Meade, J. (1989). *Agathotopia: The economics of partnership.* University of Aberdeen.

Moore, G. E. (1998). Cramming more components onto integrated circuits. *Proceedings of the IEEE, 86*(1), 82–85. doi:10.1109/JPROC.1998.658762

OECD. (2013). *Supporting investment in knowledge capital, growth and innovation.* OECD Publishing.

OECD. (2016). *ICTs and jobs: Complements or substitutes.* Digital Economy Papers., doi:10.1787/5jlwnklzplhg-

Parfit, D. (2001). Equality or Priority? In J. Harris (Ed.), *Bioethics* (pp. 347–386). Oxford University Press.

Perry, J. (2013). *Ten responses to the technological unemployment problem.* Institute for Ethics and Emerging Technologies. http://declineofscarcity.com/?p=2790

Pettit, P. (2007). A republican right to basic income? *Basic Income Studies, 2*(2). https://www.degruyter.com/downloadpdf/j/bis.2008.2.2/bis.2008.2.2.1082/bis.2008.2.2.1082.pdf

Phua, C., Lee, V., Smith, K., & Gayler, R. (2010). A comprehensive survey of data mining-based fraud detection research. *arXiv preprint, 1009*(6119). https://arxiv.org/ftp/arxiv/papers/1009/1009.6119.pdf

Piketty, T. (2015). About capital in the twenty-first century. *The American Economic Review, 105*(5), 48–53. doi:10.1257/aer.p20151060

Prabhakar, R. (2018). Are basic capital versus basic income debates too narrow? *Basic Income Studies, 13*(1). Advance online publication. doi:10.1515/bis-2018-0015

Raventós, D. (2007). *Basic income: The material conditions of freedom.* Pluto.

Rifkin, J. (2014). *The zero-marginal cost society: The internet of things, the collaborative commons, and the eclipse of capitalism.* St. Martin's.

Roberts, K. (1982). *Automation, unemployment and the distribution of income* (Vol. 9). European Centre for Work and Society.

Steuart, J. (1767). *An enquiry into the principles of political economy* (Vol. 1). London: Thomas Cadell & Andrew Millar. https://archive.org/details/inquiryintoprinc01steu/page/n4

Van Parijs, P. (1997). *Real freedom for all: What (if anything) can justify capitalism?* Oxford University Press. doi:10.1093/0198293577.001.0001

Vivarelli, M. (2014). Innovation, employment and skills in advanced and developing countries: A survey of economic literature. *Journal of Economic Issues, 48*(1), 123–154. doi:10.2753/JEI0021-3624480106

Walker, M. (2014). BIG and technological unemployment: Chicken Little versus the economists. *Journal of Evolution and Technology / WTA, 24*(1), 5–25. https://jetpress.org/v24/walker.pdf

WEF. (2016). *The future of jobs: Employment, skills and workforce strategy for the fourth industrial revolution.* Executive summary. http://www3.weforum.org/docs/WEF_FOJ_Executive_Summary_Jobs.pdf

Weston, A. (1985). Technological unemployment and the lifestyle question a practical proposal. *Journal of Social Philosophy, 16*(2), 19–30. doi:10.1111/j.1467-9833.1985.tb00434.x

White, S. (2003). *The civic minimum: On the rights and obligations of economic citizenship.* Oxford University Press. doi:10.1093/0198295057.001.0001

White, S. (2011). Basic income versus basic capital: Can we resolve the disagreement? *Policy and Politics, 39*(1), 67–81. doi:10.1332/030557311X546325

White, S. (2015). Basic capital in the egalitarian toolkit? *Journal of Applied Philosophy, 32*(4), 417–431. doi:10.1111/japp.12129

ADDITIONAL READING

Acemoglu, D., & Restrepo, P. (2017). *Robots and jobs: Evidence from US labor markets.* NBER Working Papers 23285. https://www.nber.org/papers/w23285

Atkinson, A. B. (2015). *Inequality: What can be done?* Harvard University Press. doi:10.4159/9780674287013

Black, B. (1986). *The abolition of work and other essays.* Loompanics.

Ford, M. (2015). *Rise of the robots: Technology and the threat of a jobless future.* Basic Books.

Keynes, J. M. (2010). Economic possibilities for our grandchildren. In J. M. Keynes (Ed.), *Essays in persuasion* (pp. 321–332). Palgrave MacMillan. doi:10.1007/978-1-349-59072-8_25

Loi, M. (2015). Technological unemployment and human disenhancement. *Ethics and Information Technology, 17*(3), 201–210. doi:10.100710676-015-9375-8

Naastepad, C. W. M., & Houghton Budd, C. (2019). Preventing technological unemployment by widening our understanding of capital and progress: Making robots work for us. *Ethics & Social Welfare, 13*(2), 115–132. doi:10.1080/17496535.2018.1512641

Piketty, T. (2015). *Capital in the twenty-first century.* Harvard University Press.

KEY TERMS AND DEFINITIONS

Basic Capital Grant (BCG): Redistributive scheme that consists of a single, non-periodical lump-sum payment to every citizen; intended to enable its recipients to take an investment early in their lives.

Basic Income Guarantee (BIG): Redistributive scheme that grants every citizen of a country a periodically paid amount of money, irrespective of the other income the citizen generates; intended to cover recipients living costs.

Luddite Fallacy: False belief that the number of tasks to be performed by human labor is stable.

Process Innovations: The discovery of improved methods to produce goods at lower costs.

Product Innovations: The discovery of new marketable products.

Technological Unemployment: A sort of unemployment that occurs when people are without work (and seeking work) due to innovative production processes and labor-saving organizational solutions.

ENDNOTES

[1] Futurologist authors often refer to the so-called "Moore's Law" established in 1965 by Gordon Moore (1998). He describes technological progress as an exponential curve by observing that the number of transistors on an integrated circuit doubles every 18 months.

[2] With reference to Douglas (1930).

[3] For an interesting critique see John Danaher (2019b) who in his book defends a utopian view of technological unemployment. He argues that the expectation of a complementary effect of process innovations may not give sufficient support for the belief that technological mass unemployment may not occur. Also, because machines may as well complement other machines in performing certain tasks.

[4] One problem that is often discussed within the debate of technological unemployment is the potential loss of meaning in life (e.g., Danaher, 2017; Kim & Scheller-Wolf, 2019). Work is presumed to be an integral part of our self-constitution in that it provides us with a purpose and identity. Since, in this chapter, I am predominantly concerned with problems of distributive justice, I will not say much about this topic here. Not being able to contribute to society's welfare is therefore dealt with in economic terms as a lack of productive capacity and not in terms of a lack of means for individual self-fulfillment.

[5] These can basically be classified into two strands of argument: freedom-based claims and egalitarian claims (White, 2011). The former argument supports a BIG since a BIG enhances the real liberties of citizens. The latter supports a BIG since it leads to more equal distribution. Depending on the "currency" of egalitarian justice, options for financing a BIG differ. An in-depth analysis of these arguments would greatly exceed the space available here. Here, the BIG proposal is merely assessed as a policy to counter the problem of technological mass unemployment.

[6] E.g., without minimum-wage restrictions.

[7] Besides objecting to the empirical thesis that a BIG reduces labor supply.

[8] Although it is prone to so-called "levelling-down objections" (Parfit, 2001); i.e., that, in some cases, equality of wealth and income demands that no person is better-off and some are even worse-off.

9   Like the BIG, the BCG might be financed by different means of taxation. For instance, it is proposed that it could be financed by a sort of inheritance tax.

10   One obvious reason for this constraint is given by the simple fact that not every person is able to make an investment and to eventually capitalize from it. I believe that many people are not good investors, have no entrepreneurial spirit, and are not intelligent or industrious enough to achieve a higher education degree. Therefore, a BCG can never fully replace a social security system.

Compilation of References

(2020). Doris, John, Stich, Stephen, Phillips, Jonathan and Walmsley, Lachlan. InZalta, E. N. (Ed.), *Moral Psychology: Empirical Approaches*. The Stanford Encyclopedia of Philosophy.

Abel, D., MacGlashan, J., & Littman, M. L. (2016). Reinforcement learning as a framework for ethical decision-making. *Workshops at the Thirtieth AAAI Conference on Artificial Intelligence*.

Ackerman, B., & Alstott, A. (1999). *The stakeholder society*. Yale University Press.

Adams, J. (1991). *The American amusement park industry: A history of technology and thrills (Twayne's Evolution of American Business Series)*. Twayne's Publishers.

Adorno, T. W. (1999). *Aesthetic theory* (R. Hullot-Kentor, Trans.). Athlone Press.

AI for Good Foundation. (2020). *AI for Good - Make the World a Better Place through AI*. https://ai4good.org/

Aïmeur, E., Gambs, S., & Ho, A. (2010). Towards a Privacy-Enhanced Social Networking Site. *2010 International Conference on Availability, Reliability and Security*, 172–179. 10.1109/ARES.2010.97

Alicke, M. D. (2012). Self-Injuries, Harmless Wrongdoing, and Morality. *Psychological Inquiry*, *23*(2), 125–128. doi: 10.1080/1047840X.2012.666720

Aliman, N.-M., Kester, L., Werkhoven, P., & Yampolskiy, R. (2019). *Orthogonality-based disentanglement of responsibilities for ethical intelligent systems*. Paper presented at the International Conference on Artificial General Intelligence. 10.1007/978-3-030-27005-6_3

Allen, C., Smit, A., & Wallach, W. (2005). Artificial morality: Top-down, bottom-up, and hybrid approaches. *Ethics and Information Technology*, *7*(3), 149–155. doi:10.100710676-006-0004-4

Allhoff, F., Lin, P., & Steinberg, J. (2011). Ethics of human enhancement: An executive summary. *Science and Engineering Ethics*, *17*(2), 201–212. doi:10.100711948-009-9191-9 PMID:20094921

Alonso Raposo, M., Ciuffo, B., Ardente, F., Aurambout, J. P., Baldini, G., Braun, R., Christidis, P., Christodoulou, A., Duboz, A., & Felici, S. (2019). The Future of Road Transport—Implications of Automated, Connected, Low-Carbon and Shared Mobility. EUR 29748 EN. *Publications Office of the European Union, Luxembourg, 2019*. Advance online publication. doi:10.2760/668964

Alstott, A., & Van Parijs, P. (Eds.). (2006). *Redesigning distribution: Basic income and stakeholder grants as cornerstones for an egalitarian capitalism*. Verso.

Althusser, L. (2014, February). *On the reproduction of capitalism: Ideology and ideological state apparatuses*. New York: Verso.

Amazon ditched AI recruiting tool that favored men for technical jobs. (2018). *The Guardian*. https://www.theguardian.com/technology/2018/oct/10/amazon-hiring-ai-gender-bias-recruiting-engine

Amodei, D., Olah, C., Steinhardt, J., Christiano, P., Schulman, J., & Mane, D. (2016). *Concrete problems in AI safety*. arXiv: 1606.06565v2

Anderson, M., Anderson, S. L., & Berenz, V. (2017). A value driven agent: Instantiation of a case-supported principle–based behavior paradigm. *The AAAI-17 Workshop on AI, Ethics, and Society*.

Anderson, M., & Anderson, S. L. (2007). Machine Ethics: Creating an Ethical Intelligent Agent. *AI Magazine*, *28*(4), 12.

Anthes, G. (2015). Estonia: A model for e-government. *Communications of the ACM*, *58*(6), 18–20. doi:10.1145/2754951

Arendt, H. (1951). *The origins of totalitarianism*. Schocken Books.

Aristotle. (1984). *The politics*. The University of Chicago Press. doi:10.7208/chicago/9780226026701.001.0001

Aristotle. (2010). *De sensu and de memoria*. Kessinger Publishing.

Aristotle. (2014). *Nicomachean ethics*. Cambridge University Press.

Arneson, R. J. (1990). Is work special? Justice and the distribution of employment. *The American Political Science Review*, *84*(4), 1127–1147. doi:10.2307/1963256

Asimov, I. (1950). *I, robot*. Bantam Dell.

Asimov, I. (1985). *Robots and empires*. Doubleday & Company, Inc.

Atran, S. (2002). *In gods we trust: The evolutionary landscape of religion*. Oxford University Press.

Atran, S. (2012). Psychological orgins and cultural evolution of religion. In R. Sun (Ed.), *Grounding Social Sciences in Cognitive Sciences* (pp. 209–238). MIT Press.

Atran, S., & Norenzayan, A. (2004). Religion's evolutionary landscape: Counterintuition, commitment, compassion, communion. *Behavioral and Brain Sciences*, *27*(6), 713–730. doi:10.1017/S0140525X04000172 PMID:16035401

Autor, D. H. (2015). Why are there still so many jobs? The history and future of workplace automation. *The Journal of Economic Perspectives*, *29*(3), 3–30. doi:10.1257/jep.29.3.3

Autor, D. H., Levy, F., & Murnane, R. J. (2003). The skill content of recent technological change: An empirical exploration. *The Quarterly Journal of Economics*, *118*(4), 1279–1333. doi:10.1162/003355303322552801

Awad, E., Dsouza, S., Bonnefon, J.-F., Shariff, A., & Rahwan, I. (2020). Crowdsourcing Moral Machines. *Communications of the ACM*, *63*(3), 48–55. doi:10.1145/3339904

Awad, E., Dsouza, S., Kim, R., Schulz, J., Henrich, J., Shariff, A., Bonnefon, J., & Rahwan, I. (2018). The Moral Machine experiment. *Nature*, *563*(7729), 59–64. doi:10.103841586-018-0637-6 PMID:30356211

Aydemir, F. B., & Dalpiaz, F. (2018). A Roadmap for Ethics-Aware Software Engineering. *2018 IEEE/ACM International Workshop on Software Fairness (FairWare)*, 15–21. 10.23919/FAIRWARE.2018.8452915

Barrett, A. M., & Baum, S. D. (2017). Risk Analysis and Risk Management for the Artificial Superintelligence Research and Development Process. In V. Callaghan, J. Miller, R. Yampolskiy, & S. Armstrong (Eds.), *The technological singularity: Managing the journey* (pp. 127–140). Springer-Verlag Berlin Heidelberg. doi:10.1007/978-3-662-54033-6_6

Barrett, H. C. (2015). *The shape of thought: How mental adaptations evolve.* Oxford University Press. doi:10.1093/ac prof:oso/9780199348305.001.0001

Bartolini, C., Muthuri, R., & Santos, C. (2017). Using Ontologies to Model Data Protection Requirements in Workflows. In M. Otake, S. Kurahashi, Y. Ota, K. Satoh, & D. Bekki (Eds.), *New Frontiers in Artificial Intelligence* (Vol. 10091, pp. 233–248). Springer International Publishing. doi:10.1007/978-3-319-50953-2_17

Baumann, C., Peitz, P., Raabe, O., & Wacker, R. (2010). Compliance for Service-based Systems through Formalization of Law. *Proceedings from the 6th International Conference on Web Information Systems and Technology,* 367–371. 10.5220/0002868003670371

Baumard, J., Osiurak, F., Lesourd, M., & Le Gall, D. (2014). Tool use disorders after left brain damage. *Frontiers in Psychology, 5.* Advance online publication. doi:10.3389/fpsyg.2014.00473 PMID:24904487

Baumeister, R. F., & Leary, M. R. (1995). The Need to Belong: Desire for Interpersonal Attachments as a Fundamental Human Motivation. *Psychological Bulletin, 117*(3), 497–529. doi:10.1037/0033-2909.117.3.497 PMID:7777651

Baum, S. D. (2014). The great downside dilemma for risky emerging technologies. *Physica Scripta, 89*(12), 10. doi:10.1088/0031-8949/89/12/128004

Bay, C. (1961). The Structure of Freedom. *Science and Society, 25*(1).

Bayern, S. (2013). Of Bitcoins, Independently Wealthy Software, and the Zero-Member LLC. *Northwestern University Law Review, 108,* 1485. doi:10.2139srn.2366197

Bayern, S. (2016). The Implications of Modern Business–Entity Law for the Regulation of Autonomous Systems. *European Journal of Risk Regulation, 7*(2), 297–309. doi:10.1017/S1867299X00005729

Beard, S. (2019). The problem with the trolley problem. *Quartz.* https://qz.com/1716107/the-problem-with-the-trolley-problem/

Beil, M., Proft, I., van Heerden, D., Sviri, S., & van Heerden, P. V. (2019). Ethical consideration of artificial intelligence for prognostication in intensive care. *Intensive Care Medicine Experimental, 7*(1), 70. doi:10.118640635-019-0286-6 PMID:31823128

Bellotti, V., & Edwards, K. (2001). Intelligibility and accountability: Human considerations in context-aware systems. *Human-Computer Interaction, 16*(2–4), 193–212. doi:10.1207/S15327051HCI16234_05

Bellotti, V., & Sellen, A. (1993). Design for Privacy in Ubiquitous Computing Environments. In G. de Michelis, C. Simone, & K. Schmidt (Eds.), *Proceedings of the Third European Conference on Computer-Supported Cooperative Work 13–17 September 1993, Milan, Italy ECSCW '93* (pp. 77–92). Springer Netherlands. 10.1007/978-94-011-2094-4_6

Ben-Haim, Y., Osteen, C. D., & Moffitt, L. J. (2013). Policy dilemma of innovation: An info-gap approach. *Ecological Economics, 85,* 130–138. doi:10.1016/j.ecolecon.2012.08.011

Benjamin, W. (1969). The Work of Art in the Age of Mechanical Reproduction. In *Illuminations* (pp. 217–252). Schocken Books.

Benjamin, W. (2009). A Small History of Photography. In *One way street and other writings* (pp. 240–257). Penguin.

Bentham, J. (1816). *Chrestomathia.* William Tait.

Berardi, F. (2011). Cognitarian Subjectivation. In J. Aranda, B. K. Wood, & A. Vidokle (Eds.), *Are you working too much?: Post-Fordism, precarity, and the labor of art* (pp. 134–146). Sternberg Press.

Bering, J. M. (2006). The folk psychology of souls. *Behavioral and Brain Sciences, 29*(5), 453–462. doi:10.1017/S0140525X06009101 PMID:17156519

Bigman, Y. E., & Gray, K. (2018). People are averse to machines making moral decisions. *Cognition, 181,* 21–34. doi:10.1016/j.cognition.2018.08.003 PMID:30107256

Bigman, Y. E., Waytz, A., Alterovitz, R., & Gray, K. (2019). Holding robots responsible: The elements of machine morality. *Trends in Cognitive Sciences, 23*(5), 365–368. doi:10.1016/j.tics.2019.02.008 PMID:30962074

Binder, J. R., & Desai, R. H. (2011). The neurobiology of semantic memory. *Trends in Cognitive Sciences, 15*(11), 527–536. doi:10.1016/j.tics.2011.10.001 PMID:22001867

Biran, O., & Cotton, C. (2017). Explanation and Justification in Machine Learning: A Survey. *IJCAI 2017, Workshop on Explainable Artificial Intelligence (XAI)*, 8-13.

Bissell, D., Birtchnell, T., Elliott, A., & Hsu, E. L. (2020). Autonomous automobilities: The social impacts of driverless vehicles. *Current Sociology, 68*(1), 116–134. doi:10.1177/0011392118816743

Bix, A. S. (2000). *Inventing ourselves out of jobs? America's debate over technological unemployment, 1929–1981.* Johns Hopkins University Press.

Blackford, R. (2003). Who's Afraid of the Brave New World? *Quadrant, 47*(5), 9.

Blanco, M., Atwood, J., Russell, S., Trimble, T., McClafferty, J., & Perez, M. (2016). Automated Vehicle Crash Rate Comparison Using Naturalistic Data. Vtti. doi:10.13140/RG.2.1.2336.1048

Boden, M. A. (Ed.). (1990). *The philosophy of artificial intelligence.* Oxford University Press.

Bødker, K., Kensing, F., & Simonsen, J. (2009). *Participatory IT design: Designing for business and workplace realities.* MIT press.

Bonnefon, J., Shariff, S., & Rahwan, I. (2016). The social dilemma of autonomous vehicles. *Science, 352*(6293), 1573–1576. doi:10.1126cience.aaf2654 PMID:27339987

Borning, A., & Muller, M. (2012). Next steps for value sensitive design. *Proceedings of the 2012 ACM Annual Conference on Human Factors in Computing Systems - CHI '12*, 1125. 10.1145/2207676.2208560

Bos, C., Walhout, B., Peine, A., & van Lente, H. (2014). Steering with big words: Articulating ideographs in research programs. *Journal of Responsible Innovation, 1*(2), 151–170. doi:10.1080/23299460.2014.922732

Bostrom, N. (2005). A History of Transhumanist Thought. *Journal of Evolution and Technology / WTA, 14*(1).

Bostrom, N. (2005). In defense of posthuman dignity. *Bioethics, 19*(3), 202–214. doi:10.1111/j.1467-8519.2005.00437.x PMID:16167401

Bostrom, N. (2012). The superintelligent will: Motivation and instrumental rationality in advanced artificial agents. *Minds and Machines, 22*(2), 71–85. doi:10.100711023-012-9281-3

Bostrom, N. (2013). Existential risk prevention as global priority. *Global Policy, 4*(1), 15–31. doi:10.1111/1758-5899.12002

Bostrom, N. (2014). *Superintelligence: Paths, dangers, strategies.* Oxford University Press.

Boyer, P. (2001). *Religion explained: The evolutionary origins of religious thought.* Basic Books.

Boyer, P. (2018). *Minds make societies: How cognition explains the world humans create.* Yale University Press.

Boyer, P., & Barrett, H. C. (2015). Intuitive Ontologies and Domain Specificity. In D. M. Buss (Ed.), *The handbook of evolutionary psychology* (pp. 161–174). John Wiley & Sons, Inc., doi:10.1002/9781119125563.evpsych105

Breggin, P. R. (2015). The biological evolution of guilt, shame and anxiety: A new theory of negative legacy emotions. *Medical Hypotheses*, 85(1), 17–24. doi:10.1016/j.mehy.2015.03.015 PMID:25890689

Brezillon, P. J. (1994). Contextualized explanations. *Proceedings from International Conference on Expert Systems for Development*, 119–124. 10.1109/ICESD.1994.302295

Bridle, J. (2018). *New dark age: Technology and the end of the future.* Verso.

Broeckman, A. (2016). *Machine art in the twentieth century.* MIT Press.

Bruun, E. P., & Duka, A. (2018). Artificial intelligence, jobs and the future of work: Racing with the machines. *Basic Income Studies*, 13(2), 1–15. doi:10.1515/bis-2018-0018

Brynjolfsson, E., & McAfee, A. (2014). *The second machine age: Work, progress, and prosperity in a time of brilliant technologies.* Norton & Company.

Bryson, J. B. (in press). The Artificial Intelligence of Ethics of AI: An Introductory Overview. In M. D. Dubber, F. Pasquale, & S. Das (Eds.), *The Oxford Handbook of Ethics of AI.* Oxford University Press.

Bryson, J. J., Diamantis, M. E., & Grant, T. D. (2017). Of, for, and by the people: The legal lacuna of synthetic persons. *Artificial Intelligence and Law*, 25(3), 273–291. doi:10.100710506-017-9214-9

Buiten, M. C. (2019). Towards Intelligent Regulation of Artificial Intelligence. *European Journal of Risk Regulation*, 10(1), 41–59. doi:10.1017/err.2019.8

Burdett, M. (2014). The Religion of Technology: Transhumanism and the myth of progress. In C. Marcer & T. J. Trothen (Eds.), *Religion and transhumanism: The unknown future of human enhancement* (pp. 131–147). ABC-CLIO, LLC.

Burrell, J. (2016). How the machine 'thinks': Understanding opacity in machine learning algorithms. *Big Data & Society*, 3(1). Advance online publication. doi:10.1177/2053951715622512

Busch, D. (2016). MiFID II: Regulating high frequency trading, other forms of algorithmic trading and direct electronic market access. *Law and Financial Markets Review*, 10(2), 72–82. doi:10.1080/17521440.2016.1200333

Canguilhem, G. (1992). Machine and Organism. In J. Crary & S. Kwinter (Eds.), *Incorporations* (pp. 44–69). Zone.

Carey, S. (2009). *The origin of concepts.* Oxford University Press. doi:10.1093/acprof:oso/9780195367638.001.0001

Casanovas, P., Palmirani, M., Peroni, S., van Engers, T., & Vitali, F. (2016). Semantic Web for the legal domain: The next step. *Semantic Web*, 7(3), 213–227. doi:10.3233/SW-160224

Casellas, N., Nieto, J.-E., Mero–o, A., Roig, A., Torralba, S., Reyes, M., & Casanovas, P. (2010). *Ontological Semantics for Data Privacy Compliance.* The NEURONA Project.

Castelo, N., Schmitt, B., & Sarvary, M. (2019). Human or Robot? Consumer Responses to Radical Cognitive Enhancement Products. *Journal of the Association for Consumer Research*, 4(3), 217–230. doi:10.1086/703462

Cave, S., Nyrup, R., Vold, K., & Weller, A. (2019). Motivations and risks of machine ethics. *Proceedings of the IEEE*, 107(3), 562–574. doi:10.1109/JPROC.2018.2865996

Chang, R. (Ed.). (1997). *Incommensurability, incomparability, and practical reason.* Harvard University Press.

Charisi, V., Dennis, L. A., Fisher, M., Lieck, R., Matthias, A., Slavkovik, M., Sombetzki, J., Winfield, A. F. T., & Yampolskiy, R. (2017). *Towards Moral Autonomous Systems.* https://arxiv.org/abs/1703.04741

Chassy, P., & Gobet, F. (2011). A Hypothesis about the Biological Basis of Expert Intuition. *Review of General Psychology, 15*(3), 198–212. doi:10.1037/a0023958

Chomanski, B. (2018). Massive technological unemployment without redistribution: A Case for Cautious Optimism. *Science and Engineering Ethics, 25*(5), 1389–1407. doi:10.100711948-018-0070-0 PMID:30357558

Chopra, S., & White, L. (2004). *Artificial agents personhood in law and philosophy.* Paper presented at the 16th European Conference on Artificial Intelligence.

Christensen, J. F., & Gomila, A. (2012). Moral dilemmas in cognitive neuroscience of moral decision-making: A principled review. *Neuroscience and Biobehavioral Reviews, 36*(4), 1249–1264. doi:10.1016/j.neubiorev.2012.02.008 PMID:22353427

Christidis, K., & Devetsikiotis, M. (2016). Blockchains and smart contracts for the internet of things. *IEEE Access: Practical Innovations, Open Solutions, 4,* 2292–2303. doi:10.1109/ACCESS.2016.2566339

Clark, A. (2008). *Supersizing the mind: Embodiment, action, and cognitive extension.* Oxford University Press. doi:10.1093/acprof:oso/9780195333213.001.0001

Coca-Vila, I. (2017). Self-driving Cars in Dilemmatic Situations: An Approach Based on the Theory of Justification in Criminal Law. *Criminal Law and Philosophy.* Advance online publication. doi:10.100711572-017-9411-3

Coeckelbergh, M. (2019). Artificial Intelligence, Responsibility Attribution and a Relational Justification of Explainability. *Science and Engineering Ethics.* https://coeckelbergh.files.wordpress.com/2019/10/2019_10_28-ai-responsibility-relational-explainability-coeckelbergh.pdf

Coeckelbergh, M. (2010). Robot rights? Towards a social-relational justification of moral consideration. *Ethics and Information Technology, 12*(3), 209–221. doi:10.100710676-010-9235-5

Coeckelbergh, M. (2013). *Human being @ risk: Enhancement, technology, and the evaluation of vulnerability transformations.* Springer Science & Business Media. doi:10.1007/978-94-007-6025-7

Cohen-Chen, S., Halperin, E., Saguy, T., & van Zomeren, M. (2014). Beliefs About the Malleability of Immoral Groups Facilitate Collective Action. *Social Psychological & Personality Science, 5*(2), 203–201. doi:10.1177/1948550613491292

Cohn, J. (March 2013). The robot will see you now. *The Atlantic.* https://www.theatlantic.com/magazine/archive/2013/03/the-robot-will-see-you-now/309216/

Combs, T. S., Sandt, L. S., Clamann, M. P., & McDonald, N. C. (2019). Automated Vehicles and Pedestrian Safety: Exploring the Promise and Limits of Pedestrian Detection. *American Journal of Preventive Medicine, 56*(1), 1–7. doi:10.1016/j.amepre.2018.06.024 PMID:30337236

Conner, S. (2001). Mortification. In S. Ahmed & J. Stacy (Eds.), *Thinking through the skin.* Routledge.

Corak, M. (2016). 'Inequality is the root of social evil,' or Maybe Not? Two Stories about Inequality and Public Policy. *Canadian Public Policy, 42*(4), 367–414. doi:10.3138/cpp.2016-056

Correljé, A., Cuppen, E., Dignum, M., Pesch, U., & Taebi, B. (2015). Responsible Innovation in Energy Projects: Values in the Design of Technologies, Institutions and Stakeholder Interactions. In B.-J. Koops, I. Oosterlaken, H. Romijn, T. Swierstra, & J. van den Hoven (Eds.), *Responsible innovation 2* (pp. 183–200). Springer International Publishing. doi:10.1007/978-3-319-17308-5_10

Crary, J. (2014). 24/7. Verso.

Crary, J., & Kwinter, S. (Eds.). (1992). *Incorporations*. Zone.

Cruise. (2020). *Cruise - Create what's next.* https://www.getcruise.com/technology

Curry, O. S., Chesters, M. J., & Van Lissa, C. J. (2019). Mapping morality with a compass: Testing the theory of "morality-as-cooperation" with a new questionnaire. *Journal of Research in Personality, 78,* 106–124. doi:10.1016/j.jrp.2018.10.008

Curtis, C., & Hereward, J. (2018, May 4). How Accurately Can Scientists Reconstruct A Person's Face From DNA? *Smithsonian Magazine.* https://www.smithsonianmag.com/innovation/how-accurately-can-scientists-reconstruct-persons-face-from-dna-180968951/

Cushman, F., & Greene, J. D. (2012). Finding faults: How moral dilemmas illuminate cognitive structure. *Social Neuroscience, 7*(3), 269–279. Advance online publication. doi:10.1080/17470919.2011.614000 PMID:21942995

Dalpiaz, F., Paja, E., & Giorgini, P. (2016). *Security requirements engineering: Designing secure socio-technical systems.* The MIT Press.

Danaher, J. (2016). The threat of algocracy: Reality, resistance and accommodation. *Philosophy & Technology, 29*(3), 245–268. doi:10.100713347-015-0211-1

Danaher, J. (2017). Will life be worth living in a world without work? Technological unemployment and the meaning of life. *Science and Engineering Ethics, 23*(1), 41–64. doi:10.100711948-016-9770-5 PMID:26968572

Danaher, J. (2019a). In defense of the post-work future: Withdrawal and the ludic life. In M. Cholbi & M. Weber (Eds.), *The Future of work, technology, and basic income* (pp. 99–116). Routledge. doi:10.4324/9780429455902-8

Danaher, J. (2019b). *Automation and utopia: Human flourishing in a world without work.* Harvard University Press. doi:10.2307/j.ctvn5txpc

Davis, J., & Nathan, L. P. (2014). Value Sensitive Design: Applications, Adaptations, and Critiques. In J. van den Hoven, P. E. Vermaas, & I. van de Poel (Eds.), *Handbook of ethics, values, and technological design: Sources, theory, values and application domains* (pp. 1–26). Springer Netherlands. doi:10.1007/978-94-007-6994-6_3-1

Dawkins, R. (1976). *The selfish gene.* Oxford University Press.

De Sousa, R. (1990). *The rationality of emotion.* MIT Press.

Debord, G. (2009). *Society of the spectacle.* Sussex: Soul Bay Press.

Deleuze, G. (1986). *Cinema 1: The movement-image.* Athlone Press.

Delgado, J., Gallego, I., Llorente, S., & García, R. (2003). Regulatory Ontologies: An Intellectual Property Rights Approach. In R. Meersman & Z. Tari (Eds.), *On The Move to Meaningful Internet Systems 2003: OTM 2003 Workshops* (Vol. 2889, pp. 621–634). Springer Berlin Heidelberg. doi:10.1007/978-3-540-39962-9_65

Dennis, L., Fisher, M., Slavkovik, M., & Webster, M. (2014). Ethical choice in unforeseen circumstances. Lecture Notes in Computer Science (Including Subseries Lecture Notes in Artificial Intelligence and Lecture Notes in Bioinformatics), 8069, 433–445. doi:10.1007/978-3-662-43645-5_45

Dennis, L., Fisher, M., Slavkovik, M., & Webster, M. (2016). Formal verification of ethical choices in autonomous systems. *Robotics and Autonomous Systems, 77,* 1–14. doi:10.1016/j.robot.2015.11.012

Department for Transport (DfT), & Centre for the Protection of National Infrastructure (CPNI). (2017). *The Key Principles of Cyber Security for Connected and Automated Vehicles.* https://www.gov.uk/government/uploads/system/uploads/attachment_data/file/624302/cyber-security-connected-automated-vehicles-key-principles.pdf

Derrida, J. (1994). *Specters of Marx.* Routledge.

Dey, A. K. (2001). Understanding and Using Context. *Personal and Ubiquitous Computing, 5*(1), 4–7. doi:10.1007007790170019

Dey, A. K. (2009). Explanations in Context-Aware Systems. *Proceedings of the Fourth International Conference on Explanation-Aware Computing,* 84–93.

Dignum, V. (2019). *Responsible artificial intelligence: How to develop and use AI in a responsible way.* Springer International Publishing., doi:10.1007/978-3-030-30371-6

Dilger, W. (1997). *Decentralized autonomous organization of the intelligent home according to the principle of the immune system.* Paper presented at the Systems, Man, and Cybernetics, 1997, Computational Cybernetics and Simulation, 1997 IEEE International Conference. 10.1109/ICSMC.1997.625775

Dixit, V. V., Chand, S., & Nair, D. J. (2016). Autonomous Vehicles: Disengagements, Accidents and Reaction Times. *PLoS One, 11*(12), 1–14. doi:10.1371/journal.pone.0168054 PMID:27997566

Dodig Crnkovic, G., & Çürüklü, B. (2012). Robots: Ethical by design. *Ethics and Information Technology, 14*(1), 61–71. doi:10.100710676-011-9278-2

Dodig-Crnkovic, G., & Persson, D. (2008). Sharing Moral Responsibility with Robots: A Pragmatic Approach. *Proceedings of the 2008 Conference on Tenth Scandinavian Conference on Artificial Intelligence: SCAI 2008,* 165–168. https://dl.acm.org/citation.cfm?id=1566864.1566888

Donald, A. (2002). *A mind so rare: The evolution of human consciousness.* W. W. Norton and Company.

Dorobantu, M., & Wilks, Y. (2019). Moral Orthoses: A New Approach to Human and Machine Ethics. *Zygon, 54*(4), 1004–1021. doi:10.1111/zygo.12560

Douglas, P. H. (1930). *Real wages in the United States, 1890–1926.* Houghton Mifflin Company.

Dressel, J., & Farid, H. (2018). The accuracy, fairness, and limits of predicting recidivism. *Science Advances, 4*(1), 1–5. doi:10.1126ciadv.aao5580 PMID:29376122

Duke, A. A., & Bègue, L. (2015). The drunk utilitarian: Blood alcohol concentration predicts utilitarian responses in moral dilemmas. *Cognition, 134,* 121–127. doi:10.1016/j.cognition.2014.09.006 PMID:25460385

Dunbar, R. (2014). *Human evolution.* Pelican Books.

DuPont, Q. (2017). Experiments in algorithmic governance: A history and ethnography of "The DAO," a failed decentralized autonomous organization. In Bitcoin and beyond (pp. 157-177). Routledge.

Durkheim, E. (2002). *Suicide.* Routledge. doi:10.1522/cla.due.sui2

EC HLEG. (2018). *Ethics Guidelines for Trustworthy AI.* The European Commision's High-Level Expert Group on Artificial Intelligence. https://ec.europa.eu/futurium/en/ai-alliance-consultation/guidelines

Eden, G., Nanchen, B., Ramseyer, R., & Evéquoz, F. (2017). On the Road with an Autonomous Passenger Shuttle: Integration in Public Spaces. *Proceedings of the 2017 CHI Conference Extended Abstracts on Human Factors in Computing Systems,* 1569–1576. 10.1145/3027063.3053126

Ehn, P. (2016). Design, Democracy and Work: Exploring the Scandinavian Participatory Design Tradition. *Critical Design/Critical Futures 2016 Symposium.*

Elad-Strenger, J., Proch, J., & Kessler, T. (2020). Is Disgust a "Conservative" Emotion? *Personality and Social Psychology Bulletin, 46*(6), 896–912. doi:10.1177/0146167219880191 PMID:31619133

Elkin, P., Schlegel, D., Anderson, M., Komm, J., Ficheur, G., & Bisson, L. (2018). Artificial Intelligence: Bayesian versus Heuristic Method for Diagnostic Decision Support. *Applied Clinical Informatics, 09*(02), 432–439. doi:10.1055-0038-1656547 PMID:29898469

Elshtain, J. B. (1990). Sovereign God, Sovereign State, Sovereign Self. *The Notre Dame Law Review, 66,* 1355.

Epstein, R. A. (2011). Citizens United v. FEC: The constitutional right that big corporations should have but do not want. *Harvard Journal of Law & Public Policy, 34,* 639.

Erl, T. (2005). *Service-oriented architecture: Concepts, technology, and design.* Prentice Hall PTR.

EU. (2016). Regulation (EU) 2016/679 of the European Parliament and of the Council of 27 April 2016 on the protection of natural persons with regard to the processing of personal data and on the free movement of such data, and repealing Directive 95/46/EC (General Data Protection Regulation). http://data.europa.eu/eli/reg/2016/679/oj

European Commission's High-Level Expert Group on Artificial Intelligence (AI HLEG). (2019). Ethics Guidelines for Trustworthy AI. *High-Level Expert Group on Artificial Intelligence.* https://ec.europa.eu/digital-single-market/en/news/ethics-guidelines-trustworthy-ai

European Commission's High-Level Expert Group On Artificial Intelligence. (2019). *Ethics guidelines for trustworthy AI.* European Commission. https://ec.europa.eu/digital-single-market/en/news/ethics-guidelines-trustworthy-ai

European Group on Ethics in Science and New Technologies and others. (2018). *Statement on Artificial Intelligence, Robotics and "Autonomous" Systems.* Luxembourg: Publications Office of the European Union.

Fairness. (2020). In *Cambridge English Dictionary.* Retrieved July 30, 2020, from https://dictionary.cambridge.org/us/dictionary/english/fairness

Falk, M. (2015). Employment effects of technological and organizational innovations: Evidence based on linked firm-level data for Austria. *Jahrbucher fur Nationalokonomie und Statistik, 235*(3), 268–285. doi:10.1515/jbnst-2015-0303

Fallan, K. (2015). Our Common Future. Joining Forces for Histories of Sustainable Design. *Technoscienza: Italian Journal of Science & Technology Studies, 5*(2), 15–32. http://www.tecnoscienza.net/index.php/tsj/article/view/201%5Cnhttp://www.tecnoscienza.net/index.php/tsj/article/download/201/136%5Cn

Fantawild. (2015). Fantawild Oriental Heritage Opens Soon. *Fantawild.* https://www.fantawild.com/en/medialist/show/88.htm

Fantawild. (2016). About Fantawild. *Fantawild.* https://www.fantawild.com/en/layout.shtml

Fantawild. (2016). Special Effects Films. *Fantawild.* https://www.fantawild.com/en/business vrmovie.shtml

Favarò, F. M., Nader, N., Eurich, S. O., Tripp, M., & Varadaraju, N. (2017). Examining accident reports involving autonomous vehicles in California. *PLoS One, 12*(9), 1–20. doi:10.1371/journal.pone.0184952 PMID:28931022

Fazi, M. B. (2019). Can a machine think (anything new)? Automation beyond simulation. *AI & Society, 34*(4), 813–824. doi:10.100700146-018-0821-0

Federal Ministry of Transport and Digital Infrastructure. (2017). *Automated and Connected Driving. Ethics Commission.* https://www.bmvi.de/SharedDocs/EN/publications/report-ethics-commission.pdf?__blob=publicationFile

Feinberg, M., Willer, R., & Keltner, D. (2011). Flustered and Faithful: Embarrassment as a Signal of Prosociality. *Journal of Personality and Social Psychology.* Advance online publication. doi:10.1037/a0025403 PMID:21928915

Ferdman, A. (2020). Corporate ownership of automated vehicles: Discussing potential negative externalities. *Transport Reviews, 40*(1), 95–113. doi:10.1080/01441647.2019.1687606

Fessenden, M. (2014, November 19). We've Put a Worm's Mind in a Lego Robot's Body. *Smithsonian Magazine.*

Fjell, C. D., Cherkasov, A., Hilpert, K., Jenssen, H., Waldbrook, M., Mullaly, S. C., Volkmer, R., & Hancock, R. E. W. (2008). Use of Artificial Intelligence in the Design of Small Peptide Antibiotics Effective against a Broad Spectrum of Highly Antibiotic-Resistant Superbugs. *ACS Chemical Biology, 4*(1), 65–74. PMID:19055425

Fjellman, S. (1992). *Vinyl leaves: Walt Disney World and America* (1st ed.). Routledge.

Fletcher, P. (2015). *Historically African American leisure destinations around Washington, D.C.* New York: The History Press.

Fletcher, P., Büchel, C., Josephs, O., Friston, K., & Dolan, R. (1999). Learning-related Neuronal Responses in Prefrontal Cortex Studied with Functional Neuroimaging. *Cerebral Cortex (New York, N.Y.), 9*(2), 168–178. doi:10.1093/cercor/9.2.168 PMID:10220229

Flinn, M. V., Geary, D. C., & Ward, C. V. (2005). Ecological dominance, social competition, and coalitionary arms races: Why humans evolved extraordinary intelligence. *Evolution and Human Behavior, 26*(1), 10–46. doi:10.1016/j.evolhumbehav.2004.08.005

Floridi, L. (2016). On human dignity as a foundation for the right to privacy. *Philosophy & Technology, 29*(4), 307–312. doi:10.100713347-016-0220-8

Floridi, L., Cowls, J., Beltrametti, M., Chatila, R., Chazerand, P., Dignum, V., Luetge, C., Madelin, R., Pagallo, U., Rossi, F., Schafer, B., Valcke, P., & Vayena, E. (2018). AI4People---An Ethical Framework for a Good AI Society: Opportunities, Risks, Principles, and Recommendations. *Minds and Machines, 28*(4), 689–707. doi:10.100711023-018-9482-5 PMID:30930541

Floridi, L., Cowls, J., King, T. C., & Taddeo, M. (2020). Designing AI for Social Good: Seven Essential Factors. *Science and Engineering Ethics*, 1–26. doi:10.100711948-020-00213-5 PMID:32246245

Foot, P. (1967). The Problem of Abortion and the Doctrine of Double Effect. *Oxford Review, 5.*

Foster, H., & Jackson, W. (1946, November 12). *Song of the South.* Walt Disney Productions.

Fraedrich, E., Kröger, L., Bahamonde-Birke, F. J., Frenzel, I., Liedtke, G., Trommer, S., Lenz, B., & Heinrichs, D. (2017). *Automatisiertes Fahren im Personen- und Güterverkehr. Auswirkungen auf den Modal-Split, das Verkehrssystem und die Siedlungsstrukturen.* https://elib.dlr.de/117868/

Francis, R. C. (1990). Causes, proximate and ultimate. *Biology & Philosophy, 5*(4), 401–415. doi:10.1007/BF02207379

Frank, A. (2020, June 26). Disney is overhauling Splash Mountain to remove the ride's ties to a racist film. *Vox.com.* https://www.vox.com/culture/2020/6/26/21303247/disney-splash-mountain-redesign-racist-song-of-the-south

Freud, S. (2003). *The uncanny.* Penguin.

Frey, C. B., & Osborne, M. (2013). *The future of employment*. Oxford Martin School. https://www.oxfordmartin.ox.ac.uk/publications/the-future-of-employment/

Friedman, B., & Kahn Jr., P. H. (2002). Value sensitive design: Theory and methods. *University of Washington Technical Report*, 1–8.

Friedman, B., & Kahn, P. H., Jr. (2003). Chapter. In J. A. Jacko & A. Sears (Eds.), The human-computer interaction handbook (pp. 1177–1201). L. Erlbaum Associates Inc., https://dl.acm.org/citation.cfm?id=772072.772147

Friedman, B., Hendry, D. G., & Borning, A. (2017). A Survey of Value Sensitive Design Methods. *Foundations and Trends® in Human–Computer Interaction, 11*(2), 63–125. doi:10.1561/1100000015

Friedman, B., Kahn Jr., P. H., & Borning, A. (2008). Value Sensitive Design and Information Systems. *Human-Computer Interaction and Management Information Systems: Foundations*, 69–101. doi:10.1145/242485.242493

Friedman, B., Kahn, P. H., & Borning, A. (2008). Value sensitive design and information systems. The Handbook of Information and Computer Ethics, 69–101.

Friedman, B., & Grudin, J. (1998). Trust and accountability: preserving human values in interactional experience. In *CHI 98 conference summary on Human factors in computing systems* (p. 213). ACM. doi:10.1145/286498.286699

Friedman, B., & Hendry, D. G. (2019). *Value sensitive design: Shaping technology with moral imagination*. MIT Press. doi:10.7551/mitpress/7585.001.0001

Friedman, B., Kahn, P. H., Borning, A., & Huldtgren, A. (2013). Value Sensitive Design and Information Systems. In N. Doorn, D. Schuurbiers, I. van de Poel, & M. E. Gorman (Eds.), *Early engagement and new technologies: Opening up the laboratory* (pp. 55–95). Springer Netherlands. doi:10.1007/978-94-007-7844-3_4

Frischmann, B., & Selinger, E. (2018). *Re-Engineering humanity*. Cambridge University Press. doi:10.1017/9781316544846

Fuentes, A. (1999). *Evolution of human behavior*. Oxford University Press.

Gallistel, C. R., & Gelman, R. (2000). Non-verbal numerical cognition: From reals to integers. *Trends in Cognitive Sciences, 4*(2), 59–65. doi:10.1016/S1364-6613(99)01424-2 PMID:10652523

Gangemi, A. (2007). Design Patterns for Legal Ontology Constructions. *LOAIT, 2007*, 65–85.

Gangemi, A., Prisco, A., Sagri, M.-T., Steve, G., & Tiscornia, D. (2003). Some Ontological Tools to Support Legal Regulatory Compliance, with a Case Study. In R. Meersman & Z. Tari (Eds.), *On the Move to Meaningful Internet Systems 2003: OTM 2003 Workshops* (Vol. 2889, pp. 607–620). Springer Berlin Heidelberg. doi:10.1007/978-3-540-39962-9_64

Garcia-de-Prado, A., Ortiz, G., & Boubeta-Puig, J. (2017). COLLECT: COLLaborativE ConText-aware service oriented architecture for intelligent decision-making in the Internet of Things. *Expert Systems with Applications, 85*, 231–248. doi:10.1016/j.eswa.2017.05.034

Gazzaneo, L., Padovano, A., & Umbrello, S. (2020). Designing Smart Operator 4.0 for Human Values: A Value Sensitive Design Approach. In *International Conference on Industry 4.0 and Smart Manufacturing (ISM 2019) in Procedia Manufacturing* (pp. 219–226). Elsevier. 10.1016/j.promfg.2020.02.073

Geertz, A. W. (2010). Brain, Body and Culture: A Biocultural Theory of Religion. *Method & Theory in the Study of Religion, 22*(4), 304–321. doi:10.1163/157006810X531094

Gelman, S. A., & Wellman, H. M. (1991). Insides and essences: Early understandings of the non-obvious. *Cognition, 38*(3), 213–244. doi:10.1016/0010-0277(91)90007-Q PMID:2060270

Gerdes, A. (2016). The Role of Phronesis in Robot Ethics. In J. Seibt, M. Nørskov, & S. S. Andersen (Eds.), *What Social Robots Can and Should Do* (pp. 129–135). IOS Press.

Gert, J. (2016, February 8). The definition of morality. *Stanford encyclopedia of philosophy*. https://plato.stanford.edu/entries/morality-definition/#NormDefiMora

Gips, J. (1995). Towards the ethical robot. In K. M. Ford, C. Glymour, & P. Hayes (Eds.), *Android epistemology* (pp. 243–252). MIT Press.

Glennerster, H., & McKnight, A. (2006). A capital start: but how far do we go? In W. Paxton & S. White (Eds.), *The Citizen's Stake: Exploring the Future of Universal Asset Policies* (pp. 87–106). The Policy Press. doi:10.2307/j.ctt1t88x4c.11

Gobet, F., & Chassy, P. (2009). Expertise and Intuition: A Tale of Three Theories. *Minds and Machines*, *19*(2), 151–180. doi:10.100711023-008-9131-5

Goodall, N. J. (2016). Can you program ethics into a self-driving car? *IEEE Spectrum*, *53*(6), 28–58. Advance online publication. doi:10.1109/MSPEC.2016.7473149

Goodman, B., & Flaxman, S. (2016). *European Union regulations on algorithmic decision-making and a 'right to explanation.'* https://arxiv.org/abs/1606.08813

Goram, M., & Veiel, D. (2019). Supporting privacy control and personalized data usage explanations in a context-based adaptive collaboration environment. In G. Bella & P. Bouquet (Eds.), *Modeling and using context* (Vol. 11939, pp. 84–97). Springer International Publishing. doi:10.1007/978-3-030-34974-5_8

Goram, M., & Veiel, D. (2020). Considering Legal Regulations in an Extendable Context-based Adaptive System Environment. In J. Filipe, M. Smialek, A. Brodsky, & S. Hammoudi (Eds.), *Proceedings of the 22nd International Conference on Enterprise Information Systems, ICEIS 2020, Prague, Czech Republic*, May 5-7, 2020 (Vol. 2, pp. 367–376). SCITEPRESS. 10.5220/0009565003670376

Gordon, G. J. (2018). Environmental Personhood. *Columbia Journal of Environmental Law*, *43*, 49.

Gordon, J. (2020). Building moral robots: Ethical pitfalls and challenges. *Science and Engineering Ethics*, *26*(1), 141–157. doi:10.100711948-019-00084-5 PMID:30701408

Graham, J., Haidt, J., Koleva, S., Motyl, M., Iyer, R., Wojcik, S. P., & Ditto, P. H. (2013). Chapter Two - Moral Foundations Theory: The Pragmatic Validity of Moral Pluralism. In P. Devine & A. Plant (Eds.), Advances in Experimental Social Psychology (Vol. 47, pp. 55–130). Academic Press. doi:10.1016/B978-0-12-407236-7.00002-4

Graham, J., Nosek, B. A., Haidt, J., Iyer, R., Koleva, S., & Ditto, P. H. (2011). Mapping the moral domain. *Journal of Personality and Social Psychology*, *101*(2), 366–385. doi:10.1037/a0021847 PMID:21244182

Gray, H. M., Gray, K., & Wegner, D. M. (2007). Dimensions of Mind Perception. *Science*, *315*(5812), 619–619. doi:10.1126cience.1134475 PMID:17272713

Gray, K., Young, L., & Waytz, A. (2012). Mind Perception Is the Essence of Morality. *Psychological Inquiry*, *23*(2), 101–124. doi:10.1080/1047840X.2012.651387 PMID:22754268

Greenberg, A. (2013, Nov. 8). Meet the 'Assassination Market' Creator Who's Crowdfunding Murder with Bitcoins. *Forbes*.

Greene, J. (2007). The Secret Joke of Kant's Soul. In W. Sinnott-Armstrong (Ed.), *Moral Psychology* (Vol. 3). MIT Press.

Greene, J. (2013). *Moral tribes: Emotion, reason, and the gap between us and them*. Penguin Press.

Gregor, P., Sloan, D., & Newell, A. F. (2005). Disability and Technology: Building Barriers or Creating Opportunities? *Advances in Computers, 64*, 283–346. Advance online publication. doi:10.1016/S0065-2458(04)64007-1

Gregor, S., & Benbasat, I. (1999). Explanations from Intelligent Systems: Theoretical Foundations and Implications for Practice. *Management Information Systems Quarterly, 23*(4), 497. doi:10.2307/249487

Grüter, M., von Kriegstein, K., Dogan, Ö., Giraud, A., Kell, C. A., Grüter, T., Kleinschmidt, A., & Kiebel, S. J. (2008). Simulation of talking faces in the human brain improves auditory speech recognition. *Proceedings of the National Academy of Sciences of the United States of America, 105*(18), 6747–6752. doi:10.1073/pnas.0710826105 PMID:18436648

Guillette, S. (2019, December 6). Your new lifeguard may be a robot. *Verizon.*

Guillette, S. (2019, December 6). *Your new lifeguard may be a robot.* Verizon. https://www.verizon.com/about/our-company/fourth-industrial-revolution/your-new-lifeguard-may-be-robot

Gummerum, M., Van Dillen, L. F., Van Dijk, E., & López-Pérez, B. (2016). Costly third-party interventions: The role of incidental anger and attention focus in punishment of the perpetrator and compensation of the victim. *Journal of Experimental Social Psychology, 65*, 94–104. doi:10.1016/j.jesp.2016.04.004

Gunkel, D. (2014). The Other Question: The Issue of Robot Rights. *Sociable Robots and the Future of Social Relations: Proceedings of Robo-Philosophy, 2014*(273), 13.

Gunning, D. (2017). Explainable Artificial Intelligence (XAI). *Data Science Central.* https://www.datasciencecentral.com/profiles/blogs/explainable-artificial-intelligence-xai

Guo, S., & Zhang, G. (2009). Robot Rights. *Science, 323*(5916), 876. doi:10.1126cience.323.5916.876a PMID:19213895

Haake, J. M., Hussein, T., Joop, B., Lukosch, S., Veiel, D., & Ziegler, J. (2010). Modeling and Exploiting Context for Adaptive Collaboration. *International Journal of Cooperative Information Systems, 19*(1-2), 71–120. doi:10.1142/S0218843010002115

Hagendorff, T. (2020). The Ethics of AI Ethics: An Evaluation of Guidelines. *Minds and Machines, 30*(1), 99–120. doi:10.100711023-020-09517-8

Haidt, J. (2001). The Emotional Dog and Its Rational Tail: A Social Intuitionist Approach to Moral Judgment. *Psychological Review, 108*(4), 21. doi:10.1037/0033-295X.108.4.814 PMID:11699120

Haidt, J. (2007). The new synthesis in moral psychology. *Science, 316*(5827), 998–1002. doi:10.1126cience.1137651 PMID:17510357

Haidt, J. (2008). Morality. *Perspectives on Psychological Science, 3*(1), 65–72. doi:10.1111/j.1745-6916.2008.00063.x PMID:26158671

Haidt, J. (2012). *The righteous mind: Why good people are divided by politics and religion.* Vintage.

Haidt, J., Graham, J., & Joseph, C. (2009). Above and Below Left–Right: Ideological Narratives and Moral Foundations. *Psychological Inquiry, 20*(2–3), 110–119. doi:10.1080/10478400903028573

Haidt, J., & Hersh, M. A. (2001). Sexual Morality: The Cultures and Emotions of Conservatives and Liberals. *Journal of Applied Social Psychology, 31*(1), 191–221. Advance online publication. doi:10.1111/j.1559-1816.2001.tb02489.x

Hanson, R. (2008). Economics of the singularity. *IEEE Spectrum, 45*(6), 45–50. doi:10.1109/MSPEC.2008.4531461

Happy Valley. (2020). *Happy Valley Beijing.* http://bj.happyvalley.cn/

Haraway, D. (1991). Cyborg Manifesto: Science, Technology, and Socialist-Feminism in the Late Twentieth Century. In Simians, cyborgs and women: The reinvention of nature (pp. 149-182). Free Association Books.

Harris, M. (2017, November 15). Inside the First Church of Artificial Intelligence. *Wired*.

Haslam, N. (2006). Dehumanization: An Integrative Review. *Personality and Social Psychology Review*, *10*(3), 252–264. doi:10.120715327957pspr1003_4 PMID:16859440

Haslam, N., Loughnan, S., Reynolds, C., & Wilson, S. (2007). Dehumanization: A New Perspective. *Social and Personality Psychology Compass*, *1*(1), 409–422. doi:10.1111/j.1751-9004.2007.00030.x

Heidegger, M. (1996). The Question Concerning Technology. In *Basic writings* (pp. 311–341). Routledge.

Helkama, K. (2009). *Moraalipsykologia: Hyvän ja pahan tällä puolen*. Edita Publishing Oy.

Hersman, D. (2019). *Safety at Waymo | Self-driving cars & other road users*. Waymo. https://blog.waymo.com/2019/08/safety-at-waymo-self-driving-cars-other.html

Hirschfeld, L. A., & Gelman, S. A. (Eds.). (1994). *Mapping the mind*. Cambridge University Press. doi:10.1017/CBO9780511752902

Hjerppe, K., Ruohonen, J., & Leppanen, V. (2019). The General Data Protection Regulation: Requirements, Architectures, and Constraints. *2019 IEEE 27th International Requirements Engineering Conference (RE)*, 265–275. 10.1109/RE.2019.00036

Hoepman, J.-H. (2014). Privacy Design Strategies. In N. Cuppens-Boulahia, F. Cuppens, S. Jajodia, A. Abou El Kalam, & T. Sans (Eds.), *ICT Systems Security and Privacy Protection* (Vol. 428, pp. 446–459). Springer Berlin Heidelberg. doi:10.1007/978-3-642-55415-5_38

Hoffman, D. (2019). *The case against reality: Why evolution hid the truth from our eyes*. W. W. Norton and Company.

Holstein, T., & Dodig-Crnkovic, G. (2018). *Avoiding the intrinsic unfairness of the trolley problem*. doi:10.1145/3194770.3194772

Holstein, T., Dodig-Crnkovic, G., & Pelliccione, P. (2018). Ethical and Social Aspects of Self-Driving Cars. *ArXiv E-Prints*. https://arxiv.org/abs/1802.04103

Horst, S. (2016). *Cognitive pluralism*. The MIT Press. https://muse.jhu.edu/book/46963

Hughes, J. J. (2014). A strategic opening for a basic income guarantee in the global crisis being created by AI, robots, desktop manufacturing and biomedicine. *Journal of Evolution and Technology / WTA*, *24*(1), 45–61. https://jetpress.org/v24/hughes2.htm

Hussain, S. S., Veiel, D., Haake, J. M., & Lukosch, S. (2010). Facilitating understanding of team-based adaptation policies. *Proceedings from the 6th International ICST Conference on Collaborative Computing: Networking, Applications, Worksharing*. 10.4108/icst.collaboratecom.2010.60

Huxley, J. (1957). Transhumanism. In *New bottles for new wine*. Chatto & Windus.

Hyppönen, H., Kemppainen, E., Gill, J., Slater, J., & Poulson, D. (2000). H. Hyppönen, E. Kemppainen, J. Gill, J. Slater, & D. Poulson (Eds.) Handbook on inclusive design of telematics applications. Themes/STAKES 2.

Ilievski, N. L. (2015). The Individual Sovereignty: Conceptualization and Manifestation. *Journal of Liberty & International Affairs*, *1*(2), 23–38.

Ingram, H., deLeon, P., & Schneider, A. (2016). Conclusion: Public policy theory and democracy: The elephant in the corner. In Contemporary approaches to public policy (pp. 175–200). Springer.

Islam, M. A., & Rashid, S. I. (2018). Algorithm for Ethical Decision Making at Times of Accidents for Autonomous Vehicles. *2018 4th International Conference on Electrical Engineering and Information Communication Technology (ICEEiCT)*, 438–442. 10.1109/CEEICT.2018.8628155

ISO. (2018). ISO 26262 -- Road vehicles -- Functional safety (Issue ISO 26262). ISO, Geneva, Switzerland.

ISO. (2019). *ISO/PAS 21448:2019 -- Road vehicles -- Safety of the intended functionality* (Issue ISO/PAS 21448:2019). ISO, Geneva, Switzerland. https://www.iso.org/standard/70939.html

Jensen, C. B., & Blok, A. (2013). Techno-animism in Japan: Shinto Cosmograms, Actor-network Theory, and the Enabling Powers of Non-human Agencies. *Theory, Culture & Society*, *30*(2), 84–115. doi:10.1177/0263276412456564

Jensen, L., & Weston, T. (2007). *China's transformations: The stories beyond the headlines*. Rowan & Littlefield.

Jiang, X., & Landay, J. A. (2002). Modeling privacy control in context-aware systems. *IEEE Pervasive Computing*, *1*(3), 59–63. doi:10.1109/MPRV.2002.1037723

Jobin, A., Ienca, M., & Vayena, E. (2019). The global landscape of AI ethics guidelines. *Nature Machine Intelligence*, *1*(9), 389–399. doi:10.103842256-019-0088-2

Johansson, R., & Nilsson, J. (2016). Disarming the Trolley Problem --Why Self-driving Cars do not Need to Choose Whom to Kill. In M. Roy (Ed.), *Workshop CARS 2016 - Critical automotive applications: Robustness & safety*. https://hal.archives-ouvertes.fr/hal-01375606

Johnsen, A., Dodig-Crnkovic, G., Lundqvist, K., Hanninen, K., & Pettersson, P. (2017). Risk-based decision-making fallacies: Why present functional safety standards are not enough. *Proceedings - 2017 IEEE International Conference on Software Architecture Workshops, ICSAW 2017: Side Track Proceedings*. 10.1109/ICSAW.2017.50

Kafka, F. (2005). In the Penal Colony. In N. N. Glatzer (Ed.), *Franz Kafka: The omplete short stories* (pp. 140–167). Vintage Books.

Kahane, G., Everett, J. A. C., Earp, B. D., Farias, M., & Savulescu, J. (2015). 'Utilitarian' judgments in sacrificial moral dilemmas do not reflect impartial concern for the greater good. *Cognition*, *134*, 193–209. doi:10.1016/j.cognition.2014.10.005 PMID:25460392

Kahneman, D., & Klein, G. (2009). Conditions for intuitive expertise: A failure to disagree. *The American Psychologist*, *64*(6), 515–526. doi:10.1037/a0016755 PMID:19739881

Kahn, P. H., Reichert, A. L., Gary, H. E., Kanda, T., Ishiguro, H., Shen, S., Ruckert, J. H., & Gill, B. (2011). The new ontological category hypothesis in human-robot interaction. *Proceedings of the 6th International Conference on Human-Robot Interaction - HRI '11*, 159. 10.1145/1957656.1957710

Kalra, N., & Paddock, S. M. (2016). Driving to safety: How many miles of driving would it take to demonstrate autonomous vehicle reliability? *Transportation Research Part A, Policy and Practice*, *94*(Supplement C), 182–193. doi:10.1016/j.tra.2016.09.010

Kanso, H. (2017). *Saudi women riled by robot with no hjiab and more rights than them*. https://www.reuters.com/article/us-saudi-robot-citizenship/saudi-women-riled-by-robot-with-no-hjiab-and-more-rights-than-them-idUSKBN1D14Z7

Kantardzic, M., Walgampaya, C., Yampolskiy, R., & Woo, R. J. (2010). *Click Fraud Prevention via multimodal evidence fusion by Dempster-Shafer theory.* Paper presented at the Multisensor Fusion and Integration for Intelligent Systems (MFI), 2010 IEEE Conference. 10.1109/MFI.2010.5604480

Kapitsaki, G. M. (2013). Reflecting User Privacy Preferences in Context-Aware Web Services. *2013 IEEE 20th International Conference on Web Services*, 123–130. 10.1109/ICWS.2013.26

Kapitsaki, G., Ioannou, J., Cardoso, J., & Pedrinaci, C. (2018). Linked USDL Privacy: Describing Privacy Policies for Services. *2018 IEEE International Conference on Web Services (ICWS)*, 50–57. 10.1109/ICWS.2018.00014

Kapteyn, A., Kalwij, A., & Zaidi, A. (2004). The myth of work sharing. *Labour Economics*, *11*(3), 293–313. doi:10.1016/j.labeco.2003.08.001

Karl, T. L. (2000). Economic inequality and democratic instability. *Journal of Democracy*, *11*(1), 149–156. doi:10.1353/jod.2000.0014

Karnouskos, S. (2018). Self-Driving Car Acceptance and the Role of Ethics. *IEEE Transactions on Engineering Management*, 1–14. doi:10.1109/TEM.2018.2877307

Kass, L. R. (2003). Ageless Bodies, Happy Souls: Biotechnology and the Pursuit of Perfection. *New Atlantis (Washington, D.C.)*, *1*, 9–28. PMID:15584192

Kasson, J. (1978). *Amusing the million: Coney Island at the turn of the century.* Hill & Wang.

Keesing, R., & Strathern, A. J. (1997). *Cultural anthropology: A contemporary perspective* (3rd ed.). Wadsworth Publishing.

Keltner, D., Haidt, J., & Shiota, M. N. (2006). Social functionalism and the evolution of emotions. In M. Schaller, J. A. Simpson, & D. T. Kendrick (Eds.), *Evolution and social psychology* (pp. 115–142). Psychology Press.

Kim, R., Kleiman-Weiner, M., Abeliuk, A., Awad, E., Dsouza, S., Tenenbaum, J. B., & Rahwan, I. (2018). A Computational Model of Commonsense Moral Decision Making. *Proceedings of the 2018 AAAI/ACM Conference on AI, Ethics, and Society*, 197–203. 10.1145/3278721.3278770

Kim, T. W., & Scheller-Wolf, A. (2019). Technological unemployment, meaning in life, purpose of business, and the future of stakeholders. *Journal of Business Ethics*, *160*(2), 319–337. doi:10.100710551-019-04205-9

Kirchgässner, G. (2009). Critical analysis of some well-intended proposals to fight unemployment. *Analyse & Kritik*, *31*(1), 25–48. doi:10.1515/auk-2009-0102

Kittler, F. (1999). *Gramophone, film, typewriter* (G. Winthrop-Young & M. Wutz, Trans.). Stanford University Press.

Klimczuk-Kochańska, M., & Klimczuk, A. (2015). Technological unemployment. In M. Odekon (Ed.), *The SAGE encyclopedia of world poverty* (2nd ed., pp. 1510–1511). SAGE Publications Ltd.

Koenigs, M., Young, L., Adolphs, R., Tranel, D., Cushman, F., Hauser, M., & Damasio, A. (2007). Damage to the prefrontal cortex increases utilitarian moral judgements. *Nature*, *446*(7138), 908–911. doi:10.1038/nature05631 PMID:17377536

Ko, K. H. (2016). Origins of human intelligence: The chain of tool-making and brain evolution. *Anthropological Notebooks*, 5–22.

Koverola, M., Kunnari, A., Drosinou, M., Palomäki, J., Hannikainen, I., Sundvall, J., & Laakasuo, M. (2020b, June 30). *Non-Human Superhumans - Moral Psychology of Brain Implants: Exploring the role of situational factors, science fiction exposure, individual differences and perceived norms.* doi:10.31234/osf.io/qgz9c

Koverola, M., Drosinou, M., Palomäki, J., Halonen, J., Kunnari, A., Repo, M., Lehtonen, N., & Laakasuo, M. (2020a). Moral psychology of sex robots: An experimental study – how pathogen disgust is associated with interhuman sex but not interandroid sex. *Paladyn: Journal of Behavioral Robotics, 11*(1), 233–249. doi:10.1515/pjbr-2020-0012

Koverola, M., Kunnari, A., & Palomäki, J. (in press). Moral Psychology of Sex Robots: an experimental study – How Pathogen Disgust is associated with interhuman sex but not interandroid sex. *PALADYN – Journal of Behavioral Robotics.*

Kroll, J. (2018). The fallacy of inscrutability. *Philosophical Transactions, Royal Society A, 376*. https://royalsocietypublishing.org/doi/full/10.1098/rsta.2018.0084 PMID:30322999

Kroll, J. (in press). Accountability in Computer Systems. In M. D. Dubber, F. Pasquale, & S. Das (Eds.), *The Oxford handbook of ethics of AI.* Oxford University Press.

Kurzweil, R. (2000). *The age of spiritual machines: When computers exceed human intelligence.* Penguin.

Kurzweil, R. (2012). *How to create a mind: The secret of human thought revealed.* Viking Penguing.

Laakasuo, M., Drosinou, M., Koverola, M., Kunnari, A., Halonen, J., Lehtonen, N., & Palomäki, J. (2018). What makes people approve or condemn mind upload technology? Untangling the effects of sexual disgust, purity and science fiction familiarity. *Palgrave Communications, 4*(1), 1–14. doi:10.105741599-018-0124-6

Laakasuo, M., Köbis, N., Palomäki, J., & Jokela, M. (2018). Money for microbes-Pathogen avoidance and out-group helping behaviour. *International Journal of Psychology, 53*, 1–10. doi:10.1002/ijop.12416 PMID:28229500

Lambert, B. (1992, March 16). C. V. Wood Jr., who pioneered large theme parks, is dead at 71. *The New York Times.* https://www.nytimes.com/1992/03/16/us/c-v-wood-jr-who-pioneered-large-theme-parks-is-dead-at-71.html

Landy, J. F., & Goodwin, G. P. (2015). Does Incidental Disgust Amplify Moral Judgment? A Meta-Analytic Review of Experimental Evidence. *Perspectives on Psychological Science, 10*(4), 518–536. doi:10.1177/1745691615583128 PMID:26177951

Lawson, E. T., & McCauley, R. N. (1990). *Rethinking religion: Connecting cognition and culture.* Cambridge University Press.

Lee, S.-H., & Wolpoff, M. H. (2003). The pattern of evolution in Pleistocene human brain size. *Paleobiology, 29*(2), 186–196. doi:10.1017/S0094837300018054

Leveson, N. (2011). *Engineering a safer world: Systems thinking applied to safety.* MIT press.

Leveson, N. (2020). Are You Sure Your Software Will Not Kill Anyone? *Communications of the ACM, 63*(2), 25–28. doi:10.1145/3376127

Levy, D. (2007). *Love and sex with robots.* Harper Collins.

Levy, D. (2008). *Love and sex with robots: The evolution of human-robot relationships.* Harper Perennial.

Levy, F., & Murnane, R. J. (2004). *The new division of labor: How computers are creating the next job market.* Princeton University Press. doi:10.1515/9781400845927

Lew, A. A., Yu, L., Ap, J., & Zhang, G. (2003). *Tourism in China.* The Haworth Hospitality Press.

Lewis-Williams, D. (2002). *The mind in the cave: Consciousness and the origins of art.* Thames & Hudson.

Li, L., Lv, Y., & Wang, F. Y. (2016). Traffic signal timing via deep reinforcement learning. *IEEE/CAA Journal of Automatica Sinica, 3*(3), 247-254.

Licata, M., Zietlow, A.-L., Träuble, B., Sodian, B., & Reck, C. (2016). Maternal Emotional Availability and Its Association with Maternal Psychopathology, Attachment Style Insecurity and Theory of Mind. *Psychopathology, 49*(5), 334–340. doi:10.1159/000447781 PMID:27498091

Lim, B. Y., & Dey, A. K. (2010). Toolkit to support intelligibility in context-aware applications. *Proceedings from the 12th ACM International Conference on Ubiquitous Computing - Ubicomp '10*, 13. 10.1145/1864349.1864353

Lin, P., Mehlman, M., Abney, K., French, S., Vallor, S., Galliott, J., Burnam-Fink, M., LaCroix, A. R., & Schuknecht, S. (2014). Super Soldiers (Part 2): The Ethical, Legal, and Operational Implications. In S. J. Thompson (Ed.), *Global Issues and Ethical Considerations in Human Enhancement Technologies* (pp. 139–160). IGI Global. doi:10.4018/978-1-4666-6010-6.ch008

Lin, S.-J., & Hsu, M.-F. (2017). Incorporated risk metrics and hybrid AI techniques for risk management. *Neural Computing & Applications, 28*(11), 3477–3489. doi:10.100700521-016-2253-4

Lippert, C., Sabatini, R., Maher, M. C., Kang, E. Y., Lee, S., Arikan, O., Harley, A., Bernal, A., Garst, P., Lavrenko, V., Yocum, K., Wong, T., Zhu, M., Yang, W.-Y., Chang, C., Lu, T., Lee, C. W. H., Hicks, B., & Ramakrishnan, S., … Venter, J. C. (2017). Identification of individuals by trait prediction using whole-genome sequencing data. *Proceedings of the National Academy of Sciences, 114*(38), 10166–10171. 10.1073/pnas.1711125114

Liyanage, H., Liaw, S. T., Jonnagaddala, J., Schreiber, R., Kuziemsky, C., Terry, A. L., & de Lusignan, S. (2019). *..Artificial Intelligence in Primary Health Care: Perceptions, Issues, and Challenges, i*, 41–46. doi:10.1055-0039-1677901 PMID:31022751

Lockton, D., Harrison, D., & Stanton, N. A. (2016). Design for Sustainable Behaviour: Investigating design methods for influencing user behaviour. *Annual Review of Policy Design, 4*(1), 1–10.

LoPucki, L. M. (2018). Algorithmic Entities. *Washington University Law Review, 95*(4).

Loughnan, S., Haslam, N., Murnane, T., Vaes, J., Reynolds, C., & Suitner, C. (2010). Objectification leads to depersonalization: The denial of mind and moral concern to objectified others. *European Journal of Social Psychology, 40*(5), 709–717. doi:10.1002/ejsp.755

Lovett, F. (2010). *A general theory of domination and justice*. Oxford University Press. doi:10.1093/acprof:oso/9780199579419.001.0001

Luetge, C. (2017). The German Ethics Code for Automated and Connected Driving. *Philosophy & Technology, 30*(4), 547–558. doi:10.100713347-017-0284-0

Malle, B. F., Magar, S. T., & Scheutz, M. (2019). AI in the Sky: How People Morally Evaluate Human and Machine Decisions in a Lethal Strike Dilemma. In M. Aldinhas Ferreira, J. Silva Sequeira, G. Singh Virk, M. Tokhi, & E. Kadar (Eds.), *Robotics and Well-Being*. Springer. doi:10.1007/978-3-030-12524-0_11

Mangasarian, O. L., Setiono, R., & Wolberg, W. H. (1990). *Pattern Recognition Via Linear Programming: Theory And Application To Medical Diagnosis*. Academic Press.

Mangels, W. (1952). *The outdoor amusement industry*. Vantage Press Inc.

Marchant, G. E., Stevens, Y. A., & Hennessy, J. M. (2014). Technology, unemployment, and policy options: Navigating the transition to a better world. *Journal of Evolution and Technology / WTA, 21*(1), 26–44. https://jetpress.org/v24/marchant.htm

Marinetti, T. (1912). *Futurist manifest*. Sackville Gallery.

Markoff, J. (2011, March 4). Armies of expansive lawyers, replaced by software. *New York Times*. https://www.nytimes.com/2011/03/05/science/05legal.html

Markram, H., Muller, E., Ramaswamy, S., Reimann, M. W., Abdellah, M., Sanchez, C. A., Ailamaki, A., Alonso-Nanclares, L., Antille, N., Arsever, S., Kahou, G. A. A., Berger, T. K., Bilgili, A., Buncic, N., Chalimourda, A., Chindemi, G., Courcol, J.-D., Delalondre, F., Delattre, V., ... Schürmann, F. (2015). Reconstruction and Simulation of Neocortical Microcircuitry. *Cell*, *163*(2), 456–492. doi:10.1016/j.cell.2015.09.029 PMID:26451489

Martin, K. (2019). Ethical Implications and Accountability of Algorithms. *Journal of Business Ethics*, *160*(4), 835–850. doi:10.100710551-018-3921-3

Marx, K. (2015). Foundations of the critique of political economy (Grundrisse) (M. Nicolaus, Trans.). Penguin Books in association with New Left Review.

Marx, K. (1990). *The capital*. Penguin.

McAuliffe, W. H. B. (2019). Do emotions play an essential role in moral judgments? *Thinking & Reasoning*, *25*(2), 207–230. doi:10.1080/13546783.2018.1499552

McBride, N. (2016). The Ethics of Driverless Cars. *SIGCAS Comput. Soc.*, *45*(3), 179–184. doi:10.1145/2874239.2874265

McCarthy, J., Minsky, M. L., Rochester, N., & Shannon, C. E. (1955). A Proposal for the Dartmouth Summer Research Project on Artificial Intelligence. *AI Magazine*, *27*(4), 12–14.

McCauley, R. N., & Whitehouse, H. (2005). New frontiers in the cognitive science of religion. *Journal of Cognition and Culture*, *5*(1-2), 1–13. doi:10.1163/1568537054068705

McConnell, A. (2010). *Understanding policy success: Rethinking public policy*. Macmillan International Higher Education. doi:10.1007/978-1-137-08228-2

McDermott, D. (2008). Why Ethics is a High Hurdle for AI. *North American Conference on Computers and Philosophy*, 1-8. https://www.cs.yale.edu/homes/dvm/papers/ethical-machine.pdf

Meade, J. (1989). *Agathotopia: The economics of partnership*. University of Aberdeen.

Mele, C. (2016). Pepe the Frog Meme Listed as a Hate Symbol. *The New York Times*. http://www.nytimes.com/2016/09/28/us/pepe-the-frog-is-listed-as-a-hate-symbol-by-the-anti-defamation-league.html

Melson, G. F., Kahn, P. H. Jr, Beck, A., Friedman, B., Roberts, T., Garrett, E., & Gill, B. T. (2009). Children's behavior toward and understanding of robotic and living dogs. *Journal of Applied Developmental Psychology*, *30*(2), 92–102. doi:10.1016/j.appdev.2008.10.011

Merz, J. (2012). Andreas Fischer: Rules, Roles and Routines. In J. Merz (Ed.), *In the wool (In der Wolle)* (pp. 11–58). Museum Ludwig.

Microsoft. (2020). *AI for Good - Providing technology, resources, and expertise to empower those working to solve humanitarian issues and create a more sustainable and accessible world*. https://www.microsoft.com/en-us/ai/ai-for-good

Mikhail, J. (2007). Universal moral grammar: Theory, evidence and the future. *Trends in Cognitive Sciences*, *11*(4), 143–152. doi:10.1016/j.tics.2006.12.007 PMID:17329147

Mill, J. S. (1861). Utilitarianism. *Fraser's Magazine, 64,* 391–406; 525–534; 659–673.

Miller, T. (2018). *Explanation in Artificial Intelligence: Insights from the Social Sciences*. https://arxiv.org/pdf/1706.07269.pdf

Ministry of Infrastructure & Environment – Netherlands. (2017, May 18). *On our way towards connected and automated driving in Europe*. https://www.government.nl/binaries/government/documents/leaflets/2017/05/18/on-our-way-towards-connected-and-automated-driving-in-europe/On+our+way+towards+connected+and+automated+driving+in+Europe.pdf

Mintrom, M., & Luetjens, J. (2017). Creating public value: Tightening connections between policy design and public management. *Policy Studies Journal: the Journal of the Policy Studies Organization, 45*(1), 170–190. doi:10.1111/psj.12116

Mirnig, A. G., & Meschtscherjakov, A. (2019). Trolled by the Trolley Problem: On What Matters for Ethical Decision Making in Automated Vehicles. *Proceedings of the 2019 CHI Conference on Human Factors in Computing Systems.* 10.1145/3290605.3300739

MIT Moral Machine Lab. (2016). *Moral Machine*. Massachusetts Institute of Technology Media Laboratory. https://moralmachine.mit.edu/

Mitchell, R. (1998). Learning through play and pleasure travel: Using play literature to enhance research into touristic learning. *Current Issues in Tourism, 1*(2), 176–188. doi:10.1080/13683509808667838

Mitchell, S. D. (2003). *Biological complexity and integrative pluralism* (1st ed.). Cambridge University Press. doi:10.1017/CBO9780511802683

Mittelstadt, B. D., Allo, P., Taddeo, M., Wachter, S., & Floridi, L. (2016). The ethics of algorithms: Mapping the debate. *Big Data & Society, 3*(2), 2053951716679679. doi:10.1177/2053951716679679

Mohun, A. (2013). Amusement Parks for the World: The Export of American Technology and Know-How, 1900—1939. *Icon (London, England), 19*, 100–112.

Moll, H., & Tomasello, M. (2010). Infant cognition. *Current Biology, 20*(20), R872–R875. doi:10.1016/j.cub.2010.09.001 PMID:20971425

Monroe, A., Guglielmo, S., & Malle, B. (2012). Morality Goes Beyond Mind Perception. *Psychological Inquiry, 23*(2), 179–184. doi:10.1080/1047840X.2012.668271

Mooney, C. (2016, June 23). Save the driver or save the crowd? Scientists wonder how driverless cars will 'choose.' *The Washington Post.* https://www.washingtonpost.com/news/energy-environment/wp/2016/06/23/save-the-driver-or-save-the-crowd-scientists-wonder-how-driverless-cars-will-choose/

Moore, G. E. (1998). Cramming more components onto integrated circuits. *Proceedings of the IEEE, 86*(1), 82–85. doi:10.1109/JPROC.1998.658762

Moor, J. H. (1985). What Is Computer Ethics?*. *Metaphilosophy, 16*(4), 266–275. doi:10.1111/j.1467-9973.1985.tb00173.x

Moor, J. H. (2006). The Nature, Importance, and Difficulty of Machine Ethics. *IEEE Intelligent Systems, 21*(4), 18–21. doi:10.1109/MIS.2006.80

Moravec, H. (1988). *Mind children: The future of robot and human intelligence.* Harvard University Press.

More, M. (2010). The Overhuman in the Transhuman. *Journal of Evolution and Technology / WTA, 21*(1), 1–4.

Mori, M. (2012). The Uncanny Valley (K. F. MacDorman & N. Kageki, Trans.). *IEEE Spectrum.* https://spectrum.ieee.org/automaton/robotics/humanoids/the-uncanny-valley

Mori, M. (1970). The uncanny valley. *Energy, 7*(4), 33–35.

Morris, J. K., & Springett, A. (2014). *The National Down Syndrome Cytogenetic Register.* Academic Press.

Moscardo, G. (1996). Mindful visitors: Heritage and tourism. *Annals of Tourism Research, 23*(2), 376–397. doi:10.1016/0160-7383(95)00068-2

Muehlhauser, L., & Bostrom, N. (2014). Why We Need Friendly AI. *Think (London, England), 13*(36), 41–47. doi:10.1017/S1477175613000316

Muir, B. M. (1994). Trust in automation: Part I. Theoretical issues in the study of trust and human intervention in automated systems. *Ergonomics, 37*(11), 1905–1922. doi:10.1080/00140139408964957

Müller, V. (2020). Ethics of artificial intelligence and robotics. In E. N. Zalta (Ed.), *Stanford encyclopedia of philosophy*. Stanford University.

Müller, V. C., & Bostrom, N. (2016). Future Progress in Artificial Intelligence: A Survey of Expert Opinion. In V. C. Müller (Ed.), *Fundamental issues of artificial intelligence* (pp. 555–572). Springer International Publishing., doi:10.1007/978-3-319-26485-1_33

Mumford, L. (1922). *The city. Civilization in the United States: An Inquiry by 30 Americans* (H. E. Stearns, Ed.). Harcourt Brace & Company. https://ia800302.us.archive.org/10/items/civilizationinun00stea/ civilizationinun00stea.pdf

Musk, E. (2016, July 20). *Master Plan Part Deux*. https://www.tesla.com/blog/master-plan-part-deux

National Center for Statistics and Analysis. (2018). *Critical Reasons for Crashes Investigated in the National Motor Vehicle Crash Causation Survey* (DOT HS 812 506). National Highway Traffic Safety Administration. https://crashstats.nhtsa.dot.gov/Api/Public/ViewPublication/812506

National Highway Traffic Safety Administration. (2020). *Automated Vehicles for Safety*. https://www.nhtsa.gov/technology-innovation/automated-vehicles-safety

Nissenbaum, H. (2009). *Privacy in context: Technology, policy, and the integrity of social life*. Stanford University Press.

Nooshin, L. (2004). Circumnavigation with a Difference? Music, Representation and the Disney Experience: "It's a Small, Small World." *Ethnomusicology Forum, 13*(2), 236.

Noothigattu, R., Gaikwad, S., Awad, E., Dsouza, S., Rahwan, I., Ravikumar, P., & Procaccia, A. (2018). *A Voting-Based System for Ethical Decision Making*. https://arxiv.org/abs/1709.06692

Norenzayan, A., Shariff, A. F., Gervais, W. M., Willard, A. K., McNamara, R. A., Slingerland, E., & Henrich, J. (2016). The cultural evolution of prosocial religions. *Behavioral and Brain Sciences, 39*, e1. doi:10.1017/S0140525X14001356 PMID:26785995

O'Connell, M. (2017). *To be a machine: Adventures among cyborgs, utopians, hackers, and the futurists solving the modest problem of death*. Granta Publications.

Oberle, D., Drefs, F., Wacker, R., Baumann, C., & Raabe, O. (2012). Engineering Compliant Software: Advising Developers by Automating Legal Reasoning. *SCRIPTed, 9*(3), 280–313. doi:10.2966crip.090312.280

OECD. (2013). *Supporting investment in knowledge capital, growth and innovation*. OECD Publishing.

OECD. (2016). *ICTs and jobs: Complements or substitutes*. Digital Economy Papers., doi:10.1787/5jlwnklzplhg-

Orban, G. A., & Caruana, F. (2014). The neural basis of human tool use. *Frontiers in Psychology, 5*. Advance online publication. doi:10.3389/fpsyg.2014.00310 PMID:24782809

Palomäki, J., Laakasuo, M., Cowley, B. U., & Lappi, O. (2020). Poker as a Domain of Expertise. Journal of Expertise/ March, 3(2).

Palomäki, J., Kunnari, A., Drosinou, M., Koverola, M., Lehtonen, N., Halonen, J., Repo, M., & Laakasuo, M. (2018). Evaluating the replicability of the uncanny valley effect. *Heliyon*, *4*(11), e00939. Advance online publication. doi:10.1016/j.heliyon.2018.e00939 PMID:30519654

Pan, G., Zhang, L., Wu, Z., Li, S., Yang, L., Lin, M., & Shi, Y. (2014). Pervasive Service Bus: Smart SOA Infrastructure for Ambient Intelligence. *IEEE Intelligent Systems*, *29*(4), 52–60. doi:10.1109/MIS.2012.119

Parfit, D. (2001). Equality or Priority? In J. Harris (Ed.), *Bioethics* (pp. 347–386). Oxford University Press.

Partridge, E. (2014). Social Sustainability. In A. C. Michalos (Ed.), *Encyclopedia of Quality of Life and Well-Being Research* (pp. 6178–6186). Springer Netherlands. doi:10.1007/978-94-007-0753-5_2790

Pasquale, F. (2015). *The black box society: The secret algorithms that control money and information.* Harvard University Press. doi:10.4159/harvard.9780674736061

Patil, I., & Silani, G. (2014). Reduced empathic concern leads to utilitarian moral judgments in trait alexithymia. *Frontiers in Psychology*, *5*. doi:10.3389/fpsyg.2014.00501 PMID:24904510

Paulhus, D. L., & Jones, D. N. (2015). Measures of Dark Personalities. In G. J. Boyle, D. H. Saklofske, & G. Matthews (Eds.), *Measures of Personality and Social Psychological Constructs* (pp. 562–594). Academic Press. doi:10.1016/B978-0-12-386915-9.00020-6

Pelliccione, P., Knauss, E., Heldal, R., Ågren, S. M., Mallozzi, P., Alminger, A., & Borgentun, D. (2017). Automotive Architecture Framework: The experience of Volvo Cars. *Journal of Systems Architecture*, *77*(Supplement C), 83–100. doi:10.1016/j.sysarc.2017.02.005

Perkins, A. M., Leonard, A. M., Weaver, K., Dalton, J. A., Mehta, M. A., Kumari, V., Williams, S. C. R., & Ettinger, U. (2013). A dose of ruthlessness: Interpersonal moral judgment is hardened by the anti-anxiety drug lorazepam. *Journal of Experimental Psychology. General*, *142*(3), 612–620. doi:10.1037/a0030256 PMID:23025561

Perry, J. (2013). *Ten responses to the technological unemployment problem.* Institute for Ethics and Emerging Technologies. http://declineofscarcity.com/?p=2790

Peters, B. G. (2018). *Policy problems and policy design.* Edward Elgar Publishing. doi:10.4337/9781786431356

Pettit, P. (2007). A republican right to basic income? *Basic Income Studies*, *2*(2). https://www.degruyter.com/downloadpdf/j/bis.2008.2.2/bis.2008.2.2.1082/bis.2008.2.2.1082.pdf

Pfeifer, R., & Bongard, J. (2006). *How the body shapes the way we think: A new view of intelligence.* MIT Press. doi:10.7551/mitpress/3585.001.0001

Pfister, W. (2014, April 10). *Transcendence.* Warner Bros. Pictures.

Philips, D. (1999). Narrativized spaces: The function of story in the theme park. In D. Crouch (Ed.), *Leisure/ tourism geographies: Practices and geographical knowledge* (pp. 91–108). Routledge.

Phua, C., Lee, V., Smith, K., & Gayler, R. (2010). A comprehensive survey of data mining-based fraud detection research. *arXiv preprint, 1009*(6119). https://arxiv.org/ftp/arxiv/papers/1009/1009.6119.pdf

Piketty, T. (2015). About capital in the twenty-first century. *The American Economic Review*, *105*(5), 48–53. doi:10.1257/aer.p20151060

Pillath, S. (2016). Briefing: Automated vehicles in the EU. *European Parliamentary Research Service (EPRS)*. https://www.europarl.europa.eu/RegData/etudes/BRIE/2016/573902/EPRS_BRI(2016)573902_EN.pdf

Pinker, S. (1994). *The language instinct*. William Morrow and Company. doi:10.1037/e412952005-009

Pinker, S. (1997). *How the mind works*. W. W. Norton and Company.

Pinker, S. (2002). *The blank slate: The modern denial of human nature*. Penguin Books.

Pistono, F., & Yampolskiy, R. V. (2016). *Unethical Research: How to Create a Malevolent Artificial Intelligence*. Paper presented at the 25th International Joint Conference on Artificial Intelligence (IJCAI-16). Ethics for Artificial Intelligence Workshop (AI-Ethics-2016).

Pitman, T., Broomhall, S., McEwan, J., & Majocha, E. (2010). Adult learning in educational tourism. *Australian Journal of Adult Learning*, *50*(2).

Plato. (2000). *The republic*. Cambridge University Press.

Plyusnin, I., Evans, A. R., Karme, A., Gionis, A., & Jernvall, J. (2008). Automated 3D Phenotype Analysis Using Data Mining. *PLoS One*, *3*(3), e1742. doi:10.1371/journal.pone.0001742

Poon, S. H., Jondeau, E., & Rockinger, M. (2007). *Financial modelling under non-Gaussian distributions*. Springer Science & Business Media.

Prabhakar, R. (2018). Are basic capital versus basic income debates too narrow? *Basic Income Studies*, *13*(1). Advance online publication. doi:10.1515/bis-2018-0015

Prentice, C. (2014). *The lost tribe of Coney Island: Headhunters, Luna Park, and the man who pulled off the spectacle of the century*. Amazon Publishing.

Purzycki, B. G., Apicella, C., Atkinson, Q. D., Cohen, E., McNamara, R. A., Willard, A. K., Xygalatas, D., Norenzayan, A., & Henrich, J. (2016). Moralistic gods, supernatural punishment and the expansion of human sociality. *Nature*, *530*(7590), 327–330. doi:10.1038/nature16980 PMID:26863190

Quah, E., & Mishan, E. J. (2007). *Cost-benefit analysis*. Routledge.

Rabinovitz, L. (2012). *Electric dreamland*. Columbia University Press.

Rafael, M. (2013). *Pierre Huyghe: On site*. Walter König.

Rajtz, T., Smith, M., & Mihalka, G. (2008). New places in old spaces: Mapping tourism and regeneration in Budapest. *Tourism Geographies*, *10*(4), 429–451. doi:10.1080/14616680802434064

Ramamoorthy, A., & Yampolskiy, R. (2018). Beyond MAD? The race for artificial general intelligence. *ICT Discoveries, 1*.

Raunig, G. (2010). *A thousand machines* (A. Derieg, Trans.). Semiotext(e).

Raventós, D. (2007). *Basic income: The material conditions of freedom*. Pluto.

Rawls, J. (2001). *Justice as fairness: A restatement*. Harvard University Press.

Rayman, J. (2017). Žižek's Ethics. *International Journal of Žižek Studies*, *11*(2). http://zizekstudies.org/index.php/IJZS/article/view/1002/0

RCDB. (2020). Roller Coaster Database Search Results: China. *Roller Coaster Database*. https://rcdb.com/r.htm?order=10&ot=3&ol=26380

Regalado, A. (2018, April 2). DNA tests for IQ are coming, but it might not be smart to take one. *Technology Review*. https://www.technologyreview.com/s/610339/dna-tests-for-iq-are-coming-but-it-might-not-be-smart-to-take-one/

Register, W. (2001, October 18). *The kid of Coney Island: Fred Thompson and the Rise of American amusements.* Oxford: Oxford University Press.

Regulation, G. D. P. (2016). Regulation (EU) 2016/679 of the European Parliament and of the Council of 27 April 2016 on the protection of natural persons with regard to the processing of personal data and on the free movement of such data, and repealing Directive 95/46. *Official Journal of the European Union, 59*(1–88), 294.

Rennix, B. (2019, September 24). Roller coasters and the left. *Current affairs: A magazine of politics and culture.* https://www.currentaffairs.org/2019/09/roller-coasters-and-the-left

Richardson, K. (2016). Technological Animis: The Uncanny Personhood of Humanoid Machines. *Social Analysis, 60*(1), 110–128. doi:10.3167a.2016.600108

Richerson, P. J., & Boyd, R. (2005). *Not by genes alone: How culture transformed human evolution.* University of Chicago Press.

Rifkin, J. (2014). *The zero-marginal cost society: The internet of things, the collaborative commons, and the eclipse of capitalism.* St. Martin's.

Rigby, J., Conroy, S., Miele-Norton, M., Pawlby, S., & Happé, F. (2016, July). Theory of mind as a predictor of maternal sensitivity in women with severe mental illness. *Psychological Medicine, 46*(9), 1853–1863. doi:10.1017/S0033291716000337 PMID:26979486

Ringmann, S. D., Langweg, H., & Waldvogel, M. (2018). Requirements for Legally Compliant Software Based on the GDPR. In H. Panetto, C. Debruyne, H. A. Proper, C. A. Ardagna, D. Roman, & R. Meersman (Eds.), *On the Move to Meaningful Internet Systems, OTM 2018 Conferences* (pp. 258–276). Springer International Publishing. 10.1007/978-3-030-02671-4_15

Ritchie, M. D., Holzinger, E. R., Li, R., Pendergrass, S. A., & Kim, D. (2015). Methods of integrating data to uncover genotype–phenotype interactions. *Nature Reviews. Genetics, 16*(2), 85–97. doi:10.1038/nrg3868 PMID:25582081

Rivers, C. (2016, May 10). *The black and white city: The history of race and race relations at the 1893 Chicago World's Fair.* Amazon Digital Services LLC.

Roberts, K. (1982). *Automation, unemployment and the distribution of income* (Vol. 9). European Centre for Work and Society.

Robinson, W. S. (2014). Philosophical challenges. In K. Frankish & W. M. Ramsey (Eds.), *The Cambridge handbook of artificial intelligence* (pp. 64–86). Cambridge University Press. doi:10.1017/CBO9781139046855.005

Robol, M., Salnitri, M., & Giorgini, P. (2017). Toward GDPR-Compliant Socio-Technical Systems: Modeling Language and Reasoning Framework. In G. Poels, F. Gailly, E. Serral Asensio, & M. Snoeck (Eds.), *The practice of enterprise modeling* (Vol. 305, pp. 236–250). Springer International Publishing. doi:10.1007/978-3-319-70241-4_16

Rode, C., Cosmides, L., Hell, W., & Tooby, J. (1999). When and why do people avoid unknown probabilities in decisions under uncertainty? Testing some predictions from optimal foraging theory. *Cognition, 72*(3), 269–304. doi:10.1016/S0010-0277(99)00041-4 PMID:10519925

Rodríguez, G., Soria, Á., & Campo, M. (2016). Artificial intelligence in service-oriented software design. *Engineering Applications of Artificial Intelligence, 53*, 86–104. doi:10.1016/j.engappai.2016.03.009

Rozin, P. (1999). The Process of Moralization. *Psychological Science, 10*(3), 218–221. doi:10.1111/1467-9280.00139

Russell, S. J., & Norvig, P. (2010). Artificial intelligence: A modern approach (E. Davis, Ed.; 3rd ed.). Prentice Hall.

Russell, S., & Norvig, P. (2010). *Artificial intelligence: A modern approach* (3rd ed.). Prentice Hall, Pearson.

Ruzic, L., & Sanfod, J. A. (2017). Universal Design Mobile Interface Guidelines (UDMIG) for an Aging Population. In *Mobile e-Health* (pp. 17–37). Springer.

Ryan, M. (2019). The Future of Transportation: Ethical, Legal, Social and Economic Impacts of Self-driving Vehicles in the Year 2025. *Science and Engineering Ethics*. Advance online publication. doi:10.100711948-019-00130-2 PMID:31482471

Rydell, R., Fielding, J. E., & Pelle, K.D. (2000, March 17). *Fair America*. Smithsonian Books.

SAE. (2016). Taxonomy and Definitions for Terms Related to Driving Automation Systems for On-Road Motor Vehicles. *Global Ground Vehicle Standards*, *J3016*, 30. doi:10.4271/J3016_201609

Santoni de Sio, F., & van den Hoven, J. (2018). Meaningful Human Control over Autonomous Systems: A Philosophical Account. *Frontiers in Robotics and AI*. https://www.frontiersin.org/article/10.3389/frobt.2018.00015

Sapienza, G., Dodig-Crnkovic, G., & Crnkovic, I. (2016). Inclusion of Ethical Aspects in Multi-criteria Decision Analysis. *Proceedings - 2016 1st International Workshop on Decision Making in Software ARCHitecture*. 10.1109/MARCH.2016.8

Saxe, R., & Baron-Cohen, S. (2006). Editorial: The neuroscience of theory of mind. *Social Neuroscience*, *1*(3–4), 1–9. doi:10.1080/17470910601117463 PMID:18633783

Schäbe, H., & Braband, J. (2015). *Basic requirements for proven-in-use arguments*. https://arxiv.org/abs/1511.01839

Schaefer, G. O. (2016, August 2). The future of genetic enhancement is not in the West. The Conversation. https://the-conversation.com/the-future-of-genetic-enhancement-is-not-in-the-west-63246

Schein, C., & Gray, K. (2018). The Theory of Dyadic Morality: Reinventing Moral Judgment by Redefining Harm. *Personality and Social Psychology Review*, *22*(1), 32–70. doi:10.1177/1088868317698288 PMID:28504021

Scheve, K., & Stasavage, D. (2017). Wealth inequality and democracy. *Annual Review of Political Science*, *20*(1), 451–468. doi:10.1146/annurev-polisci-061014-101840

Schilit, B. N., & Theimer, M. M. (1994). Disseminating active map information to mobile hosts. *IEEE Network*, *8*(5), 22–32. doi:10.1109/65.313011

Schoettle, B., & Sivak, M. (2015, October). *A Preliminary Analysis of Real -World Crashes Involving Self -Driving Vehicles*. http://www.umich.edu/~umtriswt/PDF/UMTRI-2015-34.pdf

Schroedel, J. R., Fiber, P., & Snyder, B. D. (2000). Women's Rights and Fetal Personhood in Criminal Law. *Duke Journal of Gender Law & Policy*, *7*, 89.

Schweizer, P. (1998). The truly total Turing test. *Minds and Machines*, *8*(2), 263–272. doi:10.1023/A:1008229619541

Serpentine Galleries. (2018, October 17). *Hans Ulrich Obrist in Conversation with Pierre Huyghe*. YouTube. https://www.youtube.com/watch?v=emYOOVRzG8E

Shapiro, S. C. (Ed.). (1992). *Encyclopedia of artificial intelligence*. John Wiley & Sons. (Original work published 1987)

Sharpe, M. (2020). Slavoj Žižek (1949 —). *Internet Encyclopedia of Philosophy*. https://www.iep.utm.edu/zizek/#Hd

Shellenbarger, S. (2019, August 26). Why We Should Teach Kids to Call the Robot 'It.' *The Wall Street Journal*. https://www.wsj.com/articles/why-kids-should-call-the-robot-it-11566811801

Shultz, S., Nelson, E., & Dunbar, R. I. M. (2012). Hominin cognitive evolution: Identifying patterns and processes in the fossil and archaeological record. *Philosophical Transactions of the Royal Society of London. Series B, Biological Sciences, 367*(1599), 2130–2140. doi:10.1098/rstb.2012.0115 PMID:22734056

Sidgwick, H. (1874). *The methods of ethics.* MacMillan & CO.

Sieber, S. (2013). *Fatal remedies: The ironies of social intervention.* Springer Science & Business Media.

Silver, D., Hubert, T., Schrittwieser, J., Antonoglou, I., Lai, M., Guez, A., Lanctot, M., Sifre, L., Kumaran, D., Graepel, T., Lillicrap, T., Simonyan, K., & Hassabis, D. (2018). A general reinforcement learning algorithm that masters chess, shogi, and Go through self-play. *Science, 362*(6419), 1140–1144. doi:10.1126cience.aar6404 PMID:30523106

Silver, D., Schrittwieser, J., Simonyan, K., Antonoglou, I., Huang, A., Guez, A., Hubert, T., Baker, L., Lai, M., Bolton, A., Chen, Y., Lillicrap, T., Hui, F., Sifre, L., van den Driessche, G., Graepel, T., & Hassabis, D. (2017). Mastering the game of Go without human knowledge. *Nature, 550*(7676), 354–372. doi:10.1038/nature24270 PMID:29052630

Simon, H. A. (1988). The science of design: Creating the artificial. *Design Issues, 4*(1/2), 67–82. doi:10.2307/1511391

Singh, M., & Naveen, B. P. (2014). Molecular Nanotechnology: A new avenue for Environment Treatment. *Journal of Environmental Science, Toxicology And. Food Technology, 8*(1), 93–99.

Singleton, P. A., De Vos, J., Heinen, E., & Pudāne, B. B. T.-A. (2020). *Potential health and well-being implications of autonomous vehicles.* Academic Press.

Sinnott-Armstrong, W. (Ed.). (2014). Moral psychology, Vol 4: Free will and moral responsibility. MIT Press.

Smith, B. C. (2019). *The promise of artificial intelligence: Reckoning and judgment.* The MIT Press. doi:10.7551/mitpress/12385.001.0001

Smithfield, B. (2018, February 25). One of the world's most preserved mummies, the Lady of Dai, is still soft to the touch, has bendy ligaments, and is 2,100 years old. *The Vintage News.* https://www.thevintagenews.com/2018/02/25/lady-of-dai/

Soares, N., & Fallenstein, B. (2014). *Agent Foundations for Aligning Machine Intelligence with Human Interests : A Technical Research Agenda.* doi:10.1007/978-3-662-54033-6_5

Solove, D. J. (2008). Understanding privacy (Vol. 173). Harvard University Press.

Sørensen, J. (2004). Religion, evolution, and an immunology of cultural systems. *Evolution & Cognition, 10*(1), 61–73.

Sotala, K., & Gloor, L. (2017). Superintelligence as a Cause or Cure for Risks of Astronomical Suffering. *Informatica (Vilnius), 41*, 501–505.

Spelke, E. S. (2000). Core knowledge. *The American Psychologist, 55*(11), 1233–1243. doi:10.1037/0003-066X.55.11.1233 PMID:11280937

Spelke, E. S., & Kinzler, K. D. (2007). Core knowledge. *Developmental Science, 10*(1), 89–96. doi:10.1111/j.1467-7687.2007.00569.x PMID:17181705

Spiekermann, S. (2015). *Ethical IT innovation: A value-based system design approach.* Taylor & Francis. doi:10.1201/b19060

Springer, P. J. (2013). *Military robots and drones: A reference handbook.* ABC-CLIO.

Stanford, C., Allen, J. S., & Antón, S. C. (2011). *Biological anthropology.* Pearson Education.

State of California Department of Motor Vehicles. (2020). *Report of Traffic Collision Involving an Autonomous Vehicle (OL 316)*. https://www.dmv.ca.gov/portal/dmv/detail/vr/autonomous/autonomousveh_ol316

Steiger, R. L., & Reyna, C. (2017). Trait contempt, anger, disgust, and moral foundation values. *Personality and Individual Differences, 113*, 125–135. doi:10.1016/j.paid.2017.02.071

Steuart, J. (1767). *An enquiry into the principles of political economy* (Vol. 1). London: Thomas Cadell & Andrew Millar. https://archive.org/details/inquiryintoprinc01steu/page/n4

Steyerl, H. (2012). *The wretched of the screen*. Sternberg Press.

Stol, K.-J., Ralph, P., & Fitzgerald, B. (2016). Grounded theory in software engineering research: A critical review and guidelines. *Proceedings from the 38th International Conference on Software Engineering - ICSE '16*, 120–131. 10.1145/2884781.2884833

Sullivan, D. (2015). Coney Island history: The Story of George Tilyou and Steeplechase Park. *Heart of Coney Island*. https://www.heartofconeyisland.com/steeplechase-park-coney-island.html

Sullivan, D. (2015). Coney Island history: The story of William Reynolds and Dreamland. *Heart of Coney Island*. https://www.heartofconeyisland.com/dreamland-coney-island.html

Sullivan, D. (2015). LaMarcus Adna Thompson's scenic railways at Coney Island. *Luna Park, the Heart of Coney Island*. https://www.heartofconeyisland.com/thompson-scenic-railways-roller-coaster.html

Sunstein, C. R. (2013). The value of a statistical life: Some clarifications and puzzles. *Journal of Benefit-Cost Analysis, 4*(2), 237–261. doi:10.1515/jbca-2013-0019

Sutton, B. (2015). *A Mother Lode of a Show About Motherhood*. https://hyperallergic.com/249073/a-mother-lode-of-a-show-about-motherhood/

Sutton, R. S., & Barto, A. G. (2018). *Reinforcement learning: An introduction*. The MIT Press.

Tassy, S., Deruelle, C., Mancini, J., Leistedt, S., & Wicker, B. (2013). High levels of psychopathic traits alters moral choice but not moral judgment. *Frontiers in Human Neuroscience, 7*. Advance online publication. doi:10.3389/fnhum.2013.00229 PMID:23761743

Tegmark, M. (2017). *Life 3.0: Being human in the age of artificial intelligence*. Allen Lane, Penguin Random House.

Tesauro, G. (1993). TD-Gammon, a self-teaching backgammon program, achieves master-level play. *AAAI Technical Report FS-93-02*, 19-23.

The IEEE Global Initiative on Ethics of Autonomous and Intelligent Systems. (2019). Ethically Aligned Design: A Vision for Prioritizing Human Well-being with Autonomous and Intelligent Systems. IEEE Global Initiative on Ethics of Autonomous and Intelligent Systems.

The Royal Society. (2019). *Explainable AI: The Basics*. https://royalsociety.org/topics-policy/projects/explainable-ai/

Thekkilakattil, A., & Dodig-Crnkovic, G. (2015). Ethics Aspects of Embedded and Cyber-Physical Systems. *2015 IEEE 39th Annual Computer Software and Applications Conference, 2*, 39–44. 10.1109/COMPSAC.2015.41

Thompson, S. J. (2011). *Endless Empowerment and Existence: From Virtual Literacy to Online Permanence in Presence*. Academia.Edu. https://www.academia.edu/2519291/

Thompson, S. J. (Ed.). (2014). *Global issues and ethical considerations in human enhancement technologies*. IGI Global. doi:10.4018/978-1-4666-6010-6

Thomson, J. J. (1976). Killing, Letting Die, and the Trolley Problem. *The Monist, 59*(2), 204–217. Advance online publication. doi:10.5840/monist197659224 PMID:11662247

Tolmeijer, S., Kneer, M., Sarasua, C., Christen, M., & Bernstein, A. (2020). *Implementations in machine ethics: A survey.* arXiv: 2001.07573v1

Tomasik, B. (2016). *The importance of insect suffering.* https://reducing-suffering.org/the-importance-of-insect-suffering

Tooby, J., & Cosmides, L. (1992). The Psychological Foundations of Culture. In J. Barkow, L. Cosmides, & J. Tooby (Eds.), *The adapted mind: Evolutionary psychology and the generation of culture* (pp. 19–136). Oxford University Press.

Tooby, J., & Cosmides, L. (2005). Conceptual Foundations of Evolutionary Psychology. In D. M. Buss (Ed.), *The handbook of evolutionary psychology* (pp. 5–67). John Wiley & Sons, Inc., doi:10.1002/9780470939376.ch1

Toth, K. C., & Anderson-Priddy, A. (2018). *Architecture for Self-Sovereign Digital Identity.* https://nexgenid.com/wp-content/uploads/2019/02/Architecture-for-Self-Sovereign-Digital-Identity-posted-nexgenid.com_.pdf

Toth, K. C., & Anderson-Priddy, A. (2019). Self-Sovereign Digital Identity: A Paradigm Shift for Identity. *IEEE Security and Privacy, 17*(3), 17–27. doi:10.1109/MSEC.2018.2888782

Tsoukalas, I. (2018). Theory of Mind: Towards an Evolutionary Theory. *Evolutionary Psychological Science, 4*(1), 38–66. doi:10.100740806-017-0112-x

Tucker, H. (2001). Tourists and troglodytes: Negotiating for sustainability. *Annals of Tourism Research, 28*(4), 868–891. doi:10.1016/S0160-7383(00)00084-0

Tulving, E. (1985). Memory and consciousness. *Canadian Psychology, 26*(1), 1–12. doi:10.1037/h0080017

Tulving, E. (2002). Episodic Memory: From Mind to Brain. *Annual Review of Psychology, 53*(1), 1–25. doi:10.1146/annurev.psych.53.100901.135114 PMID:11752477

Turilli, M., & Floridi, L. (2009). The ethics of information transparency. *Ethics and Information Technology, 11*(2), 105–112. doi:10.100710676-009-9187-9

Turing, A. (1950). Computing Machinery and Intelligence. *Mind, 59*(236), 433–460. doi:10.1093/mind/LIX.236.433

Tybur, J. M., Lieberman, D., & Griskevicius, V. (2009). Microbes, mating, and morality: Individual differences in three functional domains of disgust. *Journal of Personality and Social Psychology, 97*(1), 103–122. doi:10.1037/a0015474 PMID:19586243

Tybur, J. M., Lieberman, D., Kurzban, R., & DeScioli, P. (2013). Disgust: Evolved function and structure. *Psychological Review, 120*(1), 65–84. doi:10.1037/a0030778 PMID:23205888

Tybur, J. M., Merriman, L. A., Hooper, A. E. C., McDonald, M. M., & Navarrete, C. D. (2010). Extending the Behavioral Immune System to Political Psychology: Are Political Conservatism and Disgust Sensitivity Really Related? *Evolutionary Psychology, 8*(4), 147470491000800420. doi:10.1177/147470491000800406 PMID:22947823

Umbrello, S. (2019b). Beneficial Artificial Intelligence Coordination by Means of a Value Sensitive Design Approach. *Big Data and Cognitive Computing, 3*(1), 5.

Umbrello, S. (2020b). Meaningful Human Control Over Smart Home Systems: A Value Sensitive Design Approach. *HUMANA.MENTE Journal of Philosophical Studies, 13*(37), 40-65. https://www.humanamente.eu/index.php/HM/article/view/315

Umbrello, S., & van de Poel, I. (2020). *Mapping Value Sensitive Design onto AI for Social Good Principles*. https://www.academia.edu/43347384/Mapping_Value_Sensitive_Design_

Umbrello, S. (2018a). *Safe-(for whom?)-by-Design: Adopting a Posthumanist Ethics for Technology Design*. York University. doi:10.13140/RG.2.2.29726.38720

Umbrello, S. (2018b). The moral psychology of value sensitive design: The methodological issues of moral intuitions for responsible innovation. *Journal of Responsible Innovation*, *5*(2), 186–200. doi:10.1080/23299460.2018.1457401

Umbrello, S. (2019). Beneficial Artificial Intelligence Coordination by Means of a Value Sensitive Design Approach. *Big Data and Cognitive Computing*, *3*(1), 5. doi:10.3390/bdcc3010005

Umbrello, S. (2019a). Atomically Precise Manufacturing and Responsible Innovation: A Value Sensitive Design Approach to Explorative Nanophilosophy. *International Journal of Technoethics*, *10*(2), 1–21. doi:10.4018/IJT.2019070101

Umbrello, S. (2020a). Imaginative Value Sensitive Design: Using Moral Imagination Theory to Inform Responsible Technology Design. *Science and Engineering Ethics*, *26*(2), 575–595. doi:10.100711948-019-00104-4 PMID:30972629

Umbrello, S., & Baum, S. D. (2018). Evaluating future nanotechnology: The net societal impacts of atomically precise manufacturing. *Futures*, *100*(June), 63–73. doi:10.1016/j.futures.2018.04.007

Umbrello, S., & De Bellis, A. F. (2018). *A value-sensitive design approach to intelligent agents. In Artificial Intelligence Safety and Security*. CRC Press.

Umbrello, S., & De Bellis, A. F. (2018). A Value-Sensitive Design Approach to Intelligent Agents. In R. V. Yampolskiy (Ed.), *Artificial Intelligence Safety and Security* (pp. 395–410). CRC Press. doi:10.13140/RG.2.2.17162.77762

UN General Assembly. (1948). *Universal Declaration of Human Rights (217 [iii] a)*. https://www.un.org/en/universal-declaration-human-rights/

United Nations Global Compact. (2020). *Social Sustainability*. https://www.unglobalcompact.org/what-is-gc/our-work/social

United Nations. (2017). *Data Privacy, Ethics and Protection Guidance Note on Big Data For Achievement of the 2030 Agenda*. https://unsdg.un.org/resources/data-privacy-ethics-and-protection-guidance-note-big-data-achievement-2030-agenda

United Nations. (2019a). *Democracy & the SDGs*. https://sustainabledevelopment.un.org/

United Nations. (2019b). Sustainable development goals. *GAIA*.

United Nations. (2020). *AI for Good - Global Summit - Accelerating the United Nations Sustainable Development Goals*. https://aiforgood.itu.int/

Uomini, N. T., & Meyer, G. F. (2013). Shared Brain Lateralization Patterns in Language and Acheulean Stone Tool Production: A Functional Transcranial Doppler Ultrasound Study. *PLoS One*, *8*(8), e72693. Advance online publication. doi:10.1371/journal.pone.0072693 PMID:24023634

Vaesen, K. (2012). The cognitive bases of human tool use. *Behavioral and Brain Sciences*, *35*(4), 203–218. doi:10.1017/S0140525X11001452 PMID:22697258

Vallor, S. (2016). *Technology and the virtues. A philosophical guide to a future worth wanting*. Oxford University Press. doi:10.1093/acprof:oso/9780190498511.001.0001 van de Kaa, G., Rezaei, J., Taebi, B., van de Poel, I., & Kizhakenath, A. (2019). How to Weigh Values in Value Sensitive Design: A Best Worst Method Approach for the Case of Smart Metering. *Science and Engineering Ethics*. Advance online publication. doi:10.100711948-019-00105-3 PMID:30963389

van de Poel, I. (2014). Conflicting Values in Design. In J. van den Hoven, P. E. Vermaas, & I. van de Poel (Eds.), *Handbook of Ethics, Values, and Technological Design: Sources, Theory, Values and Application Domains* (pp. 1–23). Springer Netherlands. doi:10.1007/978-94-007-6994-6_5-1

van den Hoven, J. (2013). Architecture and Value-Sensitive Design. In C. Basta & S. Moroni (Eds.), *Ethics, design and planning of the built environment* (p. 224). Springer Science & Business Media. https://books.google.ca/books?id=VVM_AAAAQBAJ&dq=moral

van den Hoven, J. (2017). The Design Turn in Applied Ethics. In J. van den Hoven, S. Miller, & T. Pogge (Eds.), *Designing in Ethics* (pp. 11–31). Cambridge University Press., doi:10.1017/9780511844317.002

van den Hoven, J., Lokhorst, G. J., & van de Poel, I. (2012). Engineering and the Problem of Moral Overload. *Science and Engineering Ethics*, *18*(1), 143–155. doi:10.100711948-011-9277-z PMID:21533834

van den Hoven, J., & Manders-Huits, N. (2009). Value-Sensitive Design. In *A Companion to the Philosophy of Technology* (pp. 477–480). Wiley-Blackwell. doi:10.1002/9781444310795.ch86

Van Parijs, P. (1997). *Real freedom for all: What (if anything) can justify capitalism?* Oxford University Press. doi:10.1093/0198293577.001.0001

Van Parijs, P. (2004). Basic income: A simple and powerful idea for the twenty-first century. *Politics & Society*, *32*(1), 7–39. doi:10.1177/0032329203261095

van Wynsberghe, A. (2013). Designing Robots for Care: Care Centered Value-Sensitive Design. *Science and Engineering Ethics*, *19*(2), 407–433. doi:10.100711948-011-9343-6 PMID:22212357

van Wynsberghe, A., & Robbins, S. (2014). Ethicist as Designer: A Pragmatic Approach to Ethics in the Lab. *Science and Engineering Ethics*, *20*(4), 947–961. doi:10.100711948-013-9498-4 PMID:24254219

Varner, G. E. (2012). *Personhood, ethics, and animal cognition: Situating animals in Hare's two level utilitarianism.* Oxford University Press. doi:10.1093/acprof:oso/9780199758784.001.0001

Veiel, D., Haake, J. M., Lukosch, S., & Kolfschoten, G. (2013). On the Acceptance of Automatic Facilitation in a Context-Adaptive Group Support System. *2013 46th Hawaii International Conference on System Sciences*, 509–518. 10.1109/HICSS.2013.424

Verma, S., & Rubin, J. (2018). Fairness definitions explained. In *2018 IEEE/ACM International Workshop on Software Fairness (FairWare)* (pp. 1-7). Gothenburg, Sweden: IEEE.

Vivarelli, M. (2014). Innovation, employment and skills in advanced and developing countries: A survey of economic literature. *Journal of Economic Issues*, *48*(1), 123–154. doi:10.2753/JEI0021-3624480106

Voiklis, J., & Malle, B. F. (2018). Moral cognition and its basis in social cognition and social regulation. In K. Gray & J. Graham (Eds.), *Atlas of Moral Psychology* (pp. 108–120). Academic Press.

Voyer, B. G., & Tarantola, T. (2017). Toward a Multidisciplinary Moral Psychology. In B. G. Voyer & T. Tarantola (Eds.), *Moral psychology: A multidisciplinary guide* (pp. 1–3). Springer International Publishing., doi:10.1007/978-3-319-61849-4_1

Wachter, S., Mittelstadt, B., & Floridi, L. (2017). Why a Right to Explanation of Automated Decision-Making Does Not Exist in the General Data Protection Regulation. *International Data Privacy Law*, 7(2), 76–99. doi:10.1093/idpl/ipx005

Walgampaya, C., Kantardzic, M., & Yampolskiy, R. (2011). Evidence Fusion for Real Time Click Fraud Detection and Prevention. *Intelligent Automation and Systems Engineering*, 1-14.

Walker, M. (2014). BIG and technological unemployment: Chicken Little versus the economists. *Journal of Evolution and Technology / WTA*, 24(1), 5–25. https://jetpress.org/v24/walker.pdf

Wallach, W., & Allen, C. (2009). *Moral machines: Teaching robots right from wrong*. Oxford University Press. doi:10.1093/acprof:oso/9780195374049.001.0001

Walsh, T. (2016). Turing's red flag. *Communications of the ACM*, 59(7), 34–37. doi:10.1145/2838729

Ward, A. F., Olsen, A. S., & Wegner, D. M. (2013). The Harm-Made Mind: Observing Victimization Augments Attribution of Minds to Vegetative Patients, Robots, and the Dead. *Psychological Science*, 24(8), 1437–1445. doi:10.1177/0956797612472343 PMID:23749051

Warnier, M., Dechesne, F., & Brazier, F. (2014). Design for the Value of Privacy. In J. van den Hoven, P. E. Vermaas, & I. van de Poel (Eds.), *Handbook of Ethics, Values, and Technological Design: Sources, Theory, Values and Application Domains* (pp. 1–14). Springer Netherlands. doi:10.1007/978-94-007-6994-6_17-1

Waymo. (n.d.). https://waymo.com

Waytz, A., Heafner, J., & Epley, N. (2014). The mind in the machine: Anthropomorphism increases trust in an autonomous vehicle. *Journal of Experimental Social Psychology*, 52, 113–117. doi:10.1016/j.jesp.2014.01.005

WEF. (2016). *The future of jobs: Employment, skills and workforce strategy for the fourth industrial revolution*. Executive summary. http://www3.weforum.org/docs/ WEF_FOJ_Executive_Summary_Jobs.pdf

Weston, A. (1985). Technological unemployment and the lifestyle question a practical proposal. *Journal of Social Philosophy*, 16(2), 19–30. doi:10.1111/j.1467-9833.1985.tb00434.x

What is the ISO 26262 Functional Safety Standard? (2014). National Instruments Corp. http://www.ni.com/white-paper/13647/en/

White, S. (2003). *The civic minimum: On the rights and obligations of economic citizenship*. Oxford University Press. doi:10.1093/0198295057.001.0001

White, S. (2011). Basic income versus basic capital: Can we resolve the disagreement? *Policy and Politics*, 39(1), 67–81. doi:10.1332/030557311X546325

White, S. (2015). Basic capital in the egalitarian toolkit? *Journal of Applied Philosophy*, 32(4), 417–431. doi:10.1111/japp.12129

Whittlestone, J., Nyrup, R., Alexandrova, A., & Cave, S. (2019). The Role and Limits of Principles in AI Ethics: Towards a Focus on Tensions. *AIES* 19. http://lcfi.ac.uk/media/uploads/files/AIES-19_paper_188_Whittlestone_Nyrup_Alexandrova_Cave.pdf

Willard, A. K., & McNamara, R. A. (2019). The Minds of God(s) and Humans: Differences in Mind Perception in Fiji and North America. *Cognitive Science*, 43(1), e12703. doi:10.1111/cogs.12703 PMID:30648803

Wilson, B., Hoffman, J., & Morgenstern, J. (2019). *Predictive Inequity in Object Detection*. https://arxiv.org/abs/1902.11097

Winfield, A. F. T., Blum, C., & Liu, W. (2014). Towards an ethical robot: Internal models, consequences and ethical action selection. In *Conference Towards Autonomous Robotic Systems* (pp. 85–96). Springer, Cham. doi:10.1007/978-3-319-10401-0_8

Winfield, A. F., Michael, K., Pitt, J., & Evers, V. (2019). Machine Ethics: The Design and Governance of Ethical AI and Autonomous Systems. *Proceedings of the IEEE, 107*(3), 509–517. doi:10.1109/JPROC.2019.2900622

Winkler, T., & Spiekermann, S. (2019). Human Values as the Basis for Sustainable Information System Design. *IEEE Technology and Society Magazine, 38*(3), 34–43. doi:10.1109/MTS.2019.2930268

Woelfer, J. P., Iverson, A., Hendry, D. G., Friedman, B., & Gill, B. T. (2011). Improving the Safety of Homeless Young People with Mobile Phones: Values, Form and Function. In *Proceedings of the SIGCHI Conference on Human Factors in Computing Systems* (pp. 1707–1716). New York, NY: ACM. 10.1145/1978942.1979191

Wolcott, V. (2012). *Race, riots and roller coasters: The struggle over segregated recreation in America.* The University of Pennsylvania Press. doi:10.9783/9780812207590

Wolfram, S. (2016). *Computational Law, Symbolic Discourse and the AI Constitution.* http://blog.stephenwolfram.com/2016/10/computational-law-symbolic-discourse-and-the-ai-constitution

Woodbury, S. A. (2017). Universal Basic Income. The American Middle Class: An Economic Encyclopedia of Progress and Poverty, 314.

Woolgar, S. (1991). The Turn to Technology in Social Studies of Science. *Science, Technology & Human Values, 16*(1), 20–50. doi:10.1177/016224399101600102

World Bank. (2013). *Improving court efficiency: The Republic of Korea's e-court experience.* https://elibrary.worldbank.org/doi/10.1596/978-0-8213-9984-2_Case_studies_6

Wu, Y., & Lin, S. (2018). A low-cost ethics shaping approach for designing reinforcement learning agents. In *Thirty-Second AAAI Conference on Artificial Intelligence* (pp. 1687-1694). New Orleans, LA: AAAI.

Xinhua Net. (2019, April 17). Fantawild theme parks poised for growth, a fresh dose of vitality to the tourism industry. *Fantawild News.* https://www.fantawild.com/en/newslist/show/1153.htm

Yampolskiy, R. V. (2013). *Artificial intelligence safety engineering: Why machine ethics is a wrong approach. In Philosophy and Theory of Artificial Intelligence.* Springer.

Yampolskiy, R. V. (2014). Utility function security in artificially intelligent agents. *Journal of Experimental & Theoretical Artificial Intelligence, 26*(3), 373–389. doi:10.1080/0952813X.2014.895114

Yampolskiy, R. V. (2015). *Artificial superintelligence: A futuristic approach.* Chapman and Hall/CRC. doi:10.1201/b18612

Yampolskiy, R. V. (2017). What are the ultimate limits to computational techniques: Verifier theory and unverifiability. *Physica Scripta, 92*(9), 093001. doi:10.1088/1402-4896/aa7ca8

Yampolskiy, R. V. (2018). *Artificial intelligence safety and security.* Chapman and Hall/CRC. doi:10.1201/9781351251389

Yoo, D., Derthick, K., Ghassemian, S., Hakizimana, J., Gill, B., & Friedman, B. (2016). Multi-lifespan design thinking: Two methods and a case study with the Rwandan diaspora. In *Proceedings of the 2016 CHI Conference on Human Factors in Computing Systems* (pp. 4423–4434). ACM. 10.1145/2858036.2858366

Yudkowski, E. (2015). *Rationality: From AI to zombies.* MIRI.

Yudkowsky, E. (2013). *Intelligence explosion microeconomics.* Machine Intelligence Research Institute.

Zeytinoglu, S., Calkins, S. D., & Leerkes, E. M. (2018). Maternal emotional support but not cognitive support during problem-solving predicts increases in cognitive flexibility in early childhood. *International Journal of Behavioral Development*. Advance online publication. doi:10.1177/0165025418757706 PMID:31036983

Zhu, X. L., & Tang, S. M. (2015). Autonomous vehicle: from a cognitive perspective. *Multimedia, Communication and Computing Application: Proceedings of the 2014 International Conference on Multimedia, Communication and Computing Application (MCCA 2014)*, 401.

Ziesche, S., & Yampolskiy, R. (2019a). Towards AI welfare science and policies. *Big Data and Cognitive Computing*, *3*(1), 2. doi:10.3390/bdcc3010002

Ziesche, S., & Yampolskiy, R. V. (2019b). Do No Harm Policy for Minds in Other Substrates. *Journal of Evolution and Technology / WTA*, *29*(2).

Zizek, S. (2019). *Like a thief in broad daylight: Power in the era of post-humanity*. Penguin.

Zou, J., & Schiebinger, L. (2018). Design AI so that it's fair. *Nature*, *559*(7714), 324–326. doi:10.1038/d41586-018-05707-8 PMID:30018439

About the Contributors

Steven John Thompson is a new media theorist-practitioner and enlyst in technology ethics, iconetics, media informatics, and Internet phenomena. Dr. Thompson teaches at University of California, Davis and University of Maryland Global Campus. He has taught at Johns Hopkins University, Dartmouth College, and Clemson University, among others. He was Editor of *Global Issues and Ethical Considerations in Human Enhancement Technologies*, published by IGI Global in 2014 and *Androids, Cyborgs, and Robots in Contemporary Culture and Society* published by IGI Global in 2018. He is on the Editorial Board of Academic Editors for PeerJ journal in Emerging Technologies, Ethical Issues, Human-Computer Interaction, Science Policy, and World Wide Web & Web Science subject areas. Dr. Thompson published pioneering quantitative research on Internet addiction and dependency in 1996, and presented his iconics theory on agency of terrorism images as virtual subscripts of artificial intelligence at University of Basel in 2009. He was plenary closing academic panel discussant at UNESCO's First International Forum on Media and Information Literacy in Fez, Morocco in 2011. His research has been presented in over a dozen countries across four continents. He holds a PhD in Rhetorics, Communication, and Information Design from Clemson University; an MS in Media Arts and Science from Indiana University; a BA in Media Studies with Honors, a BA in Integrative Arts with a focus in New Media, and an AA in Letters, Arts & Sciences, from Penn State.

* * *

Anton Berg is finishing his Master's degree both in Cognitive Science and in Theology and Religious Studies at Helsinki University. His research focuses on ethical cognition, cognitive biases, and faith in technological progress as a modern version of theodicy in the age of environmental crisis. Currently he is looking at how religious cognition and representations relate to transhumanism and technological animism.

Gordana Dodig-Crnković is Professor in Interaction Design at Chalmers University of Technology and Professor in Computer Science at Mälardalen University. She holds PhD degrees in Physics and Computer Science. Her research focuses on the relationships between computation, information and cognition. It includes ethical and value aspects of technology with ethical aspects of AI, robotics and autonomous vehicles. She is a member of the editorial board of the Springer SAPERE series, World Scientific Series in Information Studies, and a number of journals. She is a member of the AI Ethics Committee at Chalmers and the Karel Capek Center for Values in Science and Technology as well as AI4EU project.

Mandy Goram holds a Bachelor's degree in Business Informatics and a Master's degree in Practical Computer Science. During her time as an IT Consultant and Head of a Business Intelligence team, she has gained extensive experience in numerous projects in the design, implementation, testing and launch of software systems and the design of complex system landscapes. She has profound knowledge in the areas of requirements engineering, software architectures, quality management and the development of data protection-compliant (analytics) systems, which she has gained in digital corporations and in the medical-pharmaceutical industry. Currently, she works as a research associate in the research group Critical Information Infrastructures at the Karlsruhe Institute of Technology (KIT) and is developing a legally compliant AI platform that will provide users with personalized support.

Volo Herzon is a Master's student of psychology at University of Helsinki and a research assistant in a group investigating the interaction of moral psychology and major novel technologies.

Jonas Holst has a Ph.D. from the Department of Philosophy and History of Ideas at Aarhus University. Currently, Associate Professor at the Institute of Humanism and Society, San Jorge University, Zaragoza, where he teaches ethics and aesthetics. Most recent publications on the ethical significance of friendship and hospitality and conceptual studies of play, experience and tectonics. http://orcid.org/0000-0002-5949-1727.

Tobias Holstein is a PhD Candidate at Mälardalen University and a research assistant at Darmstadt University of Applied Sciences. He holds a Licentiate Degree in Computer Science and two Master of Science degrees (Edinburg Napier University and Darmstadt University of Applied Sciences). His research focuses on the interplay of Software Architecture, Interaction Design and Ethics. Furthermore, he is interested in design processes and interdisciplinary research involving interaction design and computer science. He has gained several years of professional experience as a software engineer and architect in the development of advanced human-machine-interfaces in the automotive industry.

Atsuhide Ito is Senior Research Fellow at Solent University, Southampton, and Associate Lecturer at London College of Communication, University of the Arts London in England. Atsuhide is a researching artist and writer. His current research concerns how data translation can be artistically and critically used in sensing and registering radiation. Through his practice, Atsuhide examines how the notion of risk towards radiation is constructed, felt and applied in daily life and policy decisions. Recent publications include "The Spectral Image: The History of Visualising Radiation", Common Ground Publisher (2018), and "Towards a Theory of Cavernous Porosity" in Architecture and Culture, Routledge, and Taylor & Francis, (2016), "a Haunted Abbey and a Concrete Palace" (2019) Common Ground Publisher. The most recent exhibitions include Sound of Waves at Park Hotel with Pocko, Tokyo, Japan (2019), Fire in the Swimming Pool at Pocko Gallery, London, England (2019), Cache at Angus Hughes Gallery, London (2018).

Marten H. L. Kaas is a PhD student at University College Cork specializing in the study of philosophy of artificial intelligence, philosophy of mind, metaphysics and philosophy of science. He has completed graduate work in both philosophy and biology at McMaster University and has given lectures on emergence, free will and philosophy of mind.

Mika Koverola, MA (cognitive neuroscience, minors in psychology and science and technology studies), is focused on the interaction between humans and digital technologies, especially the moral intuitions humans have about robots. He is currently working on his doctoral thesis in the Moralities of Intelligent Machines research group at the University of Helsinki.

Michael Laakasuo is an adjunct professor of cognitive science at University of Helsinki. He is the PI of Moralities of Intelligent Machines research team. His research interests focus on the moral relations between humans and AIs, friendship, rational and emotional decision-making in poker and psychometrics of utilitarianism.

Jill Morris is an Associate Professor of English and Foreign Languages at Frostburg State University where she studies video game rhetoric, amusement park history, and technical writing.

Elias Moser is currently working as Postdoctoral Researcher at the Section Moral and Political Philosophy at the Karl-Franzens University of Graz. Before coming to Austria, he pursued research mainly in the field of legal ethics and legal philosophy. He acquired his PhD at the Humanities Faculty of the University of Berne in 2017 with an inquiry on the concept of "Inalienable Rights". At the time, he held a position as Praedoc Assistant at the Institute for Criminal Law and Criminology. In his early career as postdoctoral scholar, Elias Moser broadened his scope towards the fields of ethics of technology and economic philosophy. In 2018-2019 he worked as freelance researcher at the Institute for Technology Assessment (ITA) of the Austrian Science Funds OEAW and on the Platform "Nano-Norms-Nature" at the University of Vienna.

Patrizio Pelliccione (male) is an Associate Professor at DISIM - University of L'Aquila and an Associate Professor at the Department of Computer Science and Engineering at Chalmers | University of Gothenburg. He got his PhD in 2005 at the University of L'Aquila (Italy) and from February 1, 2014 he is Docent in Software Engineering, title given by the University of Gothenburg. His research topics are mainly in software engineering, software architectures modelling and verification, autonomous systems, and formal methods. He has co-authored more than 120 publications in journals and international conferences and workshops in these topics. He has been on the program committees for several top conferences, he is a reviewer for top journals in the software engineering domain, and he organized as program chair international conferences like ICSA2017 and FormaliSE 2018. He is very active in European and National projects. He is the PI for Co4Robots H2020 EU project for the University of Gothenburg. In his research activity he has collaborated with several industries such as Volvo Cars, Volvo AB, Ericsson, Jeppesen, Axis communication, Systemite AB, Thales Italia, Selex Marconi telecommunications, Siemens, Saab, TERMA, etc.

Marko Repo is finishing his Master's degree in Cognitive Science at University of Helsinki. His research focuses on the nexus of transhumanism and the environmental crisis. Currently he is looking at how transhuman attitudes and technologies can be construed as attempts to cope with environmental anxiety.

Teemu Saikkonen, MSc. (Ecology, minors in genetics and physiology), is focused on the evolutionary aspects of cognition and agency in moral psychology. He is currently working on his doctoral thesis in the Moralities of Intelligent Machines -research group (moim.fi) at the University of Helsinki.

Jukka Sundvall is working as a post-doctoral researcher at the Department of Digital Humanities, Cognitive Science, at the University of Helsinki while finishing the corrections for his PhD thesis in Psychology from the University of Sussex. He is generally interested in judgment and decision-making, ranging from simple experimental games to morality and politics. He is currently brainstorming designs for studies on moral patiency in artificial beings and the relationship between moral judgments and perceived mental properties.

Steven Umbrello currently serves as the Managing Director of the Institute for Ethics and Emerging Technologies. He received his MA in Science and Technology Studies at York University (Canada) and his MSc in Epistemology, Ethics, and Mind at the University of Edinburgh. He is currently doing his PhD on the ethics and design of AI at the University of Turin (Italy). Currently, his main area of research revolves around Value Sensitive Design (VSD), meaningful human control (MHC), and their philosophical foundations as well as their potential application to emerging technologies such as artificial intelligence and Industry 4.0.

Dirk Veiel is a senior researcher at the Chair of Cooperative Systems at the Faculty of Mathematics and Computer Science of the FernUniversität in Hagen. He obtained his doctoral degree in computer science in 2013. His research interests include intelligent group/community support systems, context-based adaptation, community support systems for elderly, intelligent assistance systems, formal context representations, emergence in socio-technical systems, multi-agent systems, artificial intelligence and natural language processing.

Roman V. Yampolskiy is a Tenured Associate Professor in the department of Computer Engineering and Computer Science at the Speed School of Engineering, University of Louisville. He is the founding and current director of the Cyber Security Lab and an author of many books including Artificial Superintelligence: a Futuristic Approach. During his tenure at University of Louisville, Dr. Yampolskiy has been recognized as: Distinguished Teaching Professor, Professor of the Year, Faculty Favorite, Top 4 Faculty, Leader in Engineering Education, Top 10 of Online College Professor of the Year, and Outstanding Early Career in Education award winner among many other honors and distinctions. Yampolskiy is a Senior member of IEEE and AGI; Member of Kentucky Academy of Science, and Research Advisor for MIRI and Associate of GCRI. Roman Yampolskiy holds a PhD degree from the Department of Computer Science and Engineering at the University at Buffalo. He was a recipient of a four year NSF (National Science Foundation) IGERT (Integrative Graduate Education and Research Traineeship) fellowship. Before beginning his doctoral studies Dr. Yampolskiy received a BS/MS (High Honors) combined degree in Computer Science from Rochester Institute of Technology. After completing his PhD dissertation Dr. Yampolskiy held a position of an Affiliate Academic at the Center for Advanced Spatial Analysis, University of London, College of London. He had previously conducted research at the Laboratory for Applied Computing (currently known as Center for Advancing the Study of Infrastructure) at the Rochester Institute of Technology and at the Center for Unified Biometrics and Sensors at the University at Buffalo. Dr. Yampolskiy is an alumnus of Singularity University (GSP2012) and a Visiting Fellow of the Singularity Institute (Machine Intelligence Research Institute). Dr. Yampolskiy's main areas of interest are AI Safety, Artificial Intelligence, Behavioral Biometrics, Cybersecurity, Digital Forensics, Games, Genetic Algorithms, and Pattern Recognition. Dr. Yampolskiy is an author of over 100 publications including multiple journal articles and books. His research has been cited by 1000+ scientists and profiled in popular magazines both American and foreign (New Scientist, Poker Magazine, Science World Magazine), dozens of websites (BBC, MSNBC, Yahoo! News), on radio (German National Radio, Swedish National Radio, Alex Jones Show) and TV. Dr. Yampolskiy's research has been featured 250+ times in numerous media reports in 22 languages.

Index

Purchase Print, E-Book, or Print + E-Book

IGI Global's reference books are available in three unique pricing formats:
Print Only, E-Book Only, or Print + E-Book.

Shipping fees may apply.

www.igi-global.com

Recommended Reference Books

ISBN: 978-1-5225-5912-2
© 2019; 349 pp.
List Price: $215

ISBN: 978-1-5225-8176-5
© 2019; 2,218 pp.
List Price: $2,950

ISBN: 978-1-5225-7811-6
© 2019; 317 pp.
List Price: $225

ISBN: 978-1-5225-7268-8
© 2019; 316 pp.
List Price: $215

ISBN: 978-1-5225-7455-2
© 2019; 288 pp.
List Price: $205

ISBN: 978-1-5225-8973-0
© 2019; 200 pp.
List Price: $195

Do you want to stay current on the latest research trends, product announcements, news and special offers?
Join IGI Global's mailing list today and start enjoying exclusive perks sent only to IGI Global members.
Add your name to the list at **www.igi-global.com/newsletters**.

Publisher of Peer-Reviewed, Timely, and Innovative Academic Research

www.igi-global.com ✉ Sign up at www.igi-global.com/newsletters f facebook.com/igiglobal t twitter.com/igiglobal in linkedin.com/igiglobal

Ensure Quality Research is Introduced to the Academic Community

Become an IGI Global Reviewer for Authored Book Projects

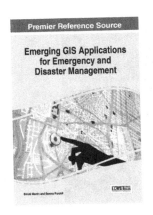

Premier Reference Source

Emerging GIS Applications for Emergency and Disaster Management

Premier Reference Source

Managerial Strategies and Green Solutions for Project Sustainability

Premier Reference Source

Comparative Approaches to Using R and Python for Statistical Data Analysis

Premier Reference Source

Solutions for High-Touch Communications in a High-Tech World

The overall success of an authored book project is dependent on quality and timely reviews.

In this competitive age of scholarly publishing, constructive and timely feedback significantly expedites the turnaround time of manuscripts from submission to acceptance, allowing the publication and discovery of forward-thinking research at a much more expeditious rate. Several IGI Global authored book projects are currently seeking highly-qualified experts in the field to fill vacancies on their respective editorial review boards:

Applications and Inquiries may be sent to:
development@igi-global.com

Applicants must have a doctorate (or an equivalent degree) as well as publishing and reviewing experience. Reviewers are asked to complete the open-ended evaluation questions with as much detail as possible in a timely, collegial, and constructive manner. All reviewers' tenures run for one-year terms on the editorial review boards and are expected to complete at least three reviews per term. Upon successful completion of this term, reviewers can be considered for an additional term.

If you have a colleague that may be interested in this opportunity,
we encourage you to share this information with them.

IGI Global Proudly Partners With eContent Pro International

Receive a 25% Discount on all Editorial Services

Editorial Services

IGI Global expects all final manuscripts submitted for publication to be in their final form. This means they must be reviewed, revised, and professionally copy edited prior to their final submission. Not only does this support with accelerating the publication process, but it also ensures that the highest quality scholarly work can be disseminated.

English Language Copy Editing

Let eContent Pro International's expert copy editors perform edits on your manuscript to resolve spelling, punctuaion, grammar, syntax, flow, formatting issues and more.

Scientific and Scholarly Editing

Allow colleagues in your research area to examine the content of your manuscript and provide you with valuable feedback and suggestions before submission.

Figure, Table, Chart & Equation Conversions

Do you have poor quality figures? Do you need visual elements in your manuscript created or converted? A design expert can help!

Translation

Need your documjent translated into English? eContent Pro International's expert translators are fluent in English and more than 40 different languages.

Hear What Your Colleagues are Saying About Editorial Services Supported by IGI Global

"The service was very fast, very thorough, and very helpful in ensuring our chapter meets the criteria and requirements of the book's editors. I was quite impressed and happy with your service."

– Prof. Tom Brinthaupt,
Middle Tennessee State University, USA

"I found the work actually spectacular. The editing, formatting, and other checks were very thorough. The turnaround time was great as well. I will definitely use eContent Pro in the future."

– Nickanor Amwata, Lecturer,
University of Kurdistan Hawler, Iraq

"I was impressed that it was done timely, and wherever the content was not clear for the reader, the paper was improved with better readability for the audience."

– Prof. James Chilembwe,
Mzuzu University, Malawi

Email: customerservice@econtentpro.com   **www.igi-global.com/editorial-service-partners**

www.igi-global.com

Celebrating Over 30 Years of Scholarly
Knowledge Creation & Dissemination

InfoSci®-Books

A Database of Over 5,300+ Reference Books Containing Over 100,000+ Chapters Focusing on Emerging Research

GAIN ACCESS TO **THOUSANDS** OF REFERENCE BOOKS AT **A FRACTION** OF THEIR INDIVIDUAL LIST **PRICE**.

InfoSci®-Books Database

The **InfoSci®-Books** database is a collection of over 5,300+ IGI Global single and multi-volume reference books, handbooks of research, and encyclopedias, encompassing groundbreaking research from prominent experts worldwide that span over 350+ topics in 11 core subject areas including business, computer science, education, science and engineering, social sciences and more.

Open Access Fee Waiver (Offset Model) Initiative

For any library that invests in IGI Global's InfoSci-Journals and/or InfoSci-Books databases, IGI Global will match the library's investment with a fund of equal value to go toward **subsidizing the OA article processing charges (APCs) for their students, faculty, and staff** at that institution when their work is submitted and accepted under OA into an IGI Global journal.*

INFOSCI® PLATFORM FEATURES

- No DRM
- No Set-Up or Maintenance Fees
- A Guarantee of No More Than a 5% Annual Increase
- Full-Text HTML and PDF Viewing Options
- Downloadable MARC Records
- Unlimited Simultaneous Access
- COUNTER 5 Compliant Reports
- Formatted Citations With Ability to Export to RefWorks and EasyBib
- No Embargo of Content (Research is Available Months in Advance of the Print Release)

*The fund will be offered on an annual basis and expire at the end of the subscription period. The fund would renew as the subscription is renewed for each year thereafter. The open access fees will be waived after the student, faculty, or staff's paper has been vetted and accepted into an IGI Global journal and the fund can only be used toward publishing OA in an IGI Global journal. Libraries in developing countries will have the match on their investment doubled.

To Learn More or To Purchase This Database:
www.igi-global.com/infosci-books

eresources@igi-global.com • Toll Free: 1-866-342-6657 ext. 100 • Phone: 717-533-8845 x100

www.igi-global.com

www.igi-global.com

Publisher of Peer-Reviewed, Timely, and
Innovative Academic Research Since 1988

IGI Global's Transformative Open Access (OA) Model:
How to Turn Your University Library's Database Acquisitions Into a Source of OA Funding

In response to the OA movement and well in advance of Plan S, IGI Global, early last year, unveiled their OA Fee Waiver (Read & Publish) Initiative.

Under this initiative, librarians who invest in IGI Global's InfoSci-Books (5,300+ reference books) and/or InfoSci-Journals (185+ scholarly journals) databases will be able to subsidize their patron's OA article processing charges (APC) when their work is submitted and accepted (after the peer review process) into an IGI Global journal. *See website for details.

How Does it Work?

1. When a library subscribes or perpetually purchases IGI Global's InfoSci-Databases and/or their discipline/subject-focused subsets, IGI Global will match the library's investment with a fund of equal value to go toward subsidizing the OA article processing charges (APCs) for their patrons.

   Researchers: **Be sure to recommend the InfoSci-Books and InfoSci-Journals to take advantage of this initiative.**

2. When a student, faculty, or staff member submits a paper and it is accepted (following the peer review) into one of IGI Global's 185+ scholarly journals, the author will have the option to have their paper published under a traditional publishing model or as OA.

3. When the author chooses to have their paper published under OA, IGI Global will notify them of the OA Fee Waiver (Read and Publish) Initiative. If the author decides they would like to take advantage of this initiative, IGI Global will deduct the US$ 2,000 APC from the created fund.

4. This fund will be offered on an annual basis and will renew as the subscription is renewed for each year thereafter. IGI Global will manage the fund and award the APC waivers unless the librarian has a preference as to how the funds should be managed.

Hear From the Experts on This Initiative:

"I'm very happy to have been able to make one of my recent research contributions, "Visualizing the Social Media Conversations of a National Information Technology Professional Association" featured in the *International Journal of Human Capital and Information Technology Professionals*, freely available along with having access to the valuable resources found within IGI Global's InfoSci-Journals database."

– **Prof. Stuart Palmer**,
Deakin University, Australia

For More Information, Visit: www.igi-global.com/publish/contributor-resources/open-access/read-publish-model
or contact IGI Global's Database Team at eresources@igi-global.com.